I0818125

PRAISE FOR *CALLED TO SERVE*

Don Hodel is a man of faith, family, and country. He has always been a strong but kind and thoughtful leader who sets an extraordinary example for those who know him and have worked with him. I know, because many decades ago he asked me to serve as his deputy solicitor when he was chosen by President Ronald Reagan as his Interior Secretary. You could not help but admire Don, as he faced every challenge, and there were many, with great wisdom. He was always principled. And as I look back, I never recall him losing his temper or patience. There is much to learn from someone who has led a full and good life, in public service and business, as his outstanding book accounts. I am honored to have worked with Don and to call him my friend. There is so much to learn from him and his outstanding book. I wholeheartedly encourage as many people as possible to read it and share it with family and friends.

Mark R. Levin
Author and broadcaster; *The Mark Levin Show* (Westwood One)
Life, Liberty & Levin (Fox News)

Having witnessed Don's significant contribution to President Reagan's successful energy and natural resources policies, it was delightful to learn of his consistently conservative Republican life before and after serving Reagan. He was President of the Harvard Young Republican Club. Oregon State Republican Chairman. Reagan's Oregon Campaign Chairman in 1968. Reagan's Secretary of Energy, and later of the Interior Department in the 1980's. Throughout, a solid principled Reaganite who has been serving on President Reagan's Alumni Association Board for the last 35 years.

Lou Cordia
Executive Director, President Ronald Reagan Alumni Association

In this heartfelt and inspiring memoir, former Secretary Don Hodel invites readers on a chapter-by-chapter journey through the defining moments of his remarkable life. From his earliest days to his service at the highest levels of government, Don shares the lessons learned along the way with warmth, humility, and wisdom. Having known him for over 30 years, I was able to experience much of this in real time. In fact, there hasn't been one major decision in my life during that time when I haven't sought his guidance and wisdom. With stories that reflect a life grounded in integrity, character, faith, tenacity, endurance, and professionalism, this book offers more than just a look into a public servant's path—it presents a blueprint for living with purpose. If you're looking to read about a life well-lived and values worth emulating, this book is well worth the read.

Kay Coles James

Director, U.S. Office of Personnel Management, George W. Bush Admin.
Assoc. Director, White House Office of National Drug Control Policy and
Assist. Secretary Health & Human Services, George H. W. Bush Admin.
President, the Heritage Foundation (2018 – 2021)
currently Founder & President, The Gloucester Institute

Don Hodel has written an insightful autobiography which includes a historical and three-dimensional look inside my father's administration where he served in two Cabinet Secretary roles. Don was and is a true Reaganite and I congratulate him on his memoir.

Michael Reagan

Columnist and radio host; author, *The City on a Hill*

Don Hodel is one of the unsung heroes of the modern conservative movement. From his early days as President of Harvard College's Young Republican Club, through his legal career, as the CEO of several private sector companies, as Chairman of the Bonneville Power Administration, and as Ronald Reagan's Secretary of Energy and of the Department of the Interior, Don proved to be a master of substance, as well as of effective style. Reading his candid autobiography is reading the story of a man of true faith who confronted extraordinary personal challenges but always came back to fight again for the ideas he believes in. Both as a senior government official and as a true leader of the modern conservative movement at Pat Robertson's Christian Coalition, Jim Dobson's Focus on the Family, and at the James Madison Center for Free Speech, Don led by example and inspiration. Read his book and learn about a man who trusts in God and who believes in the American system.

Edwin J. Feulner
Founder & President, The Heritage Foundation
(1977 – 2013 & 2017 – 2018)

Called to Serve

My Path to President Reagan's Cabinet and Beyond

Donald P. Hodel

Called to Serve: My Path to President Reagan's Cabinet and Beyond

The information in this book is based on actual events in the author's life based on their personal recollection. The names and identifying characteristics of individuals and places may have been changed to maintain anonymity.

Cover photo: Cynthia Johnson via Getty

Peak Press, an Imprint for GracePoint Publishing (www.GracePointPublishing.com)

GracePoint Matrix, LLC
624 S. Cascade Ave, Suite 201
Colorado Springs, CO 80903
www.GracePointMatrix.com
Email: Admin@GracePointMatrix.com
SAN # 991-6032

PEAK PRESS

A Library of Congress Control Number has been requested and is pending.

ISBN: (Paperback) 978-1-966346-27-2
eISBN: 978-1-966346-28-9

Books may be purchased for educational, business, or sales promotional use.
For distribution queries contact Sales@IPGbook.com
For non-retail bulk order requests contact Orders@GracePointPublishing.com

DEDICATION

To my son, David B. Hodel
and
to Aaron, Brennan, and the late Christopher Hodel, my grandsons for whom this book was originally written in answer to the question they might someday ask:
"Grandpa, how did you become a Cabinet officer?"

Additional Books by Donald P. Hodel

Crisis in the Oil Patch: How America's Energy Industry Is Being Destroyed and What Must Be Done to Save It

Every strong-willed, visionary leader needs an administrator to implement decisions, and who will also minister more directly to the needs of the people in the organization. The level of authority should not be held in competition with the leader but seen as complementary to what the leader is uniquely called to do.

-Anonymous

CONTENTS

PREFACE

Almost twenty years ago, I began putting my recollections to paper regarding how I became a Cabinet Secretary for President Ronald Reagan. In doing so, I attempted to answer in book form a question that I could imagine my grandsons asking someday: "Grandpa, how did you become a Cabinet officer?"

From time to time over the ensuing years I added additional recollections, a few or many pages, including things my parents told me regarding their early history, along with other things as I remember them from my life and activities. But over time I lost track of what I had written.

In the last couple of years, a dear friend and longtime associate, Joel Vaughan, encouraged me to finish the book. He even took on the task of reconciling and integrating all those things I had written in the past and putting them in reasonable order. He pointed out where I had left holes and where things were duplicated and encouraged me to edit and keep writing to complete a single narrative. Without his dedicated assistance, unfailing support, and encouragement, there would be nothing at this point other than several very disjointed and essentially useless chapters.

I first met Joel when I went to the Christian Coalition in 1997, and he soon became my special assistant there. He later worked in a similar role for me with Summit Power Group when I officed in my home, and he has also served with me in various other capacities.

Joel's dedication, organizational skills, research, and fact-checking were invaluable. Without his contributions this autobiography would be significantly less accurate and interesting. While the words within are mine, I am grateful to Joel for making this happen. With typical modesty he wanted none of this to be included in the book, but he has earned it, and it stays.

I also want to thank my longtime friend and business partner, Earl Gjelde, who reviewed the manuscript as it neared completion. Earl provided key details regarding events that occurred during the years we worked together.

My family's history regarding my father's brothers and sisters was greatly augmented (and in some cases corrected) by my great-niece Jennifer Corbilla's research on FamilySearch.com, and she has a more accurate tale with correct dates and names, having spent many hours combing the records. Otherwise, I have written my recollections of what my parents told me, and I know they are not completely accurate, no doubt, because I heard many of these things as a child, understanding them through a child's perspective, and repeating them until they became my version of our family's history. As I used to say in a humorous way, "This is close enough for government work."

A special thanks to the team at Peak Press: publisher Michelle Vandepas, director Tascha Yoder, editor Laurie Knight, and proofreader Erin Tackitt. They were instrumental in making my life story into a much more professional and finished product.

I disagree with the modern trend in publishing and journalism style guides that have ceased beginning the names of official positions with capital letters. Today, one does not have a meeting with the President, he instead has a meeting with the president. That was not the case during my education and government career.

In this book I will follow the modern guides for most common noun titles, such as county chairman, board of directors, etc. However, for official government titles used as common nouns, I prefer to use what I learned as the appropriate practice: President, Vice President, Secretary, Senator, Congressman, Administrator, etc.

I have written the bulk of this autobiography, and edited portions written earlier, at age eighty-eight and older, almost entirely from memory. This being the case, some details and dates may be transposed or mistaken. However, I have tried to be as honest and accurate as memory allows. A quote or an event may not have occurred exactly as I include it in the book or at the time I place it from memory, but it did take place and, I think, essentially the way I have written it.

One thing that struck me as I wrote was the way in which I felt led to take on new assignments and challenges from time to time in my life. It felt then as if those opportunities sought me out. For example:

- I did not pursue the job in the legal department at Georgia-Pacific, I was recruited.
- I did not seek to be a county Republican precinct organizer or secretary or county chairman but took each job because no one else would.
- I attempted to avoid being drafted as Republican state chairman, but, again, no one else came forward.
- I turned down the chairmanship of Senator Bob Packwood's campaign.
- I declined to be chairman of the Reagan for President campaign in the Oregon Primary in 1968, although I eventually ran the campaign from a subsidiary position.
- I had never thought of going to the Bonneville Power Administration when the people seeking to fill that position sought me out.
- After three years at Bonneville as Deputy Administrator, I tried, unsuccessfully, to persuade my predecessor to remain in the role rather than arranging to have me succeed him.
- I attempted to decline the invitation from my friend Jim Watt when he asked me to become his Under Secretary of the Interior.
- My only aspiration in Washington once I joined Jim was to do a good job and return to Oregon when his term was over. Instead, the job in the President's Cabinet came calling when my friend Tom Reed was assigned by President Reagan to find a new Secretary of Energy.

- Although I tried to decline the honor, I returned to Interior as Secretary during President Reagan's second term, succeeding Judge William Clark, because Clark insisted I do so.
- Pat Robertson sought me in 1997 to succeed Ralph Reed as head of the Christian Coalition. (That turned out to be the least rewarding of the various exciting jobs that I held. In retrospect, I have often thought I would have been well-advised to decline that one, but I took it at the time because I felt that I was called to do it. And, many good things flowed from it, not the least of which was the almost three decades association with Joel Vaughan, as stated above.)
- Jim Dobson encouraged me to become a Focus on the Family board member, which eventually led me to take one last challenging and rewarding assignment, the presidency of Focus on the Family.

Each of these, at the time they came into my life, were heady assignments, partly because for many of them, including both Cabinet positions, I was far younger than was typical for such positions, and although I had not sought them and even tried to decline some of them, once the decisions were made, I pursued them with enthusiasm. I enjoyed the opportunities to serve and attempted to do each to the best of my ability.

The other thing I noticed when writing was that I could not have had whatever success I had without the loyal and capable support of men and women who mentored me or assisted me in all of these positions. I fully understand that no executive can succeed solely by his own decisions and actions. I will not be able to name and thank all of them as we go through this book, but I will never forget that I accomplished what I did because of their amazing advice and support.

My deepest gratitude goes out to my parents who were supportive and encouraging as long as they lived; my brother, Les, who set an example of excellence and diligence; teachers, especially in high school, who encouraged me; associates, like Earl Gjelde, my close friend for nearly sixty years now, who became my essential right arm in Washington and later my partner in consulting after leaving DC, and about whom I cannot say enough good things; my college roommate Don Pearlman, whose loyalty and steadfast assistance beginning in the Harvard Young Republican Club through my Cabinet jobs was invaluable; political figures who boosted me along the way, especially my great friend Jim Watt, without whose intervention I would never have gone to DC or have become a Cabinet officer; men I worked for, like Frank Breuer at Georgia-Pacific, who taught me key management lessons; and Russ Richmond at Bonneville, who tutored me for three years in how to be BPA Administrator as well as how to exist and work within the federal bureaucracy; and Tom Reed, who was my link to President Reagan and the key to my being selected to be Secretary of Energy.

I realize that in naming these people I have overlooked so many others who saw something in me that made them want to help me succeed. If they ever see this book, I apologize for not naming them here. All I know is that I have been greatly blessed by these friends and mentors.

I have written in more detail about my various positions in the chapters that follow, and I leave it to others to judge whether I was more—or less—successful in these posts. Again, all I can say is that I did my best at the time with what I knew.

Finally, I must make absolutely clear that most of these positions would never have occurred and none of them would have been even a fraction as enjoyable or fulfilling without the unfailing encouragement and supportive assistance given to me by my loving wife, Barbara. In the end, much of this story was as equally her biography as mine. Underlying it all is a love story. Rest assured, she could not have been more a part of my story, our story, than she was, and it would never have happened without her.

Donald Paul Hodel
April 2025

Positions, Titles, Honors
(In rough chronological order)

Education

Grant High School, Student Body President, Valedictorian
Portland Junior Symphony, violin
Harvard National Scholarship
Harvard-Radcliffe Orchestra, violin
BA, Harvard College
Juris Doctorate, University of Oregon School of Law

Professional

Attorney, Davies, Biggs, Strayer, Stoel and Boley
Attorney, Georgia-Pacific Corporation
Chairman, Clackamas County Republican Central Committee
Chairman, Oregon Republican Central Committee
Tri-County Chairman, 1968 Oregon Reagan for President
Deputy Administrator (COO), Bonneville Power Administration
Administrator (CEO), Bonneville Power Administration
Board of Directors, Electric Power Research Council
Founder, Hodel Associates, Inc.
Board Member, North American Electric Reliability Council
Under Secretary, US Department of the Interior
Secretary, US Department of Energy
Secretary, US Department of the Interior
Presidential Citizens Medal
Cofounder, Managing Director, Summit Power Group
Member, Electric Power Research Council, Advisory Board
President & CEO, Christian Coalition
President, Council for National Policy
Chairman, Independence Institute
President, James Madison Center for Free Speech
President & CEO, Focus on the Family
President & CEO, Family Policy Alliance
President, North American Electric Reliability Council
National Energy Award, U.S. Energy Association
Chairman & Chairman Emeritus, Summit Power Group

Corporate Boards of Directors
American Electric Power Company
Columbia Gas
MAPCO
Integrated Electrical Services
Salem Radio
Phillips Publishing (Regnery Publishing, Human Events)
The Federalist Society

Honorary Doctorate Degrees
LLD Pepperdine Law School
LLD Alabama A&M
LLD Liberty University

CHAPTER 1

SON OF IMMIGRANTS

I never set out in life to become a Cabinet Secretary. In fact, I set out to be President. Here is how it all came about.

My grandparents on both sides, the Hodels and the Brodts, were first generation Canadians who emigrated from Europe. In the late 1800s, Canada sought to bring people into central Canada, the provinces of Manitoba, Saskatchewan, and Alberta, to populate the area and to farm its vast expanse of potential wheat production. The Canadian government offered them an opportunity to acquire large farms in return for moving to Canada and settling there. This was not an easy life for them. Farming is hard work and the winters there are even more severe than along our own northern border states, where, likely due to the somewhat milder winters, today most Canadians live near the United States-Canada border, while our states closest to the border are sparsely populated.

Both of my parents were born in Canada. My father, Philip Ernst Hodel, was both amazed and amused to learn only in his late fifties, when he was investigating his family's genealogy, that his middle name was not Earnest. Dad was born in rural Saskatchewan, about thirty miles north of the town of Regina. He was born in February 1904, on either the thirteenth or fourteenth. I do not recall which day was correct, but Mom referred to him as "My Valentine."

My mother, Theresia Rose, who went by her middle name, was born on October 25, 1905, in Regina, to Carl and Marie Brodt. She was their oldest child, with two brothers and three sisters. Mom enjoyed being in school plays and, I gather, was popular in school. I was told that she was an attractive blonde with an outgoing personality.

The custom at that time among many ethnic groups was that if a husband died, an unmarried brother of his would marry the widow and become a father to his brother's children, a tradition found in the Bible. This happened in my father's family. Dad's mother, Louise, married Franz Hodel. They had seven children, the oldest named Peter. When Franz died, Louise married his younger brother, Adam, my grandfather, a widower, who fathered eight more children by her (in addition to eight by his first wife), of which my father was third youngest and their only mutual child to survive past infancy. Peter was twenty-two years older than my father and likely left home before my dad was old enough to remember him, but they became acquainted over time, perhaps when Pete visited.

Dad's father, Adam, was multilingual, speaking seven languages, because his father (my great-grandfather) had been an itinerant medicine man who traveled throughout southern Europe. So, my grandfather picked up the languages of the countries he lived in, as well as English. He lived in the Bucovina region of what later became Romania, although several countries have dominated it even during my lifetime in the troubled Balkans.

Dad told me stories of how immigrants in that part of Canada had come from all over Europe and settled in small communities of their peers and fellow countrymen. However, the Canadian government only wrote to them in English, and several of those communities had no one who could read or understand the government's letters. Often, people traveled all day by horse (or by horse and buggy) to see my grandfather so he could translate letters for them, and they would not be able to return to their homes before nightfall. So, they slept in blankets on the dirt floor of my father's home. He told me he remembered getting up many days and finding the floor covered with sleeping strangers his father was helping.

I have no idea whether they paid my grandfather for his assistance, but I doubt that was the case because these people were very poor. It obviously pleased my dad that his father helped them, and it was passed on to me to want to do the same kind of thing. I remember fondly thinking of my grandfather's hospitality to people in need of help.

In 1918, when my dad was fourteen, the world was swept by a severe influenza pandemic. It is estimated that 500 million people (out of 1.5 billion people in the world) were infected and that approximately fifty million people died worldwide. As we so well recall the panic and despair from the more recent COVID-19 pandemic, 1918 was far worse. Fear of catching the flu was everywhere and there were no vaccines.

Dad told how grave diggers would dig a grave while the family of a deceased flu victim waited with the casket at the other end of the field. Then they would switch ends of the field while the family brought the casket, held the grave-side service, and placed the casket in the grave. After the family had covered the casket with at least six inches of dirt and moved away from the grave, the grave diggers would return and finish filling the grave, but they would not get near the family for fear of catching the flu.

Dad and Pete, along with their mother, survived the flu, and they were the only two of her children to do so. Dad's father was either already dead or died at the same time. Since Pete was nowhere near Regina at that time, it meant that my dad, at age fourteen, became the sole support of his mother. He took a job in a drug store. As a boy, it made me sad to think of him at such an early age having such responsibility, but it also made me enormously proud to think of him shouldering the load and doing his best to do what was required.

I recall several anecdotes my father told me about those times, including that as soon as he went to work, the druggist told him he was free to eat as much candy as he wanted, but that he could not take it out of the drug store or give it to his friends. Dad said that for the first week he thought he had died and gone to heaven, as he ate lots of candy. By the end of the week, however, he was sick of candy. In fact, to his dying day he rarely ate it. An object lesson I took from that was the potential for aversion therapy. If one wanted to get rid of a desire, one could overindulge it for a brief time. Later I applied that process very effectively to stopping smoking.

The pandemic coincided with part of Canada's prohibition era, when only drug stores could dispense whiskey, and only by doctor's order. Dad, as a young teenager, had the task first thing in the morning of pouring drinks for the alcoholics who came there to get their "prescriptions" filled. This made a profound impression on him about the evils of drink, and the dangers of addiction. He was grim and determined whenever speaking of it to me when I was a young boy. It made an impression on both me and my brother, Les. Dad drank only socially, never to excess, and drank less and less as he got older, eventually not imbibing at all.

I remember my father telling me that he was the top student in his high school class. I admired him for that, and I wanted to emulate him. He said that he learned shorthand so that he could take notes as fast as the teacher spoke. On one occasion the teacher looked up from speaking and saw my dad sitting there with his pencil on his desk, having stopped writing. The teacher got up in a huff and came over to discipline him, looked over Dad's shoulder, did a double take and then said, deflated, "Oh, shorthand!" and walked back to his desk.

This story always appealed to me because it illustrated the importance of being prepared when an opportunity arrived. One should not wait for the challenge and *then* seek to become prepared. In fact, I am sure this is the element of the Horatio Alger stories I read as a boy that appealed to me. The hero was always doing something useful even when not in immediate need of a skill. Then, when opportunity presented itself, he was ready.

My parents met at church in Regina, where Dad's family moved when he reached high school. Dad was five feet eight inches tall, about average for men at that time in the twentieth century. Mom was five seven, tall for a woman in her day. In fact, she told me that when he showed interest in her she was dismissive and said, "He's too short for me." Eventually, however, things reached the point between them where Dad went to her father and asked for permission to propose.

Years later, when I was old enough to understand and remember the story, Mom spoke with genuine distress about her father's reaction when Dad asked. "Why would you want to marry *her*?" he asked. "She can't even boil water!" Dad was not deterred, however; she accepted, and they became engaged.

I have never forgotten how pained Mom was by her father's thoughtlessness, even long after he had died. That was a deeply felt hurt—even for me—and it affected me all my life by making me not want to hurt people that way. In fact, to have any chance of avoiding hurting people, I had to learn to control my sharp and cutting tongue.

Dad was too poor to even think about going to college, and job opportunities were very slim in Regina after he graduated from high school. So, in 1924 he went south to Portland, Oregon, to find work. He told me that his brother Peter lived there and wrote and told him there were jobs available. Dad and Mom were engaged by that time, and their understanding was that he would go away to find work and return in a year to marry her.

Dad found a job with Huntington Rubber Mills, a company that made rubberized diapers, bottle caps, and heels and soles for shoe repair shops. In those days many people had their shoes re-soled as often as necessary, provided the uppers were still in good shape. Dad started by going door-to-door selling rubberized diapers. He did not like that job, but he learned a lesson that was not lost on me when he told me the story. It is important to be willing to do *any* job in order to be responsible and earn one's living. No honest job is too demeaning if it is the only one you can find. To put it another way, it is much more important to work at *anything* than to be unemployed.

My father's example was a great inspiration to me. He was a self-made man and diligently worked long hours throughout his career. He always encouraged me in my life and career and showed real pleasure regarding my hard work and was proud of my successes. In addition to being a true gentleman, he was kind, a man of strong character, and he was hard working. He was my inspiration, and he was the motivation in my life until he died. I wanted to please him, and, as I have said before, he was generous in his praise for my efforts and successes. I was blessed to have a father like him as my mentor and example.

I observed both of my parents and saw what worked for them. They both were bright, strong, special individuals. They always kept teaching me—in little ways, by subtle means, ways that I did not even realize at the time. And they taught me solid values—ethics, primary principles, and the meaning of right and wrong, which built the foundation in me that guided my life.

In June 1925, Dad returned to Regina to marry Mom and bring her back to Portland. There is an amusing story that shows how little some people in the US knew about Canada—and Canadians—in those days. He returned to his church after a three-week absence, during which he had gotten married. A woman asked, "Why, Mr. Hodel, you haven't been to church for several weeks. Have you been ill?"

"Well, no," he said, "I went to Canada to get married."

The woman gasped and said, "You married an *Indian*?"

This story always got lots of laughs when it was told to family and friends, because Mom, as a tall blonde, looked Scandinavian.

Leaving Regina and all her family and friends was difficult for such a gregarious person as my mother. She was very attached to her friends, whom she made—and kept—in large numbers. She became very homesick, and it was not her style to suffer in silence. She told Dad, repeatedly, how she missed her friends and wanted to go back home.

Mom soon became pregnant and, on May 1, 1926, my brother, Leslie Earl Hodel, was born. In June, Dad arranged for Mom and baby Les to travel by train, the only real, long-distance travel option in those days, back to Regina for six weeks to visit family and friends. That seems like a long visit now, when people often commute across the country for even a day or two by airplane, but in those days by train the trip took three days each way. It was also very expensive and difficult, especially for a young mother. It meant sitting up for that long with a baby. That was not easy! If she was making the journey, she was going to make the most of it.

When Mom returned from Canada, she was in tears about her desire to go back to Regina *to live*. Dad, a wise man, said that he would save money so that she could go back for a visit in two years, and he promised that if after that she still wanted to move back to Canada, they would do so. She took that trip, but found that after those two years, her friends in Canada had married and gone off in different directions, so the atmosphere in Regina could no longer compete with Portland, where she had made many new friends. She returned to Portland, happy to stay there, and, fortunately for me, I was born an American citizen nine years after my brother.

I believe my dad expected how Mom would feel after two years. However, it was equally clear to me that he would have kept his promise if it had turned out she wanted to return to Regina. The lessons learned from that story were important components of my own remarkably happy marriage to Barbara: Honor your wife; be sensitive to her needs and desires; seek reasonable solutions to her problems; make no dictatorial demands; and keep your promises.

Soon after first arriving in Portland, my parents both applied, studied for, and received their United States citizenship. Dad was a great patriot. He loved the United States of America and the freedom and opportunity it provided to all of us. While he never said negative things about Canada, he taught his sons to be patriots, and he certainly imparted to me the idea that *we owe something back* to a country that has provided us so much freedom and opportunity. In later life I looked back and realized that my dad shared with me the concept expressed by Edmund Burke: "All that is necessary for evil to triumph is for good men to do nothing." I often quoted Burke in speeches I made as a Cabinet officer.

Dad told me that he had a strong, early bias toward President Franklin D. Roosevelt, who was very popular with Canadians. Dad was poor at the time and barely made it through the Great Depression, but he did not see financial success as wrong. The more he listened to FDR speak, however, the more he thought that FDR was stigmatizing Americans who had economic success and trying to turn other people against them, and that led him to become a

Republican, which is how I was reared and remained throughout my life. I grew to be a committed conservative, so that wing of the Republican Party became my home.

My father was often so quiet and reserved with strangers that they thought he was shy or maybe even unfriendly. In fact, he had an earthy sense of humor. He did not like dirty jokes, but he enjoyed somewhat risqué or off-color humor. I remember after he got a small fishing boat that he had a name painted up on a slat of wood and affixed it to the bow—*Numbut*. When asked why he chose that name, he said, "If you sat on those hard wooden seats for very long, you'd know why." He liked jokes that caused the listener to think and where he did not say anything off-color, but one could figure out what was meant.

Dad became president of Portland's Downtown Kiwanis Club, and I once attended a luncheon where he introduced the Queen of the Portland Rose Festival. In her remarks she commented on how hard the seats were on the floral float she had ridden during the three or four hours of the festival's parade. When my dad got back up to the lectern he commented, "Gee, and I always thought the saying went, 'Uneasy rests the *head* that wears the crown!'" The audience loved it.

His actions like that influenced me years later in my own speaking opportunities, both in school and during my career. Growing up, I had to learn where the line should be drawn in such jokes, and in my teenage years I crossed it a few times, but I never wanted to offend. Over time I figured out how to amuse people without insulting or upsetting them, and it was a benefit when I later had a great number of speaking opportunities.

When I was CEO (chief executive officer) of the Bonneville Power Administration and emceed the dedication of its new Ross Control Center on a very misty day, my father would have been proud when I joked to the audience, "You may not realize it but these metal chairs on the stage have a dish shape, and each time I get up to introduce someone a puddle forms on the seat. I sure hope my shorts are colorfast!"

By the time I was in President Ronald Reagan's Cabinet, the sense of humor I learned from my father was a useful tool for dealing with people, both individually and in groups, as well as to sometimes handle an awkward situation. I remember a speech I gave in Pennsylvania at the request of a US Congressman who needed someone "important" from Washington, DC, to speak at one of his events. After my remarks, there was a Q&A period, and a fellow got up and asked a pretty hostile question about a decision I had made as Secretary. He went on and on about why my decision was wrong. I listened patiently, but at some point, it was obvious the audience was becoming embarrassed at someone who was talking so long and treating the speaker so rudely. Finally, he finished with a flourish, "How could you make such a terrible decision?!"

Realizing that a full explanation would take far too long, I stood silent for what seemed like several seconds and then said, kind of hesitantly, "Well... it seemed like a good idea at the time." The audience exploded in laughter, and I went on to the next question.

In my first press conference as Secretary of the Interior, I was asked if I was going to turn the buffalo around on the Department's official seal to face to the right, like Jim Watt, two Secretaries before me, had done with some decorative items. With the original seal on the lectern in front of me, I leaned over to look at it from above and my view was, of course, reversed from that of the audience. "Why, that buffalo *is* facing to the right," I said and pointed to my right with my right hand. Everyone laughed and I went on to the next question.

I was born on May 23, 1935, and in my early years, we lived in Portland's Richmond grade school district. Several things happened in my early life, which, in retrospect, are significant.

First, my father came home from a Kiwanis Club meeting one day, not long after my fifth birthday, with a story. He was very impressed that he had met a man, Gust Anderson, who was a Representative in the Oregon State Legislature. I think back to that vivid memory and believe that I likely concluded that if my father was proud to meet such a person, he would be very proud of me if

I became a successful politician. My dad's approval meant so much to me.

Not long after that, our family was at our cabin on the Tualatin River near Portland. It was a summer day in 1940, and I overheard my parents discussing the awful war taking place in Europe. Those were the early days of the Second World War. No doubt reflecting my mother's emotions, I remember being upset that such bad things were happening.

I exclaimed, "Oh, why can't they just get along?" Even at that young age, I was a fixer. I wanted to please my mom and to help those distant people to live in harmony. I later expressed myself as wishing that I could be President so that I could solve people's problems and do good. I have mentioned this a few times over the years and, most of the time, people have reacted as if my declaration was so unusual for someone that young that they found it difficult to believe.

Another aspect regarding WWII was that, although Dad did not know it at the time, the US Government had a secret weapons program, the Manhattan Project, which built the atomic bombs that led to the end of the war. Dad had a security clearance to provide components but was not told exactly what they were for. After the war he learned that the parts Huntington Rubber Mills produced were for operating the fuel rods that were used to control the reaction in the atomic pile which generated the weapons grade uranium.

A second memory which had a powerful impact on my life and attitude occurred when my mother explained to me that we had relatives in Germany, where horrible things were happening during the war. In the dark of the night, without warning, someone from the "government" could knock on the door and take parents away from their children, never to be heard from again. This was a terrifying thought to me—imagining life at that age without Mom and Dad. From that moment I became distrustful of too much government power, and, while believing that a well-intentioned leader could do good things, government on the whole was inherently dangerous, even potentially evil.

I remember thinking at the time that if I wanted to do good, I could become either a pastor or President—not bad for a five-year-old. And I reached the rational conclusion that I could do more good for more people as President than as a pastor; therefore, President it was. And for the next fifteen years, I never wavered from that goal.

My family's favorite photo of me as a boy (Family photos)

My career goal became more complex and more sophisticated when my godfather, "Uncle" Gerdau Roeder, around that same time in my young life, taught me to say that I wanted to be not a politician but a statesman. In his estimation, politicians could not be trusted, and statesmen were respect-worthy leaders. I did not know exactly what a politician was but becoming both a statesman and President seemed quite reasonable to me. He also told me that most men in politics were lawyers. That was not totally accurate, even though a good number of people in public life were lawyers, but I did not know that or even care. If Uncle Gerdau thought becoming a lawyer was a good thing for me to do, then I was ready to do it.

Uncle Gerdau and his wife, "Aunt" Elsie, were not related to us but were my parents' closest friends. My parents attended the same church where Uncle Gerdau was the pianist. He was very talented and could sight-read anything set before him almost flawlessly, yet he could not play from memory. He also was a very upright man of solid integrity, and I remember having the thought that I did not want to do anything to displease him.

When I was an early teenager, thirteen or so, my dad became very ill (if I knew then what it was, I have forgotten) and he and Mom took a six-week trip to Arizona for the sunshine to recover. For those six weeks I lived with Uncle Gerdau and Aunt Elsie. I got to school by riding my bicycle a couple of miles each way. It was a different era from now when people worry so much about their kids getting hurt or kidnapped. I loved the responsibility of getting myself to school. And I felt very much at home with the Roeders.

Deciding at a very early age to go to college was easy for me. One miserable, cold, rainy, winter day in Portland, I was in the car with my mother as she drove past a group of construction workers digging a ditch beside the road. Seeing them out in the cold and rain, slogging through the muck, I shuddered, and said with feeling, "Oh! I'd *hate* a job like that!" Without missing a beat my mother said, "Well then, Baby, you better go to college!" Just like that, my mind was made up, and I never doubted that my choices were either working in a muddy ditch for the rest of my life or going to college. That was pretty simplistic, of course, but decisive for me.

I would have later, no doubt, reached the same decision about the necessity of going to college if I wanted to pursue my goal of being a lawyer on the way to becoming a statesman, but as a child I was far too unsophisticated to understand that college was a prerequisite to admission to law school. It didn't matter to me, either. It was enough that I could avoid the wet, cold ditch in the middle of winter if I went to college. The fact that it served my ultimate goal as well was just an added benefit.

Uncle Gerdau also gave me another essential for reaching my goal. He stated that the best lawyers came from Harvard, so I had better plan to go there. I am not sure where he got his information, but I accepted as truth all that he said. And while not all leaders went to Harvard, sure enough, in my lifetime I found that many leading lawyers, judges, and statesmen had done so.

What intrigues me in retrospect is that I actually believed I could achieve the goal of becoming President of the United States. My information was woefully inadequate and often faulty, but working with the facts I had been given, my efforts were entirely reasonable. What amazes me as I look back is how my life was set on a course by broad goals and seemingly minor bits of information that weren't even all that accurate. My desire to help people was a response to my mother's emotional reactions to war, and my career path was shaped by Uncle Gerdau's words, which I grabbed hold of and made mine, confident that if I succeeded in politics it would make my father proud. I wanted to be a Harvard educated lawyer so that I could become a statesman, even President, so that I could help people. I had absolutely no idea, however, what other kind of preparation it would take to pursue that path.

I remember later in life my dad saying that when he heard I wanted to go to Harvard and become a lawyer, he readily approved of my idea, realizing that in a week or so, any boy my age would want to be something else. He said that had he thought it possible or likely that I was serious, he might have raised some red flags, due to the cost.

Dad, an excellent student in high school, had not gone to college because it was too expensive. His family had no money with which to send him. And even though he was the top student in his class, he did not get a scholarship. I remember him telling me that there was one scholarship offered to students in his class, but, to his regret, it went to a boy whose father could have afforded to send him to college anyway.

Harvard, based on what he knew of it, seemed like an elite school not suited to the likes of us. Although my parents were somewhat better-off financially by the time I reached college age, it was still a huge burden for them, one year, including travel, equaling almost 30 percent of my dad's annual income. As I progressed through grammar and high school, I came to realize that Harvard was among the most expensive schools in the country and that I ought to seek a scholarship to help pay for my education. I had not yet focused on the fact that law school came after college and that Harvard College was not the same as Harvard *Law* School. I began to plan early on, studying dutifully, getting good grades, and engaging in extracurricular activities that would look good on a college application.

From kindergarten until midway through fifth grade, I attended Richmond Grade School in southeast Portland. This was also the school my brother, Les, had attended nine years ahead of me. As is so often experienced by younger siblings, Les had been a top student and my teachers simply expected me to be like him, so, motivated by my parents and this expectation and, of course, by my plans to attend Harvard, I did my homework and got straight *A*'s (with one *B)* in four years of high school. Fortunately, I found that if I did my homework, my memory was good enough that I could do well on tests.

Richmond was in a tough neighborhood with many immigrants: Italian, Jewish, and German. My parents were immigrants, too, of course. But because they spoke excellent English, I never knew if anyone thought of us as immigrants, and neither did I, until my brother commented on it years later.

One important lesson I learned early was when I got into a fight in the second grade and, while friends told me that I had won, it really hurt. I decided that if winning hurt that much I would not get into any more fights. I made it a point to seek common ground and to find ways to defuse angry situations.

Les studied piano as a boy, eventually becoming a very good pianist, and my parents expected me to take music lessons as well. I do not recall a discussion of what instrument I would study, but I think their leaning was toward the piano for me, too. After all, we were not well-off, and we already had a piano. However, one day about a year before I started going to school, the radio was on, and I heard some music that I really liked. I said to Mom, "That is what I want to play." I did not know until she told me that the instrument was the violin; and soon, they bought a half-size violin and took me to lessons. I do not recall how well I did, but I remember my father saying, later, that I never made the squeaks and squawks usually expected of beginning violinists.

Fairly early in my life with the violin, it seemed to my mother that I was progressing past the abilities of my first teacher, and she managed to get me an audition with Frank Eichenlaub, Portland's foremost violin teacher. He would not take just any pupil. He had to see talent and believe there was serious intent on the student's part before he would take them. As I recall, I was the youngest of all his pupils at the time I started.

For thirteen years, I studied violin, even after I knew that music would not be my career. My parents felt that continuing lessons was a good way to reinforce what I was learning. As an eighth grader, with Mr. Eichenlaub's encouragement, I auditioned for and became a member of the violin section of the Portland Junior Symphony, which consisted mostly of high school students. The next year, I also played in the high school orchestra. Even earlier, I played as a soloist for various groups around the city, mostly women's clubs. My mother always drove me to these recitals and attended them.

Playing the violin in high school (Family photos)

Midway through my fifth-grade year, my parents found a house to buy in Portland's Laurelhurst district, a middle-class neighborhood. My new homeroom teacher did me no favor when she welcomed me to my new class by introducing me and holding up my transfer report card that showed straight *A*'s. Imagine how popular that made me right off the bat. It was about this time in my life that I made the conscious decision that if I had to choose, I would rather be respected than liked.

I think that attitude was solidified when the first question I got from one of my new classmates at Laurelhurst was, "How many cashmeres do you own?" I did not even know what a cashmere was! Of course, I soon learned that they were very expensive sweaters that I knew were out of our price range. I never owned or even asked my parents for one. In fact, when my mother later got wind of the fashion expectations of my new classmates, I recall a discussion, the essence of which was the question, "Do you want a cashmere?"

I said, "No, they are too expensive." In saying that, I knew that I would never be a part of the so-called in-group. Since she wholeheartedly agreed cashmeres were too expensive, that was the end of the matter. I emotionally and mentally stuck out my chin as if to say, "I won't conform to your elitist notions of fashion."

I came from a well-read home, and schoolwork was easier for me than for most of my classmates. Getting *A*'s came almost naturally, if I listened in class. I was determined to excel at my studies and earn the respect of my classmates whether or not they became my friends. I did not want to seek friends who valued someone based on how many cashmeres they owned. I decided that I would not worry about them liking me, but I was determined to be worthy of their respect whether they gave it or not. I could not control their attitudes or responses, but I could control my actions.

After finishing eighth grade, I went to Grant High School, because our house was in that district and students were required to attend the school in the district where they lived. Grant was a fairly large school with about 2,400 students and over 600 students in my class.

In high school I was highly verbal and had a problem with talking in class, possibly because I would finish my work early and have extra time. I generally felt that I had something interesting to say, even if at times I became a bother to others. In geometry, for example, I was prone to annoy my seatmates in such a way that the teacher, Mrs. Young, eventually moved all the other students into the first five rows and put me in row seven, separating me from the others by a row of empty seats. She did not think much of me at that point.

Mrs. Young also happened to be my homeroom teacher, which meant that first thing in the morning I went to her room so she could take attendance and make announcements before we students headed off to other classes for the rest of the day. When the first six weeks had passed, report cards were distributed to the students by their homeroom teachers. That morning, Mrs. Young looked at me as I walked in the door, having reviewed my report card containing straight *A*'s except for one *B*, and said, "Y'know, Hodel, if you'd shape up, you could get a scholarship." It was obvious that she had not thought of me as having that potential until she saw my grades, even though I was doing excellent work in her geometry class. She simply found it hard to believe that someone who was as much of a nuisance as I had been to her could possibly be a good all-around student.

Quite often in the evenings I was on the phone with my two closest friends, Bruce and Danny, and occasionally others who asked for my help in the math classes that we shared. I enjoyed helping others, not only because it made me feel good, but I knew that doing so also helped me better understand and retain what we were studying.

In the same vein, I tried to help my classmates who were struggling. Many years later, at my sixtieth high school reunion, a woman I had not known well in high school, but who was in one of my classes, came up to me and thanked me for helping her in that class. She told me that she was terribly nervous about having to stand before the class and make presentations and that the other boys would make faces at her and try to embarrass her. She recalled that I told her to ignore those guys and look at me, and that I always looked back at her with a friendly and encouraging expression. All those years later she was still emotional about how much that had meant to her.

I was naturally curious about how things worked, but even more so regarding people, what made them who they were. I learned to read people, how to motivate them, and how to create a genuine sense of comfort. I knew that if I could avoid offense in what I said and use personal mannerisms to show that I was sincere, open, and caring, I could help others feel good about themselves, which also made me feel good. Using self-deprecating humor often eased tension and added to a sense of geniality. I also worked hard to remember a person's name when I met them and used it often in order to get it in my mind.

All through high school I continued to get top grades and was also involved in outside activities. I enjoyed the extracurricular things, but I also wanted them to add to my resume for the scholarship I wanted at Harvard. As a sophomore, I resigned from the Portland Junior Symphony, much to my mother's and Mr. Eichenlaub's consternation. It was prestigious to be a part of this excellent music group, and to drop out after only two years was hard for them to accept.

Instead, that year, I tried out for the Grant High basketball team, along with a lot of other boys. The coach put us through a series of practices and slowly reduced the number of boys who still had a chance to make the team. I survived all the cuts but the last one. So, in the end I didn't make the team. I'm pretty sure I was cut because in one of the last scrimmages I came down with two rebounds under the basket and went back up with what should have been easy layups, but I missed them both! Agony!

Whether or not that was the reason I didn't make the team, I later came to believe that missing those layups was the best thing that could have happened to me, because I was able to attribute my failure not to some arbitrary or unfair action by the coach, but to my own failure to convert easy baskets. It also taught me, again, that no one wins them all. Losing and failing are part of life and learning to deal with that fact and moving on is a critical part of growing up and preparing for success in life.

I also realized that it might have been much better to have tried out a year earlier as a freshman so that I would have had that experience when it came to my sophomore year. At the time, I was disappointed not to make the team, but in retrospect it was a great blessing. The practice schedule would have kept me from many other activities that helped me eventually earn a scholarship to Harvard, proving Mrs. Young's earlier prediction.

In sophomore social studies class, one of the assignments was to do a research paper on career alternatives. I chose to examine what it meant to be a lawyer. After all, my long-term goal of becoming a statesman required it, I thought. What I discovered only reinforced my commitment to my plan. And it clearly had the potential to result in a better quality of life than being a violinist. Out of many thousands of lawyers, a high percentage achieved both financial security and recognition, whereas out of thousands of musicians, only a handful excelled and lived well financially. Whether or not a political career developed, I was impressed by the vision of a senior lawyer in his community being recognized as a good and generous man of wisdom who could be sought out for his general advice as well as his legal assistance.

As I progressed in high school, I began to seek lessons and opportunities for leadership, which, as we know, both statesmen and Presidents must have. As other experiences came into my life, I continued my progress toward that childhood goal.

CHAPTER 2
LEARNING TO LEAD

When I had just begun my sophomore year at Grant High School I saw a notice for a new organization, Junior Achievement, which sounded interesting. "JA," as it was known, sought to teach high school students in one school year what it takes to start, operate, and then close a business, all through the forming of short-term, practice companies, with business leader-advisers assisting the students. When I mentioned JA to my dad, a businessman, he really liked the idea, and he encouraged me to get involved.

At the first meeting, kids from different high schools were divided into about thirty groups of fifteen or so each and designated a "company." We were told about JA and what we would do over the next eight months. Then we were to elect our company officers. I knew immediately that I wanted to be president of my company. We had only a few minutes of getting acquainted and very little time to discuss a few issues—and there was no campaigning; but I was pleased that the other students in my company elected me as president from among those who had been nominated.

In later years, I have tried to look back and recall just what I did that allowed me to project some quality or qualities that made a majority of the others in the room vote for me. I knew from experiences in grade school that appearing to *want* to be president was a good way *not* to get it. There is a natural reluctance to elect someone who wants a position too strongly. To this day I remember the sense of awareness of how I had to conduct myself to increase the chances that I would be elected. I also suspect that when someone mentioned the possibility of electing me, I conveyed, probably by my body language, that I would take the job if it were offered.

I imagine now that there were a few things that would have prompted someone to nominate me, as well as vote for me, although I knew no one prior to that night. First, I dressed neatly, although not stylishly. I customarily wore gray chinos and one of my father's white, long sleeve dress shirts with my sleeves rolled up halfway, and a pin below the top button at the collar, which I left unbuttoned. That was my "uniform." Businesslike and sharp looking.

Next, I learned not to be a disruption, as I had been in Mrs. Young's class. I was careful not to talk just to be talking. I waited until an issue had been reasonably well covered and then would do something that I often did later in my career. I would summarize where it sounded to me the group had come out, putting my shaping on it so that it was a complete package. I think that was a unique gift I had, and it was part of me even at that stage of my life.

Third, I did not pass up any opportunity to say something funny, as long as it was positive and brief and didn't look like I was trying too hard. I employed a timely comment connected to whatever was being said that could lighten the mood, but never in a disruptive or disrespectful way.

Finally, and perhaps most importantly, I truly felt and showed genuine respect for everyone with whom I was talking and tried to project that in the way I addressed people or responded to their comments. In other words, I always tried to project self-respect, respect for others, and seriousness sprinkled with appropriate humor on occasion, qualities which I knew instinctively, even then, people want to see in their leaders.

I tried to show leadership that wore well among others, being sincere in my views, kind in persuasion, and gracious in implementation. I wanted to attract followers in a way that engendered loyalty, not turned them off. I was competitive, not for the sake of winning, but to excel, and for the satisfaction of competing and doing my best. I sought to be the final decision maker by accepting responsibility. As with my childhood goals, I was not there to simply "win" or to be in control of others, but to do the right thing and to help others.

I have focused on this JA election because it contained many of the elements that cropped up over and over in my life and helped propel me into positions of leadership. One way or another, people with whom I dealt perceived that I was smart, but not too smart; competent, but not arrogant; congenial, but not weak; and a team builder, not an autocrat; and they wanted to be on that team.

I usually felt that I really had something to contribute in the way of getting people to work together for a common objective. To me there were few things in life that provided as much satisfaction as achieving some goal we had set as a group and then worked for collectively as a team. This was particularly true where people were divided and needed to be brought together, or in those cases where there were willing people with great attitudes but who were disparaged by their associates and not given much to do that was useful. Over and over, I found that by befriending an individual and really assessing what they could do best, and then putting them to work doing it, I not only found a top performer, but I made a lifelong friend.

I was not a directive leader. I did not relish setting a goal for a group and telling people exactly what they were to do. My leadership style, which I described as collegial, was characteristic in every such position I filled through my life and career. That is, I gathered the key people on any given issue, discussed the objectives and alternatives with them, and tried to come to a consensus. However, if after a reasonable time it became clear to me what we needed to do (and almost always that was also the point at which most of the group was in agreement) rather than saying, "This is what we will do" and giving an order, I would say something like, "Well, then, it seems to me that what we need to do is..."

My closest staff in any of my positions could tell when I had reached a decision and, unless there was something new to say that had not already been covered, the time for discussion was over.

Among the only times I can recall losing my temper was when someone either continued to assert his own position after my decision had been conveyed or passive-aggressively did not follow. On one of those occasions, fortunately a one-on-one meeting, I slapped my hand on a glass-topped conference table so hard that I was relieved to find that I had neither broken the glass nor injured my hand. But I regretted almost immediately losing my cool that way, and to this day it is something I vividly remember—and still with regret.

Over time, however, I realized that my desire to lead, which eventually became a calling, did not mean that I had to be president of the country or of an organization. I found that I was most comfortable working for a visionary leader who I felt was competent and worthy, and who would let me do the actual operation of the organization. Making a team function smoothly was my desire and my strength.

My desire to lead was satisfied by having the ability and delegated authority to pull the levers and push the buttons that ran an organization, and I was very comfortable implementing faithfully the decisions made by the leader. I never aspired to be in the spotlight with the attention on myself. There were times that I had no real alternative other than to accept a top position, but my most satisfactory jobs in my career were serving as "number two." I experienced that role several times in my life, most notably at the Bonneville Power Administration in my thirties, the US Department of the Interior in my forties, and later, the Christian ministry Focus on the Family in my sixties. And while I later became CEO of each of those organizations, I found the COO role (chief operating officer) to be much more personally satisfying.

In JA, for three years, I was, however, president of each company in which I was involved. At the midyear point in all three years, I was reelected president even though the standard JA recommendation was that we should change presidents at midyear. I think most of my team members agreed that the job I was doing as president was good for all of us. In addition, the presidents from all thirty or so of the JA companies in Portland were formed into a group called the Portland Junior Achievement Association. It was like a Chamber of Commerce for the JA companies, and out of all the company presidents, I was elected president of that group, too, even though Grant High School was not generally liked by the other high schools in Portland because its students were thought to be snobs.

When my family moved into the new district, causing me to attend Grant, unlike my brother, who had gone to Franklin High School, he said in jest, but giving voice to the general reaction toward Grant students, "If Don goes to Grant, I'll never speak to him again!" Unlike any other high school in Portland at that time, Grant had quite a homogeneous student body in terms of economic status. We were almost all from the middle class, some low end and some high end. There were a few from poor homes and a few from very wealthy homes, but by and large the vast majority came from the middle of the middle class. This led to a sense of belonging and a measure of confidence about oneself and one's compatriots at school, presenting a certain air to outsiders.

Some of the other ten high schools in Portland had two incompatible cultures, and one could feel that when talking with students from there. One such school drew about half its students from the very wealthy community of Portland Heights, situated on the top of the West Hills overlooking Portland and, in my opinion, their kids were snobbish. The other half came from the closest thing to slums that Portland had at that time, the bottom of the hill areas where Portland's oldest, often run-down homes were.

In my junior year at Grant, I became involved in student government, although not joining the governing clique composed of the "cashmere sweater" crowd. While I had some friends among them, I was definitely not one of them, and I spurned any chances to join their clubs before ever being asked. Perhaps I thought I would not be invited and would avoid the shame of seeking to be invited and not succeeding. Also, however, it was common knowledge that there was drinking and smoking going on in parties held by that group, and I wanted no part of anything that might sully my reputation and interfere with my chances of earning a scholarship to Harvard.

So, as an "outsider" I ran for assistant treasurer of the Grant High School student body in January 1952, my junior year. The assistant treasurer automatically moved up to treasurer the next semester and treasurer was a good stepping-stone to student body president, something that I wanted, but dared not admit to openly, for the reasons I explained earlier in writing about JA.

Each candidate for assistant treasurer was required to speak to an assembly of the entire student body for one minute on an assigned subject, which, that year, was: "Why We Should Support the United Good Neighbors" (a community-wide charitable fund-raising organization). The student body constitution required a majority of the votes to win. There were several candidates for the position and a runoff between the top two would be required if no one achieved an absolute majority on the first ballot.

Each candidate for all positions on the student council (which included assistant treasurer) spoke to the student body at the same assembly, beginning with the lowest offices. The school's 2,400 students filled the auditorium, while candidates for office were required to sit in chairs at the back of the stage, in plain view, while each of the other candidates came forward about fifteen feet or so to the microphone to speak.

My father helped me prepare for the speech, which came in at just under the one-minute limit, and I remember it being a good speech, including a touch of humor. When it was my turn to walk forward to speak, however, I was so nervous that I felt like I could not breathe. I thought I was going to collapse for lack of air. Afterward, I could not recall taking a single breath during the entire one-minute speech. That panic did not deter me from getting involved in such things is a testimony to my youth and enthusiasm.

Fortunately, I received a majority of votes on the first ballot and no runoff (a final vote to choose between the top two vote getters in cases where no one received a majority on the first ballot) was required. As assistant treasurer I automatically became a member of the student council. I performed my duties diligently, which mostly meant working with the treasurer, sharing responsibility counting the money that came into the student body from the sale of student identification cards and tickets to various events, and making the bank deposits.

It was clear that an outsider's views were not welcome the day I attended my first student council meeting. A matter was under discussion, and I offered a comment, to which one of the in-group seniors gave a scornful look and said in a totally disparaging way, "Who cares what *you* think?" That made me furious, though I did not show it. To this day, my anger still rises just thinking about that total disrespect.

The experience also increased my determination to seek to be respected rather than liked. At the same time, I learned to keep quiet unless I had something very important to say, which was not often. To this day when I am in groups where I am not an insider or the boss, I try to be very careful never to say something that might expose me to ridicule and rejection.

The other impact the severe put-down had on me was that it caused me to want *never* to treat someone else that way, reminiscent of my mother's painful experience with her father. I already had a basic attitude of respect for others, but after that painful slight I tried more than ever always to show my respect, although I am sure there were occasions where someone pushed me past my limits. I felt that even if people were uninformed, I owed them the courtesy of hearing them out. This attitude even influenced my treatment of the media later in life because often the questions one gets, especially on complex matters, are based on ignorance of the subject. When I was head of Bonneville Power, I often gave speeches about the electricity supply situation in the Pacific Northwest, talking about kilowatts and kilowatt hours in describing our electric supply. After one such speech a young reporter came up to me and asked, "What's a 'kilowatt'?" At that moment I knew I was headed for trouble when he wrote his story no matter how good his intentions were.

Through Junior Achievement I was gaining leadership experience and skills, but that was of no importance to the majority of my schoolmates, who knew nothing about JA and, of course, had no idea that I was involved in it—whatever it was. At Grant High School I was still that outsider without any cashmere sweaters who kept getting top grades but didn't make the basketball team.

While the in-group held those views, I was doing what came naturally in befriending others. I acknowledged anyone I recognized by saying hi as we passed in the hallway, whether they were in my class or not, even to those in the classes behind me. This was not common among my classmates who followed the more traditional approach of pretty much ignoring everyone in the classes behind them. I liked being recognized by others, and it pleased me to make others feel good by recognizing them and to this day it still does. I also enjoy an opportunity to tell people something good said by others about them, and I cannot remember ever gratuitously telling someone that anyone else had been negative or critical about them. I felt the injury of my self-perceived rejection by the in-group, and not only did I not want anyone to get that feeling from me, but I also hoped in some small measure to offset the similar slights my in-group classmates dished out to others on a daily basis.

In the spring of 1952, my junior year, an announcement was made that the American Field Service (AFS) was offering summer scholarships to a hundred or so young men and women across the US to spend six weeks with a family in a European country. The vision of AFS, which was founded by a group of pacifists from WWI who had volunteered to drive ambulances at great personal risk, was that international understanding would lead to brotherhood and world peace. My school counselor, Mrs. Whitted, suggested that I would be ideally suited for such an opportunity. The only question was, could my parents afford it since the scholarship did not cover any of the cost but was simply the opportunity to participate? The cost was substantial, about $800, at a time when $10,000 per year was a good income and a year at Harvard cost less than $4,000.

My parents thought it would be a wonderful learning experience for me and the fact that they were first generation Canadian

Americans with a German-Swiss background undoubtedly influenced them. I filled out the applications, expressed a preference for West Germany, and waited. I was accepted along with three other boys from Portland, and 101 other students from around the country.

My summer in Germany was wonderful, and very "stretching" for a young Oregon high school student. I lived with the Mueller family in Bad Cannstatt, a suburb of Stuttgart in southwestern Germany. I became close friends with their son, Gerhard, who was a year and a half older than me. We kept in touch for the rest of our lives, and Barbara and I visited him and his wife on the way to the World Energy Conference in Munich in 1971, and again when we traveled to the Balkans to speak on behalf of Campus Crusade for Christ in April 2000. (In my speeches there I felt it necessary to explain that the Department of the Interior in the United States oversees natural resources, unlike some European countries where the "interior" agency is the government's internal police watchdog.)

Barbara referred to Gerhard as "Don's German brother," and his daughter, Miriam, as "our German daughter." In 1981, Miriam lived with us as an exchange student, although she was not part of any program. That was the first year we lived in Arlington, Virginia, when I was Under Secretary of the Interior. Later she visited us in Colorado on several occasions, once with her husband and children. In August 2023, seventy-one years after my summer as Gerd's "brother," he sent me an email inviting me to his ninetieth birthday bash in Stuttgart that September. I would have enjoyed being with him for such a milestone birthday; however, I just did not feel up to traveling all that way to spend only a few minutes with him when he was surrounded by all his loving family and local friends. He died a year later, and I was saddened when Miriam informed me of his passing.

When I came back from Europe at summer's end, many teachers, especially those with introductory social studies classes, asked me to come and talk to their classes about my experiences over the summer in Europe. In September, I had automatically succeeded to the position of student body treasurer, so I was introduced before each of these classrooms to which I spoke as the treasurer of the student body who had spent six weeks in Europe as an exchange student. In this way I probably spoke to all the freshmen and most of the sophomores at our school. I had an interesting story to tell, and I made sure it held their attention and was humorous. The question-and-answer sessions gave me a chance to interact with other students and treat them with the respect that I genuinely felt.

That fall, Grant High School appeared to be following in its tradition of winning the state high school football championship, having been the dominant team for years. The team was undefeated for each of the prior two years. But winning the state championship for the third straight year was not to be, as eligibility rules were strict, and it turned out that one of our substitute players lived two blocks outside the Grant district. Unfortunately, this became known after Grant had already played and won its first four games. The official decision of the league was that Grant had to forfeit those four games even though the ineligible player contributed nothing to those victories. Instead of those four wins, we suddenly and shockingly had four losses, and even though we won all the rest of the games, there was no chance of making the playoffs. Fury reigned among Grantonians. Letters were written and rallies were held, all to no avail, and yet the mood at Grant that prevailed was: "Rules are rules, however stupid they may seem, and we will abide by them." It really was an impressive reaction considering the intensity of the disappointment.

As January approached, I had the opportunity to file a petition to be a nominee for student body president. I wanted the title for my resume, and I craved the respect that I felt would follow being elected. I was less enthusiastic about the work it would entail, but I didn't really dwell on that. The two biggest deterrents were the burden of getting my name on the ballot, which required a petition to be signed by something like fifty or one hundred students, and my recognition that I was likely to lose if I did get on the ballot.

One day while I was still undecided about what to do, Burke Rice, son of a major bank president in Portland, came up to me in the hall between classes. Burke was our senior class president, and definitely one of the inmost of the in-group, but someone who actually treated me respectfully, and thus we were on quite friendly terms.

I am sure Burke was trying to be nice to me, but he said something like, "Don, I don't know if you're thinking about running for student body president, but I don't think you should because you know you don't belong to any of the important clubs and you probably would lose. You know (Jim) Damis and (John) Narver are going to run." Again, I think Burke said this in all sincerity, as a friend. He truly seemed concerned that I would be embarrassed by losing to the popular Damis and Narver, who were cocaptains of the basketball team, and were cocaptains and the stars of our martyred football team. They were the epitome of Big Men on Campus.

I was very much offended by Burke's comments though I showed no such emotion to him. I thanked him politely for his advice and told him I appreciated his thoughtfulness in warning me. My close buddies with whom I did things, like double-dating and going to movies, who also were not in the right clubs, told me I was an idiot to run, because they were sure I would lose and, further, they saw no reason why I or anyone would even want to be student body president.

Immediately after speaking with Burke, I went to my friend from the high school orchestra and junior symphony, Joanne McMath, who was very much in the in-group and probably my best friend among them, and told her that I wanted her to circulate my petition for student body president and get enough signatures for me to be placed on the ballot. She was very reluctant, saying that she was afraid I would suffer hurt feelings from my inevitable loss. I told her that I was not asking her advice, I just wanted her to do it. I was uncharacteristically insistent, and she recognized that I saw it as a test of our friendship. She finally gave in and said she would help. I am pretty sure she was embarrassed to be circulating a petition for someone she felt had no chance to win.

Joanne did her job very well, obtaining the necessary signatures needed for my nomination. In January, at the all-school assembly Damis, Narver, and I each made required speeches (three minutes this time), but unlike my previous school election, candidates for president had no assigned topic. This was a campaign speech, and I prepared carefully. Even now, I am impressed with what I recall of both the content and the delivery of my speech. My theme was that I would *like* to talk of the football victories that Grant had won, but instead I would talk of four losses, which made me prouder to be a Grantonian than all the victories in our school's storied history. I praised the players, students, their parents, and our faculty for the responsible and unusual way in which we accepted the decision that deprived Grant of another state championship. It was an emotional speech, and I was told later by friends that even many senior girls who would never vote for me were in tears as I spoke.

Going in, I expected that, considering the heavyweight competition, the best I could hope for was a runoff and, of course, in a runoff I knew that the combined Damis-Narver votes would probably beat me. But when the votes were tallied, contrary to everyone's expectations, including mine, it was a landslide—for me! I was told later by a friend involved in counting the ballots, that I garnered a majority in every class except the senior class, where, with Damis and Narver also being seniors, I won a plurality of the votes. Among the freshmen, I was told that I won an overwhelming 90 percent, although knowing how hard it is to get that high a percentage of votes in any election, I suspect it was actually less.

The winners' names (but not the number of votes) for all positions were posted on a large signboard hanging in the center hall of the school. I was standing there when the tally was completed, and I saw my name posted as the winner. Although I was excited about winning, my first thought was, *Oh my goodness, now that I've won the job, I have to do it.* With all the activities I was engaged in, I had a moment of panic about how I was going to get everything done.

Decades later, at our high school class's fiftieth reunion, Judson Jones, an avid friend of Damis and Narver, perhaps after a few too many drinks, said, "The only reason Hodel won was because Damis and Narver split the vote." Even though I was then in my seventies, I was annoyed by his statement. Several times that night and thereafter I wanted to point out to him that in order to win, one had to have an absolute majority of the votes, therefore, I beat Damis and Narver *combined* on the first ballot, which was a lot harder than beating either of them individually. I never said anything to Jones and a few years later I learned that he had died, so I was glad I had let it lie that night, but I still had the impulse deep inside me to set the record straight. The fact that I'm including this anecdote here shows how strongly I feel about the disrespect I experienced both before the election and fifty years later at the reunion.

Shortly after the election, Marilyn Adkins, who was one of my debating team partners and a close friend of my high school girlfriend, told me that she was standing in center hall with a bunch of senior girls looking up at the posted results when one of those who was in the in-group said in frustration, "Oh, dear, he just doesn't have my sympathy," to which Marilyn said, "Y'know, he doesn't really need it."

It may also have been Marilyn who told me about another interesting dialogue that took place in center hall at that same time. The student body president was traditionally expected to kiss the girl who was chosen to represent Grant High School as the Portland Rose Festival Princess. When some senior girls looked up at the election results—probably not happy that I had won—one of them suddenly said, "Oh, my gosh, that means he has to kiss the princess." Another asked, "Do you think he knows how?" Marilyn knew from my girlfriend that I did in fact know how to kiss a girl and she found the comment uproariously funny. It did, however, confirm to me that I had been very careful about my reputation and did not behave in public in any way that would have hinted about such things. By the way, I chose not to continue the tradition of kissing the girl selected as Grant's princess because it seemed inappropriate to me.

I was recognized by the teachers as a straight *A* student by the time I ran for student body president. I know now that teachers talk about students, although I did not know it then. But I was the beneficiary of a reputation as a top student. I had several of the toughest teachers in the school and they were genuinely gracious to me.

I was a good student who treated them with respect, enjoyed their courses, and showed that I did. One of the little tricks I used was telling myself that I liked each course even though occasionally I wasn't so sure about that. Again, I now know how much that kind of attitude impresses the teachers to want to help and encourage such students.

My senior English teacher, Miss Anderson, was a graying woman, about five feet two inches tall, who was probably in her mid-fifties. At age seventeen I could correctly guess a fellow student's age within a few months, but guessing the age of anyone over thirty was pretty much out of my skill set. Her reputation was that of being the toughest English teacher in the school. I remember being apprehensive when I was assigned to her class because I knew she would be tough, and I wanted top grades in order to stay on course for a scholarship to Harvard.

Early in September, Miss Anderson assigned homework on a particular topic and, the next day, she went to the blackboard and began writing questions to which we were supposed to write the answers on paper—there were no personal computers in those days, of course. For some reason the answers were very clear to me, and I wrote them down as fast as she did the questions. As she finished the last question, she turned toward the class and saw me very obviously setting my pencil down in the trough at the top of my desk while all of my classmates were still writing. She looked at me, raised her eyebrows, and mouthed silently, "Are you finished?" I nodded with a slightly embarrassed and apologetic smile, not wanting to look smug or self-satisfied. She promptly turned back to the board and wrote two more questions, one of which was an essay question that required a longer answer. I don't think my classmates ever knew that the last two questions, and tough ones at that, were my fault. Fortunately, when she graded the papers, she found my answers to be good enough for an *A+*. From that point on, I could basically do no wrong in her class, and I worked hard never to disappoint her because I was pleased I had earned her respect and strongly wanted to keep it. Little did I know how that would pay off in January when I was elected student body president.

The afternoon of the day I was elected, I walked into Miss Anderson's room immediately after lunch for her 1:00 p.m. class. She got me aside as I arrived and said very quietly so as not to be overheard by my classmates as they entered, "I know all the work you are going to have to do as president, and sometimes you will have to miss lunch. I don't want you to do that, so if you need to bring your lunch into class with you go ahead and do it. I'll just let you sit in the back where you won't disturb others."

"And" she went on (to my utter astonishment since this came from a strict disciplinarian and the toughest senior English teacher), "if you are not able to get your homework done, just let me know, and I will not call on you." I could hardly believe my ears! With those words she took away a great deal of my concerns about the burdens of the job. As it turned out, I did not want to take advantage of her truly gracious offer, so I don't recall that I ever used it. I managed to get all my homework done and still participate in Junior Achievement, where I had company president duties, along with the Portland Achievers Association president responsibilities, and complete the student government things I had to do.

The student body presidents and vice presidents of all ten high schools in Portland were formed into the Portland Interschool Council which was created by the school system to allow some cross fertilization of ideas among the schools. It met just a few times during the semester, at which time the group elected its president. Regardless of the general attitude toward Grant High School, as a direct result of my being in Junior Achievement, I was also elected president of the Interschool Council. Why me? Somehow I was able to strike a balance between being willing but not wanting it too much, which made people recognize that I *could* do it and that I *would* do it, but I was not *asking* to do it.

The reason JA helped was that one of the other student body presidents was also in JA and, as president of his company, knew me from the Portland Achievers Association. He nominated me based upon the way in which we had worked together in JA, which

I took as a great compliment. As a result of becoming president of the Portland Interschool Council, I also was invited to speak to local Kiwanis and Rotary Clubs. When I spoke to the Kiwanis Club, of which my father had once been president, he was in the audience, and it was one of the proudest days of his—and my—life.

CHAPTER 3
HARVARD

In spring of my senior year of high school, Harvard notified Mrs. Whitted at Grant High School that I had been accepted for admission and, further, that I had received one of the thirty-two Harvard National Scholarships awarded that year. It was the highest scholarship offered by Harvard. It was for a "full ride," meaning it included tuition, room, and board, worth at least $3,000 per year, which would have covered everything except my travel to and from Massachusetts. Unfortunately, Harvard had a strict policy against awarding assistance to students from families they determined were able to pay for themselves. Thus, the scholarship was (like the American Field Service) "non-stipendiary," meaning that I was listed as a recipient of this highly coveted scholarship, but I would receive no financial assistance as long as my father continued to earn his same annual salary. Dad was then making $12,500 per year, and the Harvard standard at that time was that a family with one child at home that made over $8,000 per year would not get a stipendiary scholarship. It was, however, like an insurance policy. If my father died or became unemployed, my scholarship would take over and pay for everything.

In those days it was generally assumed that the Ivy League schools knew who was applying to one or more of them and that if they really wanted someone it would affect the incentives they offered. So, I always suspected that if I had also applied elsewhere in the Ivy League, such as to Yale or Princeton, Harvard might have seen fit to bend its rules and offer me money with my prestigious scholarship. As it was, with Harvard being my only choice, they knew they had me. Dad was not insulted by the fact that I received no actual accompanying cash, and he never once complained or objected. His sense of justice made him see the fairness of the principle even as it cut against his interests. And, with his own experience at my age when his family did not have the money to send him to college, he surely was proud that Harvard deemed him able to send me.

In 1953, commercial air travel was by propeller planes only. It was also expensive, so there was no thought of my flying to Boston. Just as I had done the summer before on my way to New York for the boat trip to Germany in the AFS summer exchange student program, I traveled by train, for three nights and part of four days, across the country. The first two nights and three days were from Portland to Chicago on Union Pacific, and the coach seats reclined almost to a bed, a lot like first class air travel today on international flights with footrests, almost a flat recline, etc. It still was hard to sleep on the train, in part because of the excitement. Then, when we got to Chicago it was necessary to transfer by Parmelee Transfer (basically a limousine service) from the Union Pacific station to the New York Central station.

The eastern trains were terrible, having dirty, old, straight-backed seats with little padding. I rode to Boston sitting up in coach class for seventeen hours on that stretch, arriving very weary around 9:00 a.m. Fortunately, the first couple of days at school were spent signing up for classes, buying books, getting furniture for your room, and so on, so I was able to rest some and get ready before classes began. I was also energized because it was exciting to begin this new adventure.

Freshmen at Harvard lived in "The Yard," meaning Harvard Yard, a walled-in, gated area the size of two or three good-sized city blocks. Just inside the walls for much of the yard were freshman dorms, called halls, the administration building, Widener Library, and the hall where we had our meals. I was assigned to Wigglesworth Hall, named for a father and son who both were students in an earlier century. Room E-10 was my home for the year, along with my two roommates, fellow Grantonians Don Pearlman and Jim Damis, neither of whom were my friends in high school.

We decided to room together because we were intimidated by warnings Harvard sent to incoming public-school graduates about our being unable to compete with the prep school students, who allegedly had a much better education than the public schools could possibly have given us. We also expected that the preppies would be snobs, who would look down on us (which was true). We made the rooming decision even though we did not know each other well, we did not like each other, and Don made it clear that in the election for student body president he had voted for John Narver rather than either one of us. But as the old axiom goes, the devil you know is better than the devil you don't, and at least we all three were from Grant, and we all were sons of immigrants.

Don's father had immigrated to the United States from Estonia at the age of twelve, sent by his family to avoid the tsar's pogroms (persecutions) against Jews. He traveled with his brother, two years older, through Ellis Island and crossed the US by train to reach relatives in Portland. He later went into the furniture business with his brother and, when I knew Don, his father was the co-owner of Pearlman Brothers Furniture store. Years later when Barbara and I purchased a new house, we bought our furniture from Mr. Pearlman's store.

Jim Damis's father was an immigrant from Greece. He had worked his way on a ship to the United States as a teenager. I recall being told he was seventeen years old, and that he found work as a waiter in a Greek restaurant while he went to law school at night. Through hard work and dedication, he managed to get through law school and, by the time Jim was in high school, had become a successful lawyer in Portland with an extensive clientele in the Greek community. The Damises were not wealthy, but he was able to put his two sons and a daughter through college, both boys to Harvard and the daughter to a prestigious eastern girls' school.

Mr. Damis was a warm and generous-hearted man I instantly liked the first time we met, which was at the time that Jim and I were talking about rooming together. He spoke in broken English, so much so that I had great trouble understanding him. My heart overflows with admiration even now as I think of this man who worked so hard and tenaciously to better himself and provide for his family and to see them educated at the best colleges in his adopted country. No doubt he reminded me of my own father and his appreciation of the opportunity provided by this great country of ours.

Throughout high school I had made all *A*'s except for one *B* in the first quarter of first-year Latin, and at graduation I was selected to be class valedictorian. I thought that meant I had graduated first in my class (out of almost 600 students) but I was wrong. I never learned why I was named valedictorian or by whom, but I assume it had to do with my wide-ranging extracurricular activities and having been student body president, in addition to my grade point average.

Pearlman was also a top student in our class, but with no outside activities to his credit. We hardly knew each other but were naturally competitive people. One day early in our freshman year, we were standing in our room, looking out of the window, as we thought back to each of our classes from high school to reconstruct our grades so that we could determine who had the better grades. Each of us could list the grade received in every class in high school without referring to a transcript. It turned out that he had beaten me because he had one less *B* grade than I did, giving him something like a 3.94 GPA, while I had a 3.91.

It's kind of odd how things work. Through rooming together for four years, Don and I became the closest of lifelong friends. He was best man at my wedding, and later an absolute life saver when it came to filling out the seemingly endless forms required by the government before I could be appointed to the positions I held in Washington, DC. Eventually, I persuaded him to join me in Washington as my executive assistant when I became Secretary of Energy and to follow me back to Interior when I became Secretary there.

Don was very serious about life and about everything he did, hardworking and smart. But he lacked a sense of humor. Jim Damis and I—and others—teased Don unmercifully, as only college companions will do. He took it all very seriously and responded as if our jests were serious statements, although many were entirely made up, with no basis in fact. One day, Don told us that rather than go outside and play when he was a boy he had preferred to stay inside and listen to political news on the radio. Jim then came up with the line, "Don, if you had gone out and played when you were a little boy…" and followed with whatever jibe he was thinking. Don was also teased and taunted by fellow students.

A subject that led to many attacks was his staunch defense of US Senator Joe McCarthy. At the time, McCarthy asserted that there were numerous secret Communist sympathizers or actual party members in the State Department. Initially, even noted liberals including Robert F. Kennedy supported the Wisconsin Senator's anti-Communist work. At some point McCarthy got offtrack and became increasingly erratic, which brought the scorn of the establishment and the hostile media, which attacked him viciously.

Don's support of McCarthy was red meat to a bunch of college freshmen and other students who found this out about him. They would stop by our room to argue with him about that or anything else they could think of. They knew nothing other than what they had read in the press or heard about and would make up accusations about McCarthy to throw at Don.

Don never gave an inch. He fought them tooth and nail, and accusation by accusation. When they made up things having no truth to them, Don would defend McCarthy intelligently, constructing his own explanations for McCarthy's actions based upon what he did know.

While I was not a vocal McCarthy supporter, I was strongly anti-Communist, remembering my father's warnings vividly. Before I went to college, he gave me a list of groups suspected by the FBI of being Communist or Fascist subversive organizations. He had the list due to his security clearance because of the work done by Huntington Rubber Mills during WWII for the war effort. He pointed out that while many sounded good by name, in reality they were anything but, and he added that many well-meaning

Americans had joined them, not realizing what they were only to have that come back to haunt them later. One would have to have grown up during the Cold War to truly understand the gravity of those conversations we had.

With Dad and John Harvard (Family photos)

The interminable arguments Don Pearlman faced became a burden to Damis and me because of the disruption to our room. Finally, Jim and I sat Don down to teach him how to respond when people teased him. We told him that these guys were making up stuff to throw at him just for the fun of baiting him. He stated that he knew that already, so we told him that he simply should not argue back against false arguments. He just had to dismiss them and the best way to do that was to wait until his opponent finished some outrageous accusation about McCarthy and, after a short pause, look at him very dismissively, possibly even rolling his eyes and say, “F--- you.” In other words, don’t dignify the ridiculous attack by responding to it; instead, reject the attacker. Don learned that lesson well and soon the "bear baiters" found that the fun had gone so they stopped interrupting the peace and quiet of our room. Don put up with teasing with a doggedness and determination that I admire now more than ever. He just kept chugging along.

In high school, Jim was an outstanding football and basketball player and a star sprinter on the track team. He earned multiple varsity letters in those sports, the kind of person others popularly referred to as a jock. As soon as we got to Harvard, he went to daily football practices, having easily made the team. Almost all of his friends were athletes, so Pearlman and I met many of them when they came by our room.

Jim, though, had problems at Harvard. He used up so much energy practicing football that he had a hard time adjusting to the academics with what little time he had left. He flunked out at the end of his freshman year. Harvard had a rule that, in order to be readmitted, you had to spend a year working before you could reapply. Then, if you could persuade the admissions committee that you had learned your lesson, they would let you back in. Jim went through all that, was readmitted, and graduated a year after Don and I did, before he went on to law school—at New York University, I think. He became a star flanker in football and was named to the Ivy League all-conference team in his senior year.

With Jim out of school for what would have been his sophomore year, Don and I continued to room together for the next three years until we graduated. I came to admire and appreciate his steadfastness in all things and found that he was influencing me philosophically. My natural inclination going back to my childhood was to be distrustful of government and to be a political conservative, and Don cemented those strong leanings with factual and philosophical justifications.

And then came politics for which, of course, we shared an affinity, both finding it fascinating. The difference was that I was not eager enough to go looking for political contacts. Don, on the other hand, had a passion for politics and, like anything else about which he was passionate, pursued it by seeking to get to know key people. In this way, he and I were a good team. He needed some of what I brought to the table: presence and leadership skills, which I had proven to have in high school; but without Don's contacts and networking skills I would have watched from the sidelines. He was the consummate "back room" politician but needed a front man. I was a natural front man and happy to let him do the heavy lifting.

Don, I think, could have projected the leadership persona had he wished, but he was content to work behind the scenes, mapping our moves, and positioning me to be selected for leadership positions. We helped each other get where we both wanted to go in terms of having a political presence at Harvard, something he strongly sought and which I also wanted but would not have been willing to sweat and strain over. Over the four years at Harvard, we came to appreciate each other and respect our complementing gifts.

Don's loyalty was of legendary proportions, and he was among the most devoted and trustworthy people I have ever known. This quality, coupled with his top-notch intellect, is what caused me to invite him years later to join me in my Cabinet posts. I was totally confident that he would always be watching my back to head off the kind of political backstabbing that is prevalent in politics. His single-mindedness did not make it easy for others to work with him, but it made him invaluable to me throughout my tenure in Washington, DC.

After a post-government career as a Washington, DC, lawyer at the prestigious firm Patton-Boggs, Don died from cancer in the summer of 2005 at age sixty-nine, and I was honored to be asked to be among those who spoke at his funeral in Portland. It is hard—then and now—for me to say enough good things about Don Pearlman.

As it turned out, Don and I were more than able to hold our own with the preppies at Harvard, although I did not know it at first. The college at the time gave out grades after seven weeks, rather than only at the quarter's end, so as to alert students to their progress, and with time left so that they could study harder if needed. I had trouble settling down to study at first, not really knowing how to do so. Getting good grades in high school had been easy for me, which allowed my attention to become focused on the extracurricular activities I felt were so important. So, at Harvard I was studying about six hours a week, which was a lot for me, but I expected I would have to work even harder or I might have trouble.

You can imagine my elation and relief when I got my seven-weeks grades, which were two *A*'s, a *B*, and a *C*+. My *B* professor said I would easily be able to raise that to an *A*, and my *C*+ instructor said that would easily become a *B*. Wow! I was excited and impressed and, yet, downhearted at the same time. Getting no money from the scholarship continued to gnaw at me. Then, doing so well with my grades without seriously studying was further proof to me that I merited the scholarship, which increased my resentment. Finally, those good grades encouraged me falsely to believe that I did not need to study much at all, which I have regretted for the rest of my life as a missed opportunity that could never be recaptured. Although things turned out well for me and my family, I have sometimes wondered how much more I might have accomplished, or how much better I might have performed in each of my jobs, or simply how much more of a well-rounded a person I might have been, if I had not wasted the learning opportunity of those college years.

Harvard put a strong emphasis on writing, and we had been told that this was another area where we, as public-school graduates, would not be able to compete. I had written very few papers in high school but at Harvard I had to write at least one 500- to 1,000-word paper for each class. I was fortunate to have a strong vocabulary due to my parents' having been very well-spoken, both with good vocabularies of their own, which I observed and absorbed while growing up. And fortunately, I could type. This was long before word processors came along,

Pearlman and I collaborated on a few papers, which, for me, was a great learning experience. I was very literate and wrote well, as did he. The difference was that Don weighed each word with greater care, in the manner that I later learned to do as a lawyer. At that time of my life, however, I tended to toss words onto the page the way they sounded in my mind's ear. This meant that we had significant stylistic differences, which we debated word-by-word. The results were papers in which every thought and every word had been discussed and weighed for its accuracy and value to our presentation. I remember that one of our "section men" (graduate students who were assigned several individual members of a large class to mentor and grade) wrote across the top of our paper, "You guys will have a blast in law school!" which we took as a compliment but also knew was his commentary on the stodgy style of the paper we had written. He gave us an *A* because it was extremely well done, but stylistically, it was about as exciting as reading the phone book.

Sometime in the fall of 1953, Pearlman and I became acquainted with John Roger Thomson, who was six foot two and handsome, with a great presence. John had established a close relationship with two previous "wheels" in the Harvard Young Republican Club, or HYRC, as it was commonly known. They were Bill Rusher, a founder and first president of the HYRC, and Roger Allen Moore, the sixth or seventh president, a top-ranked student in the Harvard Law School and member of the student-run journal of legal scholarship *Harvard Law Review*, a most prestigious position that was acquired only through merit. Both Rusher and Moore were active in the National Young Republican Federation.

William A. Rusher was an impressive, articulate, solidly conservative man, then in his early thirties, which was an advanced age to me as an eighteen-year-old freshman. He was at that time counsel to the US House of Representatives Committee on Un-American Activities, which, like McCarthy's efforts in the Senate, was investigating Communist infiltration into the American government. Bill was staunchly anti-Communist, as were Don and I. Harvard, of course, was already such a liberal school that Bill claimed to have received a letter while he was a student there addressed simply to "Bill Rusher at The Kremlin on the Charles." True or not, it was a fair indication of what we thought of the political leanings of Harvard. Rusher later became editor of the conservative magazine *National Review*, founded by another titan of the right, William F. Buckley Jr.

Pearlman and I joined the HYRC and became part of John Thomson's faction, which was mentored by Rusher and Moore. We attended meetings but did little else in the HYRC during our freshman year. In the fall of our sophomore year, however, the leadership of HYRC fell into hands of young men who were neither conservative enough, nor loyal enough, to follow either Thomson's example or the mature leadership provided by Rusher and Moore. John was encouraged by Rusher and Moore to coordinate a coup that would replace the existing leadership with a solidly trustworthy conservative who was totally loyal to Bill and Roger.

The plot was simple: Elect John as president of the HYRC along with a slate of equally loyal and conservative officers. Pearlman had already committed us to following John's leadership (which meant following Rusherr's and Moore's leadership). As part of our efforts, we asked some of our friends to join HYRC, which was already the largest political club on the campus, thereby swelling its ranks significantly. Then all that was needed was to turn out our votes at the next meeting and elect the new team, which worked as planned.

Rusher and Moore wanted to control the HYRC because it was part of the Massachusetts Council of Young Republican Clubs. The HYRC sent five delegates and five alternates to every meeting of the "Mass. Council," as it was known. The ten of us who went were smart and articulate, and we coordinated our actions. We were fully engaged and also very effective, giving the HYRC a significant impact on the Mass. Council as desired by Rusher and Moore (and their associates in the national YRs). The Mass. Council was by far the largest YR group in New England and usually managed to control or at least influence the New England Council of YR clubs. Again, the Harvard club sent delegates to the Regional Council and helped control the regional organization.

For several years, the New England Council of YR clubs managed to significantly influence who was elected president of the Young Republican National Federation for a two-year term at the national group's biennial convention. Working with others, including an amazing political campaign organizer named Clif White, this group of successful political operatives was referred to nationally as the "Syndicate" by both friends and foes and for several years controlled the national YRs.

F. Clifton White Jr. , a decade later, masterfully put together the successful Draft Goldwater for President movement in 1964. A respected conservative political consultant, White was the consummate grassroots voter organizer. His posthumously released memoir, *Politics as a Noble Calling*, is an exemplary instruction manual on political organizing.

In order to perpetuate our control of the HYRC, as John Thomson's term as president ended during our junior year, I became the Syndicate's designated—and successful—presidential candidate. Pearlman and I had invited two club activists to be our roommates, Tom Stalker, who was a great friend of Bill Rusher and John Thomson, and Bill Smith, a student I recruited at the team's behest to be part of our faction because we saw him as a natural leader among freshmen HYRC members.

In fact, we took over the HYRC in the fall of 1954 in time to be part of the successful effort in 1955 to elect Charlie McWhorter as president of the YR National Federation. Charlie had been one of the prime founders of the HYRC with Bill Rusher. Charlie went on to work for AT&T but committed apostasy when, as national YR president, he met and spent some time with President Dwight D. Eisenhower, literally falling under Eisenhower's spell, who, though a popular President, was not a philosophical conservative. Ike neither appeared to understand the risks of a too powerful federal government nor seemed particularly concerned with the degree of Communist infiltration into the US Government. That happened to be an area of particular expertise for Bill Rusher, due to his work with the House Committee on Un-American Activities. Charlie remained a friend to his former colleagues, but he was clearly no longer viewed as a conservative.

My initial reaction to all this had been the thrill of victory and intrigue, but it rapidly turned to distaste for conniving and seeking positions simply for the sake of holding the positions. We played what I came to identify as "position politics." By that I meant simply seeking to capture and hold the position without making any contribution to the party. When the battle over my successor turned ugly—because it was between Stalker and Smith—with the Syndicate backing Stalker, but Smith winning, the needless hostility turned me off to such politics, and I vowed never again to be involved only for the sake of getting elected. *Seek the position to make a difference, or don't seek it at all,* was an attitude that played into much of what I did in the future.

When Pearlman and I were back in Oregon during the summers, he encouraged me to join him in going to various Republican activities. Most of these were through the Oregon Young Republicans. Our contacts in the Syndicate gave us a lot of information about the YRs in Oregon, and Don and I got in touch with them. This was interesting because the YRs in Oregon were almost always at odds with the Syndicate; partly because Oregonians were generally more liberal, and partly because they were mavericks who would not play ball with a machine like the Syndicate. Therefore, they were almost always on the outside looking in when the key jobs were filled at the YR National Federation. The one exception was a fellow named Wes Phillips who was ambitious and figured out that the Syndicate had control and, therefore, was the team to join. While the Syndicate did not fully trust him—he appeared to be an opportunist rather than a loyalist—they were willing to work with him. Wes would enter my political life years later, as well. We got to know, from a distance, several GOP leaders in Oregon because the YRs with whom we associated were invited to Republican state central committee functions.

One incident that stands out happened in the summer between Pearlman's and my junior and senior years, when we were at a state party function, and he pointed out someone to me and said, with great significance, "He's very close to the state chairman!" I remember how impressed I was by that, but just nine years later I found that the job of state chairman was much less impressive *if you were the person who held it.*

Also, that summer before my senior year, I attended the 1956 Republican National Convention in San Francisco, where

President Eisenhower was renominated. Because of my connection to the YR Syndicate, I was appointed head of the page pool. Pages run errands, assist convention organizers, and help keep order on the floor. For that week, I lived on Coca-Cola, hot dogs, and adrenaline.

As I recall there were a couple of hundred young men and women serving as pages at that convention, an average of almost four for each state. Each day, a different third of the pages were assigned to me for general duty throughout the convention hall. This was more fun for them than just sitting with the delegates from their state and watching the proceedings.

I was so focused and intent that I somehow learned the name of virtually every one of the pages who were assigned to me. They were sufficiently responsive to my control that if a message was being sent by a delegation from one side of the hall to a delegation in another, I could have prevented that page from delivering it in a timely fashion for the message to serve its purpose. I neither did that nor was I asked by my contacts to do so, but I was in a position to do so had it been deemed necessary.

The biggest operation the pages did—at my direction—was to control demonstrations on the convention floor. The floor was set up with wide aisles between the rows of delegates from the states, and another wide, open space in front of the stage. There was also a passageway around the back of the stage. A demonstration that filled the aisles and the space in front of the stage, but with nowhere else to go, soon died out. So, when Eisenhower (the incumbent) was nominated, I had the pages guide the enthusiastic demonstrators around the back of the stage in a constant flow of people so that the demonstration went on for more than just several minutes because the demonstrators could repeatedly keep moving past the stage.

When former Minnesota Governor Harold Stassen, a quadrennial candidate for President in those years, was nominated, I had the pages simply block off the passage behind the stage and, with no way to keep moving, for that and for other more political reasons, his demonstrators quickly lost their enthusiasm.

This experience at my first national convention was one of the many breaks and learning opportunities I gained during my formative political years for which I now am very thankful.

CHAPTER 4
LOVE AND LAW

Three things occurred on Saturday, December 4, 1954, that affected my life forever. I was a sophomore at Harvard, and it was a day I will never forget.

First, I had been deputized by our faction in the HYRC to take the lead in recruiting a freshman named Norman William Smith to join us. The plan was that I would drive him to the Massachusetts Council's annual Christmas party and, during the evening, enlist his support for our team. We had decided that Bill was a promising young leader in his class. I could not afford a car in college, but a Harvard alumnus who owned a rental car company allowed any Harvard student with a valid and clean driver's license to rent without the usual twenty-five-year-old age requirement for renting a car. Two YR friends and I shared the cost of the car for me to take Bill to the "recruiting" Christmas party. I would have the drive and the time at the party to sell him on joining our team.

Second, earlier that afternoon was the annual reunion of the 1952 class of the American Field Service summer scholarship students who, like me, had spent six weeks between our junior and senior years of high school in Europe. Many of that group were by then attending colleges in the Boston area and someone managed to connect us all in that era before cell phones and emails and set up the reunion, which took place in a meeting hall at Harvard.

Third, two girls attending the reunion, Kay Harrington and Marinda Kelly, were students at Wellesley College, a prestigious all-female school located about thirteen miles from Harvard. The girls had no car but had somehow managed to get themselves to Harvard for the reunion. Unfortunately for them—but very fortuitously for me—they had no idea how they were going to get back to campus.

Harvard was a men's college at the time, and I had already figured out as a sophomore that the eligible (i.e., attractive) girls at the adjacent Radcliffe College (which years later became part of Harvard) had been swiftly taken by upperclassmen. Thus, with no prospects to date at Radcliffe, it occurred to me that, having a car for the evening, I could assist these two girls in getting back to their dorm and, in the process, establish a "beachhead" for future dating opportunities—if not with either of them, perhaps with one of their friends. The two ladies were delighted to have a ride back to Wellesley. It was nearly dinnertime when we left Harvard and, with no food at the reunion, none of the three of us had eaten. So, we decided we would go for a bite once we arrived back at Wellesley.

When we arrived at their dorm, Bates Hall, I went inside with them and walked down a long flight of stairs to the waiting area. Kay had forgotten that she had been scheduled for "bell duty" to serve as the dorm receptionist that afternoon. And her roommate, knowing that Kay was not around, kindly filled in for her. And that was when, as I walked down the stairs to the reception desk, I saw Barbara Beecher Stockman for the first time. She wore a bright yellow sweater and an ankle-length, green corduroy skirt. I was immediately—and strongly—attracted to her. And from that moment on my life would never be the same.

Barbara had also missed dinner in the dorm due to filling Kay's shift at the desk. So, the three girls and I decided to go to their favorite local sandwich shop in the town of Wellesley. Once we had ordered, one of the girls, noting I was wearing a suit and tie, asked why I was so dressed up. When I explained that I was on my way to a Christmas party they immediately asked if I was taking a date. When I said that I was not, they reacted as if they were really upset. How could I not take a date to a Christmas party? They did not know, of course, that I had a political assignment that night.

Trying to sound like I needed their sympathy, I answered, “I don’t have anyone I can ask to go with me.” Simultaneously, Barbara and Marinda each said, “I’ll go with you.” Kay said nothing, already having double-booked dates for that night and trying to figure out how to extricate herself from *that* problem.

Barbara was sitting directly across from me in the booth, and I was already very attracted to her and hoped to get to know her better. As soon as she and Marinda spoke, I looked directly at *Barbara* and asked, “How long will it take you to change?” I was so focused on Barbara by that point that I acted as if I had not even heard Marinda say she would go.

I knew I had to be back to Harvard to pick up Bill at the scheduled time, and with having to drive the girls back to their dorm, I had about twenty minutes I could spare. I have no doubt that Providence intervened, when Barbara answered, calmly, confidently, and without hesitation, “Twenty minutes.”

“You’re on,” I said to Barbara, trying not to go overboard in showing how happy I was that she would go with me.

On many occasions over the subsequent fifty-eight years together, Barb and I reflected on that day and wondered what might have happened if she had said she needed *more* than twenty minutes to get ready. Knowing how committed I was to keeping my obligations, I have always believed I would have said, regretfully, that I could not wait that long.

We got back to Bates Hall, and I sat down to wait, fearing that my plans could be stymied if Barbara took longer than twenty minutes. No worries. At almost exactly twenty minutes Barbara came into the reception area ready to go. She looked great, wearing a shapely, gray checked dress and a pair of red high-heeled shoes. Later I learned both dress and shoes were borrowed from her roommate, Kay. Trading outfits, it seems, was a common practice in their dorm.

We were ready to go, but I still had that “small” complication of my original purpose for the evening. I had not forgotten that I was supposed to recruit Bill for our team in the HYRC sometime during the ride or at the Christmas party. Now, I was bringing a date.

As soon as Barb was in the car, I explained, with sufficient details so that she would know why I had a car and what I hoped to accomplish. I also asked her to be as attentive to Bill as if she were his date. I did not want to make him feel awkward or disrespected. I was very relieved when she calmly agreed. As she later said, she was just happy to be going unexpectedly to a Christmas party. It wasn't as if we had a prearranged date, and I had suddenly changed the terms.

At the party Barbara was wonderfully gracious and sociable, readily paying attention to Bill and not acting as if she was actually there with me. She had nothing invested in a relationship with me and she enjoyed the party immensely. She danced with Bill and with me. She was very attractive and gracious, and he liked her, too. Bill brought Barbara tasty items and beverages from the refreshment table, and so did I. It is entirely possible that the favorable impression Barbara made on him helped him decide to join our club.

Meanwhile, my YR associates at the party were totally flabbergasted that I was being so attentive to Barbara. They knew I did not have a date for the party, and I had not had a chance to explain why she was with us. So, they just assumed that Bill had brought her. Thus, it appeared that I was committing the unpardonable sin of trying to bird dog his date, as we called it, cutting in on him as a means of trying to cut him out.

As it happened, I was successful in *both* of my missions that evening. Bill agreed to join our YR group and later was even elected as my successor as president of the HYRC. (Bill's election was a bitter fight between him and Tom Stalker, both of whom were Pearlman's and my roommates at that time.) At any rate, after the party I made a beeline back to Harvard to drop Bill off and then drove Barbara back to Wellesley.

I received my first lesson in college dating rules that evening. No self-respecting girl would dare return to her dorm until the last moment before the 1:00 a.m. curfew. Doing so would be a certain sign that her date was substandard. So, Barbara and I sat in the rented car and chatted until 12:59 a.m.

As we talked, several topics came up. I learned that Barbara was born in Pittsburgh, Pennsylvania (on September 19, 1935), and reared in Evanston, Illinois, until halfway through high school, finishing in Salisbury, Maryland, and accepting a scholarship to Wellesley. I later learned that she descended from New England royalty being related to John Alden of Miles Standish fame and to author Harriet Beecher Stowe.

We also discussed the topic of dating in general, and, in due course, that of showing affection, namely kissing. Still in keeping with my self-imposed life of moderation as a means of protecting my image, which I adopted back in high school in Oregon, yet desperately hoping I would not offend Barbara, I said, confidently, that I did not kiss on the first date, although even then I think that was hardly the norm for couples on first dates. But then, as now, I was a bit old-fashioned.

Only later did I learn from Barbara that she viewed my pronouncement as a personal challenge, which prompted her to ask, "What would you do if a girl kissed you first?"

"Kiss her back," I muttered, whereupon she, calmly and without fanfare, slid across the flat, bench seat and kissed me. And, yes, I kept my promise and kissed her back.

With that bold and direct, yet flirtatious, move on Barb's part, I was absolutely smitten. Here was this very pretty girl who had deftly handled what could have been an awkward situation at the party with wonderful poise—and then also initiated a good night kiss!

As I left that night on my short drive back to school, I suddenly exclaimed out loud to myself, "That's the girl I'm going to marry!" And the rest, you might think, is history. Well, while that is true, there is more to the story.

As I soon learned, Barbara was engaged to another fellow at the time I met her, and he was not enrolled in a Boston area institution of higher education. Her fiancé was overseas in the US Navy, but he had graciously encouraged her to enjoy the full college experience, which included dating. He had to know that it involved a risk that she would meet someone to whom she became attracted and that, of course, is what happened. But it was a decision that turned out to be fatal for his intentions toward Barbara, or better said, for her intentions toward him.

We had been dating for about three months when I realized that I was falling deeply in love with Barbara and was interested in a long-term—really a lifelong—relationship with her. Besides loving her I also confirmed what I had concluded that first night that she had all the things I could want in a wife—she was smart, articulate, beautiful, poised, and on and on. During those three months I talked with her at great length about whether she knew her fiancé well enough to marry him. I somewhat boldly suggested that she did not. I had learned that because of their age difference of six years, her parents had been wary of the relationship, and that Barbara had only seen him perhaps forty-five times over a *six*-year period, most of those at her house and in the presence of her mother! My opinion, which I freely shared with her, was that she couldn't possibly know him well enough to know that she wanted to spend the rest of her life with him.

Perhaps due to what I was telling her, or perhaps because Barbara realized that she was falling for me, without mentioning it to me, in late January she wrote her fiancé an honest letter about the situation. He replied, quite correctly, that she had to choose. If she wanted to remain engaged to him, she had to stop dating me, and if she wanted to continue dating me, they would have to end their engagement.

I remember vividly the night that she and I went with some of her friends to one of their homes near Wellesley. Barbara had told me she had received a letter from her fiancé, and we needed to talk. We went into the dining room while the rest of the group was in the living room. There, she told me that she had written to her fiancé about how she was becoming quite attached to me, and she even read aloud the key parts of his return letter. I knew that this was a critical moment in our relationship. If she decided that she wanted to remain engaged, I would have to bow out. I strongly wanted her to choose me but felt that I had to be very careful not to push her to decide in my favor. I did not want to risk her later feeling that I had caused her to make the wrong decision. And I told her that very clearly, saying that of course, I strongly hoped she would continue our relationship, while promising to stop pursuing her if she picked him. I will be forever grateful that she chose me.

Barbara and I each grew up in churchgoing families, but, regrettably, we did not live according to Christian teachings regarding our relationship while in college. Midway through our senior year, and about six months before we were planning on getting married, Barbara became pregnant. I deeply regret what the stigma of a premarital pregnancy did to Barbara. At one point, she said something that made it plain we had been raised to value morality and had ignored it. Actually, it was I who ignored it and persuaded her to go along.

Since that time, I have (tearfully) shared with a few close associates my regret over how I so disrespected Barbara by persuading her to engage in sexual intimacy before we were married. Even now, I am filled with deep regret as I write this for what I put Barbara through, and I am still filled with gratitude for her serenity in the face of this major change in her life. Fortunately, there were never any recriminations expressed between us, and I knew that I was the person most responsible for what happened.

The pregnancy was a major trauma to us, and even more so to our parents, each of whom held the traditional—and proper—view of courtship and marriage. We were blessed during this terribly difficult time, however, because both Barbara's parents and mine loved us and supported us in spite of what we had done. I deeply regret causing them such grief and I remain thankful for the loving way in which they stood by us at that painful time, and how the rest of our lives unfolded thanks to their love and support when we felt that we (especially, I felt that I) least deserved it.

In addition to our moral failure, underlying everyone's attitudes were concerns over what an unplanned pregnancy meant for our future: *Would I be able to go to law school? Would our rushed marriage be short-lived?* (Something we understood to be quite common in such circumstances.) *Was this the end of what we thought were my promising prospects as a Harvard graduate and aspiring lawyer?* We did not consider putting the baby up for adoption, and abortion was, of course, a felony at the time, and I thank God that in my pre-Christ life, that was not even an option.

As soon as we learned that Barbara was pregnant, we went to the clerk's office in Cambridge and got married, on December 10, 1956, continuing to live in our respective dorms. A couple of weeks later, we visited Barb's parents in Salisbury, Maryland, for the Christmas holidays. They were wonderful. There was no question they were dismayed at our situation, but they put as good a face on things as possible.

Even though we had had the civil ceremony in Cambridge, Barbara's mother insisted that while there we go through a formal marriage observance in her Episcopal Church. At the time I was so consumed by my feelings of guilt that I did not want any public attention focused on us, but I am grateful that she persisted and that we acquiesced. Later, after we had come to faith in the Lord, Barbara and I were glad that we had gone through the religious observance of our marriage. The formal blessing of our marriage and public acknowledgment made it seem less furtive and no longer something we were trying to hide, although the impulse to do so remained strong.

In January, we returned from being with Barb's parents and were shocked to learn that she had unknowingly violated a strict Wellesley policy that prohibited married women from living in the student dorms. Although she was a good student on scholarship, she was told she had to leave school. This was another embarrassing experience for her, and a disheartening one for her mother, a Wellesley graduate, who had been thrilled at the prospect of her daughter following in her footsteps and earning a Wellesley degree, and on a scholarship awarded as the daughter of an alumna.

We rented a very small, one-room apartment in an old house near Harvard, and I took a part-time job working in the Harvard Co-op selling men's accessories so as to reduce the additional costs paid by my parents. This entire episode was a reminder to me for the rest of my life that letting emotions govern the making of decisions can be devastating and burdensome not just to me but to everyone with whom I am associated. However, it left me with a debt of gratitude to Mom and Dad for their unfaltering support through this difficult time. They were wonderful parents who encouraged and supported me throughout my life and who gave me the momentum to seek to achieve success, but it is easy to encourage and support someone who is doing good things. The test of love comes in the face of a major error in judgment and a lapse in morals.

After I was in the Cabinet and Barb and I began giving our Christian testimony in public, we decided to include the details of our unplanned pregnancy. We felt that it was important to show audiences that people in our positions were not perfect and that we had lived very common lives. In addition, it was the truth. We found that audiences resonated with that part of our past, and showing how Christ forgave us also told them that He also would be there for them in troublesome times. I decided that to give my descendants a more complete picture of my life, and to show that it was not all just sweetness and light, I needed to include this low point, as well.

I have often said that marrying Barbara was the best decision I ever made. First of all, we had a wonderful, loving relationship. There is nothing better or more pleasing in life. In addition, I have no doubt that I would never have had the career I had without her total support and encouragement along the way.

Barbara was serene and supportive at every step of our lives. She willingly moved with me across the country to Oregon and away from her parents on the East Coast. Soon, she became like a daughter to my parents. They loved her and she loved them in return. My mother on occasion would tell me, "I hope you realize what a gem you have in Barbara!"

Barbara made my life happy and fulfilling and was always supportive and encouraging when I felt called to take on a new task or job, even if it was full of risk or involved moving away from a place she loved, such as from Oregon to the nation's Capital. In Washington, DC, she made it her mission for our home to be a safe haven for me. She told me that for as long as we were there, she would take care of all our personal affairs so that I could devote my full time and attention to my work, which involved significant pressure and long hours. She did a wonderful job of dealing with all of our personal matters and never once found it necessary to ask for me to become involved. She always said that her goal in life had been to be a good wife, and she succeeded beyond all expectations.

Barb was a distinguished woman in her own right and an asset to me in all ways. During my career, she accompanied me to numerous official and social functions, attended many of my meetings, and traveled with me on almost all trips, including internationally. Staff and friends referred to us as "Team Hodel," which captured the closeness and devotion which we exhibited toward each other and the manner in which she conducted herself. Throughout our marriage, she willingly avoided commitments or social engagements for herself in order always to be available to accompany me. And throughout our lives together, she arranged her schedule to enable us to spend as much time together as possible. She was truly amazing and wonderful.

Unfortunately, many modern couples today cannot appreciate the importance of the role Barbara played in my career. I truly regret that she subordinated any possible desire she might have had to have a career of her own, but she made plain to me that she liked the role she had decided to fill. She chose her role in life, and she lived it to the fullest. One day, the tables would turn, and our lives would center around Barbara, but more on that in a later chapter.

And Barbara was completely selfless. At my earlier mentioned fiftieth high school reunion, Barbara and I planned to attend, flying to Portland from Denver, as we had settled in Colorado after my time in Washington, DC. However, a few days before we were to leave for the reunion, she tripped on a curb in front of the dry cleaners and fell flat on her face. The next day she was seriously black and blue around the eyes, on her cheekbones and forehead, and across the bridge of her nose. She looked as if she had been bludgeoned.

I offered to cancel the trip to my reunion to avoid the embarrassment she might experience, but she would not hear of it. Off we went, and in she walked, with makeup substantially, but not entirely, covering the bruises. I was so proud of her and at the same time felt great sympathy and admiration for her, because I knew how difficult it would have been for me to attend looking like that. We had a great time, and her bruising essentially disappeared as she participated without apparent embarrassment. It reminds me of the poise with which she handled the very first time we were together when she accepted the role of befriending Bill Smith at the YR Christmas party.

Being married during my last semester at Harvard, I seriously applied myself to my studies for the first time since freshman year and my grades promptly rose. That proved to me that had I studied diligently throughout college I would have learned a great deal more. It is unfortunate that I didn't take advantage of that wonderful opportunity.

After I graduated, we moved to Oregon, where our first son, Philip, was born on August 7, 1957, shortly before I entered law school in September. My parents were a great help during the move. They drove from Oregon to Massachusetts, and then down to Barb's parents' house in Maryland, using their car to transport our belongings to Oregon. They paid for Barb and me to fly to Oregon because, by then, she was nearing her third trimester. They did all this without one word of criticism from my father and only, at worst, an occasional, but rare, pained look from my mother.

We chose to live in Oregon so that I could attend law school at the University of Oregon School of Law in Eugene. I knew that I wanted to practice law in Oregon, and I was assured by two Oregon lawyers with whom I spoke that a degree from the U of O was a better choice for a law career in the state than to stay in Massachusetts and go to Harvard Law, even given Uncle Gerdau's and my long-standing opinion that it was the best school.

I did not even apply to Harvard Law School for two additional reasons. The first was that I really could not afford to go there. Also, I had a higher score on the LSAT (Law School Admission Test) than Don Pearlman who *was* applying to Harvard Law, and if I got admitted but chose not to go and he did not get admitted, he might think that my applying there capriciously took a place he otherwise could have had. I just could not risk that with my best friend.

I applied to several schools, including the University of Oregon, and to Willamette, also in Oregon. And I also submitted applications to Boalt Hall at the University of California (not in Oregon obviously but still a top school), plus a couple of others, and was accepted by all. I enrolled in Oregon, my top choice. Don Pearlman was not admitted to Harvard and ended up going to and graduating from Yale Law School. He began practicing—also in Oregon—a year later than I did because he spent a year after graduation clerking for a federal district court judge in Nevada.

Law school was a terrible grind. I studied as I never had before, and I placed intense pressure on myself to succeed. Although I started out with above average grades, they were declining so badly each quarter (to just a little above a *C* average over the next two quarters) that by the end of the first year I became discouraged and discussed it with Barbara, saying, "If I can't do better than this, I ought to quit." She understood my concerns but encouraged me to stay the course. I knew that was sound advice.

Barbara was amazingly supportive and accepting through it all, never uttering even one word of complaint. We moved into a small student housing apartment that was sparse but affordable. She did all the baby duty with Philip, except that I tried to help her get him to sleep at night. Once he had fallen asleep, however, he was all hers. I did not get up if he cried during the night, actually sleeping with a pillow over my head, and in that era, before fathers were expected to share more of the homemaking tasks, I never changed diapers, I'm embarrassed to say, for either of our two sons. Barbara was then, as throughout our lives together, the totally supportive teammate whom I relied upon in every way.

Fortunately, at the beginning of my second year in law school, a fellow student, Kaye Robinette, told me that he was looking for a study partner and suggested that we study together. Kaye taught me how to study law. Of greatest importance, he explained to me how to outline the material in each course. I was determined to succeed in law school, and I concentrated intensely on outlining each course. The result was that without intending it or even fully realizing it, I had substantially memorized my outlines in all four courses.

Kaye and I got together at his house the night before each exam to review and discuss our outlines. That way, we helped fill in or modify each other's outlines to make them complete and accurate. Of course, that review was a great refresher before each exam. Kaye was very able and perceived the kinds of issues in courses that would be good exam questions, and we would discuss how best to answer those questions as part of our preparation.

Exams were given on Monday, Tuesday, Thursday, and Friday for four hours each morning, beginning at 8:00 a.m. and finishing promptly at noon. The typical exam had eight questions which meant that students should take no more than thirty minutes on each question. We learned during our first exam the year before that if you took too much time on one question, you would not have enough time left to write good answers to the later questions. We wrote our answers by hand, in ink, in those blue examination books with lined pages that most every student of higher education is familiar with—at least those who preceded the laptop computer age.

The exams I remember were in Decedents' Estates (i.e., Wills and Trusts), Bills and Notes, Real Property, and one other. I felt pretty good after the first exam, but when it came to the second exam, Real Property, it was a disaster!

For years the senior professor at Oregon Law School was K. J. O'Connell, affectionately known to students as "KJ." He taught property courses and was widely known for giving difficult exams. Then in the spring of 1958 (near the end of my first year) it was announced that he had been appointed to the Oregon Supreme Court and was leaving school at the end of the quarter.

Sometime over that summer, law school Dean Orlando John Hollis made his selection, and Professor Richard Kelly, who had been teaching the Real Property course at Creighton Law School, was chosen to replace KJ. There was general dismay among the students who were not shy about saying things like, "No one can replace KJ," "KJ gave the hardest exams," and so on. Such statements were so common and unguarded that it is almost certain that Professor Kelly had heard them, which likely influenced the difficulty of the first exams he administered at Oregon Law beginning that fall.

My first exam under Professor Kelly, Real Property, came in November of my second year—the end of the fall quarter. When I opened the Real Property exam, I found eight questions. So far, so good. Then, as I read the first question, I saw that it was exceedingly complex and difficult, so much so that I was nearly in shock trying to get a handle on what the issues were. I tried to sort out all the pieces, identify the legal issues, and write a cogent answer. Ordinarily, I wrote rapidly and was able to analyze a question quickly. However, I was agonized to see that I had used almost an hour and a half figuring out and writing the answer to just the first question.

I turned to the second question and, if anything, it was worse—more complicated. By the time I had answered five questions—the last two hurriedly—I had less than half an hour remaining in the exam. Fighting panic, I knew I did not have time to write full answers to the remaining three questions so I just wrote a brief statement on each stating how I would go about answering them, describing that it was a question of such and such and which cases I would bring to bear on each. I knew, of course, that I had written totally inadequate answers to those questions.

I was dismayed and disheartened as I turned in my blue book, convinced that I had flunked the exam. I never stayed around after a test to stand on the law school steps and discuss with my classmates that day's exam. In this case I should have done so, as I would have learned that I was by no means alone in my reaction. In fact, panic was widespread among those who had taken the test, but of course I did not hear that, and Kaye did not either, so we could not calm each other's fears of having failed. I was devastated.

When I got home, I shared my anguish with Barbara and went to bed virtually in tears, so distraught that I seriously thought of quitting law school and not even bothering with the remaining exams. After lying there feeling miserable, finally I decided that since I had come this far and worked so hard, I would finish the exams. If I had done as badly as I thought, I would have plenty of time to quit law school once I got all of my grades.

Fortunately, when I went back to Kaye's house to study for our next exam, we discussed how hard Professor Kelly's exam had been. Since Kaye agreed that it was impossibly difficult, I felt a little bit better about how I might have done, but I could in no way feel good about it. So, we simply moved on to do the best we could with the next day's exam.

The two remaining exams were by no means as difficult as the Real Property exam. In fact, Kaye had pointed out during our study time at least five questions that he thought might be among the eight on the Decedent's Estates exam—and they were! Talk about being prepared for a test…

After the last exam Barb, Philip , and I drove from Eugene to my parents' home near Lake Oswego for Christmas. I was pretty discouraged because I was so aware of how poorly I had done on that Real Property exam. About a week after we returned home, my grades arrived in the mail. Astoundingly, I had earned straight *A*'s! I literally could not believe it! I learned that Kaye had gotten three *A*'s and a *B,* which hardly seemed fair since he had taught me how to outline and had helped me study for the exams. .

When we got back to school, I found out that my having made straight *A*'s had become common knowledge and it made me somewhat of a celebrity among the students and the faculty, as it had been done only once in the prior five or six years. Kaye and I went to see our professors to get their feedback on our exams.

The Decedents' Estates professor said that when grading our books, he wondered if we had somehow gotten hold of a copy of the questions before the test because our answers were so thorough and on target. We told him how we had studied together, and that Kaye had suggested that certain issues would make for great exam questions.

But there was more. When Professor Kelly told us about our scores on his exam, and that I had scored only twenty-six out of a possible one hundred, while Kaye scored only twenty-three, he explained that we both got *A*'s because the next highest grade was a seventeen! He graded on a curve, aware that the exam was truly "impossible." It worked, however, to accomplish one of his goals, as he never ever again heard a word about how K. J. O'Connell gave the toughest exams.

My straight *A*'s raised my grade point average enough that all I needed in my remaining five quarters of law school was to get all *B*'s and two more *A* 's to achieve an overall *B* average. If my average continued to be at least a *B* (3.0) for the next five quarters, I would be able to write a thesis and earn not just a Bachelor of Laws degree, but a Doctor of Jurisprudence degree, which was the honors degree at U of O Law School at that time. To qualify me for the JD degree, my thesis had to be of publishable quality.

I now had a specific goal in sight—to reach a *B* average. Sure enough, by the end of the second year in law school I had achieved the *B* average, and I began my thesis on the subject, Punitive Damages in Oregon. There had been many cases in the state, and it took a great deal of research and study, while at the same time I was editor of the law review. Law review editors are usually chosen because they are first in their class. I was not the top overall, but they made an exception because of my straight *A*'s and my writing ability, and probably because of my level of interest. I was eager to do it, while others were less so.

In the winter quarter of my third year, I took Conflict of Laws from Dean Hollis. I wrote a decent exam but received only a *C*, dropping my overall average below a *B*. I went to see the dean. He had me sit down and began the interview by saying, "Mr. Hodel, that was a miserable performance," drawing out the word to be *mizz-er-a-ble*. I was devastated. I still remember intensely the feeling of mortification that swept over me. We then went through the exam question by question to see what I had answered versus what he had expected. I felt truly injured by his approach, which was to make every assumption against me where there was the slightest room for interpretation or the smallest ambiguity. I missed my much-needed *B* by a mere two points. I did not, however, argue with him because I knew that that would be futile and, ultimately, counterproductive. So, I listened carefully to what he thought would have been better or more complete answers, eliminating any opportunity for him to perceive an ambiguity that he could score against me. While I felt he focused on many technicalities that were picayunish and unfair, I listened well.

In the next, and final, quarter of law school, I earned two *A*'s and two *B*'s, which exceeded the necessary 3.0 GPA. One of the *A*'s was in the second half of the dean's course in the exam for which I consciously wrote the answers in the way I knew he wanted them, and it paid off. I received the highest score in his course that quarter. So, when I graduated, I was the only one in my class to receive the Doctor of Jurisprudence degree and my law review article on punitive damages was not just *publishable*, it *was* published—all one hundred pages—in the *Oregon Law Review*.

A few years later the University of Oregon decided to confer a JD degree as a matter of course on all those graduating from law school, requiring only a passing grade point average and no thesis. They offered to replace my diploma for a fee of $50 with one stating that I had earned a JD degree "with honors," which would have distinguished my diploma from the others. Since I felt no one ever looked at such things, I decided to save the $50.

My friend Don Pearlman worked hard to keep his grades up to the 3.0 requirement during his third year at Yale Law School, and he also wrote a thesis of the required "decidedly superior quality" at Yale, so that he would receive a JD. We therefore continued our friendly competitor progress from high school, into Harvard, and through law school as well.

One of the fearsome obstacles, actually the most intimidating obstacle, to becoming a member of the Oregon State Bar was the bar exam. It was given only once a year and only about 70 percent of those taking it passed. Bar review courses were usually four to six weeks of overall review of the various subjects that would be covered on the bar exam. They were intended to refresh the applicants' memories and point out some of the most effective techniques for writing the exams. Dean Hollis prided himself on a high passing rate for graduates of U of O Law School among "his" graduates. He did not believe that we needed to take a bar review course and was disdainful of any who did. While the dean may not have liked it, I was determined to take the bar exam only once! I did not want to risk having to repeat it a year later, so I entered the bar review course in Portland at the local Northwestern College of Law, a night school that Dean Hollis considered inferior in every way. For the next six weeks, from the end of school until the bar exam in mid-July, I devoted myself to intense study.

The bar exam was grueling. I saw that one of the reasons the dean made our exams in law school four hours long and with tight time pressure was to make the bar exam seem easier. It consisted of "only" three hours in the morning and three hours in the afternoon for two days, and another three hours in the morning of the third day. I lived at an intense level of stress all during that period.

The exam was held in Salem, the state capital, and I went with apprehension, not sleeping well the night before. The exam had one low point for me. I had finished answering a question on conflicts of law (where a matter involves the laws of more than one state) with a few minutes to spare and I did something that I had never done in law school or did on other questions on the bar exam, I looked back over the question and realized—to my horror—that I had misread it. It involved an automobile accident in state *A* with parties who lived in state *B*, while the medical treatment occurred in state *C*. But I had written the answer as if the accident had occurred in state *B* and the parties lived in state *A*! I nearly fainted from panic. In the three or four minutes remaining I quickly wrote an addendum to my answer that stated, in effect, that I had placed the accident in the wrong state and that the principles I had discussed were still the correct principles, but the results would have differed from those I had written. When I later learned that I had placed second on the exam among the several hundred taking it, I concluded that I had not been docked for my near disastrous misreading of the question.

When the bar exam was over, I was completely fatigued and wrung out. I had lived on adrenaline for three years of law school and a double dose during the intense preparation time for the exam.

Now it was over—almost. I could let down a little and wait for the results that would be released just prior to the annual bar convention in the city of Seaside.

For the rest of my life, I planned—and encouraged others to do the same—exciting events immediately following times, or seasons, of high stress. My theory, which I had learned from experience, was that in times of letdown our bodies and emotions internally relax and, therefore, are particularly susceptible to illness from viruses. I did not want to face getting sick after a particular challenge or triumph, so we always had something going on, scheduling times of rest and recuperation slowly in the midst of continued activity.

Barbara and I decided to go camping for four days before I started to work at the law firm where I had interned. We took the family tent, a portable crib for Philip, who was almost three, and we went up the Clackamas River to North Fork Crossing campground. As it turned out, we had the campground completely to ourselves for four days. The closest we came to not being alone was a couple of times hearing a dirt bike buzzing up the logging road some distance behind us.

Our camping trip coincided with the biggest heat wave of the year. In Portland the temperatures approached one hundred degrees. Barbara, who hated hot weather, could not believe how comfortable it was in the mountains. We had chosen the prime camping spot, right next to the stream, where we could hear the sound of water gurgling over the rocks. The pool in front of our camp—all three feet deep of it—was very cold, but warm enough one day that we were able to skinny-dip while Philip napped in his portable crib. The breeze during the day kept us comfortable, and at night temperatures lowered considerably. It was so wonderfully cool that we had to sleep in flannel sleeping bags. For Barb, this was heaven. I think her positive attitude toward camping for the rest of her life was solidified right then. It was private, fun, and cool! What more could you want?

The following week, I went to work. I had suggested to my mother in jest sometime earlier that maybe I ought to think about another graduate school program I could enter to avoid having to start practicing law right away. She did not even flinch before saying, "Not on your life, Baby. It's time for you to get a job!"

CHAPTER 5
LAWYER

During the spring of 1959, when I was finishing my second year of law school, a scholarship was created at the school to be awarded to a second-year student who exemplified a significant public service potential and who had excellent grades. Named for former Oregon Governor Paul Patterson, a graduate of the school who had died in a plane crash a couple of years earlier, and funded by some of his friends and supporters, the scholarship of $1,000 would go to one student each year. While my class standing was probably no higher than sixth at the time, thanks to my straight *A*'s in the fall quarter and all *B*'s in the second quarter, I was nominated (along with some others) for the inaugural scholarship and interviewed by a committee that included Dean Orlando Hollis and Judge Alfred Theodore "Ted" Goodwin of the US Ninth Circuit Court of Appeals, who also was a graduate of the school. Fortunately, I won the scholarship, which was quite significant financially. At the time, tuition was only $84 per quarter and books ran another $200 to $250, so basically, $1,000 was a full scholarship and then some for my coming third and final year.

As a man with a family, I still needed a job that summer before my third year of school began in the fall, and I wanted one as intern in a local law firm so that I could gain experience and, of course, earn money for the last year of school. I spent the previous summer working with my father at Huntington Rubber Mills thanks to his boss, Mr. Bellows, feeling favorable toward me.

Dad knew David L. Davies, the senior partner in the prestigious Portland law firm Davies, Biggs, Strayer, Stoel, & Boley, the largest law firm in Oregon. Clients included US National Bank, US Plywood Corporation, numerous lumber companies, Northwest Acceptance Corporation, a finance company, the local Bell telephone company, and so on. These were class *A* clients that paid large annual retainers. As the largest law firm in Portland, Davies was considered by its partners and young associates to be the *most* prestigious in the entire State of Oregon.

Years earlier, David Davies had been a lawyer for Huntington Rubber Mills. Dad called Mr. Davies, asking if he would be willing to interview me and at least give me some advice on what I might do to find a summer job as an intern with a law firm. After the interview, during which he seemed to be impressed by two things, my Harvard undergraduate degree and my straight *A*'s, Mr. Davies offered me a summer job. I accepted with gratitude.

As soon as classes were concluded in June, Barbara and I bundled up Philip and all our worldly goods and moved from our little apartment in Eugene to Portland for the summer so that I could begin my internship. We rented a very small apartment in an old building on 15th and Mill Street, which was a mile or so walk from the office and thus saved us from needing a second car or paying bus fare.

The other intern that summer was Barry Biggs, son of Hugh Biggs, the second named partner. Barry would not be hired full time because of the firm's policy that no children of partners could become permanent employees. Barry and I became good friends, and I learned a lot about the firm from him. While interning, I knew I wanted full-time employment at the firm after I graduated the following June. Barry was able to clue me in that the firm would not make an offer unless the applicant first made clear that he *wanted* to work there and *would* accept a job offer if it were made. They never wanted to be in a situation where someone could say, "I was offered a job, but turned them down."

Toward the end of summer, I asked for another appointment with Mr. Davies and told him I did not know what their opinion of me was, but that I definitely wanted to begin my career as an attorney there. He warned me that I would not become rich practicing law and reminded me that the firm preferred to hire Ivy League graduates, and, finally, that they *wanted* to offer me a job. This provided much comfort to me as I entered my final year of school. We talked about some other things and finally he said, "You haven't asked me about your pay!"

I responded, "Mr. Davies, I know that this firm pays its new associates as well or better than any in Oregon and that you will be fair, and I am just pleased to be able to come and work here." (On the other hand, I had the good sense and maturity to realize that if I got on board and did the job, better pay would follow, regardless of my starting salary.) He seemed enormously impressed by that and by the fact that I did not ask about vacation benefits, retirement, or other such things. He subsequently told my father how impressed he was because so many young men those days were coming in demanding or negotiating for salary, benefits, retirement, and the like.

Mr. Davies told me that the starting pay would be $475 per month, and I replied that I was grateful for that. To my surprise, when I arrived in June after taking the 1960 bar exam, I found that my starting pay was *$500*, something I could not have achieved no matter how much bargaining I had done. The firm had simply decided that was the level of salary competition they had to meet, and so they raised the starting pay level. In early September I learned that I had passed the bar exam, which brought with it a degree of assurance that my income would be increasing again. I received a $500 bonus at the end of my first year, and a $75 per month increase for the next year.

I don't know how things are done today, but in those days, firms generally had two categories of attorneys: partners and associates. Partners (a status reached at the Davies firm after six years) had ownership in the law firm and some form of profit-sharing agreement, with the newer partners receiving smaller shares than more senior ones. Associates were simply employees of the firm and were paid a monthly salary, plus an annual bonus.

Upon starting work at the firm as a first-year associate, I had to decide whether I wanted to be a trial lawyer or a general lawyer. I had some inclination toward a trial practice because of the excitement of the courtroom combat, but realized I would really dislike the fact that in order to do well one had to prepare carefully and fully for the trial, essentially with the intensity I experienced preparing for exams in law school, while knowing that most cases are settled on the courthouse steps just before the trial even begins in the courtroom. I knew myself well enough to understand that sooner rather than later I would get very frustrated with that process and, as a result, find it very difficult to be properly prepared if a case actually went to trial. Therefore, I opted for business law practice. Had I chosen trial law, I likely would not have had anything like the career path that followed. Working with businesses prepared me for the next step in my career, full-time corporate law.

In my second year at the Davies firm, Barbara and I took some big steps. First, we decided that we wanted to live in a house rather than an apartment. We bought a small (900 sq. feet), three-bedroom house in Lake Oswego, in Clackamas County, entering into a thirty-year mortgage.

We also felt that it was time to expand our family. Within thirty days of my passing the bar Barbara was pregnant, and on June 13, 1961, our son David Beecher Hodel was born—a month early. Our first son, Philip Stockman Hodel, had been named for our fathers, Stockman being Barbara's maiden name. David was simply a name that we both liked, and Beecher was a family name that Barbara's mother favored strongly because it came from her side of the family and was historically very distinguished.

We probably were responsible for Dave's early arrival by deciding, with Barbara eight months pregnant, to attend automobile races at the Portland Speedway on a very hot June day. We stood around in the heat and dust into the evening, carrying Philip or chasing him around. Barbara was feeling quite ill by the time we got back home and soon she went into labor. We did not know it at the time, but our family was complete.

Playing with my two boys (Family photos)

While at the Davies firm, I worked very hard and was well-received by its clients, including the US National Bank. I did a lot of credit work for the bank (reviewing loan documents, helping collect overdue accounts, representing the bank in cases where the party filing bankruptcy owed money to the bank, and so on), and by my third year at the firm I was overseeing younger associates and assigning them work. I was clearly on track to become a partner.

Things that sometimes happen in our lives that might seem small at the time can have big impacts later on. During law school I was a member of a legal fraternity whose alumni often held fund-raising events to help their local chapter function. In early 1963, midway through my third year at Davies, I received a telephone call from a man named Bill Moshofsky. That he called me was flattering in itself, since he was older and well-established as a lawyer and one of the more distinguished graduates of the University of Oregon Law School. Bill enlisted me to help put on what proved to be a successful fundraising dinner in Portland for our legal fraternity in Portland.

I had been practicing in the Davies firm since September 1960, and while working on the fraternity dinner I got to know Bill fairly well. He was a pleasant and likable man who was serving at that time in the legal department of Georgia-Pacific Corporation, a national producer of timber products, headquartered at the time in Portland. Not only was G-P *not* a client of the Davies firm but it was a much-disliked rival of our large client US Plywood. There had been a long and nasty lawsuit only a few years earlier between the two companies, leaving a lot of bad blood between their law firms as well.

In early October 1963, I received another call from Bill. This time, he asked if I would be willing to go to lunch with him and Frank Breuer, who was general counsel at Georgia-Pacific. Bill was moving upstairs to the executive suite under the title of assistant to the president and trying to find his replacement for the legal department. I had no interest in leaving the Davies firm to become an in-house counsel. In-house lawyers were generally viewed by private practitioners like those of us at Davies as less prestigious. Bill was undeterred when I told him that I was not likely to be interested. He said, "Well, we'd love to have lunch with you, anyway."

During lunch, I was quite impressed with their description of working conditions in the legal department of G-P: only one night per week, except in emergencies. At Davies, I had been working three nights each week, plus every Saturday, and every second or third Sunday. I had two young sons and a wife, whose company I really enjoyed, and I had little time to be with them.

I characteristically had not mentioned money at lunch, but Breuer made plain that he would not give someone a raise simply to lure them away from their current employer. He acknowledged that the annual pay at G-P would likely be *less* than at a law firm, but the stock options available to G-P lawyers could make up a lot of the difference. (As it turned out the G-P stock that had vested at the time I eventually left the company was worth $30,000 net, and I left at least three-quarters of my options "on the table" because they had not yet vested. So, Frank was surely right about that.)

After lunch, I went back to the law firm with mixed emotions. I was tempted by what was a pretty sure offer from Breuer, one with a much more family-oriented work schedule, but at the same time I was on track at Davies to achieve my long-held goal of becoming a law partner (in just another three years) and, also, there was the likelihood that my salary at G-P would not increase as rapidly as at the law firm.

I was in a quandary, knowing that if I even mentioned that I was considering an outside offer, it would be a sign of disloyalty and would damage my career there. But I had one friend at Davies with whom I could talk privately, Dick Franzke. He and I had shared an office for the first few months he was at the firm. He had felt like a total outsider because, unlike most of the lawyers at the firm, he had no Ivy League experience, and some made it plain that they looked down on him. Since I did not feel that way, even though I was a college Ivy Leaguer, he and I became pretty good friends.

That afternoon, I went into Dick's office and told him about the lunch, adding that I was intrigued by the offer. He nailed the issue with two questions:

"Why are you here?" he asked.

"I expect to become a partner in three years," I said.

"So, you become a partner, so what?"

Bingo! All at once he focused my attention on the reality that becoming a partner simply meant I would be making more money, but my workload and working conditions would not change significantly. First of all, I knew myself well enough to realize that I would not work fewer hours than the team I was on or fewer hours than my boss. I could fit into that pattern, make a lot of money, perhaps $500,000 a year by the time I was forty-five (about $5 million in 2024), but I would hardly know my wife and kids.

I laid it all out to Barbara when I got home that night. She was totally supportive of whichever direction I chose to go, although she was definitely intrigued with the idea that I would have more time at home with her, Philip, and David if I accepted the offer from Frank Breuer at Georgia-Pacific.

Also, that night, I called my parents and discussed this situation with them. Dad made my decision even easier for me. First, he commented that he had had several offers over the years but had always been afraid to take them because of the risk involved, and the fact that there was no one to take care of Mom, Les, and me if something happened to him or if the deal went bad. He could not afford to risk giving up the bird in the hand. Although he did not regret his decision to stay with Huntington Rubber Mills for his entire career, he recognized that his financial future might have been much more rewarding, and his work conditions much more enjoyable, if he had taken the risk of a new job.

Then, Dad said that while he did not think it would be necessary, I could feel free to take the chance and make the move, with the assurance that if it did not work out he and Mom would help us financially until we got back on our feet. With his encouragement and support, and Barbara's willingness, I called Frank Breuer the next day and said that I wanted to join Georgia-Pacific's legal department, which I did on November 11, 1963.

The "Georgia" in Georgia-Pacific was more than casual or a geographic designation. There was a quite strong southern flavor to the leadership, reflecting that the company was founded in Augusta, Georgia. I used to say that when the phone rang and the voice said, "Don" I would answer "Yes." However, when it spoke with a distinct southern accent my response was "Yes, *Sir*!"

Frank Breuer was a wonderful man to work for. He was gentle but firm, kind but tough, knowledgeable, and considerate of his team. I reported to him for over six years—November 1963 to September 1969—and grew to greatly admire and respect him. During that time, he often invited me into his office to engage in a discussion of how to handle a particular matter regarding managing the legal department, often personnel related. He also confided in me regarding some of the more difficult decisions he had to make in dealing with the top management of G-P. I felt greatly complimented by his involving me in these discussions.

Frank also gave wonderful guidance about the role of a lawyer. He emphasized that our job was not to tell the client what he could not do; it was to tell him how to do *legally* what he wanted to do. During this time, I benefited greatly from our meetings. I now realize this was my first experience in serving side-by-side with a leader I trusted and respected, and in seeing myself as his number two, even though it was an unofficial post, it was great preparation for those official roles that came later.

Suddenly, instead of working six days and three nights each week, plus some Sundays, as an attorney with Davies, at G-P, I now had every night free except Monday, plus I worked very few Saturdays; and no Sundays were required by my job. I had more time with my family, and, as it turned out, more time to dabble in politics.

Politically, life had been quiet for me after returning to Oregon and becoming a lawyer. Because I had been so turned off by the events at the HYRC with the fight over my successor and because I was so totally obsessed with law school, I did not have any political connection in Oregon during those three years. The closest had come in the fall of 1958 when we went to vote in Eugene and I noticed that there were no names on the ballot in our precinct for the position of precinct committeewoman. I wrote in Barbara's name as a joke. Little did I know that one vote would be enough for her to tie with one other write-in candidate for the position. A few days after the election she received two phone calls. One was from the clerk of elections office saying that she had tied, and that if she and the other write-in candidate did not have a resolution, the clerk would simply flip a coin and notify the winner.

Barbara had no interest in serving and said so. Fortunately, shortly thereafter the phone rang again, and it was the other candidate, who had for years *been* precinct committeewoman. She had routinely won the position each year by writing in her own name and with that one vote won in a unanimous landslide—one to zero. She was almost frantic about the possibility of losing. Barbara quickly assured her that she would happily withdraw her name, that I had written it in as a joke, and that she did not want to disrupt the woman's career in elective politics. Years later, when I was active in statewide Republican affairs, the woman came up to me and told me how grateful she was to Barbara for her generosity.

While I was still with the Davies law firm, there were several young associates who were members of what had been formerly a Toastmasters speaking club called the Trumpeters. Meetings were held over breakfast, and three "table topics" were assigned to the group, from which each member was required to choose one topic on which to speak extemporaneously for one minute. At the end of the meeting, every presenter was evaluated by the group on choice of topic, speech delivery, posture, gestures, eye contact, and other speech techniques. The local chapter had been disaffiliated by Toastmasters International after one of their district governors dropped in on one of their meetings and noticed that they were not following the policy of refraining from the subjects of religion and politics. The chapter was a purely political group, originating out of Republican activities. They still felt that the Toastmasters format was ideal for keeping up their members' interest and enthusiasm, so, undeterred, they simply reconstituted themselves as the "Trumpeters" and continued the chapter with the same format as before.

I was invited to attend a Trumpeters meeting by one of the young associates at the Davies law firm, during my first year there. Things went well and soon I was invited to join the group. Trumpeters reawakened my interest in politics. It was an invaluable experience and strengthened my ability to speak effectively in public, something that I became good at and certainly needed throughout much of my life.

Trumpeters also gave me instant access to men who had become active in Oregon Republican affairs. These included many who would later serve in the party, the state legislature, and elsewhere in the state government, such as Republican chairmen at the state and county levels. I got to know on a first name basis Oregon's Attorney General, Secretary of State, one US Senator, and several state and federal judges. One standout early on was future US Senator Bob Packwood, who was just getting ready to make his first run for public office when I joined the group.

Bob graduated from Grant High School two years before me and, when I was a senior, tried to recruit me to attend his alma mater, Willamette University, but of course I was headed to Harvard. When he later decided to run for the US Senate, he was by that time a member of the Oregon House of Representatives, and I was Republican state chairman. He won in an upset and represented Oregon in the Senate from 1969 to 1995.

Packwood was forced to resign his Senate seat in the mid-1990s after allegations of sexual harassment were made, as reported in the *Washington Post*, by several women, some of whom were former members of his office staff. His own redacted diary allegedly contained reference to his having made the unwanted advances. There is no justification for his actions, which were evidently admitted in his own words. Nonetheless, Bob was very helpful to my early political career, and, for that, he has my gratitude.

By the fall of 1963, with the next Presidential election on the horizon, I decided that I wanted to learn how to do grassroots political work. I checked and found that the position of Republican precinct committeeman in my precinct was vacant. I thought that filling that opening would allow me to learn what door-to-door politics was all about. However, the primary election in which candidates for precinct committeeman (or committeewoman) could be elected was not until the coming May. So, being a lawyer, I decided to examine the Oregon State Statutes that govern party structure and learned that the county central committees had the authority to appoint people to fill vacant precinct posts.

I learned the location and time of the next central committee meeting and went there to ask to be appointed. To my astonishment the Clackamas County chairman was Dr. Paul Dutton who had been our family's dentist for many years while I was growing up. He was by then in his seventies and retired from dentistry. He was wonderfully well-intentioned but substantially miscast as a politician. In fact, the central committee was limping along with most party positions in the county unfilled. The good doctor was basically a caretaker trying to hold together a weak and discouraged organization.

When I presented my request to be precinct committeeman, the old warhorses on the central committee advised me that they could not appoint me, having been informed—falsely—by the (Democrat) county clerk that they had no such authority. It was not my style to argue, so I mentioned that I had examined the appropriate statutes and believed that they did indeed have that authority. They were unconvinced, so I withdrew my request and went home.

A few days later, I was surprised when Dr. Dutton called and asked me to be the emcee at the upcoming annual dinner for the county Republican central committee. I was both intrigued and excited by the prospect, but I knew it was quite unusual for this role to be offered to a complete outsider who was only twenty-eight years old and had done nothing at all for the county party. I told him I was not qualified and that surely there must be some party activists who would love to be emcee. However, he was undeterred, thereby proving my point that he was miscast as a politician. I was sure he was going to upset some people. Finally, after considerable hesitation and genuine efforts on my part to dissuade him, I accepted.

My parents came to the dinner which was held in late November. There were forty or fifty other attendees, including almost all Republican candidates in the county for the 1964 spring primaries, as well as the few GOP officeholders from the county. My parents told me how proud they were of me to be invited to be emcee, which, of course, pleased me immensely. I worked hard preparing and did a careful and thorough job, as well as an entertaining one. My observation of my father's gift of humor plus the experience and training in Trumpeters paid off in a big way. Now I imagine that I must have seemed awfully young and inexperienced, but I was prepared and poised enough that people were impressed.

A few days after the dinner, Dr. Dutton called me and said that the position of precinct organizer for the county party was open, and he wanted me to take the job. He was desperately looking for new blood and he clearly saw me that way. I objected, pointing out that I had sought the position of precinct committeeman so that I could learn *how to be* a good precinct committeeman, but I did not see myself taking on the leadership role in the precincts for the entire county. There was no way I could hope to do the job in all 273 precincts, most all of which, I learned, were without incumbents. For several weeks he and I talked back and forth until, finally, I said to him, "OK, I will take the job but only until we can find someone who is *qualified* to do it." He readily agreed probably because he knew it would be up to *me* to find my successor.

In December, not long after joining Georgia-Pacific, Barbara and I accompanied Don Pearlman and his wife, Shirley, to a Young Republican Christmas party in Salem. I remember sitting with Barbara in the back seat of Don's car and, as we crossed over the Tualatin River on I-5 traveling south (it's funny how some memories remain in one's mind like a video), I mentioned to Don that I had been asked to take the job of precinct organizer for the county. I felt confident he would be impressed that it was a good steppingstone to political influence, but his reaction was a typical Pearlmanesque response. In a grumbling voice he said, "What would you want to do *that* for?"

Despite my friend's pessimism, I accepted the position at a county executive committee meeting in January 1964. Among the members of the executive committee were Sylvia Phillips, vice chairman, and Gerry Coleman, finance chairman. Very quickly, Sylvia, Gerry, and I became the de facto leadership of the central committee. We would agree on the items we felt needed to be on the central committee meeting agendas, and Sylvia would meet with Dr. Dutton to get his approval and advise him on how each matter ought to be handled. This worked quite effectively for a few months, and during that time, I struggled, having no idea how to fill precincts in anticipation of the upcoming general election in November.

But I did not let lack of training keep me from giving it my best effort. The first thing I did was get copies of the precinct maps for the whole county. Clackamas, the third most populous county in the state, was about forty miles long, north to south, and about sixty miles, east to west. It was heavily urbanized in those areas adjacent to Multnomah County around Portland and in the cities of Milwaukie, Lake Oswego, West Linn, and Oregon City.

Next, I spread the maps out on a four-by-eight sheet of plywood set on sawhorses I set up in our living room. Our living room then became the precinct headquarters for the county. Barbara never once complained or in any way objected to my conversion and occupation of her living room in this fashion. This was simply another major burden wholly accepted by her in the aid of whatever my calling happened to be. She just walked and worked around the clutter and kept our two young boys from smashing into it during the day when I was gone. The good side for both of us was that when I was working on the precinct job I was at home, not away at night and weekends as I had been while working for the law firm.

In addition to contacts made through the Trumpeters, my mother also helped build my political profile. She and Dad were living in Clackamas County in their house on the Tualatin River, near Lake Oswego. She was a member of the Lake Oswego Women's Republican Club, one of the most active Republican women's clubs in the state. Mom was not an officer (because she did not want to be that involved) but she was very active in the club's activities. We had moved to Lake Oswego after I started work with the Davies firm, and for quite a while after I became involved in local politics and the Clackamas County Republican central committee, I was introduced by people to others as "Rose Hodel's son." That certainly helped me become acquainted with and accepted by the older Republican activists in the area.

I had begun smoking cigarettes during the summer of 1952 when I was sailing across the Atlantic on my way to Germany with the American Field Service. Most of the other students on that ship were in college already, while we one hundred AFS exchange students were still in high school. Some of the college students in the group ran a mock Republican political convention. I got involved and was offered cigarettes from the (older) college guys I was working with—the smoke-filled room was a reality—and thus began my smoking experience. During my senior year in high school, therefore, I smoked occasionally, but seldom and mostly in the privacy of my home with my parents (my dad was a lifelong smoker) because I did not want to set a bad example for younger students who might see me smoking. As treasurer—and soon president—of the student body, I continued to be concerned about having a clean reputation.

At Harvard, however, I was away from scrutiny and there was no reason to refrain. I chain-smoked, and quit, and chain-smoked, and quit, many times. When I came out of college, I continued that stop and start routine. Usually, I would quit because of the cost of the cigarettes—not cheap even then—and due to my assumption that it must have been bad for my health, only to start again when one of the new fathers in the Davies law firm came by to pass out cigars, which, among so many young, usually newly married lawyers, seemed to occur every three months or so. A few days or a week or two later after the free cigar I would buy another cigar while in the mood for one. Then I would buy a couple, and soon I was smoking up to five cigars a day, which was expensive and smelly, and worse for me than cigarettes. Then I would bum a cigarette or two and, finally, I would buy a pack and be back to chain-smoking a pack and a half a day. Making matters worse, Barbara also smoked.

In those days it is important to note that public hostility to smoking was just beginning to build. People could smoke almost anywhere: in offices, elevators, restaurants, even in airplanes. In fact, it was in January 1964 just two months after I joined G-P that the first US Surgeon General's report stating that smoking was hazardous to one's health was published. I did not need that study to tell me that smoking was bad for me. I had begun to notice that smoking made my lungs feel constricted and that I was waking up in the morning with a headache that only went away after my first cigarette of the day.

When I left the law firm in November 1963, to work at Georgia-Pacific, I faced a new reality when it came to smoking. I became the fifth lawyer in the G-P legal department but the only smoker. During the first couple of weeks, I continued to smoke and occasionally, Tom Withycombe, one of the other lawyers, would bum a cigarette from me. By this time, I knew that I really wanted to quit smoking, and I realized that the fact that none of the other lawyers habitually smoked was a perfect environment in which to do that; and then I thought, *What if Tom becomes a smoker because I have them available, and then if I quit, I will have cigarettes being smoked around me and available to borrow from him.* At that point I decided if I ever wanted to stop, I needed to quit for good and do so immediately.

Being an "experienced quitter" by this time made me aware of some of the pitfalls. So, I decided to use my own type of aversion therapy, reminiscent of my father's *unplanned* break from eating candy as a boy. I decided that I would smoke heavily for three days and my last cigarette before bedtime on that third day would be my last cigarette—ever. So, for those three days I smoked continuously from the moment I got up in the morning right through meals and in the evening until I went to bed. I intentionally inhaled deeply. By the third night I was feeling so ill from the smoke that I could hardly wait to get to bed so that I could stop smoking. And I continued to feel nauseated for the next two or three days. That was the key to quitting successfully.

I vowed that I would never put another cigarette or cigar to my lips, knowing that the odds were high that if I did I would begin smoking regularly again. In the more than sixty years since making that vow, I am very grateful that I have kept it. For several years after I quit, Barbara continued to smoke, finally quitting when she was very sick from a bout with peritonitis.

Whenever I tell this story I am reminded of my late friend Rich DeVos, cofounder of Amway, who was fond of joking during his speeches: "*You* don't smoke. The *cigarette* smokes. You're just the sucker!"

CHAPTER 6
POLITICIAN

I had emceed the county dinner at Dr. Dutton's invitation in November 1963, just a couple of weeks after I had gone to Georgia-Pacific, and shortly after that he asked me to be the precinct organizer for the entire county—273 precincts. As I wrote earlier, I finally agreed to try to do the job until we could find someone who was qualified to do it.

Helen Cannon was secretary of the county Republican central committee and had been around many years before I got involved. She saw that I had no idea how to even get started and suggested that I get in touch with three women—Frances Davisson, Clydia Magaurn, and Margaret Lavachek—for advice on what to do about finding precinct captains. Frances was the immediate past county chairman. Clydia ran the annual Lake Oswego Women's Republican Club Country Fair, a rummage sale fundraiser for the central committee. Margaret was the wife of Lew Lavachek, a wealthy land developer, and a good friend of Frances and Clydia. All three lived in Lake Oswego and, therefore, knew my mother because of her participation in the Lake Oswego Women's Republican Club.

I called Frances and asked if I could meet with her and the others to talk about recruiting people to fill precincts. She let me know she was working and had no time to do anything, but she graciously agreed to meet if I could set it up. I called the others and got the meeting set. When we got together, they were open with their advice, but it was clear that their working days were over. They told me which potential precinct committeemen or women to call on a precinct-by-precinct basis, and even evaluated their abilities, but they made it quite clear they would not make any calls themselves. It was also becoming obvious to me what Dr. Dutton had been up against.

When Frances stepped down as chair and left him the job, all her Republican women friends took the opportunity to retire with her. They were worn out from having fought the good fight for many years. They were relieved not to be phoning, going to meetings, licking stamps, stuffing envelopes, and trying to go door-to-door. Some of them were getting on in years and while their hearts were still loyal to the Grand Old Party, they simply did not have the energy any longer. They might do it for a friend, like Frances, or Clydia, or Margaret, but not for a politically inexperienced older dentist and certainly not for a twenty-eight-year-old upstart who had let himself get talked into trying to fill 273 precincts, which meant I had to find twice that many people.

Even with Frances's ideas, I made very little progress, and by mid-March the county had precinct committeemen or committeewomen in only about 10 percent of the precincts. No one who knew anything about being a precinct person wanted to get involved, so the recruiting process was slow—and dismal. I could only try to do it in my spare time.

One day, while walking down the street in downtown Portland, I bumped into Wes Phillips (not related to Sylvia), an activist I had known for several years through the Young Republicans. As I related earlier, he had wanted to be part of the national Young Republican Syndicate I had worked with while I was at Harvard, but he had not made it into the group. We greeted each other cordially and stopped to talk.

Wes was pleased to learn that I was precinct organizer for Clackamas County and disclosed, to my surprise, that he had been Clackamas County chairman just a few years earlier. In fact, he was Frances Davisson's predecessor. I told him how much difficulty I was having finding precinct men and women. He said that he had many friends out there (meaning in Clackamas County) and that he would be willing to help. I was delighted. He also said something that gave me the impression he might consider becoming chairman again if we needed someone.

I was very encouraged by Wes's offer to help fill precincts and the possibility that he might provide some leadership as chairman, if the need arose. I was very fond of Dr. Dutton, but he was not equipped to be county chairman. I could hardly wait to tell Frances. I phoned and told her about my conversation with Wes and, much to my astonishment, she was both alarmed and outraged! "Why," she said, "this is terrible! He may be planning to come in and take over the county party again. He was a *terrible* chairman, and we cannot afford to have that happen."

She immediately called an emergency meeting with Margaret and Clydia, where I was required to brief them all on my meeting with Wes. His offer to consider filling the chairman's role if that were needed was perceived by them as absolute proof that he was planning a takeover—a totally unacceptable scenario. Suddenly, I did not have to make the calls to fill precincts—they made them. They were determined to recruit friends who would vote at the election in June should Wes try to become involved.

With their help, precincts suddenly began to fill. They were good organizers. They knew lots of people and the rallying cry of "Stop Wes Phillips!" worked wonders. Other retirees also jumped in and harnessed themselves to the cause.

Frances and her friends let me in on the background of their hostility to Wes. While he was county chairman, he had committed an unpardonable sin. Clydia Magaurn had, as I wrote earlier, been in charge of the Country Fair and raised approximately $12,000 each two years to be used for Republican Party purposes. The money was deposited in an account belonging to the party central committee, but it was clear that Clydia and her friends, like Frances, Margaret, and (even) my mother, were very proprietary. It was *their* money; they had raised it; they cared deeply about how it would be used; and they wanted to be involved in those spending decisions. Phillips, however, chose to ignore them and to spend the money without following their advice.

I seem to recall that Wes thought the most useful thing would be to give individual candidates for office financial help in their campaigns, while those women (fondly known to Barbara and me afterward as "Those Women") did *not* want the money given to candidates because they felt the candidates would waste it. In a day when $4,000 was sufficient to run a good campaign for the state legislature, $12,000 was *a lot* of money. They wanted to spend it on newsletters or handouts supporting *all* the candidates in the county. Wes attempted to force the situation and get their support for his approach, but they refused, so he simply did what he wanted. They in turn mounted a campaign against Wes at the next election where he was defeated by Frances , which is how she came to be Republican county chairman. Obviously, I knew none of this when I first talked with Wes on the street that day and innocently came back excited to tell Frances about his coming to my rescue

Precinct elections were held at the time of the primary election in May. Those who were elected then were eligible to vote at the June central committee meeting. We worked to file the names of candidates that had been recruited for precinct posts so that their names appeared on the ballots in the primary. That way, at the organizing meeting in June they would be eligible to vote for officers. By June, we had approximately 60 percent of the precincts filled, and we turned out a large number of those workers to the meeting, just to be sure that Wes Phillips didn't sneak in with some hidden cohorts and steal the election.

At some point during the spring of 1964, Gerry Coleman and Sylvia Phillips decided that Dr. Dutton had to be replaced with someone who was better suited to the job, and I agreed. I admired Dr. Dutton for his heart and his spirit, but it was apparent to me that even he would be relieved if he could pass the burden on to someone else.

At one of our "pre-meeting" meetings, Gerry and Sylvia began talking about how to replace Dr. Dutton at the June meeting where county officers were elected. They were visualizing some kind of surprise move where their candidate, Gerry, would suddenly be nominated, and Dr. Dutton would learn that he would not be reelected. This was so similar to the way we had operated in the Young Republicans back at Harvard that I was repelled by it and did not want to have anything to do with it. After all, I was involved because Dr. Dutton had invited me and pushed me forward. At the same time, I knew they were right about the need for new leadership.

Rather than surprise Dutton with a takeover, I told them that I thought he would welcome a chance to be rid of the job, and I suggested that they let me talk with him. They were nervous that if I failed to persuade him and he chose to run that we would have a mess on our hands. I responded that as precinct organizer I probably could influence a majority of the votes. It was apparent to Sylvia and Gerry that I was potentially the most powerful factor in the central committee because, within reason, I had the votes (so long as I had the support of Frances, Clydia, and Margaret). Finally, they agreed that I should talk with Dr. Dutton.

I went to see Dr. Dutton at his home. We spent some time talking about him and how generous he had been to me, and about the future of the party. I mentioned the good job Gerry Coleman was doing as treasurer, which received a very positive reaction from Dr. Dutton. I gently raised the question of whether Dr. Dutton would like to see Gerry be chairman and got an overwhelmingly positive answer. He was excited at the thought. I suggested that if he called Gerry and urged him to accept the role, Gerry might just do it. Dr. Dutton could hardly wait to call Gerry.

As soon as I finished my meeting with Dr. Dutton, I called Gerry to alert him to expect the call and to respond appropriately. And that's what happened. Dr. Dutton had the pleasure of selecting his successor and persuading him to take the job, and he did not ever know or need to know that for a time there was thought of a plot to replace *him*. I felt good about all that then, and I still feel good when I think of it.

In both the national and Oregon Republican parties, 1964 was a battleground year. Conservatives rallied behind US Senator Barry Goldwater from Arizona, while liberal Republicans were sold on Governor Nelson Rockefeller of New York. In those days there were only fifteen or sixteen states whose delegates to the national convention were selected by popular vote in a primary election. Most were selected in state conventions or by party caucuses. Oregon was a small state in population, but it was the last highly visible primary before California, at that time the second largest state after New York. Oregon was, therefore, thought to be very important because it gave momentum and news coverage just prior to California's primary.

Goldwater was winning the nomination state-by-state, but Rockefeller had a chance to win Oregon, which could give him a big boost to help him win California and bring Goldwater's momentum to a halt. Rockefeller poured resources into the Oregon primary. In the end he won the Oregon primary at a cost of five dollars for each vote he received! That was an astonishing amount in a day when twenty cents or forty cents were big expenditures per vote.

The primary engendered great controversy and hostility among the party faithful, and right in the middle of it all I was trying to recruit precinct workers. Many I talked to wanted me to first declare which Presidential candidate I was for before they would commit to being a committee person. I refused, stating firmly and clearly that I would support the nominee whoever won, that my job was to help elect Republicans, and that I was not going to take sides in the primary fight between Rockefeller and Goldwater.

Later I learned that I did this so well that the Goldwater supporters were convinced I was for Rockefeller and the Rockefeller supporters were convinced I was for Goldwater. That was not quite the result I was aiming for, but at least it made it possible to recruit some precinct workers. What it showed, I think, is that the partisans felt so strongly about their man that anyone who was not for him was against him and that is how they categorized me. There was no room for someone who was neutral.

At the county central committee election in June, we elected Gerry Coleman as chairman and Sylvia Phillips as vice chairman. Sylvia and Gerry both had strong reservations about Goldwater and, especially, about the local people who were supporting him.

I was elected secretary. After that, I sometimes joked that being party secretary for Clackamas County was the best job I ever had in politics: "It didn't matter what happened at the meetings. It was whatever I wrote in the minutes that was the official record." Barbara often cautioned me, correctly, that my saying that could leave the listener with the idea that I did not perform my duties accurately or truthfully, but she fully knew that I did. And it is also true that what I wrote was the official record.

I have never disclosed to anyone other than Barbara where I really stood in the Presidential nomination contest during that time, but it is relevant to the story of how I became a Cabinet officer. My heart was with the conservative movement, Goldwater, and my mentor Clif White, all the way. I did not like Nelson Rockefeller or what he stood for. I voted for Goldwater twice in 1964, once in the Oregon Primary and once in November. Both times he lost.

As a member of the Harvard Young Republican Club and eventually its president, I was a trusted associate of the National YR Syndicate. As a result, conservative leaders such as Bill Rusher and Clif White became mentors and friends. In fact, of all the members of the Syndicate and all the people they launched in Republican politics, I was the one who achieved the highest ranking, a Cabinet position, and not once but twice. Their association was helpful to me, and it was a source of pride among my friends at the top of the Syndicate that I reached the positions that I did. The HYRC activities gave me real political experience but, perhaps more importantly, it gave me key figures in a national Republican establishment as friends or mentors. And those people uniformly supported Reagan when he entered politics after they had worked for Goldwater in 1964.

Don Pearlman and I were in touch with Clif in 1963 when he was organizing the whole draft Goldwater campaign—with Goldwater as a semi-reluctant candidate. Later, I learned that Clif had had to persuade the Senator simply not to do anything that would take him out of the running. As his potential nomination came closer, however, Goldwater began to realize it could happen and he began to get involved. But at first it was Clif and his team doing it all, without any help (or interference) from Goldwater.

After President John F. Kennedy was assassinated on November 22, 1963, about eight months before the 1964 nominating convention and almost one year before the general election, Don and I called Clif and urged him to consider *not* pushing for Goldwater. Our assessment, which proved to be correct, was that Goldwater was a perfect opponent for JFK, a northeastern liberal, who was then considered to be soft on national defense, but he would get clobbered by now-President Lyndon Johnson, who succeeded Kennedy and unquestionably would be the Democrat nominee in 1964.

We felt that Johnson would immediately take advantage of the public sympathy that followed his accession to office after a beloved, martyred President—and he did, of course. He also portrayed himself as a fiscal conservative, turning out the lights in the White House to save money, and promising to take strong action in Vietnam, while painting Goldwater as a trigger-happy "mad bomber," who just might precipitate nuclear war.

When Goldwater was nominated for President at the Republican Convention held at the Cow Palace in San Francisco, the national party was, as I wrote earlier, as badly divided as Oregon, and the liberals in the press exploited that division. After losing the nomination, Rockefeller refused to endorse Goldwater, and his supporters took their cue from him. Oregon Governor Mark Hatfield made public statements separating himself from Goldwater.

Goldwater did not help matters at all after the convention. He removed Clif White and installed an inexperienced team of people from his home state as his campaign team. I don't believe that Clif or anyone could have saved Goldwater, but it would have been a much better effort had the candidate stuck by Clif. Goldwater surely did not know how to get his message across in a winsome manner and his team had no national experience.

After the convention I became the Clackamas County liaison to the Goldwater campaign. In that liaison role I discovered an amazing group of women (almost all the activists were women) who were, in many cases, brand new to the political process, brought into the party because of Goldwater and the fire for the cause he espoused. They saw things in black and white with no gray areas. They did not see why compromise made sense or was in any way necessary. Their campaign style was in your face and aggressive. In fact, I had to cajole more than a few of my hard-won precinct workers to stay the course after being angered and upset by door-to-door Goldwater campaigners who felt the precinct representative was not doing enough to support the candidate.

I was sympathetic to the intent of these overly intense campaigners and their emotions even though I deplored their tactics. On a positive note, among them were stalwart conservatives I would respect the rest of my life. In serving respectfully in the liaison capacity, it turned out that I was, also, cementing my relationships with people I would see often in the future and who would support me in future political positions.

LBJ and the Democrats continued to label Goldwater a warmonger, including creating a television commercial featuring the mushroom cloud of an exploding nuclear bomb, which sealed Goldwater's fate and Johnson's election in a huge landslide. It was a major defeat for conservatives.

Election Day 1964 also brought political disaster to every Republican candidate in Clackamas County. It was not because a large number of Democrats turned out to vote, but because so many Republicans chose to stay home. Embarrassed at the things the press highlighted about Goldwater, they simply did not show up at the polling places and vote, which meant that we lost every down-ballot race in our county.

Sylvia Phillips and Gerry Coleman were so dismayed that they announced, right after these disastrous election results in our county, that they were resigning. I tried unsuccessfully to get them to reconsider. When they would not, the remainder of the central committee designated a nominating committee. I was a member, and we began a search for a new chairman and vice chairman. We tried all the likely individuals who seemed capable of doing the job and generating support—other than Wes Phillips, of course.

Finally, in desperation someone suggested that maybe I should do it. I genuinely tried to resist, stating the truth: I was too young and too poorly connected with the key political types in our county and state. I had the votes if I wanted them, and I could easily win if it came to a contest, but I doubted my ability to engender the support among the movers and shakers in Clackamas County that was needed to do the job well.

On the other hand, I had spent a lot of time and energy trying to recruit people to the precinct positions. I hated to see them abandoned and felt like I would be doing so if I quit along with everyone else. Finally, after everyone who *should* have taken the job turned it down, I reluctantly agreed to do it "until we find someone better qualified." With my decision, Sylvia Phillips agreed to stay on as vice chairman. And in early January 1965 at age twenty-nine, at an otherwise uneventful meeting of the Clackamas County Republican central committee, I was unanimously elected as county chairman.

A few days later, my mother phoned, well aware that for the past year or so I had been introduced to a lot of people in Lake Oswego as Rose Hodel's son. She launched right into her message. "Well, Baby, you've arrived. Today I was introduced as 'Don Hodel's mother.'" It was a turning point that we both recognized. She was proud of me, and I was pleased to make her proud.

As county chairman, I automatically became one of the seventy-two members of the Republican state central committee, which consisted of the Republican county chairman and vice chairman of each of Oregon's thirty-six counties. The night I was elected county chairman, after Barbara and I had returned home, I was standing in front of the chest of drawers in our bedroom unloading my pockets, getting ready for bed, and I said to her, "If I ever wanted to be elected Republican state chairman, Clackamas County is the best place from which to do it." It was the third largest county by population, in Oregon, and, although it was located next to the state's *largest* and most urban county, Multnomah (i.e., the city of Portland), in the eyes of the rural counties, it did not have all the negatives related to the big city urban area.

I inherited a county executive committee of a dozen or so members that consisted of several people in their fifties and sixties and, maybe, a few who were even older. I was at least twenty years younger than the next *youngest*, which actually helped me appeal to younger voters, and brought in a lot of new people to the county party. One of the best was Don Lindsay, a computer company owner-operator who agreed to serve as our finance chairman. We brought in other young people and hired a bright, ambitious young man, Gary Putnam, from the college YRs, to be our county executive director. He was actually the person who coined the term, *Those Women.*

I should point out that Those Women was not meant in any way to be disrespectful. In many organizations, and especially in churches, if not for the group of women who roll up their sleeves and get busy organizing and doing things, nothing would get done. In Gary's case, however, he was constantly hassled, in his estimation, by them as they tried to tell him what to do and how to do it.

Clydia Magaurn and her friends ran the usual Country Fair fundraiser in 1965 and again raised a lot of money. Since the Wes Phillips fiasco, however, the money had been deposited in a separate account controlled by Clydia. I will always count it as a singular feat that, before I was finished as county chairman, Clydia and her friends offered to let me decide how to spend that money! I never took them up on it, though, always consulting with them regarding how to spend it in a way that we all agreed was best. I took it as a real compliment, however, and a sign of having earned their trust that they were willing to let me decide. They all were as old as my mother, in addition to being her friends, and I treated them with the same respect and grace as I did her. They appreciated it and rewarded me with their support, friendship, and trust, which is pleasing to recall all these years later.

At the first meeting of the state central committee, I met a lot of new people. I was not only among the newest members, I was also the youngest, in some cases by several decades. The state chairman was Governor Hatfield's handpicked choice, Peter Gunnar. I later learned that he had been state chairman once before but had hatched an overly ambitious fundraising program that bankrupted the state committee.

That summer, Gunnar approached the state central committee with a plan for a major door-to-door fundraising campaign to support a slick magazine and campaign effort in 1966. I was very supportive and sold our county committee on participating. We put teams in the field door-to-door soliciting contributions. We did well and sent the proceeds and the names and addresses of the donors to the state party. One day, several weeks into the campaign, I called the state office to get an accounting on what we had turned in. I was stunned to learn that they could not tell me. Further, I learned that they did not have records of who had given what.

I was shocked. Without those records it would be impossible to carry out the promises we were making to donors about delivering their magazines. At that point, with the support of the Clackamas County central committee, I stopped sending any further money to the state central committee. I set up a separate bank account for our central committee into which we placed our funds from the program until I could get proof that the state would be able to fulfill its promises.

Gunnar wanted that money in his state coffers because he was spending money as fast as it was coming in. But instead of using the money to establish the magazine and do other things promised in the program, he was paying salaries—including his own. As far as I knew, he was the first paid state chairman of the party, and I became very suspicious that our efforts were simply going to pay the staff. I got in touch with the chairmen of a couple of other big counties and discovered that when they found out what was happening, they also set up separate accounts and withheld *their* funds from Gunnar.

At the January 1966 state central committee meeting in Salem, the major item on the agenda was the fundraising program. Jim Allison, Washington County chairman, was a firebrand and was really angry at Gunnar. Jim was neither inclined to pull his punches nor was he likely to be tactful. He was a good twenty years older than me, but I convinced him to let me be the spokesman for the large counties who were concerned about the program and were withholding their funds. I did not want things said in public that would show up in the press and hurt our party and our candidates.

During my presentation, I tried to say in nonconfrontational tones that the program was not working, that money was being spent by the party faster than it was being raised, and that we needed to redirect the state party's course. I did say, "Back in August the chairman said this was a 'go for broke' program. Well, we've made it." In fact, about two-thirds of the counties, probably twenty-four out of thirty-six, mostly the less populated ones, had not done anything, so they were oblivious to the faults we had encountered. Gunnar, of course, disputed my assertions and convinced them that our objections were not valid.

When the time came for a "vote of no confidence" in Gunnar's program, he had the support of two-thirds of the members. However, he lost the votes of every large county in the state. Pete, therefore, was saved by the well-intentioned, but unknowledgeable small counties who trusted his assurances that there were no problems with his fundraising program. That night on television a very astute political commentator from one of the Portland television stations said that while the vote had been heavily in favor of Gunnar, when he (the commentator) analyzed the vote and saw that those counties representing the huge majority of the state's total population voted against him, he realized that the question was how long Gunnar could survive as chairman.

As soon as the meeting was over, an angry Travis Cross, Governor Hatfield's press spokesperson (and sidekick), who was furious about my having made Gunnar's alleged malfeasance a public issue, came up to me and said, "You have opposed the Governor's party chairman!" He almost shouted at me. I tried to point out that I had done it in a gentlemanly and low-key fashion compared to what would have happened if I had let others handle the issue. That did not help placate Cross. And not liking personal confrontations of any kind, I was quite saddened by his criticism.

When I got home, I informed Barbara that I likely had committed political suicide by offending the Governor and his insiders, and that my future in politics was probably at an end. I felt mildly sorry it had come to that, but I was convinced that I had done the right thing and had spoken honestly to the members of the central committee.

Five months later, by June 1966, Gunnar ran out of money to pay his salary and keep the party afloat. Not only had the money we turned in been spent on daily operations and payroll, but the party's prior debts had not been paid. As best we could determine, the state party was $11,000 in debt (over $100,000 in 2025 dollars). A very large source of funds had dried up when the largest counties stopped sending revenues to the state central committee. He could go no further and, having abandoned his own grandiose fundraising schemes, decided to call it quits. He announced that he would not seek reelection in July 1966 at the central committee election.

Gunnar named a nominating committee consisting of five or six people and—to my surprise—he included me. Then I realized that he probably did that to minimize my chances of succeeding him. That was OK with me, since I was one of the newest county chairmen and only thirty-one years old. No one—especially me—thought of me as a potential Republican state chairman.

Perhaps in part because I believed that my political future had been abbreviated by crossing the Governor and in part because I had spent a pretty intense couple of years being active, I decided that I had spent enough time in politics, and it was time to get out. I went to my friend Don Lindsay, whom I had persuaded earlier to be the county finance chairman. Don was doing a great job raising money and devising ways to spend it effectively in support of Republican candidates. I told him I was not running for reelection at the June 1966 Clackamas County party organization meeting and urged him to take the job. He was very reluctant but finally decided that he would do it rather than see all his good work go to waste.

I did not put him in a position where he had a fight to get the job. If he had had to contest the position, he probably would have walked away. I had worked the committee well and carefully, and he was strongly supported. He was unanimously elected and proceeded to do an outstanding job as county chairman.

In the fall of 1966 as a result of a lot of good work and the ebb and flow of politics, Clackamas County had amazing success in supporting Republican candidates for office. I don't recall the exact numbers, but in a county where Democrat voters outnumbered Republicans by many thousands, we won a majority of the votes in the county for all but one of twelve Republican candidates. Don Lindsay deserved a lot of credit due to his excellent leadership and the campaign materials that he sent out. They were attractive and persuasive; and because he was a computer expert, he was ahead of the competition in being able to target households without duplicating the mailing so that the limited financial resources of the county went further and were more effective.

The chairwoman of the nominating committee for the state party in search of Pete Gunnar's successor as state chairman was Dortha Moore, Oregon's national committeewoman (there is one woman and one man from each state on the Republican National Committee). Dortha had been in that role for at least a decade at that time and was well liked and respected. She and the remainder of the committee talked to at least one hundred people who were legitimate prospects to be state chairman. Not one of them would take the job. The large debt, the mess Pete had made, the low reputation of the party, and lawsuits Gunnar had brought against conservatives all made the job very unattractive to anyone with any kind of reputation and stature. After several weeks of failing to find any qualified person who would even consider accepting the job, Dortha called me. She pointed out that we were having no success in finding a nominee and asked if I would consider taking it if we simply couldn't find anyone else.

"I am really too young and not qualified," I said. "We need to find someone who has the necessary stature." We talked about our options. Clearly, Dortha had talked with the rest of the nominating committee, and she assured me that they agreed with her that unless someone unexpectedly appeared, I was the best alternative at this point. The election was to take place in a couple of weeks, and we simply could not go into that meeting with no nominee. It would make the party look even weaker and it would likely lead to a nasty battle among unqualified candidates. Finally, I agreed that if we could not find someone qualified to take the job, I would do so until we found someone who was.

The meeting of the state central committee was set for July 22, 1966, where the new state chairman would be elected. With only two weeks to go before the meeting, the chances of finding a candidate continued to look bleak. Then, one day, I heard a news report that State Senator Bob Smith, a good, solid conservative from eastern Oregon, might be considering running. I called Dortha Moore and told her that I had heard that Bob might be interested in the job and said to her, "We need to get him. He would be great."

"Oh, no!" Dortha said. "He's from my part of the state and he has a wonderful political future. This job has never been a stepping-stone to anything."

There was a long pause as I remained silent. After a moment she obviously realized that she was talking to the guy she had talked into taking the job she had just labeled "never been a stepping-stone to anything." She then backpedaled and tried to reassure me that it was a perfect role for me. The fact was, I knew what she was saying was true, and I wasn't agreeing to be the candidate in order to seek a political future.

Years later, when I was in President Reagan's Cabinet, Barbara and I attended a reception held in conjunction with a meeting of the Republican National Committee. As I entered the large Washington, DC, hotel ballroom, standing with her back to me chatting with someone was Dortha Moore. I walked over, put my hand on her shoulder and, before she turned to see who it was, I whispered, "That job has never been a stepping-stone to anything." She turned, and with great laughter we renewed our friendship.

Barbara had arranged for a sitter to stay with Philip and David so that she could accompany me to that state central committee meeting where I was to be elected state chairman. We were both getting excited about that. Although it was a very troubled position, for me it was a big step up in the political process and in one sense I had little to lose. Everyone who mattered knew what a mess the party was in, so if I failed, it would not be a surprise. If I succeeded in any measure, it was all gravy. But I drove down to the meeting of the state central committee alone while Barbara stayed home with Philip who, at age twelve, had broken his jaw in a bicycle accident.

When the time for the election arrived, at the last minute a county chairman from southern Oregon decided to throw his hat in the ring, in part, I'm sure, because he felt that I was too new—and too young—to do it. He was, of course, right. I went to Dortha and said I was willing to withdraw to avoid a fight that might divide the state central committee. She—and the other committee members—would not hear of it. They contended that I was better qualified than he, although I always thought that might be due to their "not invented here" syndrome. They had looked extensively and found no one, so they settled on me, and no one was going to come along at the last minute and undo what they had decided.

There was a flurry of activity as Dortha enlisted the aid of none other than Travis Cross, the Governor's aide, who only six months earlier had chewed me out for damaging the party by opposing Pete Gunnar. But by then, Governor Hatfield had been nominated for the US Senate and was in a tough race. Every little thing that might affect it one way or the other was of concern. A fight and the election of someone from southern Oregon may not have seemed to be helpful. There may, also, have been recognition of the fact that I was a recognized conservative by the state party activists and Hatfield was in trouble with them. If I were chairman and supportive of Hatfield it could be of great help to him. A cadre of people, including Cross, descended on my prospective opponent and persuaded him to drop out. I was the sole nominee and, therefore, elected unanimously as Republican Party state chairman at the age of thirty-one. And during my brief term in that role, my would-be opponent became one of my strongest supporters.

What an amazing turn of events. Only nine years earlier I had been impressed when Don Pearlman pointed out the person who was "*close to* the state chairman" and here I *was* the chairman! My brother, Les, and his wife, Gladys, and their kids were driving back from a camping trip, had the car radio tuned to a news station, and were totally surprised to hear that I had been elected. I had not thought to say anything about it to Les.

The job really was a mess, however. There's an old spiritual that begins, "Nobody knows the troubles I've seen," and it surely applied to the Republican Party of Oregon when I was elected. It turned out that the party was in debt more than $30,000 with no income. It had promised thousands of contributors to produce and deliver the glossy magazine. Three issues had been printed and distributed, and the donors had been promised four issues in return for their donations. But the party was totally broke, and the last issue of the magazine would cost about $2,500 to print and distribute. The state party was also suing a group of conservatives who called themselves the "United Republicans of Oregon" in order to prevent them from using the name *Republican* during an election that was going to be close, and with a party that was in disarray over the disagreements spawned by Pete Gunnar's divisive actions as chairman.

I was soon invited to speak to the Trumpeters, as they were excited about having one of their own members be the new state chairman. The introduction of course emphasized my election to the position. When I stood up to speak, I paused briefly and began, "Gentlemen, I have just gotten my hands around the biggest can of worms I have ever seen!"

I had to act quickly, and one of the first things I did was to direct our attorneys to drop the lawsuit against the United Republicans of Oregon. If they wanted to use the name, so be it, the more the merrier—and it saved additional legal costs.

Next, I had to find a way to produce and distribute one more issue of the magazine. I called State Rep. Monty Montgomery, the Republican leader in the State House. He personally loaned the party the $2,500 to print that magazine and all he asked was that I promise not to leave the job until he was paid back. I met that promise right after the first of the year.

Ten thousand of the $30,000 total debt was owed to the Republican National Committee because they had arranged for a speaker to come to Oregon for a fundraiser and that was their share of the proceeds. Gunnar had stiffed them. I called the RNC, truthfully explained the situation and asked them to forgive the debt, which, after some back and forth, they did. Other bills, I addressed one at a time and either paid them off from the occasional miscellaneous contributions we received or persuaded the creditor to reduce the amount. I attribute part of my success in this to my years doing credit work for the US National Bank of Portland when I was a lawyer with the Davies firm, where I learned that a creditor, if properly approached, would often accept a smaller assured payment than go to the trouble and expense of suing in hopes of getting more.

I also had to raise money for the state party and for our candidates for office. But asking for money from potentially large donors was a *major* problem for me, and likely one reason I always enjoyed being in the number two role more than being the CEO who had to carry the main fundraising responsibility. First, asking for money always felt like begging to me. Second, I did not really understand the process of fundraising. Third, I was acutely aware of the fact that I was young and inexperienced. I sometimes would call on a "fat cat," as the best donors to the party were called, and if I were lucky, he would give me $100. But I had no doubt that if I had been a person of more senior stature, he would have given $1,000.

Of course, we were also in the middle of the 1966 election campaign. I spent a significant amount of my time speaking to conservative audiences that were quite hostile to Governor Hatfield because of his opposition to the Vietnam War. Most Republicans, including me, felt that we ought to try to win the war rather than oppose it. Hatfield's opponent, Congressman Bob Duncan, was a reasonably conservative Democrat and a supporter of the war, which made things difficult for Hatfield. I gave more speeches supporting Hatfield than for anyone else during that campaign. I simply stated the truth, that on that one issue I disagreed with

Hatfield, but on a whole host of other issues, I disagreed with Duncan. Over and over, I made the point that if Duncan were elected, he would vote with the Democrats on every issue but that one, which was a persuasive argument with my conservative audiences.

As chairman, I tried to help our candidates as much as possible, even if I did not agree with their positions. I felt that the party chairman should not discriminate against any Republican candidate. When a conservative friend chided me for supporting Hatfield, I responded that I believed that was my job, and if I could not do that, I should resign the position rather than not live up to my obligation to support all Republicans.

With Senator Mark Hatfield and Barbara (Bonneville Power Administration/Department of the Interior)

I decided that I needed to visit every county, but there was no money to reimburse me for my travel. I drove our 1965 Ford Mustang to every county where we had any kind of organization. I had to do this on the weekends because I could not take time off from work, as I was still working full time at Georgia-Pacific. I figured out later that my nine months as state chairman cost me about $500 in unreimbursed out-of-pocket expenses. Considering that my G-P salary was about $12,000 a year, $500 was a lot of money.

Supporting our candidates came in four primary areas: I tried to keep the party's debt from embarrassing them; I worked to keep a public lid on the negative things about the party; I spent a lot of time on the phone talking to people in the party to keep them involved and voting; and I gave many speeches in support of their campaigns. These were all experiences that I would use later in my career.

CHAPTER 7
GOVERNOR REAGAN

The 1966 elections were great for Republicans in Oregon. Under Don Lindsay's leadership we won virtually everything in Clackamas County, including a State Senator, three out of four State House seats, and several county offices, such as commissioner, assessor, and others. It was the best Republican record in our county of any election in anybody's memory.

Statewide, the party did even better. We won control of the State House of Representatives and almost took over the State Senate. We won the Governorship, an open US Senate seat (Hatfield), and two of the four Congressional seats. It was a good year to be state chairman. I could not claim any credit for those successes, except for saying that I stayed out of the way. However, in the period of good feeling that followed such a victory, I did get more than my share of plaudits.

One of the reasons we won the State House was through the efforts of Bob Packwood. When he ran for the state legislature in 1962, many of his key supporters were Trumpeters, of course. In 1965 Bob approached Howell Appling, a past Republican Secretary of State, and asked for financial help in traveling around the state to recruit other state legislative candidates.

Bob was a member of the Junior Chamber of Commerce, and he devised a brilliant strategy for recruiting potentially successful candidates. The Jaycees, as they were widely known, were young business and professional types who were active in their communities. Bob would travel to a town where he knew a few Jaycees and ask each of them to name five or six people they would like to see in the state legislature. He would also ask some prominent Oregon citizens the same question. He later said that almost without exception the same name or two would show up on almost everyone's list. He would then go to that person and tell him that he could run and win a seat in the state legislature because he had solid support.

Bob offered to provide at least $4,000 for each campaign and to give the candidate and campaign team training in how to run for office and win. It was a brilliant strategy, and he really deserved a lot of credit for achieving Republican control of the state legislature in that amazing 1966 election year by attracting and helping good, solid candidates.

In spite of "my" success, however, I never wavered from my goal of finding a qualified successor as state chairman. My prime candidate was Irving Enna, Multnomah County chairman. Irving was a friend of mine, a member of Trumpeters, and old enough to be my father, which, at my age, was not that old. He was an insurance agent, and, in fact, he had sold me a large life insurance policy. I liked him a lot and we were colleagues on the state central committee.

I decided to persuade Irving that he should take the job, which was easier than I had expected. Previously, the nominating committee, on which I served, had interviewed Irving for state chairman. At that time, he had declined because he was in the middle of several personal and business obligations. Those hurdles had passed but his reluctance had not, because he did not want to oust *me*. However, I convinced him that I would be delighted to step aside if he would be willing to succeed me, and he agreed. Then it was up to me to get him elected—unanimously, if possible, in order to increase his chances for a successful chairmanship. That was not easy since the counties outside the metropolitan Portland area did not like the idea of the state chairman coming from the biggest city in the state.

Each county in Oregon had two equal votes on the state central committee, but urban areas were much smaller geographically than the rural areas and, therefore, easier for candidates to campaign in. This made the people living in rural counties feel neglected by candidates for office. People from rural counties were quite used to driving many miles to the nearest city or even into Portland to shop at Christmas, whereas people in the big city would sometimes object to driving across town to a meeting. I had promised Leland Burnap, county chairman in Baker County, over 300 miles from Portland, that I would try to hold a meeting in his county before leaving office. So, I scheduled an April 1967 meeting in the town of Baker. It was at this meeting that I intended to have Irving Enna elected state chairman.

There was considerable grumbling from the central committee members about the difficulty of getting to Baker, which was nearly a five-hour drive from Portland, and at least that far from other parts of the state. To make their travel easier, and to reduce the complaining, I arranged for a Greyhound bus with comfortable seats—and a toilet in the back—to leave from Portland, an easy place for most of them to reach, and many decided to ride the bus. In fact, the contingent from southern Oregon that had initially objected to my election all came up to Portland and joined the bus ride. During my tenure as chairman, I had managed to gain their trust and confidence. They were among my strongest supporters, a fact that was very pleasing. They did not, however, like the idea of Irving succeeding me because of the ingrained resentment of the large urban areas by the less populated counties. The bus ride turned out to be a wonderful means of bringing people together.

After an hour or so the bus made a rest stop. One senior member of the committee got off the bus and bought several bottles of bourbon, ice, mixer, and paper cups. The party got rolling in a big way after that. I did not drink, but those who did had a high old time—literally. And politically, they bonded (and banded together) and spoke openly about their concerns regarding the party. The next day at the state central committee meeting, their new unity and my candidate coalesced. Irving was elected unanimously, and a solid working relationship was established. It was tremendously pleasing to me to feel that I had helped bring about harmonious relations between people who had been at least distant if not downright hostile.

Suddenly, I was without a political position again, but that did not last long. Bob Packwood approached me in late summer 1967 and asked me to be his campaign chairman in his 1968 race to become Oregon's junior US Senator (i.e., if he won, that meant Hatfield would quickly become the state's senior Senator in Washington after only two years in office). I told Packwood no. "I have promised Barbara that I am going to reduce my political involvement," I explained. I probably leaned on that a little heavily, but I did not want to just say that I was not interested in getting involved in his campaign. Bob was considerably liberal for a Republican, and I was uneasy about that, even though we had been friends for some time. In any event, he accepted my reasoning, while we continued to see each other at the weekly Trumpeters meetings.

Bob's invitation to me was quite a surprise, as I had not exactly been encouraging to him when he first decided to run. As state chairman, I was invited to attend the Governor's periodic Coordinating Council meeting, which consisted of the Republican leadership of the state, including Packwood as a leader in the State House. During one meeting in the spring of 1966, he took me aside and told me that he was planning to run against longtime incumbent Senator Wayne Morse in the next cycle. I could not believe it. If ever there was a Senator who was entrenched and apparently unbeatable, it was Morse. He had first gone to the Senate as a Republican. He was known for his lengthy speeches and one-man filibusters but was very liberal even for an Oregonian. Finally, he switched parties, first to Independent and then to Democrat. He had strong labor union backing and appeared to be invincible. Against this background, when Bob asked, "Well, what do you think?"

I said, rather tactlessly, "You've got to be kidding!"

He was not kidding. He ran a great campaign and ultimately won, but the rest of that story comes later.

Around 1960 or so, the State of Oregon had adopted a statute requiring the Secretary of State to place on the Presidential primary election ballot the name of any person who was prominently being mentioned as a prospective candidate. The only way someone could get his name off the ballot was to sign an affidavit stating that he was "not now and never would be" a candidate for President. In 1966, the subject of Presidential politics came calling again in Oregon, and in a way that would dramatically affect both my future and that of the country.

Late in the 1964 election season, a B-movie actor and corporate spokesman had given a stunning, pro-Goldwater televised speech that captured the hearts of millions of conservatives, including mine. One of the watershed moments in the conservative movement in my lifetime was that speech by Ronald Reagan that aired on national television October 27, 1964, supporting Goldwater. At that time, I could not remotely imagine the long-term, profound effect that speech would have on America and, not so incidentally, on my life and career.

The speech was titled, "A Time for Choosing," but it has forever since been referred to by Reaganite conservatives simply as "The Speech." Reagan had been a popular speaker to various groups around the nation for several years and criticized an arrogant government bureaucracy, while also highlighting the dangers of encroaching Communism. That evening, he combined those themes into a speech that became a career-maker, electrifying the party faithful and, especially, its Goldwater supporters.

With LBJ's landslide victory, it had been far more Ronald Reagan's year than Goldwater's. In fact, after watching The Speech many Republicans felt the Republican National Convention that summer had nominated the wrong man for President, which the RNC delegates felt again twelve years later, in 1976, after Reagan's electrifying concession speech to nominee Gerald R. Ford at that convention.

There is no question that The Speech also laid the groundwork for Reagan's election as Governor of California in 1966 and, eventually, his election as President in 1980. But for those who have never seen it—or who saw it only sixty years ago—it would amaze them to learn that if given today it might have labeled Reagan an extremist and an angry man, both of which would now severely hurt a candidate's chances. Since he, himself, was not the candidate, however, his angry rhetoric, his hostile jabs at an arrogant bureaucracy, and his criticism of the excesses of both the federal government and of liberals in it, forever endeared Reagan to conservatives.

In 1966, Ronald Reagan was elected Governor of California. His first trip outside the state was in January 1967 to Oregon to speak at a Republican fundraiser held in Eugene. His staff scheduled this speech to test his popularity outside of California and to begin to lay the groundwork in case he should end up on the Oregon Presidential Primary ballot in 1968. Due to the statute, the Reagan organizers were pretty certain that his name would be put on the ballot, and they were definitely not willing to let him sign such an affidavit.

State Representative Monty Montgomery, who at my request had given the personal loan to meet the needs of the state party, was the new House Majority Leader and the head of the Eugene event. As state chairman, I was invited and met Governor Reagan for the first time, albeit briefly. I spent more time talking with his staff, notably a man named Tom Reed, the strategist behind Reagan's low-key campaign, a connection which turned out to be life-changing for me.

In October 1967, Reagan again came to Oregon for a speech, this time in Portland, and Tom Reed asked to meet with me. He described the particulars of Oregon's primary requirements, all of which I knew, of course, and said that he was concerned about some of the people who were already trying to create a draft Reagan movement in Oregon. They were well-meaning, enthusiastic, and exuberant, but inexperienced and naive. They were perfectly susceptible of saying and doing things that would embarrass the Governor of our neighboring state, which was not acceptable in a well-run campaign and could even hurt him in California.

The Reagan team in California felt that I could manage a more respectable campaign and asked me to be the chairman. I replied, candidly, that I was not qualified to be a Presidential campaign chairman. I simply did not have sufficient public stature. But I said that I could try to find someone who had the necessary prominence to be the Reagan chairman. Reed said that he appreciated my attitude and my help, but he continued to suggest that I was the right person for the job.

It happened that a few weeks earlier I had been meeting with Oregon Governor Tom McCall. During that meeting he said he thought Reagan was very popular and that he, McCall (even though a liberal Republican), was impressed and might support him for President. Although, he said, "He won't pay any attention to someone like me from a small state." Then he told me that one of his own big supporters and a former, very visible Rockefeller supporter in the 1964 campaign, Bob Hazen, also liked Reagan. I knew of Bob, as our fathers had been friends in the Portland Kiwanis Club.

Bob Hazen was a prominent Portland civic leader and had succeeded his father, Ben Hazen, as head of the Benjamin Franklin Savings and Loan Association which was a well-recognized financial institution in the state, and I thought he would be a good state chairman for Reagan because Bob's reputation as a former Rockefeller supporter would avoid the criticism that Reagan was being supported by far right-wing people. Bob was also well known because he was the voice of frequent radio ads for his company. When I told this to Tom Reed, he said to check it out. I called on Bob, and after some discussion—and my agreeing to help him run the campaign—he accepted. Reed was pleased.

Hazen, several other Reagan supporters, and I flew to California to meet with Governor Reagan. Our mission was to try to obtain his agreement to run, or at least his acquiescence to allow us to form a campaign committee in his name. The trip was really just window dressing so that Reed could assert that we had come to Reagan to ask him to run rather than have it appear that Reagan's staff was initiating this effort. Reagan was affable, but noncommittal, basically saying he would not try to influence us one way or the other. So, with the encouragement of the Reagan team, we pressed on in Oregon.

Bob Hazen, I would soon learn, was very busy with another role that year. He was chairman of the national association of Savings and Loans. Bob traveled a lot that year. As a result, I ended up running the day-to-day activities of the Reagan campaign in Oregon as the campaign's tri-county chairman. The title did not matter to me because once Bob gave me his full support, I was able to make all the decisions (with the help of some others I recruited, including my good friend Diarmuid O'Scannlain, who subsequently was Deputy Attorney General of Oregon, Public Utility Commissioner, and was eventually appointed by President Reagan as a Judge of the Ninth Circuit Court of Appeals, a position he held for nearly forty years and in which he remained true to his conservative philosophy in spite of enormous pressure to shift). Thus, I was the de facto Reagan chairman in Oregon.

I set up a formal committee of people who were Reagan supporters but who were decidedly centrist and mainstream, i.e., not members of what the liberal press could possibly label as the "lunatic fringe." I was so successful at that during the primary—which ultimately was won by Richard Nixon on his way to becoming President—that on radio talk shows, some of the strongest conservative activists attacked the Reagan campaign for being captured by the liberals, the only time in my career that I have been labeled as anything less than a staunch conservative.

I may have gone too far in the makeup of the Reagan committee; for example, I included such non-conservatives as Pete Gunnar, my predecessor as state party chairman, but I added him precisely because he was not possibly subject to the accusation of being a conservative.

I knew that our task was to conduct what was called a "holding action." Oregon was intensely parochial in elections. I had been told that Reagan would not come into the state to campaign, and after the success of Rockefeller's slogan in 1964: "He cared enough to come to Oregon," there seemed little chance of winning without an active candidate. I tried to persuade Tom Reed that if Reagan would simply call Governor McCall and ask for his support, we could get McCall to serve as honorary chairman of the campaign. Reed, probably wisely and rightly, perceived that that could be a mixed blessing. It might garner votes, but it would identify Reagan as further left than he was—or wanted to be—and perhaps worse, Governor McCall was a loose cannon. No one could control what he said, and he might easily create all kinds of problems for the Reagan campaign by some off-the-cuff remark.

Meanwhile, I was still working at Georgia-Pacific, having to hold down a job to provide an income for my family. I worked my full fifty-hour week in the legal department and then ran the statewide Presidential campaign in my "spare time." In all honesty, I did not spend as much time on my job as I should have. At my 1968 end-of-year review, my boss, general counsel Frank Breuer, told me that I would not be receiving as much of a raise as I would have because I spent so much time on the Reagan campaign. So, political work cost me significantly from a financial standpoint, as of course, it does many others.

Tom Reed wanted me to be able to work less for G-P so that I could spend more time on the campaign. His vision for getting me more freedom to run the campaign was for Governor Reagan to call the president of G-P, Bob Pamplin, and ask for my workload to be reduced. I worked way down the ladder from Pamplin, so I ran that idea past my boss, Frank Breuer. He said he would check, but came back saying that there was no reason for Reagan to call Pamplin, who asked, "Why would I want to talk to Reagan?" Even though at the time, Georgia-Pacific had major land and timber holdings in California and constantly sought assistance from the Governor, Pamplin evidently did not like the idea of playing a political influence game.

Later, I mentioned this incident to a Washington lobbyist who was incredulous at Pamplin's disinterest. He could not believe a company could be so apolitical that it would fail to take advantage of such a possibility. He said if that had been his aerospace company, the CEO would have accepted the call from Reagan, granted the work-relief request, and also *doubled* my pay in the process. But Bob Pamplin was very straightlaced. He was not about to allow an employee of G-P to slack off his work and be rewarded for it just because he was involved in politics, even if it might aid the company. His strong sense of how to behave properly set a good example for me as a young lawyer under his leadership.

In the end Reagan gathered a respectable vote in the Oregon primary, but Richard Nixon won the state's delegate count by winning a plurality of voters. Bob Hazen was elected as a delegate to the 1968 Republican National Convention, held in Miami Beach, Florida, and he recognized my assistance to him by asking me to be his alternate delegate, which was my second trip to a Republican National Convention (having served as head of the page pool in 1956).

In 1968, I still was not earning very much income. We had two young sons and significant expenses, but Barbara encouraged and supported me all the way, insisting that I attend the convention in Miami Beach, although the financial cost was very high for us.

In Florida, I quickly discovered that I had better political connections than Bob Hazen had. My friends Bill Rusher and Clif White were major cogs in the Reagan campaign and were very influential players at the convention in trying to win the nomination for Reagan. Hazen and I were the only Reaganites in an Oregon delegation bound by state law to support Richard Nixon on the first ballot. Senator Mark Hatfield was head of the delegation and also, under the state law, he was committed to Nixon.

The night of the balloting for the Presidential nominee, we knew the vote was going to be close. Nixon would either barely make it or fall just short on the first ballot. Our goal was to shake loose just enough delegates to make the latter happen, as it was apparent to knowledgeable insiders that Reagan would be nominated if Nixon could be kept from winning on the first ballot.

On the floor of the convention, the Oregon delegation sat directly in front of the South Carolina delegation, which, due to the powerful leadership of their US Senator Strom Thurmond, had pledged to support Nixon. (Then already sixty-five years old, he did not leave the Senate until he was over one hundred!) Thurmond had been a Democrat (in 1948 running for President and winning four states as a Dixiecrat in opposition to President Truman) until

1964 when he switched parties and became a Republican in order to support Barry Goldwater. Every one of the Palmetto State delegates with whom I spoke told me how they loved Ronald Reagan: "But Strom said we voted our hearts in 1964 (for Goldwater) and this time we want to *win*!" They believed Thurmond when he said, "Nixon can win," meaning the Presidency.

The press made a big deal out of the possibility that Nelson Rockefeller might be the compromise candidate if Nixon stumbled. I said then, and I say now, that Rockefeller would not have won the nomination in that convention if he had been the last candidate available. A huge majority of the delegates deeply resented him for his failure to support nominee Barry Goldwater in 1964. They would never have rewarded his treason by nominating him. In fact, to this day among longtime Republican Party activists, labeling someone as a Rockefeller Republican is an epithet.

Before the balloting for President that night, the *Miami Herald* hit the street with a late edition with a big bold headline, "Hatfield for Vice President." The story asserted that there was a "done deal" as politicos like to say, and Nixon had chosen Hatfield to be his running mate. Hatfield was a good campaigner, was well-spoken and gracious, and he was liked by the media, but he was a liberal Republican.

Bill Rusher took a copy of that newspaper and went straight to the floor of the convention to find Strom Thurmond. "Senator, you are about to be the victim of the worst double-cross of the twentieth century," Rusher said, and thrust the paper at him. Thurmond took one look at the headline and reached for the red phone at his elbow that went directly to the Nixon command center, telling whoever answered that he had to speak to Nixon immediately. When the person said something like "he's not available," Thurmond said, very clearly and distinctly, "If he does not talk to me *right now*, South Carolina will not cast its votes for him." Hearing that, they managed to find Nixon immediately.

Thurmond asked Nixon, "Is this headline true?" Nixon equivocated. Strom pressed. Nixon said that he had only *spoken* with Hatfield, and that he was one of the possible choices to be his running mate. Thurmond demanded Nixon's promise that Hatfield would not, in any circumstance, be his choice, and without such a promise South Carolina would bolt. Nixon got the message.

Had Nixon not capitulated, Ronald Reagan would have won the GOP nomination that night. The last state to be polled in the roll call of states, Wyoming, put Nixon over the top by about eleven votes. South Carolina had twenty-two votes, thus, losing those votes on the first ballot would have put Nixon eleven votes short of the nomination. On the second ballot his support would have eroded rapidly and begun to move to Reagan.

A later photo of President Reagan and me after he presented me with the Presidential Citizens Medal (The White House)

Years later, in 1982, during my meeting with President Reagan prior to his naming me Secretary of Energy, I mentioned the 1968 convention and that I had been a Reagan alternate and how close we had come to nominating him. He responded with amazing recall, confirming my recollections, saying that if South Carolina had held back its votes from Nixon, he would have won. Then he said, "You know who the two most relieved people in the whole convention were that night? Nancy and me!"

I think there was a reasonable chance Reagan might have lost to the Democrat nominee, sitting Vice President Hubert Humphrey. He was still new to the national political scene and had served less than two years as Governor, so his relative inexperience would have been used by the liberal media to bludgeon him.

After the Republican Convention, I volunteered to work on the Nixon campaign because I thought it was important for Republicans to win the White House. However, I was never asked to do anything. That was fine with me. I was completely out of politics, and I did not miss it. When I was in, I was in it wholeheartedly and devoted myself fully (when I was not working at my paying job). Now that I was out of politics, I was relieved, and ready to concentrate on my family, my law career, and my financial future. By the beginning of 1969 my salary was about $17,500 per year and I had options for 30,000 shares of stock, which were subject to forfeiture in the event I left before the end of five years. I continued my membership and participation in Trumpeters as the closest thing to politics that I did.

Bob Packwood ran a tough, grassroots Senate campaign in 1968 against the incumbent, Morse. While no one had given him much chance in the beginning, Packwood excelled during the debates and narrowly won, by a margin of 3,293 votes out of 813,999 that were cast. Morse called for a recount. The labor unions sent organizers into Oregon to represent Morse, while Packwood enlisted the volunteer assistance of many young lawyers to represent him. Members of the Trumpeters were obvious candidates, and I was asked to handle two counties in southern Oregon: Jackson and Josephine. At my own expense, I drove down there, taking my family with me. I do not recall why we decided to take the boys out of school, but it was probably because Barb wanted to go with me, and we had no way to leave them at home.

The two counties could not have been more different. Jackson County used punch card ballots, and the recount was completed there in a few hours with only a one or two vote difference in the outcome from the original count. Josephine, on the other hand, had paper ballots marked in pencil by hand. The Morse representative and I sat down with the county election board and started the recount. I was well-versed in the applicable election laws thanks to the work of a team of lawyers led by a brilliant attorney named Jack Faust, who was a friend of Packwood's and also a Trumpeter.

My instructions were to mirror the Morse representative. If she challenged a particular defect when it was a Packwood vote, I was to challenge similar Morse votes. Things started off innocently enough. The statute covering voting stated that a vote was to be cast by marking an *X* in the box beside the candidate of choice. Suddenly the Morse representative challenged a Packwood vote where the voter had marked with an *X* that extended beyond the borders of the box. I then did the same with the Morse ballots. Then she objected to a ballot where the tail of the *X* extended outside the box, and, again, I countered with a similar challenge. She challenged a ballot where the voter had used a check mark rather than an *X*. I began doing the same.

Sometime during the second hour it became apparent that, at the pace we were going, the recount was going to take several days. We each were challenging almost every ballot cast for the other side and so we and the Election Board agreed to challenge all the ballots. Doing that preserved both sides' rights to review all the ballots in the event the statewide recount made the race close enough that the Josephine County votes could affect the outcome. That did not occur, and in the rest of the state Packwood *gained* enough ground so that Morse eventually conceded.

Suddenly, the Trumpeters became a hotbed of highly successful politicians. Bob Packwood was Oregon's junior US Senator. Trumpeter Lee Johnson had been elected Oregon Attorney General in 1966, and Clay Myers was elected Secretary of State that year as well. Several members were also state legislators and city council members. I had become Republican state chairman in the summer of 1966, although, stepping down a year later, but I was succeeded by another Trumpeter, Irving Enna.

One night during our stay in Grants Pass for the recount there, Packwood stopped by to talk about how things were going. He did not seem to hold a grudge over my refusal to run his campaign, perhaps because of my willing and loyal support during the recount. That relationship with him would soon prove to be instrumental to my future.

CHAPTER 8
POWER

The best political job in the Pacific Northwest (PNW) is Administrator of the Bonneville Power Administration (BPA). I didn't know that in 1968 when I was asked during the Reagan campaign what I wanted in the way of a federal job if Reagan won. The real answer was "none," but I kiddingly said, "Bonneville Administrator."

I answered that way because a couple of years earlier a former BPA Administrator, Charles F. Luce, had become Under Secretary of the Interior to Secretary Stewart Udall during the Johnson Administration and, following the New York blackout of 1965, had become chairman and CEO of Consolidated Edison, one of the nation's largest electric utilities, serving New York City and environs. My limited knowledge was that Bonneville played a similar role for the Pacific Northwest, so I thought that would be a pretty good, high-paying *management* job; and it was headquartered in Portland. Lots of good reasons for a lighthearted answer.

I began working at Georgia-Pacific in November 1963 and after a while I realized that I really wanted to manage things rather than simply practicing law. However, Georgia-Pacific was a company run by CPAs. In their eyes lawyers were sometimes necessary but they were not suitable as executives. To become a manager at G-P would have required me to move to a small town, probably somewhere in Oregon, and become, at best, an assistant manager at a sawmill and hope to be successful and eventually be promoted. Besides having to relocate my family, this would have meant a substantial cut in pay, and a big change in my family's lifestyle. I simply wasn't willing to subject them to that.

What little else I knew about Bonneville came from three sources. First, from my brother, Les, who had gone to work for Portland General Electric (PGE) when he came out of college in the late 1940s. Second, Ted Fryou, a longtime friend of my parents, was treasurer of PGE and I had listened as he talked with them about some of PGE's problems with BPA. Finally, and more significantly, Georgia-Pacific was an industrial customer of BPA, and I had been sent to BPA a few times to sit in for G-P in customers' meetings when Chuck Luce was Administrator.

Over time, after becoming Deputy Administrator at BPA, I learned that as soon as the 1968 election was over and Nixon was President, the investor-owned (private) utilities in the Pacific Northwest wanted to influence the Nixon Administration in selecting the new Administrator and Deputy Administrator at Bonneville. These were the only two political appointments at BPA. It was pretty much understood that under Democratic Presidencies the public power utilities had the greater political influence, and during Republican Presidencies the private utilities had the upper hand. Before going to BPA, I knew none of this, so it was a total surprise when, late in the spring of 1969, I got a call from Les, who was by then an executive at PGE. He said that he had been approached by PGE's CEO, Bob Short, who asked, "Would your brother have any interest in being appointed Deputy Administrator at BPA?"

Les told me that and asked what I thought. Without even *having* to think about it, I told him that I was definitely interested, but that I really had no idea what the job involved. I just knew that it sounded like it would give me a chance to be a manager.

I quickly updated my resume—which was not that long—and made an appointment to meet Mr. Short later that same day. When I was invited into his office, I gave him my resume. It was a "standing interview," meaning neither of us sat down, which told me it would not be a long meeting. He read my resume as I stood there and finally muttered, loud enough for me to hear, "With *this* resume we ought to run you for President," which I took as simply a nice way of saying that he was impressed.

A couple of weeks later I got a call from Short, and he asked how well I knew Senator Bob Packwood. He said that it looked like the Nixon Administration was trying to court Packwood, being that he was Oregon's new US Senator. That meant that Packwood might have a big say over this appointment. I briefly told Mr. Short the things I had done to help Packwood become a Senator—as I described in the previous chapter. He suggested I call and try to learn if Packwood were asked, would he support me.

Now, I had recently heard from a friend of mine who knew Packwood quite well that he had asked Bob to support *him* for an appointment in the Nixon Administration. Packwood was very cautious in his response to my friend, asking things like, "Who else is under consideration?" and then saying that he would have to think about it. I assumed this meant Packwood was being careful about making recommendations for government jobs, and that I might get the same cool reception. I had no idea how he might feel after I had declined to lead his senatorial campaign. I had told him the truth: I promised Barbara I would cut back on my political activities. And then, within a very few months, I had agreed to run the Reagan campaign. I thought the new Senator might feel insulted or disrespected by that. I told Short that while I knew Packwood well, he had been cautious about endorsing a friend of mine, but that I would call and find out how he felt about me.

When I reached Senator Packwood on the phone, after brief cordialities, I said I had been told that he was likely to have substantial influence with the President on appointments. And then I told him there was a move afoot to appoint me as Deputy Administrator of BPA.

"Oh, great!" he said with enthusiasm, "What can I do to help?" I was very surprised and also pleased by his warm response. I said that as far as I knew, I just needed to be able to say that he would be supportive, if asked. I then told Bob Short of Senator Packwood's reaction.

What I did not know then, but figured out later by piecing together comments I heard from time to time, was that the four Pacific Northwest investor-owned electric utilities were trying to work together on a unanimous recommendation of two people to lead BPA. They had already agreed that their choice for Administrator would be a man named Bob Timm from the State of Washington, and that the deputy should, therefore, be from Oregon. However, they did not want to replace the current Administrator, Russ Richmond, until a critical regional electric power development agreement in which BPA played a major role had been completed.

Richmond and other leaders of the Pacific Northwest utility industry had been working for several years on a region-wide, ten-year Hydro-Thermal Power Program (HTPP) for the PNW, projecting electric load growth for the entire region and assigning responsibility among the utilities for the building of power plants to meet that load. Richmond had been appointed during the Lyndon Johnson Administration and would ordinarily have been replaced by Nixon as soon as he was elected. However, Richmond was essential to the completion of the HTPP negotiations because he was very influential with the public power agencies that had to agree to the plan for it to be acceptable to the region and to the PNW political delegation in Washington, DC.

So, the utilities decided that since they could not afford to lose Richmond, their goal—as I was told—was to "find a young lawyer from Oregon who could learn the job fast and be able to help bring Timm up to speed as soon as the HTPP was signed and Richmond was replaced." However, the HTPP agreement was not finalized until October 1969, nine months after Nixon was sworn in as President, and during that time, Bob Timm grew impatient. He had good political connections inside the Administration and secured an appointment to a position in Washington, DC. So, after the HTPP was signed and there was no agreed-upon candidate for Administrator, no one continued to push for Richmond to be replaced. He remained head of BPA, which turned out to be a blessing for me and a very significant factor in my career.

I include all of this background to further explain what had been happening in the search for a Deputy Administrator. Each time one utility came up with a possible candidate, another utility objected, and by May 1969 they had eliminated everyone who had been on the list of possible deputies. They were getting desperate to find someone to appoint as deputy to learn the job. That's what finally led Bob Short to call my brother and ask if I might be interested. I never found out how they had even heard of me.

After giving Short my resume, and the calls regarding Packwood's support, a couple of weeks passed before I heard anything more, and I really did not think too much about it. It seemed like a long shot, and since I had a good job, going to work at BPA involved the risk that it would only be for the term of Nixon's Presidency, which at the time did not look like a sure thing for a second term. That raised the question, *What happens after Nixon loses and I'm replaced at BPA?*

In June, Bob Short called and said that I had a problem. Someone at Pacific Power and Light (PP&L), the largest investor-owned utility in the Pacific Northwest—and one that was very politically influential—was not happy about my becoming deputy at BPA. Bob did not know exactly why, but possibly there was a concern that my brother worked for PGE. Both utilities were headquartered in Portland and were competitors. On the other hand, PP&L's objection could have been something I had done while I was involved in Republican politics. Bob asked me if I knew anyone at PP&L. Years earlier I had met the CEO, a wonderful man named Don Frisbee, although, I was unsure if he would even remember me.

It was interesting how I knew Frisbee. As I have said earlier, I was a prominent alumnus of the Portland Junior Achievement program. The director of JA, who somehow remembered me even seven years later in my last year of law school, invited me to speak at a JA banquet in Portland. I was quite flattered and happy to accept in order to show my appreciation for what I had learned in JA and to give something back to a program that had been such a great experience for me. I was on the program that night along with several others, including Don Frisbee, who gave the main address.

After the banquet, he was complimentary about my remarks and he handed me his business card, saying, "When you graduate, give me a call." By the time I graduated I had already agreed to go to work for the Davies law firm, so I never followed up on his invitation. Now, suddenly, I needed to talk with him to try to find out if PP&L was going to oppose my becoming Deputy Administrator at BPA.

Fortunately, Frisbee took my call and graciously assured me that he remembered me. I explained why I was calling, adding that I knew enough about politics in Oregon to realize that if the leadership at PP&L opposed me, it would be a waste of time for me to seek political positions.

Frisbee could not have been nicer. He assured me that I had no problem at PP&L and said he would be happy to support me. When I reported this to Bob Short, he thought the deal was done. But once the regional support was cleared, there was still the all-important interview in Washington, DC, that had to happen first. What I did not know at the time was that this interview would alter the course of my life in ways I could not imagine.

In late July or early August 1969, I was notified that I needed to go to Washington, DC, to be interviewed by Secretary of the Interior Walter Hickel. At my own expense I flew to Washington where it became clear that, for such a relatively low-level job, the Secretary never intended to meet with me. And it turned out that the same thing was true for the next person in line, the Assistant Secretary for Water and Power, Jim Smith. This gives you a pretty good idea of the importance the people in Washington, DC, gave to BPA. As a result of the bigwigs not being interested, I was interviewed by thirty-one-year-old James Gaius Watt, Deputy Assistant Secretary for Water and Power.

Watt had been named Deputy Assistant Secretary at the young age of thirty. He had initially gone to Washington in his early twenties as an assistant to US Senator Milward Simpson of Wyoming. Senator Simpson was elected in November 1962 and was the father of that state's future US Senator Alan Simpson. After Watt left Simpson's staff, he became a lobbyist for the US Chamber of

Commerce, remaining there until Nixon was elected, at which time he received his appointment at Interior.

Upon entering Watt's outer office, I met Jim Smith and his confidential assistant, Mary Ann Wilkinson, who was very cordial and easy to talk with. She was altogether grandmotherly yet unmistakably professional. She was official, yet pleasant, and I liked her at once. After a few minutes, Watt told her to send me in. He sat behind the desk, leaning back in his chair, as I entered. I had not even taken my seat when he asked rather bluntly, "Why do you want this job?"

"I don't" was my direct response. After a short pause, I continued, "I have a good job, now, but I'm interested in the opportunity to serve in a management position."

Later, as I got to know Watt better, I realized that I could not have responded in a more effective way to impress him. He respected people who were not intimidated by his direct approach. I also learned that he loved having that (young) Deputy Assistant Secretary assignment. He was a natural leader and wanted as much responsibility as he could obtain.

After my successful interview with Watt, there remained one hurdle to overcome. Russ Richmond had said that even though he knew he was slated to be replaced as soon as the HTPP was approved, he would not take just anyone as his deputy and that he had to approve any proposed nominee. Returning to Portland, I scheduled an interview with him.

In comparison to meeting Watt, I remember little about the interview with Richmond, which is odd considering their back-to-back influence on my career as I served as number two to each man. Richmond was congenial but direct in his questions. It was apparent that I knew essentially nothing about electricity. Of course, I had the further obstacle of being a lawyer in a 3,000-employee organization whose professional staff included 800 engineers with a very small legal department. However, he apparently was satisfied that I could be taught and told Smith and Watt he would accept me.

My appointment was made by Secretary Hickel effective October 1, 1969, which is the day I walked in the door to BPA at the age of thirty-four. That position was a major turning point in my life and career. It gave me experience in the electricity industry, helped me become a recognized energy expert, and eventually helped me to be nominated in January 1981 by President Reagan for my first job in Washington, DC, as Under Secretary of the Interior, before joining his Cabinet twenty-one months after that.

Upon arriving at the Bonneville Power Administration, I began the most intense learning curve in my life. I had a Harvard education, a University of Oregon law degree, good legal experience, and I had served in political leadership roles, but I had never held a major management position in a large organization. Further, I had no background in electricity. What I had was an aptitude for math, a fair understanding of physics, and an eagerness to learn.

BPA had been created in 1937 under President Franklin D. Roosevelt in order to market the power produced by two federally owned dams on the Columbia River which were then under construction, Grand Coulee and Bonneville. It was somewhat similar to the Tennessee Valley Authority.

Privately owned utilities in the Pacific Northwest had opposed building either of those dams because they correctly believed that it threatened their dominance of the electric utility industry in the PNW. In an effort to stop the dams from being built, they stated that the increased electric output was not needed by them, and they would not buy it.

Faced with that situation, FDR persuaded Congress to create BPA to find or create markets for the power from the dams, and as stated in the bill, to do "such other things as were necessary for the operation of an electric power system." Among the other things deemed necessary by the government was building an electric transmission network, which between 1937 and 1969 had grown to become the largest high-voltage transmission grid (i.e., the most miles of lines built and operated by a single system) outside the Soviet Union, which of course was government-owned (like everything else there) and had to supply power to the country with the largest land mass in the entire world. To have a market for the power it created, BPA actively promoted the creation of multiple public agencies—municipal (city-owned) electric utilities, PUDs (Public Utility Districts in Washington State and People's Utility Districts in Oregon), and rural electric co-ops (RECs) throughout the Pacific Northwest including Idaho and western Montana.

Henry R. "Russ" Richmond was a longtime BPA employee; in fact, he was the first Administrator to work his way up through the organization. It would have been very easy for him to sequester me in a corner somewhere as the new deputy foisted on him by the new Republican Administration. Instead, he did an amazing job of mentoring me and arranging for me to get a crash course in electricity and computer technology, including sending me to a week-long computer school in California.

Richmond created a team of five BPA staff members to teach me about electricity, two of whom deserve special mention here. Portland Area Manager John Alberthal had the primary responsibility of shadowing me on a daily basis and helping me learn the ins and outs of the operation.

A young engineer, Earl Gjelde (JELL-dee), was also on that team and became a good friend over my eight years at BPA. At one point under President Jimmy Carter, Earl served as Acting Administrator of BPA. He was (and is) a brilliant and talented professional. As an indication of how highly I thought of Earl, when it became apparent that I was going to be appointed Secretary of Energy in 1982, I asked him to come to Washington and serve as my chief operating officer. And when I later became Secretary of the Interior, he was my second in command there, too, as I had been to Jim Watt.

In both jobs he ran the department for me. After I left government service, Earl and I became business partners (a plan we had discussed years earlier when I left Bonneville and he was still working there), and we conducted all dealings between us on handshakes—no written contracts. Over time we added other shareholding partners, which required written contracts to govern the relationships, but Earl and I remained the closest of friends, as were Barbara and his wife, Sandra. As I wrote about Don Pearlman earlier, I simply cannot adequately describe Earl's gifting and what he has meant to me in my various posts.

When I went to Bonneville, I continued wearing the same business attire that I had as a young lawyer—and with the same determination as I had dressed to look in high school (casual, but still a little nicer than those who purposely dressed so casually as to appear uncaring). I arrived at the office wearing dark suits and white shirts, with conservative patterned ties, and dress shoes.

When I was in college, those of us representing the Harvard Young Republican Club dressed in a very conservative manner as well—charcoal gray suits and white shirts with dark ties. (Someone once looked at a group of us and said something like, "What's this, an undertakers' convention?") When I was in the Davies law firm the same attire was standard. That is also how I dressed at Georgia-Pacific, so, when I went to BPA, there was no reason to change. I was always aware that I was much younger than almost all of the people with whom I was involved and that it was wise not to highlight my youth, especially with people who were reporting to me.

While at BPA I went to the Nordstrom across the street to purchase some new clothing, and the salesclerk tried to get me to become "more stylish" by wearing colored shirts and new, more fashionable, very wide ties with large knots (which had just become the thing to wear for those who fancied themselves stylish). Barbara even indicated that she thought maybe I should try it, even though all the people with whom I worked at BPA were very traditional engineering types.

One evening, she and I were invited to attend an event at Waverley Country Club in Portland. This was a gathering of the top executives (and their wives) of the largest companies in the city. There were maybe one hundred civic leaders present at the dinner. Barbara and I were at least twenty years (or more) younger than everyone else there. I wore my standard dark (blue) suit, white shirt, and conservative (red, I think) tie. As we walked in the door I saw immediately that I was dressed just like *every one* of the other executives there. Only one man was dressed differently: the conductor of the Portland Symphony, who wore a white suit! The moment we walked through the door, and I saw the crowd, I leaned toward Barbara and muttered (so only she could hear), "Please don't *ever* again suggest I dress more stylishly!" And she did not.

Throughout my career I resisted the casual Friday (and worse) look, feeling that clients, customers, and coworkers should see professionally dressed executives, and that they, at least subconsciously, would have less respect for those they felt did not present themselves properly. I know that I always saw people who were too casual in their appearance (i.e., not dressing for the role they had, whether formally, in uniform, or in laborer's work clothing) as very likely to be too casual about their performance. Such people created a reduced expectation on my part, and I had to be persuaded that they were better at their job than their appearance suggested.

I also focused on my professional attitude and behavior. I genuinely believed that all people deserve respect, and I felt it was only right to show that by how I treated them. This meant to me that I needed to greet them with a sincere smile. Knowing that sometimes if I was distracted by problems, my smile might be fleeting, I practiced so that I knew what my face felt like when I was giving a warm smile so that I could reproduce it even when my mind was otherwise distracted. I might be troubled by something else that was going on, but the person I was meeting would not know that. I did not want to give them any reason to think that I was unhappy with (or did not respect) them. Both in how I dressed and the way I behaved, I felt that I was arming myself to be able to convey the message that I wanted to send to others.

Finally, I had learned a few years earlier, at age twenty-eight, that I was allergic to alcohol, even in small amounts. I thought I perhaps had serious stomach problems, but the doctor finally figured out that alcohol triggered the acid-producing nerve in my stomach and until the alcohol had been passed from my system, I suffered acid indigestion. What could have been a hindrance in the era of the three-martini lunch, actually helped me, as I always had my edge when I got back to the office after lunch or, later when we were in Washington, after multiple official receptions and dinners. It made it somewhat awkward when I was on official trips to foreign nations where alcohol was so much a part of socializing, but my staff was careful to emphasize that I was unable to drink and that my not doing so was in no way intended to show disapproval of their drinking.

Immediately upon joining BPA and for as long as Richmond was there, he had me attend all of his meetings, listening and absorbing. When I needed help understanding something, I waited until the meeting was over to ask someone, usually John Alberthal, to explain it.

Every morning, the first thing I did was go into Russs office. He spent thirty minutes or so imparting his experience and wisdom to me regarding management techniques, electric utility issues, relationships with the customer utilities, key figures in the industry and within politics, and even how to live my life. It was an intense and very wonderful experience for me. Russ was almost a generation older than I and could not have been nicer to me or more encouraging if I had been his own son. Nothing I did after BPA would have been the same if Russ had not spent so much time and energy training me. I will always be tremendously grateful to him for all that he did. I loved working with Russ, who became more than a mentor to me. He became a friend, even a father figure.

Along the way, I became more and more comfortable in my job, so much so that I was able to share humor with Russ. He laughed when, after the adoption of the Hydro-Thermal Power Program shortly after I arrived, I kiddingly said, “Gee, it didn’t take *me* long to get this signed.”

Russ had a great sense of humor, which was often on display in his office and in meetings. It was a revelation to me when, by observing Russ in action, I learned that even in the executive office of a large organization people could have fun and tease and joke. Until that time, whenever I had been included in an executive level meeting, it was a serious occasion. Executives tended to be reserved when there were non-executives in the meeting. But with Russ, and now that I was an executive myself, I found that it was

OK, in fact it was common for humor to be present at appropriate times.

On one occasion, at an all-employees meeting in the BPA auditorium, I presented Russ with his twenty-year service pin and joked with him a little, though very respectfully. The employees thoroughly enjoyed seeing the boss being teased. After receiving his pin, Russ took the microphone to make a few remarks. He paused for effect, then turned toward me sitting to his right on the stage and said, "Don, I don't care what everyone else says, I think you're doing a great job!" That, of course, brought down the house! And I was laughing as hard as anyone. Clearly, the employees enjoyed seeing the banter between the boss and his deputy.

After I had spent several months on the job under his tutelage, Russ decided that I was ready to take on my first BPA speaking opportunity. The audience was the Public Power Council, which included the public-owned electric utility agencies: municipalities, RECs, and PUDs. These utilities were important customer groups for BPA and, naturally, with BPA's history, they were very supportive of Democrat Administrations and eager to get to know the new Republican guy at Bonneville.

Public speaking was something with which I had quite a bit of experience through Trumpeters and my political activities up until that point. However, I was quite nervous about this, my maiden speech on an energy subject *and* representing Bonneville before a potentially skeptical audience. They were polite and friendly, and as far as I knew, I avoided any major mistakes. Afterward, a much older man came up and told me that it was the best speech he had ever heard. I knew flattery when I heard it, and his was *extreme* flattery. So, I was very suspicious about his motivation. John Alberthal was in the audience and, perhaps more credibly, also complimented me on my presentation. Later, I learned that the "extreme flatterer" was notorious for his effusive praise of anyone who "mattered" because he was in the business of selling insurance to utilities. Making friends was part of his marketing technique. This information confirmed my initial skepticism about his flattery.

The moment John complimented me, however, I immediately realized that I had just reached a major transition moment in my life. I could no longer rely on other people's compliments about my speeches. I was second in command of a major organization, and almost no one—and definitely no one working for me—was going to criticize me to my face. From that point on, and pretty much for the rest of my life, I knew that I had to evaluate my own public speaking performance. I suggested to Barbara that she could fill that role for me; however, she found it difficult, as being critical of me went against her instincts, but she did her best.

I remained very critical of my speeches throughout my career. Once, when I was in the Cabinet, Earl Gjelde and I were walking along the hallway, returning from a big meeting where I had spoken, when I grumbled that I had not done a very good job with my speech. I asked Earl what grade he would give me, and he pleasantly offered a *B*, which he thought was pretty good. I did not care for that as, by the time I reached that level, I felt that all my speeches had to be *at least B*'s, preferably *A*'s; thus, a *B* was my lowest acceptable performance.

Over the next two years following my maiden speech, Russ continued mentoring me and encouraging me about the progress I was making. In turn, I applied myself diligently to learning all that he had to teach me. I was given additional speaking opportunities to industry and outside groups, which helped to establish me as a credible leader at BPA in the eyes of the company's stakeholders.

Tennyson wrote, "In the spring a young man's fancy lightly turns to thoughts of love." But if you were at the Bonneville Power Administration, in spring your thoughts turned—not so lightly—to Congressional budget hearings, because that is when the committees on Capitol Hill in Washington, DC, began preparing and vetting the coming year's federal budget. A massive amount of detail had to be produced for the committees and then organized and presented in a clear and convincing manner. This was not easy for anyone involved. It was very much like preparing for final examinations in college or law school.

We basically lived in a two-year budget cycle. The year before a federal election, agency expenditures would climb as members of Congress wanted to show their constituents how valuable the members were. Then, the year after an election, the Administration in Washington, whether Republican or Democrat, would tend to try to clamp down on appropriations.

My first exposure to that grueling process was in 1970, although that year I was strictly an observer, watching how it was done. Ever the teacher, Russ took me along on his trips to Washington and had me attend every meeting and hearing that dealt with our budget, which included a huge amount of information, data, and numbers. Because the electric load was growing and new power sources were being added to the system, BPA needed to build additional high voltage transmission lines while maintaining existing lines and installing and upgrading transformers and circuit breakers. The electricity production learning curve I had been on remained very steep.

I attended both the House and Senate versions of the hearings, and it was very exciting and new territory for me. Having been involved in politics for much of my adult life, I then found myself visiting the seat of our nation's government in an official role, far beyond anything I had envisioned even a year earlier. I was meeting Senators and Congressmen and key political appointees. It was exciting and eye-opening to me.

My second year at BPA for the appropriation hearings, as part of my learning process Russ assigned specific budget items for me to present to the committees. Again, he did an excellent job of giving me experiences that prepared me for larger responsibilities. I was becoming much more comfortable with the breadth and depth of BPA and with the numbers that were such an integral part of the operation. I learned that I did not need to know how to design an electric power transmission system. What I had to be able to do was to explain in layman's terms, for the benefit of members of Congress, what was needed and why.

At one of my early hearings, Russ had given me a particular project to present. The Senator asked a question that I could not answer. Russ enjoyed teasing me over the incident while reporting to the top staff about the hearings, telling them about what happened to me, saying, "Don had the answer to 100 questions. Unfortunately, the Senator asked question number 101."

Russ introduced me to the key US Senators from Washington State, both of whom were Democrats, as that party controlled both Houses of Congress at the time. Democrats Warren Magnuson (second in seniority in the Senate Appropriations Committee, a very powerful position) and Henry "Scoop" Jackson, Chairman of the Senate Interior Committee, later known as the Senate Energy and Natural Resources Committee. Jackson became a good friend of mine, in no small measure due to Russ's strong support of me.

Russ also taught me that knowing the key staff of these Senators and Representatives was more important than knowing the officeholder himself. Many of the main decisions were essentially handled by trusted top staff. Talking to the Senator or Representative was usually a waste of time if the staff was opposed to what you were trying to "sell." Many a visitor to Capitol Hill does not understand this and thinks that visiting a Senator is what matters. In most cases that is not so, unless you already have their staff on board.

Three years into my tenure at BPA, in early 1972, Russ's wife, Peggy, encountered some health issues and he decided to retire. He said that he did not want to risk spending the next few years working only to lose Peggy before they had the pleasure of enjoying retirement together. This likely affected my decision, years later and for the rest of my working life, to encourage Barbara to spend as much time with me as possible. She attended my meetings when it was OK for her to do so once I was in the Cabinet, as well as traveling with me whenever possible. This had to be at our personal expense, but we simply were unwilling to be separated any more than was absolutely necessary.

Russ told me that he wanted me to succeed him as Administrator, which was bittersweet to me. I liked things just the way they were. I very much enjoyed being COO to a wise and knowledgeable leader. I did not want him to leave BPA, and I did not *want* his job if that meant *he* was leaving. As a way of persuading Russ to stay, I assured him that as far as I was concerned, he did not have to come into the office every day as long as I could reach him by phone for advice on the big issues. I felt confident that I could run the day-to-day activities just fine, thanks to his expert training, but I wanted the comfort of being able to let him make the big decisions.

I also protested that he had wonderful relationships with key people in the electric industry and with the politicians who were most critical to BPA's operations and, although I knew many of them, I was still very young compared to almost all of them and I had neither the clout nor the contacts he had established over many years. He told me that the very moment I became Administrator all those contacts would immediately become mine. In due course I learned that, once again, Russ was very wise and what he said was correct.

During my time working with Russ Richmond, I never intentionally did or said anything that could remotely seem disrespectful toward him, but at this point in time I made a comment that gave him the wrong impression. I said, "You know, if I had wanted to get rid of you as Administrator, I did not have enough influence to get it done. But now, I think I might have enough clout to keep you from retiring." I said this partly in jest, to point out how popular he was with all the key constituents and the leaders in government, even the Republican Administration. I said this to him in hopes it would encourage him not to retire.

The next morning Russ came to the office visibly upset; frankly, I had never seen him like this. And worse, it was all because of what I had said! He told me that he expected more loyalty from me than to threaten to block his retirement. When I realized how seriously he took my comments, I knew that he was absolutely determined to retire to spend time with and take care of Peggy. I immediately apologized for seeming to want to thwart his genuine desires and offered to assist in any way that I could. Later in life, I would experience firsthand exactly how Russ felt about caring for his wife, but that is for another chapter.

Russ skillfully managed his departure and my appointment. He worked with Jim Smith (the Interior Department's Assistant Secretary for Water and Power, who had been too busy to meet with me three years earlier, but who had become a friend), and the key members of the Pacific Northwest Congressional delegation in both parties, so that by the time of the 1972 Presidential election, the decision had been made. His retirement and my appointment were both scheduled for December, a month after the election.

Before beginning its second term in office, the Nixon Administration made an unnecessary and foolish decision to demand that all its federal agency appointees tender their resignations in writing. There were a couple of reasons this heavy-handed demand for resignations was ridiculous. First, it was unnecessary because all Presidential appointees in any Administration serve "at the pleasure of the President," which means that he can simply tell them to leave at any time. No resignation is necessary. Second, it was foolish because it insulted Nixon's loyal appointees who were suddenly threatened with a loss of their position, which made them insecure at best, even if their resignations were not accepted. For me that meant submitting a letter resigning as Deputy Administrator, which meant almost nothing since I would be appointed Administrator in a few days.

With Russ Richmond upon his retirement from BPA (Bonneville Power Administration/Department of the Interior)

On the day I became BPA Administrator, December 1, 1972, the weather turned very cold in the region, which caused the electric loads to rise rapidly. At the same time, several dams froze over, causing electricity production to be diminished. Freezing rain damaged some of our lines, further limiting the amount of power we could transmit across the mountains to the cities on the West Coast. At the same time, cold weather meant increased need for electricity to heat homes, buildings, and factories. This increase in demand and decrease in supply meant that we could not meet our load requirements, and we had no alternative but to reduce the load by decreasing the supply to our industrial customers—as provided for in their contracts with us.

As a result, I had to direct BPA to implement the largest power curtailments in its history. Contracts for "interruptible power" then in place with large aluminum company smelters helped greatly at the time, because those contracts allowed BPA to temporarily reduce electric service to *them*, which allowed BPA to serve other customers without interruption. As long as the normal power supply was resumed before the aluminum pots cooled to the point of solidifying, the consequences were minimal. In order to be able to interrupt their supply of power in this way, BPA sold the power to these "interruptible customers" at a low price. The process saved BPA a great deal of money we would have had to spend to guarantee around-the-clock power deliveries in all circumstances, and the savings more than reimbursed the companies for their occasional loss of production. It was a win-win for all parties, especially the public, whose power was substantially less costly than it would have been, and BPA could supply power to the average customer more often than would otherwise have been possible. Critics of BPA complained that the big aluminum companies were getting too good a deal. They focused only on the price BPA charged for interruptible power compared to the price for the more reliable power supplied to everyone else and ignored the savings to everyone from the interruptible power supply contracts.

Our unprecedented curtailments led to news stories about the power crisis, and I had to be prepared to handle reporters' questions. One humorous situation arose when I asked Carl Blake, the man who maintained the official power supply figures at BPA, "How big will our load be today, Carl?"

I don't remember the figure this many years later, but he replied with an exact number, such as, "10,397,472 (kilowatts)."

I was amazed at the precision of his answer, and asked, "How can you be so specific?"

"Because that's all the power we've got," he said, with a rueful smile.

Four days later, on December 4, we held Russ Richmond's retirement celebration, almost like a roast where many warm and humorous remarks and presentations were made about his tenure. Finally, it was his turn to speak, and his own humor again was on display. His opening remarks were, "Well, Don, just four days ago I left you a nice, smooth-running organization…" I did not hear how that sentence ended because the roar of laughter drowned it out. Everyone knew that the weather was beyond the control of the incoming BPA Administrator.

CHAPTER 9

TRAGEDY AND NEW LIFE

Without a doubt, two of the most life-changing experiences happened during my years at the Bonneville Power Administration, and they had nothing to do with work, electricity, or politics. As this book is about how I became a Cabinet officer, this chapter may seem surprising, but the course of my life would have been very different were it not for these events. The first of these happened in 1974 while we were living in Lake Oswego, Oregon.

At this time of our lives, Barbara and I were "cultural Christians." We went to church because it was the thing to do. But as Barbara later put it, we were churchgoing vessels with nothing in them. We had shape from our early training, but no meaning. When the boys became old enough, we took them to Sunday School. As Barb would say, in a seemingly almost embarrassed, self-deprecating way, "After all it hadn't hurt us."

As a young boy, our oldest son, Philip, began to have problems in school, which became more and more evident starting in fifth grade. But even before that, we had noticed that he had issues. At birth the doctor told us that the umbilical cord had been partially wrapped around his neck and thus he might have been deprived of oxygen. It was never determined whether this was true, or if so, if it was the cause, but even as a little boy, he just never seemed to have any perspective on things. He was small and not particularly athletic, although he played Little League baseball and made the all-star team. He began to spend long hours alone in his room listening with headphones to what we later realized was heavy metal music with destructive lyrics.

As he got older, Philip continued having behavior problems, and he started running with a bad crowd, which was a major warning sign. His issues in school never seemed serious enough to hold him back a year, but he could never quite keep up. Finally, in fifth grade and at our insistence, the school tested him, and both his teacher and the principal were surprised to learn that he was quite intelligent.

Philip's behavior problems also showed up in church and, eventually, he no longer wanted to go. I suppose there would be a diagnosis today for what plagued our son but then we were helpless, medically, psychologically, and spiritually.

At the same time, the pastor at our church began to deliver political sermons—and he was on the wrong side! At the end of each service, I wanted to demand equal time to rebut the sermon. Much later in life, when speaking to Christian audiences, I would say that since we were so displeased with the pastor, "we did what any good Christian would do, we stopped going to church." Christian audiences got the joke—that a *good* Christian would have looked for another church rather than stop going.

Philip had always been active, not afraid of taking risks, perhaps the worst example being when he fell off a bike and broke his jaw. There was a steep hill behind our house and he and his friend were at the top of it and decided to see how fast they could come down. Philip was sitting on the handlebars while his buddy was steering and braking. Part of the way down, there was a road that took off up a side hill, kind of like a runaway truck ramp on a highway. By the time they got to that point they were going so fast that the friend tried to slow down by taking the ramp.

When I looked at the place later, there was loose gravel at the start of the up ramp, and I am quite sure that when the tires hit that the bike slid sideways and crashed. Philip took the hit right on his jaw and it broke at the hinge. His mouth was wired shut so that he could not move it for six weeks. We bought a blender, and we ground up all of Philip's food, so he ate by drinking everything through a straw.

The summer after his eighth-grade year, Philip ran away and lived in the woods not far from our home for several weeks. At about that time, he asked Barbara what she thought of suicide, and she said that she felt it was also running away from one's problems rather than dealing with them. We had no idea what to do about someone who was asking such questions.

Before the start of his freshman year in high school, we decided we had to do something to try to get Phil on a proper path. We decided to send him to Shawnigan Lake School, a private boarding school on Vancouver Island in British Columbia, Canada, which focused on discipline and academics. I had learned of Shawnigan through my lifelong friend, François Elmaleh, who had gone there and excelled. He felt it had changed his life very much for the better.

Philip did not fight against going and I think he was willing to try it because it would get him away from the stress in our house. And we thought he might do better being away from us. He and I were not getting along, and that was partly because I was an over-achiever, and I could not relate to his chronic malaise. I now realize, of course, that we all needed help.

My career was going very well at the time, but my family was struggling terribly. Barbara had very bad experiences with Phil, trying to argue him out of the things he was doing. She later acknowledged that she even screamed at him out of frustration, something that was completely out of character for her. She later would say that she must have hoped that by raising her voice she might get through to him and cause him to listen. We tried to reason with him about doing drugs, but his attitude was, "If you haven't tried it, don't knock it."

Philip continued to spiral out of control. We were pretty sure he was using both alcohol and drugs. We had no idea at first about Philip's drug use, but we knew he was going to beer parties and coming home drunk. But even when we finally learned about his drug use, we had no idea what to do about it. He told us that drugs were easier to find at school than alcohol. At one point even he recognized his hapless situation, telling me, "Dad, even going to parties all the time isn't fun."

We became concerned that he would drive a car while under the influence of alcohol or drugs and injure or kill either himself or an innocent person. So, we made a deal with him: If he were too drunk or too stoned to drive, he was to call us, and we would come and pick him up. He kept that deal. We had to go and get him more than once. However, that was only a small bandage on a very large problem.

We were naively and falsely comforted, however, when he returned from Canada after his junior year. He seemed to be far more positive about life, more at peace. We didn't know that his coming back so much less troubled should have been a source of concern. When someone who is possibly suicidal suddenly becomes relaxed and almost happy, it is a huge warning sign. He had made his plan, and he had solved his problems. We thought his attitude was a good sign. Little did we know.

That summer I told Philip that we had decided not to send him back to Shawnigan for his senior year and he said, "Good, because I wouldn't go back." No anger. No hostility. Just a simple and clear statement. And we were OK with that because he did seem better.

Everything came to a tragic head on Philip's seventeenth birthday, August 7, 1974. We had a family party at our home, with my parents and my brother and his wife, but Philip did not show up. Les and Gladys had left, and we were talking with my parents about the problems with Philip. I had just said that I was hopeful that if we could just get him through this next year he would be on the right track. At that moment there came the knock at the door that we had been dreading. There were two policemen on our front porch. They made sure we were the Hodels and then said that we'd better sit down.

Barb later told me that she had thought, *Oh dear, here it comes, he's wrecked the car.* But that was not what they had come to tell us. They said that Philip had been found hanging from a tree. It was not a cry for help. He had clearly and carefully planned it to succeed on his first attempt.

After I became a Cabinet officer we began giving our Christian testimony in public, and whenever Barbara told this part of our story it was at that line, "hanging from a tree," that Barbara's voice quavered, even thirty years later. Obviously, a mother never stops hurting when she is vividly reminded of her grief. And I assure you, neither does a father.

Philip had told his friend Jeff that he planned to kill himself on his seventeenth birthday, but he had made similar comments before, so Jeff didn't take it seriously. That meant that after Philip's suicide Jeff felt he was personally responsible for not saying anything. He was very troubled, and his father brought him to see us. I did my best to console him, first telling him that there was no way for him to know that this time Philip was serious, and then I pointed out to him that even if he had told us it might have done no good. We would not have known what to do.

We were totally overcome—with grief, with shock, and with guilt. We suffered grief, of course. Shock came from never having known anyone who had experienced suicide—and we certainly did not know that *kids* ever killed themselves. And we experienced tremendous guilt, because with a suicide everyone who is related or close feels guilty, and the parents feel it most of all. It was futile to ask ourselves, *What could we have done differently to save our son?* but we could not keep from coming back to that question over and over.

I tried to compartmentalize it all. I went back to work the next day, a truly insensitive thing to do to both Barbara and David, leaving them to deal with their grief without me there. I have viewed that with regret as a mistake ever since, but in retrospect, I realize that I had no reservoir of strength from which to draw, for me or for them.

David was almost four years younger than Philip. But whereas Philip had absorbed large amounts of our time and worry, Dave was a wonderful son, the compliant one. Unlike Philip before him, he had been a very happy baby, a ray of sunshine, without either the incubator or the colic problems that had made little Philip's early months so miserable for him. It is sad, but true, that the easy child gets much less attention than the difficult child. It was certainly true for Dave.

After Phil's death, Dave, of course, became our main focus, which must have been difficult for him. He was hurting from the suicide of his brother but also was hiding his feelings out of his concern for Barb and me. And he had a tender heart. The day I went back to work after Phil's death, Dave phoned me and, while hurting terribly himself but knowing how anguished I was, said something to the effect that he "was there for me" and that he loved me.

Our religious training from our childhoods came back, and we wanted to have a memorial service for Philip. However, by that time, we had no church. So, we went searching and found a Lutheran church we knew about because Uncle Gerdau, my godfather, had once been the organist there. The pastor was already booked for that week, but when he heard our request, he rearranged his schedule to do a service for us. He may have been influenced by the fact that he, too, had lost a son, not through suicide but due to cancer. He was able to identify with us in a special way.

On the next Sunday, two days after the memorial service, we went to his church and began attending regularly—not because we felt obligated, but because we were desperately seeking comfort. The people in that congregation launched what we later thought of as a "rescue operation" for us. They did everything they could do for a family that was hurting: sympathy notes, phone calls, flowers, anonymous gifts of food left on our front porch, and when we were at the church, they hugged us. Years later we realized that we *first met* Jesus Christ in those people.

Since I was somewhat prominent in Portland due to my job at BPA, there was a brief newspaper article about Philip's suicide. Business associates, friends, and acquaintances reached out to us with sympathy and many of them shared their own pain with us. Some of them had runaway children, and when they heard about Philip it made them fear that their missing children might have committed suicide and were never coming back. We at least knew the finality of Philip, although any boy we saw in public who resembled him caused our hearts to start. Others had children who had been prevented from committing suicide and were institutionalized, possibly for the rest of their lives.

At the time, we prayed to a God we hardly knew for relief from our broken hearts. And we were looking for answers. But with suicide, there are no answers, only questions. We were attending church because we *wanted* to and because our hearts were stripped bare, and we were hearing things we had never heard before—not that other preachers hadn't said them.

One Sunday, Barbara heard the pastor say, "Jesus Christ died for your sins," and she realized that he was speaking about *her* and about *her* sins. She had never considered herself a sinner before. She thought, *I'm a good person.* But then she realized that when you are considering whether you are a sinner you have to judge yourself by God's standards, not your own, and not in comparison to other people.

Finally, she realized that if Christ's death on the cross meant that her sins were forgiven, it was false pride to say that she could not forgive herself. It was like saying her standards were higher than God's. And when she came to understand that, she began to feel her burden lifting, as though someone were assisting her, and she became that Christian vessel filling up with the gift of faith.

For me, there was no sudden revelation, no blinding flash, no Road-to-Damascus experience. But as we continued to attend church on Sunday mornings, I began to feel a growing relationship with the Lord. And then, one Sunday, the pastor was speaking from First Corinthians 15:12–19, where the Apostle Paul writes that some are preaching that Christ was not raised from the dead. He laments that if what they are preaching is true then we who believe in Christ are the most miserable of all people, for we have hope in Christ only in this life!

It hit me like a ton of bricks! The Resurrection is everything! It distinguishes Christianity from all other religions. It cleared away *my* sins. *My* burdens were lifted.

As Barbara and I looked back on those times, we believed that our coming to Christ was the reason our marriage stayed together. We were told that after losing a child, over 90 percent of marriages break up, especially after suicide. We believed we knew why: The guilt is unbearable.

I sometimes woke up in the night weeping over all the things that I did or did not do as a father that might have contributed to Philip's suicide. The guilt was so severe that the impulse to look for someone else to blame was nearly overwhelming. At that same time Barbara was going through the same anguish. Imagine how she would have felt if I had said, "Philip's suicide was really your fault." Or, what if she had said something like that to me? I came to believe that when a couple experiences suicide in the family, trying to process one's overwhelming feelings of guilt often leads to blaming the other spouse as an escape, as in, "I was partly to blame, but *you* were his *mother*, and you bear a lot *more* blame!" Had we done that, or anything like it, I believe our marriage would have suffered a fatal blow from which, eventually, it would have crumbled.

We, however, were spared, because before we said such damaging things to each other, we each came to know Jesus Christ, and while we could never shed our guilt, we could lay the *burden* of that guilt on His shoulders. And that allowed us to experience the comfort that a loving relationship provides. Many times, one or the other of us woke up in the night crying, reaching out for the other and receiving unconditional love and comfort.

We began a slow process of reordering our priorities and our perspective. We came to truly understand in our core what we had often heard and even said, namely, that status and money and power did not provide real or lasting fulfillment in life. We believe that is why we never caught "Potomac fever"—unlike so many people who go to Washington and fall in love with the aura of power and influence that surrounds that city.

Coming to Christ had an effect on every aspect of our lives, changing us from the inside out in so many ways, including its effect on our marriage. We developed the ability to forgive each other for not being perfect—or perfectible. And as we were finding forgiveness in Jesus, our surviving son, David, came to Christ also, through the encouragement of a friend of his, which made us even more proud of him and gave us a new relationship with him, too!

We began to see the beauty in helping others. Barb's paternal grandmother, Georgie, had been living with Barb's mother, who had a full-time job. When Georgie broke her hip at age ninety-three, she came to live with us because Barb's mom could not stay home to help her. Then, when we were moving to Washington, some of our friends suggested that we put Georgie in a nursing home. "After all," they said to Barbara, "she is very old and will be a great burden to you."

Later, in speaking about this advice, Barbara would say that the old us might have agreed with that, but the new us thought, No. She's not ill. She is just very old and slow moving, and, after all, she is my grandmother. She just may be one of those "least of these" Jesus talked about helping. And it worked out very well. Barb's mother was Georgie's daughter-in-law, who could do no right in Georgie's eyes, but Barb, as her granddaughter, could do no wrong. .

So, Georgie moved with us to Washington and just slowed down, and slowed down, and slowed down, until finally she came to a stop at the age of 102. But she never lost her spunk. One day around age ninety-eight, Barb noticed that Georgie had not taken a new medication the doctor had prescribed and inquired as to why. Georgie said, "I am not sure I want to take that. I understand it may be habit-forming." What a wonderful spirit.

We also began each day differently than before. Instead of reading the newspaper the first thing in the morning, we returned from exercising and began daily Bible reading. While I showered and shaved, getting ready to go to work, Barb read to me from the Bible; and then we got down on our knees together and prayed—aloud—which was hard, considering our upbringing in churches which did not encourage that kind of togetherness, as you really have to trust the person who is beside you as you pray.

My newfound faith in Jesus Christ also became evident in my work. My various positions had often been stressful and pressure-packed, but now I could remain relatively calm, and others recognized the difference. Things were seen from a new perspective. After all, if the Lord could comfort me for the loss of our son, for whom I gladly would have given up anything I had or anything I had achieved, handling job-related stress should be easy.

Let me emphasize that I am not trying to claim that we had it easy, or that we somehow thought we were perfect. To the contrary, we were still sinners, but the more we learned about Jesus Christ, and the more we came to know Him personally, the more able we were to go on. And we saw that no one was outside of His loving reach, His graceful forgiveness. Instead of lives filled with worry, distress, and dismay, we could lead lives of joy, hope, excitement, and purpose, which means that we changed the way we saw others.

Four years after losing Philip, death struck my family again, and this time it was my father. In 1971 at age sixty-seven, he began to suffer cognitive difficulties due to the onset of Alzheimer's. Just when he was beginning to anticipate retirement, he was losing the ability to do things that had always been simple. For the first year or two we knew something was wrong, although neither my mother nor I heard the word *Alzheimer's* until the day the doctor told us that was what he was suffering from.

Dad had become president of Huntington Rubber Mills, where he had worked for fifty years. But as he struggled with the need to retire, almost all his assets were tied up in his shares of stock in the company. There was no market for the stock of a small, privately held company, so he was not able to sell them. Unexpectedly, an offer for the entire company came from a buyer that was using its tax loss carryover to acquire profitable companies, paying premium prices. This presented an opportunity for Dad and the other shareholders to turn their unsaleable stock into cash.

By the time that offer came, even Dad knew that he was losing his ability to think and remember. At first, he made extensive notes so that he could refresh his memory. Then, he reached a point where he could not interpret his notes, and he would bring them to me so that I could help him understand what they meant. This was a very sad time for all of us because we could see he was seriously declining.

When the time came to negotiate the sale of the company, Les and I sat beside him, one on each side. We were a good team. Les had once been the head of purchasing for Portland General Electric during the entire time that the company built the huge Trojan Nuclear Power Plant, a billion-dollar project. He was exceedingly adept at negotiation and very bright. I sometimes joked about him being the smart brother, but it was true. I brought my experience as a lawyer to the table. Basically, Les and I did the negotiation for Dad, with his full agreement to the particulars, of course. In the end, the sale produced enough value to provide a reasonable, though not large, retirement for him and our mother through the value of the stock he owned at the time of the sale. And it was important, as well, to the other shareholders who otherwise had no way to sell their shares of stock.

Dad was still alive and working when I was appointed as Administrator of BPA, and he was very proud, especially as he stood in the picture with the whole family on the day I was sworn in. Before the sale of his company, he still went to his office every day. I drove past his office each evening on my way home from work, and if I saw his car I would often stop and talk with him. I could tell that he really could not understand the ins and outs of the various activities in which I was involved, but I would speak enthusiastically about what I was doing and about the excitement I was having. It always cheered him up.

My father had been my adviser on matters of life and business. However, when he began the long, slow slide into Alzheimer's disease, he could no longer actively engage in such discussions. Interestingly, it was not until his death that I suddenly realized that a large part of my motivation in life was to please him. To my surprise that had continued to be true even after he was no longer able to understand what was going on. It was enough for me to know that, had he understood what I was telling him, he would have been very proud of me.

It took seven years for Alzheimer's to finally take my father. The last three years got worse and worse. For longer than was good for her, Mom insisted on caring for him at home. She was attempting to keep a promise she had made to Dad years earlier when they had visited someone in a nursing home. It was a dismal environment and, as they left, Dad said, "Please, Rose. Don't ever put me in a place like that." Mom assured him that she never would.

Unfortunately, as happens too often with Alzheimer's patients, my gentle and loving father changed with the worsening of his disease. He became abusive and angry from time to time. Les and I began to fear for her life because of Dad's delusions. On one occasion she had to wrestle him to the floor and wrap him inside a throw rug to control him. On one visit, Dad took me aside and, motioning toward my mother, said, "Who is that woman?" and on another visit, "That woman is trying to kill me." No amount of assurance from me could change his mind at that moment. There seemed to me to be a substantial risk that at some point he could do something drastic and hurt her.

Finally, we were able to persuade Mom that Dad had to be placed in a facility equipped to care for Alzheimer's patients. It was really a nice place, and Mom faithfully went there every day and fed him one or more meals for the nearly three years it took for his affliction to take him. Slowly he deteriorated and finally he succumbed to pneumonia at the age of seventy-four in the spring of 1978, a few months after I left BPA.

Dad was interred in a section of Riverview Cemetery in Portland where a number of family members are buried. Mom and Les each consented to having the ashes of Philip, Dad's namesake, also buried in my father's grave. This is the same cemetery where Barbara and I bought plots for us, complete with a headstone with our names and birth dates. Only our ending dates needed to be added. Les and Gladys did the same, and Gladys died a few years after Barbara and was buried there.

My mother lived eight years longer than Dad and was in quite good health most of that time. She met a woman friend in her apartment building with whom she often traveled internationally.

Les and I encouraged her to buy a new car. She objected to doing so because it was quite expensive, and she was "so old" and didn't want to deprive us of our inheritance. We assured her over and over that she and Dad had done the greatest possible favor for us by encouraging us and supporting each of us in getting a good education and achieving financial success, and that we did not need her to hold back on anything because of her desire to leave money to us.

So, she purchased a yellow Cadillac coupe with white leather upholstery, which cost her just over $10,000 at the time, and she, with her blonde hair, courtesy of a periodic rinse, looked great in it. Many times, during the succeeding years, she told us how much she enjoyed that car.

Mom lived to see me confirmed in my various positions in Washington, first as Under Secretary of the Interior in 1981, followed by Secretary of Energy in 1982 and, finally, Secretary of the Interior in 1985. She was more than proud.

Since Barbara and I were living in Washington, DC, beginning in January 1981, our son Dave, who was a freshman at Whitman College in Walla Walla, Washington, spent his summers and Christmas holidays in Lake Oswego, living with my mother in her spare bedroom. Mom, after Dad's death, had sold their home on the Tualatin River and moved into a condominium closer to Barbara and me. She lived there for the remainder of her life.

Dave had not had a car at college before I went to Washington, but it became a necessity, since we would not be in Portland to drive him back and forth to school. So, we gave him our primary vehicle so that he could get to college and back to Lake Oswego in the summers.

I wrote earlier about going back to my job at Bonneville the day after Philip's suicide, leaving Barbara and young David at home alone to deal with their grief. When it came time to move to Washington, I once again was needlessly insensitive.

Dave was still home for Christmas vacation in early January 1981 when I received Jim Watt's call asking me to move to Washington to join the Reagan Administration as his Under Secretary. I was excited. As soon as I hung up the phone my mind was rapidly thinking about all the things that needed to be done—about the house, our cars, everything, including Dave. Unfortunately, instead of sitting him down and discussing what was going on, and seeking his understanding and support, I sprung our move on him, simply announcing, without giving him even a moment to consider the situation, "We'll give you one of our cars (so that he could get to college and back to Lake Oswego in the summers), and you'd better take all of your belongings with you when you go back to Whitman, because when you get back this summer this house may no longer be your home."

Like Barbara, who processed things carefully and thoughtfully before accepting them (versus my jumping to a conclusion, and sometimes the wrong one), Dave was shocked, to say the least. I still regret treating him like that, which must have been very distressing and destabilizing to him. Unfortunately, we cannot undo such things but only apologize. He went back to Whitman and seemingly adapted well. I went to DC, and Barbara soon joined me there, as our lives took a very different tack than previously.

I was proud of Dave then and am proud of him now as I write this, including for the ease with which he appeared to adapt to such major changes in his life. Only years later did I learn from things he said what a toll it took on him to maintain his apparent composure—both when Philip died and, later, when we moved to Washington. He made the effort and worked to avoid causing me concern because he was so supportive, but it was much more difficult for him than I realized at the time.

As an adult, I think Dave always doubted that I truly admired him for so many things, but I really did—and do—including his integrity. I was a hardworking, ambitious father with high expectations, and he was much gentler and congenial. It was hard for him to cope with my personality. He has always exhibited an interest in and talent for the arts (music, theater, etc.), but I think he felt that I wanted him to be an overachiever in the business world. While I would have been proud of him for that, I would never have preferred that to his exercising the giftings God put inside him, and being a man of good character, a loving husband, and a good father to his own three sons, which is far more important in the real world—and for eternity.

When David reads this, I hope he will know how much I love and respect him and appreciate all that he did to be supportive, and that I regret I was not more aware at the time. I love him deeply.

Dave was staying with my mother on a Monday night in the fall of 1985 during a school break when she suffered a major stroke. As soon as I heard, I made travel plans for Barb and me to get to Oregon on Thursday, but on Wednesday Les called to tell me that she had flatlined. All her vital signs were gone, and she was simply being kept alive by the devices to which she was attached.

Les asked if I wanted Mom to be kept alive until I arrived the next day, and I assured him that I did not, since seeing her alive in that state would accomplish nothing in my eyes. Mom was removed from life support and died. She was buried next to my father and Philip at Riverview Cemetery.

CHAPTER 10
CHIEF EXECUTIVE

On December 1, 1972, at the age of thirty-seven, I became Administrator of the Bonneville Power Administration. For the first time in my career, I was the top executive of something significant. This was an interesting situation because all of my direct reports were at least twenty years older than I was. Further, they were all long-term BPA employees, many of them hired while Democrats occupied the White House, and here was this very young Republican sitting in the top job.

Having had three years to get to know each of the individuals as Russ Richmond's number two, I felt that I had a good sense of their strengths and weaknesses. I went out of my way to show them my utmost respect, seeking their advice on all decisions. My parents had instilled in me a conviction that all people are entitled to be shown respect, and I tried always to do that. I used my customary management style. I liked to get all the knowledgeable people in the room and discuss the issues and reach a consensus. I was simply not comfortable with a style in which the boss just told people what to do and how to do it.

The people with whom I worked in my career seemed to like my collegial approach, and I think they liked working with me because they knew that I was relying upon each of them for advice. I once told Barbara that I believed each top staff member at BPA and later at the Departments of Interior and Energy was confident that I could not have succeeded without his or her specific help. My nature also was to trust people as far as possible, but never to forget that self-interest could easily override loyalty, especially if one's job were involved.

My first task, even before I was sworn in, was to choose my own replacement as Deputy Administrator. A man named Ray Foleen was the obvious choice. He had been special assistant to Russ Richmond and the three of us worked very closely together. Ray was Russ's golfing buddy and had been at BPA for several years, which gave him a wealth of knowledge about what had been done and why. Also, I found him to be a very congenial friend. Choosing Ray had the further benefit of reassuring the top staff that I wanted BPA to continue on the course that Russ Richmond had set.

Of course, the bureaucrats at the Interior Department in Washington wanted to name someone from outside BPA, a political appointee of *their* choosing. But I convinced them to let me select Ray, making the case that I needed the kind of knowledge and support that he could provide. I did not need or want a deputy from outside who had been chosen by someone else and was likely to know even less about BPA than I did. There was no way I would have the time or ability to train a newcomer as Russ had done for me. My knowledge of BPA was simply not deep enough, and neither was my experience in what it took to manage a large, high profile organization.

As soon as I was in the job, I realized that I had not had the experience of being the head of a division or department of a large organization. I had skipped that step in my career. So, I asked the human resources director to let me know what outside training was available for someone in my situation. Actually, throughout my career I often was dismayed at the lack of training provided to people appointed to key government jobs.

The first set of development offerings I was shown, however, were for CEOs, people in positions comparable to mine, courses which seemed like no more than ego-stroking, such as tips for meeting other CEOs and learning to connect with them for networking and future dealings. That was not what I was looking for at all. I wanted to know what mid- to upper-level managers learned while moving up through the ranks. The HR team then located a course taught by the American Management Association for people who were newly promoted department or division managers, not for chief executives. Of course, I took a lot of ribbing from my staff about being the top guy yet having to take a lower-level management course. It was all good-natured teasing and funny, but it was also true.

Among the many helpful components of the course, and by far the most useful tool—one that I would go on to use for the next almost fifty years—was using a flip chart to help a group choose a path for dealing with a major problem. It became a hallmark of my management style from that day forward. Even with the teasing it often brought from my staff, my use of a flip chart proved to be the most productive and efficient way to reach consensus and identify what appeared to be our best options.

At BPA, I held meetings with my closest advisers in my office rather than in a conference room and would begin with that small group (a few to several depending on the issue) facing the flip chart, while I—with marker in hand—stood in front at the chart. I can still remember the laughter that ensued each time I got up, took the marker in hand and Ray Foleen said, "Oh, no. Here we go again with that management training stuff." Everyone who worked with me came to expect it. Virtually everyone who has worked for me since has seen me do it.

At the top of the sheet I would write, *O & A*, which stood for Objective and Alternatives. Interestingly, the natural course of many business discussions is for people to start offering solutions to *their* idea of the problem before there has been any discussion of what the problem is and certainly before there could be any agreement on the objectives before them.

It was for me a lifelong lesson on the importance of agreeing on objectives before trying to figure out how to solve a problem. After I moved on to Washington, DC, I almost always followed this same process for any major or difficult issue. Only after we agreed on our objective and spelled out our alternatives, would I ask, "How much of this is possible in the political atmosphere in which we operate?" Unfortunately, because of politics, in Washington the answer often was "not much."

The classic experience illustrating this point was a meeting regarding a proposed rate increase. BPA had almost 200 direct utility customers, divided up into basic classifications (as I described in the previous chapter), including municipalities, rural cooperatives, public utility districts in Washington, and people's utility districts in Oregon, as well as four, large investor-owned utilities which sometimes bought power and were constantly sharing BPA transmission lines for which they had to pay. The BPA Act that had created the agency, under its preference clause required that power be sold first to the public agencies (PUDs, RECs, and municipal systems), while the private utilities, financed by stocks and bonds, came after them.

I believed in having everyone in a meeting who was essential, but no more. In addition to Ray Foleen, and one or two others who came from time to time, depending on the need for their expertise, those in most of the meetings about rates in my office included three very able men.

Bernard Goldhammer had the title of power manager, and he was brilliant. Russ once described Bernie as BPA's in-house genius. It turned out that that statement offended several others who thought they were also geniuses. "So," Russ told me, "*Now* I say, 'Bernie is one of *only three* geniuses on the BPA payroll and I won't tell you who the other two are.' That way anybody else who thinks of himself as a genius is happy."

Bernie was recognized as a remarkably gifted man both inside and outside BPA, as well as an excellent negotiator. He had the ability to come up with proposals that included a little something for everyone but did not give anyone everything they wanted. Before he ever started negotiating with others, he had a clear picture of where the process would end, but he started with a proposal that was unsatisfactory to all and then let them force him to give up things they wanted until they were satisfied that they had gotten all that they could. As negotiations took place Bernie slowly gave bits and pieces to everyone so that in the end everyone got something, which made them more willing to agree. They all knew what he was doing, but he was so good at it and so congenial that they usually bought in. That allowed the representatives for BPA customers to go back to their bosses and brag about how they had forced Bernie to give them more than the initial proposal.

Hector Durocher, Bernie's deputy, was an extremely able man, but unlike Bernie, he would spend a lot of time deciding exactly where the negotiation ought to come out and he would then present that to the other parties as his only and final proposal. (Bernie retired partway through my term as Administrator, and when Hec succeeded him, he chose Earl Gjelde as his deputy.) Having decided where negotiations should come out, Hec would not budge during negotiations. The customer representatives objected to Hec, complaining to me that he was unreasonable, intransigent, and needed to be replaced. Almost any proposal Hec made in a given situation was very close to what Bernie's view of the proper result would have been, but by not giving the other parties the ability to get any wins in the process, he did not give them a chance to prove their value, which created serious hard feelings.

Doug Hansen was the Assistant Administrator for Administration, which was a long and fancy government title for our de facto chief financial officer. He was an accountant, through and through.

My special assistant, Harold Kropitizer, was a lawyer, smart and aggressive, and not afraid to speak up when he disagreed with something anyone said, including me. Any supervisor should greatly value that quality in a subordinate because it is far too easy to have people around you who are yes-men, agreeing with anything you say.

At our first meeting on the rate increase, we made no progress. Finally, I got out the flip chart and began with the question, "What is our objective?" Well, as it turned out, everyone had a different objective. Bernie wanted whichever rate proposal was acceptable to the greatest number of our customers and would raise enough revenue to meet BPA's needs. Hec wanted the perfect rate proposal, one that was fair and could be proved to be fair by allocating all the costs of the system exactly correctly to each customer. Doug

Hansen just wanted something that brought in enough money, and he was indifferent to the reaction of the customers. Others wanted rates that favored the smaller PUDs. And there may have been one or two other objectives

And then there was my position: The establishment of a defensible rate increase proposal *as soon as possible* so we could begin the process of vetting it through the customers' review committees, the Department of the Interior, and Congress. A defensible rate proposal meant one that would allocate the costs of the system in a way that could be defended as fair to the various users. Unfortunately, in such a complex system as the PNW power grid there are so many elements that the outcome will vary widely based upon which element is given the most weight.

Once the flip chart revealed these different objectives, we were able to discuss what our *primary* objective needed to be, and once we agreed on that we could discuss alternative ways of reaching that objective. In the end, a combination of Bernie's and mine won out—a proposal that raised sufficient funds to cover our costs, and which would be acceptable to the bulk of our customers, and which could be accomplished as soon as possible.

BPA's service territory encompassed five geographic sections of the PNW known as "areas" with a manager for each. One was known as the Portland Area, which covered the entire State of Oregon. An area manager's job was to stay in close touch with all of BPA's customers in his area. For instance, when there was going to be a policy change or a rate increase, his job was to explain the basis of the change and encourage the customers to support it.

If I had a specific leadership gift, it was being able to identify the strengths and weaknesses of individuals and then putting them in positions where they could be successful. Over the years I rearranged assignments for some, promoted others, and sometimes found it necessary to move a few out of their roles.

Bill Galbraith, who had been overlooked for significant promotion at BPA in the past—likely because he was not thought to be technically strong—seemed to me to have the personality that would make a very good area manager. So, I reassigned him to that role, overseeing the Portland Area. Bill turned out to be extremely capable of working with people, just as I had thought. I remember that when he was retiring several years later, he complimented me for having been able to see the good qualities in people, like him, in positions where they could make a valuable contribution to the organization. No doubt I liked hearing that because it tended to confirm my belief that almost everyone has something to contribute, if they can be placed in the right position.

Russ Richmond knew the importance of a boss using good-natured humor as a way to relate to staff members, and following his example, I tried to employ that as well. Ray Foleen once bought a new crystal, precision watch that kept the correct time to within one second per year. Being an engineer, Ray was very proud of his watch. I, on the other hand, wore an inexpensive Timex digital watch. So, occasionally, and sometimes to break the tension of a situation, I would ask Ray exactly what time it was. He would proudly tell me, right down to the second, and I would look at my watch and say, "That's what my Timex says." Ray would react just as I hoped he would, laughingly saying, "C'mon Hodel, cut that out!"

And when the teasing came my way, it helped keep things from getting too serious. Besides references to the mid-level management course, I also got teased about telling the same joke before most of my speeches when in front of a new audience. The staff who accompanied me to speeches said they were tired of hearing the same joke time after time, even if it did get a huge laugh from audiences. It was a joke that Bernie Goldhammer told me, but which has since entered more than one chief executive's repertoire. I told it like this:

When I became BPA Administrator, I found that Russ Richmond had left three envelopes in the middle drawer of my desk, with a note that they were to be opened in a time of crisis.

Well, I had been in the job only four days before a crisis arrived. So, I opened the first envelope, which included a notecard that read: "Blame your predecessor."

Somewhat later, another crisis arose, and I opened the second envelope. The card inside read: "Reorganize." I found out that reorganizing does little good, but it keeps the critics away for a while.

Finally, we had a third crisis, and I opened the last envelope. The card read simply: "Prepare three envelopes."

The most significant achievement of my tenure as head of BPA was the passage by Congress of a law authorizing BPA to self-finance. From its inception BPA was, like almost all government agencies, funded by annual budgets approved by Congress. The difference for BPA, however, was that it sold electricity and therefore *produced* income for the government. At the time I was Administrator, its revenues were about $300 million per year. The first time Russ explained that to me he said that he pictured a little man in the basement of the Treasury Department wearing a green eyeshade entering the BPA receipts in a ledger but never giving us any credit for sending it. He lamented, "So, I have to go to Congress and beg them to appropriate the funds we need to operate this system and make the money that *we* are earning for Washington."

Of course, I inherited that system from Russ and found myself in the position of having to present and justify BPA's annual budgets. Sometimes we had projects that would generate additional revenue and pay for themselves in short order, but that was not even a consideration in the appropriation process. The deciding factor in that process was the level of spending that the Office of Management and Budget (OMB) established for the entire government. Thus, a good and economically sound new power supply was weighed against other things, such as a new and critical armament for the military or some social program that might "buy" votes.

Whenever I was in Washington, I made a point to go visit the offices of the two key Senators regarding matters relating to BPA, Democrats Scoop Jackson and Warren Magnuson from Washington State. Russ had given me great access to them and their staff members. I worked on getting to know their key aides better, as well, and met with them as often as possible, another lifelong practice of mine since staff can grease or put sand in the wheels. When given a chance, I would at least stick my head in the door of the Senators themselves just to say hello. Also, of course, I would testify from time to time before their committees. I got along well with their key staff members regardless of our party affiliations. We all recognized that BPA was, in fact, not a political operation. It was a federal electric transmission agency that needed to be run as much as possible like a business.

These political friends of BPA were constantly being called upon by its Administrators, including me, to help push the appropriations through Congress that were needed to keep the electric system up and running. At the same time there was cyclical pressure for BPA every two years, like all agencies, to cut its number of employees and to reduce the budget. Meantime, increased functions related to an ever-growing power system required greater numbers of employees. But OMB resisted increases in personnel and, in fact, often imposed restrictions on areas that were critical to our operations.

I decided to try an unusual approach. I went to OMB and dealt directly with Don Crabill, the official whose job it was to oversee BPA's budget. He had set a goal of keeping the number of employees to 3,050 as part of his obligation to hold whatever agencies he was responsible for to some limit imposed on him. He would look at BPA's staffing chart and decide what he thought were jobs that could be cut. Unfortunately, he had only the budget numbers to look at and could not possibly understand the role that each employee played. Since he was requiring me to reduce the number of jobs, I proposed to him that I would keep our number of employees at 3,025 (twenty-five less than he was targeting) in return for him allowing me to decide which jobs were most important to fill. He accepted my promise and agreed to my proposal.

In federal agencies, as in businesses, there are two basic position classifications, those which are filled and those which are vacant. In any large organization, including BPA with its over 3,000 employees, retirements and deaths are a constant factor in ensuring that there are always vacant positions, so that our total number employed at any one time was always below whatever limit was set by OMB.

So instead of having OMB looking over our operations (and our shoulder) and trying to tell us where we needed specific numbers of people, we could make the decision based on our real needs. So, if we decided we had to start a new project, we would have to find positions from something else that we were already doing. It would not be easy to do that, but it was much better for us to control our own future rather than having an outsider who really did not know what was most important to our system making those cuts.

Next, it seemed to me that because BPA generated revenue and was operating as a utility more than as a typical federal agency, we had the potential to fund our own activities from our revenues. That was when I began to think about seeking legislation that would allow BPA to use its revenues to operate the system and pay its operating costs—like a utility. This, I called "BPA self-financing." If I could convince Congress to agree, we would be allowed to use the revenues we generated and would not have to seek appropriations for operating costs. No one at BPA or anywhere else gave me any encouragement because they believed that getting such a proposal through Congress and OMB would be pretty much impossible.

To begin with, in order to get a bill through Congress I had to convince essentially all of the various utilities in the Pacific Northwest, both public and investor-owned, to be supportive. Any group of utilities or even a single, politically influential utility which opposed such legislation could easily have sidetracked it. This meant that after first selling the idea to the key BPA staff, I had to persuade essentially all of our utility customers that it was a good idea. Since some people are always inclined to oppose *any* new idea that is not their own, I had to show that the proposal not only did not hurt them, but that it would actually benefit their utility.

I turned to my trusty flip chart. As I write almost five decades later, I cannot fully remember the pitch I developed, but I laid it out step-by-step in a very compelling and persuasive way and presented it to my top BPA staff, who, with their questions and suggestions, helped me modify and improve the plan and my presentation of it. Next, I scheduled presentations to groups of customers. Rather than fancy, overhead slides (today it would be PowerPoints) like so many others used, I used a simple marker and overhead projector and basically turned a big screen in front of the room into my flip chart. I started with the objective, which was to reduce the reliance upon—and the *uncertainty* of—BPA getting appropriations from Congress to do our job. Then I laid out the way in which we could achieve the goal.

At the flip chart during my final meeting at BPA (Bonneville Power Administration/Department of the Interior)

I prepared the presentation myself and, thus, invested myself in it. Therefore, I knew it well enough to be able to present it without use of notes, which made a big impression on anyone seeing it for the first time. In fact, after one presentation a bright, young lawyer who worked for one of the large municipal districts was overheard saying, "That was impressive. Can you imagine our CEO trying to make that presentation?"

My arguments made sense and came across as eminently reasonable and beneficial: to the region, to each class of customer, to BPA, and to the federal government, since it would mean appropriations would only be needed for capital projects in the future and BPA's rates would have to raise enough revenue to pay the equivalent of debt service on those costs. This last point was important to impress those in Washington, DC, who believed that because BPA's power was so inexpensive we were already getting more benefits than we were entitled to.

I first made the sale to our utility customers across the region. This took several months as I traveled around the Pacific Northwest to meet with key groups. Next, I went to the Department of the Interior and presented my proposal to the Deputy Under Secretary, Bill Lyon, who had become a friend and was a very influential adviser to Interior Secretary Rogers Morton (who served under both Presidents Nixon and Ford). Bill liked the idea, but because he understood how the system worked and resisted change, he thought there was little chance of selling it on Capitol Hill. He wished me well in the way that good friends do when they don't think there is a chance of success.

Even though he was skeptical of my ability to get Congressional approval, Bill helped me persuade Secretary Morton and others in the Department, and soon all the decision makers there were on board though it was not something they were going to risk any of their political capital to support. It seemed like they thought, "Oh, well. This is probably a good idea, but no one can get it through Congress." What they did not know was that Senators Magnuson and Jackson, along with Republicans Mark Hatfield and Bob Packwood, from Oregon, were pretty good friends of mine and, particularly Magnuson and Jackson, were very fond of BPA.

I worked my way slowly through the necessary steps of going to see the Senate staffs and making my flip chart presentation, each time doing it from scratch, so that they would see it develop before their eyes. As I mentioned above, when it unfolded that way, step by step, it was compelling, leaving the impression that it made such good sense they would be thinking, *Why wouldn't we do this?*

In order to make the presentation to the key Senators and Representatives, it was necessary for me to ignore the mandate one of Secretary Morton's underlings placed on the Department. In a memo in the Secretary's name, we were forbidden to go to Capitol Hill without specific permission on a given subject. I could not seek permission because, in doing so, the "smart guys" in the Department would have tried to tell me how to do it and restrict my presentation, and I had better relations with key Senators than they did.

One day, as I was walking from Senator Jackson's office to Senator Magnuson's office, down the hall toward me came Secretary Morton. There was nothing for me to do but keep walking toward him and as we passed, he said, "Hi, Don," and smiled. I smiled back respectfully and said, "Mr. Secretary." I was pretty sure he knew what I was doing but nothing was ever said. Partly I thought that was because he had been a member of Congress and knew how the game was played, and the staffer who tried to shut off access did not.

My approach for preparing for a typical Congressional hearing—in any of my roles which required me to do so—was to collect the staff experts into a room and have them brief me on the subject matter. As soon as I understood what was being said we moved on to the next subject. When I had any doubt about the matter, I would repeat back to the person briefing me what I thought I understood. This allowed them to say, as often was the case, "No, that's not quite right," and then re-explain it to me. Sometimes it took several iterations before I could say it correctly, but once I could do so I was ready to testify on that subject.

When I became Secretary of Energy, I followed a slightly different approach. The staff could not wait to get me into a briefing session for my first hearing. The room was set up as a hollow square with, perhaps, twelve people on each side, and at least thirty to forty people total in the room. I did not want them to ask me tough questions and have me flounder in front of them. That would lead to embarrassing leaks in the press about how the new Secretary did not know what he was talking about. So, I opened the meeting by saying something like, "OK, what is the toughest question I will be asked?" A really smart person would raise their hand and ask it, then everybody waited expectantly to see me try to come up with an answer. Instead of trying to answer, however, I would say, "That's a good question." Then I'd ask the group, "What's the best answer to it?" There would often be several staff who had good answers, and they would discuss or debate the differences among them, and I would learn not only what the best answer was, but also many of the nuances, which to the extent I remembered them while testifying, made me more knowledgeable at the hearing than anyone on the committee.

I quickly learned that however thin my knowledge of the subject might be, I almost always knew more than the Senators or Representatives questioning me in a hearing. Sometimes members of their staff were experts in a particular matter, but although they wrote the questions for their bosses to ask, they were not the ones asking the questions. I needed to be able to answer their first-level questions, and if the committee member asked a more complex follow-up or a more detailed question, I could legitimately offer to have one of my staff who accompanied me to the hearing answer it. Usually, the committee chose not to have someone else testify and simply let my staff supply the information for the record afterward.

I soon became aware that when I displayed a solid knowledge of my subject matter, and then occasionally said in answer to a detailed or technical question, "I don't know the answer to that," it actually increased my credibility. We have all experienced people coming across as insecure or, worse, pompous, when behaving as if they knew everything there was to know about a subject.

I once heard a story from John Whitaker, who was Under Secretary of the Interior under President Nixon. John once suffered, truly *suffered*, an experience when on Capitol Hill testifying on matters relating to the Bureau of Indian Affairs (BIA) and accompanied by a top official of the BIA, Wes Franklin. When Whitaker was asked a particularly difficult question, he replied, "Mr. Chairman, I don't have that specific information, but I'm sure Mr. Franklin can answer the question." Franklin, however, only sat there beside him, with his arms folded across his chest, and slowly shook his head from side to side, without saying a word. I often relayed that story to my staff who were going to accompany me to a hearing. I would admonish them, "Don't *ever* do that to me! If I turn to you for help, and *you* do not know the answer, just politely say, 'Mr. Chairman, I don't have that information at hand. May I supply it later for the record?' *Do not* leave me sitting high and dry."

In the case of promoting passage of a new law through Congress, however, my usual preparation would not suffice. In that scenario, I had to be deeply knowledgeable and persuasive, winning over Senators and Representatives who had been around Washington a lot longer than I had, and many of whom were quite pleased not only with that fact but also with themselves.

Normally, members of a committee will not support a proposal that reduces their control over an agency. Thus, one might have expected Warren Magnuson, as a senior member of the Appropriations Committee, to object, because BPA self-financing would reduce the committee's detailed oversight of BPA, but this is where the personal relationship and his support for BPA came into play. His staff, after seeing my presentation and discussing my proposal, was supportive and so was he. Scoop Jackson signed on, as did Hatfield and Packwood. This gave me crucial support from all key Senators from the Pacific Northwest. Support from the regional, bi-partisan Congressional delegation was essential in getting a regional measure through Congress. When key Senators of both parties were in agreement and no constituents were upset, Representatives in the House had no reason to oppose the matter.

The plan was to have the bill considered on the Consent Calendar, the list of bills on which there is no known objection and which are unanimously passed as a matter of course with very few members (Senators or Representatives) on the floor. Members were pre-advised of what bills were to be taken up on the Consent Calendar, which their staffs could review for potential problems. If none were found, the member did not bother to show up. It was perfunctory. The key component was to make sure that every staffer for every Senator or Representative who might have an interest in the bill was satisfied that it was OK, which meant primarily that it did not encroach on anything they cared about. The only danger to a bill on the Consent Calendar is that if even a single Senator or Representative on the floor objects, the bill is sent back to committee and may never get passed.

The day the Bonneville Self-financing Act was passed, there were only four Senators on the floor, and none of those objected. That took a lot of very specific detailed work on my and my team's part to assure any possible opponent that the bill should not be opposed for any reason by any constituency—public power, private power, or any member of Congress. Our success was demonstrated by the fact that only four members were on the floor at the time it was on the calendar for the vote, which meant that there was no one who had any objection. Basically, the same thing happened in the House, and President Gerald Ford signed my bill into law.

The passage of the Bonneville Self-financing Act was one of only two or three bills relating to the Department of the Interior which were passed by Congress that year. I heard from Bill Lyon that at the end-of-year review by the Department's legislative office, someone said they got two bills passed, before someone else corrected, "And the Bonneville bill." The first speaker replied, "But that was easy, there were only four people on the floor (of the Senate and of House) when it passed." They had not helped at all and apparently had no idea how hard I had worked to make sure there were *only* so few on the floor at that time, which meant seeing to it that every possible opponent was satisfied that it was OK.

Those present were not there for any reason related to the vote on our bill. Bill Lyon understood all that and told me the story with some amusement and as an indication of how out of touch some of the people in that legislative affairs office were.

BPA now had the right to use the revenue it generated for its operations without having to seek appropriations. And we were now *expected* by Congress to operate the system without further appropriations. I was surprised by how much the self-financing act affected the staff at BPA. Suddenly they had a vested interest in seeing that it ran like a business and generated enough revenue to cover its operating expenses, which also meant they had an incentive to keep expenses within budget.

A huge issue going on during the time I was BPA Administrator was the growing opposition to development by environmental advocates. There was a joke going around about those who opposed various kinds of development. “NIMBY” meant Not in My Backyard, and “BANANA” meant Build Absolutely Nothing Anywhere Near Anything.

Opponents vociferously attacked the validity of load forecasts made by BPA and the electric utilities of the Pacific Northwest which were included in the joint Hydro-Thermal Power Program. Those forecasts projected a rate of growth consistent with the history of the region, requiring the building of additional generating capacity virtually every year. Since there were no large hydroelectric (dam) sites remaining to be developed, that meant new electricity had to come from either coal-fired or nuclear power plants. Solar and wind power were not yet commercially feasible.

As the opposition to new plants increased, and the availability of an increased power supply was postponed, Bernie Goldhammer periodically reported to me on large industrial electric load users who had called to inquire about obtaining large power contracts with BPA. He had to inform them that we had no additional supplies scheduled to allow us to take on new industrial customers; thus he turned them away.

This kind of thing was going on at other utilities. The effect, of course, was that the loads did not grow as rapidly as the combined utilities had predicted. The NIMBYs and BANANAs and other opponents of growth began pointing to that as proof that there was no need for additional power.

What was missed in the arguments made by the opponents was that this meant a slowing of economic growth in the entire Pacific Northwest. In conversations I had with the head of the Oregon Environmental Council, a man named Don Waggoner whom I had known since high school, it became apparent that the slowing of economic growth was not only acceptable, it was his and his cohorts’ objective.

A dedicated, single interest environmentalist, Waggoner was an advocate of producing less energy and also less food in order to protect the environment. When I pointed out that if the US reduced its food production, millions of people elsewhere in the world would starve to death, his response was an indication of his priorities: "Well, they will starve someday anyway, so this just speeds it up." Though I fully disagreed with such a heartless attitude, I respected his honesty (which contrasts with what we see today from those advocating draconian measures in the name of the environment), but the fact is that things which will reduce energy and food supplies condemn millions of people to severe suffering and premature deaths.

This was early in the growing environmental movement, and I set up these meetings with Waggoner because I knew him and hoped that our having known each other would enable us to find some common ground. He made this statement in what was probably our third meeting. He strongly opposed all new energy projects. For those three meetings he always brought his right-hand man with him. After he made the statement about letting people die, his sidekick parted company with him, I think because he suddenly saw the callous inhumanity of the extreme views Don supported.

Internet searches will now produce articles that criticize the utilities and BPA for making excessive forecasts. I argue that the forecasts were correct because they were made by utilities which were charged with providing reliable electric service to all customers. Further, one of the things I noticed immediately upon joining BPA was that virtually everyone at BPA (and at the other utilities) had the same attitude of public service. We all believed electricity was one of the greatest inventions of all time and that it provided a wonderful, enjoyable, and healthy life for millions of people. Only later did the governmental attitude shift toward forcing utilities to forecast that they would meet future loads through conservation (using methods which tended to constrict economic growth to the detriment of the people at the bottom of the economic pyramid).

Another major issue occurring during my time as BPA Administrator, and one which was used to oppose me at my 1982 confirmation hearing to be Secretary of Energy, was the ultimate failure of the Washington Public Power Supply System, known as WPPSS (and usually pronounced "Whoops"). As I wrote earlier, under the terms of the 1969 Hydro-Thermal Power Program (HTPP), the utilities, both public and private, of the Pacific Northwest combined their forecasts of future electric load growth. The result was an apparent need for one new, large power plant (roughly 1,000 MW) per year for the foreseeable future and, eventually, they forecast more than one such plant every year.

The plan included sequencing the power plants according to when a plant was needed to meet the projected load growth and then assigning a utility to build it. Each of the private utilities wanted to build a plant and was allocated a project and time to complete it. None of the public agencies (cities, PUDs, RECs) was large enough to take on such a large project by itself, so they got together and created WPPSS, which was on the list for three large—approximately 1,000-megawatt—nuclear power plants.

The contract for WPPSS Plant #1 had been executed on BPA's behalf by Russ Richmond. The contracts for the next two were developed and completed by the region's utilities and signed by me on behalf of BPA while I was Administrator. The regional Congressional delegation was fully on board with the plan. Remember, as I explained earlier, Russ, a Democrat, had been retained as Administrator under President Nixon primarily so that BPA could help negotiate and complete the HTPP.

While the heads of all the utilities, and we at BPA, were pressing ahead with implementing the HTPP, opposition to new power plants and transmission lines was growing, and because of the unavailability of large blocks of power for new, large industries, the load growth was slower than forecast, but virtually no one in the utility industry believed this was a trend. They believed that the new power plants were still going to be needed roughly on the schedule set out in the HTPP if the region were to continue to grow.

It was quite obvious—then and now—that if the utilities refuse to take on new, large industrial and commercial loads, total electric loads will not grow as much as forecast, fewer jobs will be created, and fewer people will be able to find jobs, meaning fewer people will move into a region. More recent commentaries can be found discussing the overly optimistic forecasts that were part of the HTPP from the perspective of thirty or forty years later and none that I have seen make note of this aspect of what they called the "faulty forecasts."

At that time in the evolution of the environmental movement, very few people, and essentially no utility executives, thought electric utilities should be responsible for limiting the economic prosperity and jobs in the region by deciding not to build power plants. It was not their role to stunt economic growth.

In retrospect, the opponents of growth were successful, as they effectively blocked the building of new power supplies, so the utilities were forced to turn away prospective large, job-creating loads, and the demand for new power did not grow nearly as fast as had been anticipated. It was essentially a self-fulfilling prophecy: "We will stop you from building new power plants, so you will not be able to sign up new customers, and then you don't need more power."

In 1976, Jimmy Carter was elected President over the incumbent, Gerald Ford, and, of course, the expectation was that his incoming Secretary of the Interior, former Idaho Governor Cecil Andrus, would have me replaced at BPA by a Democrat. He did not like me, and the feeling was mutual, primarily stemming from the fact that, as Governor, he had once tried to force me to sell power to Idaho Power Company in violation of the BPA statute. He simply refused to acknowledge that my hands were tied by the law because the Bonneville Power Act required BPA to reserve its power for public power customers and legally BPA could only sell power to non-public customers (investor-owned utilities) that was judged to be excess to the needs of the public systems.

Andrus invited me to a meeting in his office at the Capitol in Boise and essentially demanded that I sell low-cost power to Idaho Power Company for the benefit of Idaho citizens. I tried to explain why I could not legally do so. He refused to acknowledge that I was right and remained hostile to me afterward. All he could see was that BPA power would lower the electric rates to users in Idaho, which would have been politically good for him as Governor.

Shortly after the November 1976 election, however, Senator Scoop Jackson's staff called my office, asking if I could give him a ride on the BPA airplane to Spokane, Washington, for a non-political speech. We could carry members of Congress in our planes for a government purpose but not for campaign purposes. Providing non-political transport to key Senators was, of course, a wonderful opportunity on which both Russ Richmond and I capitalized—taking any opportunity to spend an hour or two uninterrupted with Senator Jackson. I made sure that I accompanied Jackson, and the official record showed accurately that I had a meeting on the plane with him, which removed any risk that we could be criticized for flying Senator Jackson on our plane.

I hung around during and after his speech, while Scoop answered questions from the press. He was asked what was in store for BPA under a new leader since everyone expected the new administration to replace me as soon as possible. To my utter surprise he announced that he would insist that I stay on. He stated that I had done a good job of leading BPA and had not politicized the agency, so there was no need to replace me. When I subsequently asked him about his bold statement, Scoop confided that he had no confidence that Andrus would take advice from him on who should head BPA, so that meant he did not want me to leave. Once Jackson took that position no one in the Pacific Northwest Congressional opposed him. Republicans had no desire to see me replaced and the Democrats did not want to oppose Scoop. Although all the behind-the-scenes machinations were not known publicly, I took it as a very high compliment that Jackson felt that way.

However, I was now a subordinate in a department run by partisan Democrats. Unlike Russ Richmond's experience when the situation was reversed, I had zero influence with them. Anytime there was a problem I had to enlist the help of Senators Jackson or Magnuson. Of course, I felt that even I could not be calling them every day or so without wearing out my welcome.

The new Assistant Secretary for Water and Power, Joan Davenport, was the official through whom I reported to the Secretary. She distrusted the bureaucracy, although I did not understand why she felt that way as a Democrat. But it was interesting nonetheless, in that we Republicans also distrusted the bureaucracy, which was made up mostly of Democrats.

On my only visit to Joan's office, her desk had several stacks, at least a foot tall, of contracts. A lawyer before her appointment, Joan, not trusting the bureaucracy, felt that it was her duty to read through every proposed contract from any agency reporting to her. She never understood the important stuff while she buried herself in contract boilerplate language, not being able to see the forest for the trees, as the old saying goes. Those in the Department who reported to her quickly figured out that she would not have time to look over their shoulders at the significant things they were doing as long as she had *enough* contracts to read—so they loaded her down with all kinds of them. It was a great lesson in bureaucracy and how it could effectively neutralize a senior official.

With Dave, Barbara, and Mom at my BPA retirement dinner (Bonneville Power Administration/Department of the Interior)

In the summer of 1977, Congress passed legislation establishing the new Department of Energy, one of two "DOEs" created at the urging of the new President, the other being the Department of Education. President Carter signed the bill into law and nominated James Schlesinger, who had been Secretary of Defense under Presidents Nixon and Ford, a former Director of the CIA, and a former head of the Atomic Energy Commission to be the first Secretary of Energy. Schlesinger was also a great friend of Scoop Jackson. As part of the legislation, the "power-marketing agencies" of the Department of the Interior (such as BPA) were transferred to the Department of Energy.

As soon as Schlesinger was confirmed on August 9, 1977, I called Scoop and asked if he was ready for me to leave BPA, telling him, "BPA is being eaten alive by the bureaucrats in Washington, and I have no clout with them." He asked me to be patient for a few more months while he worked through the process of getting my successor cleared. It turned out that his candidate was Sterling Munro, his own executive assistant for many years, who had run Scoop's unsuccessful effort to win the Democratic Presidential nomination in 1976.

By the end of 1977 Jackson was successful in getting Munro approved by Secretary Schlesinger, and I retired from the Bonneville Power Administration—and, I thought, from government service—on December 31, 1977. It had been a wonderful, fulfilling experience but I was ready for the next chapter in my life.

CHAPTER 11
OFF TO WASHINGTON

A question I was often asked after my eight years in Washington was which job I liked best, being Secretary of Energy or Secretary of the Interior. The answer from an intensity standpoint, clearly, was Energy. It was a huge Department with a (then) $15 billion budget and 140,000 workers (125,000 contractors and 15,000 departmental employees). But it was not controversial. It was responsible for making the nuclear weapons for the US, and when it came to energy, DOE could study, fund research, and talk about energy needs and production, but had no authority to make decisions that really affected either.

Interior, on the other hand, was quite a bit smaller, with only a $6 billion budget at the time, and 70,000 employees. But it was highly controversial, a political minefield, being responsible for managing a majority of the over 30 percent of the land in America that is owned by the US Government, with the US Forest Service, an agency of the Department of Agriculture, managing the national forests. Interior controlled the leasing (or refusing to lease) millions of acres of land and millions of square miles of the continental shelf, under which rested billions of barrels of oil, billions of tons of coal, and trillions of cubic feet of natural gas. With all those resources, the ongoing wars against the combustion engine are ridiculous, political ploys for more control of Americans' daily lives. For these dynamics and for the sheer beauty of America's natural resources, national parks, and wide-open spaces, I often repeated Jim Watt's line, that the Department's responsibilities were "wrapped around the heartstrings of America."

A speech I gave in 1974 while BPA Administrator titled "Prophets of Shortage" was openly hostile to extremists in the environmental movement. In the speech, I included a section noting that they were totally—and almost solely—focused on stopping all coal electric generating plants, but I predicted, "Once they stop coal, they will turn with equal vigor to stop the use of natural gas."

While I was at the Bonneville Power Administration, I served on the board of directors of the Electric Power Research Institute (EPRI), headquartered in Palo Alto, California. It was a prestigious and important organization of all of the major electric power producers in the US in which they cooperated on research affecting the production and transportation of electricity. At one of the meetings, we were "treated" to a presentation by Ralph Cavanagh, an environmental advocate I had known since sometime in the 1970s when he was actively opposing new power projects in the Pacific Northwest. In his speech, Ralph described how the environmental movement was determined to stop the burning of coal to generate electricity, and that part of that strategy was to cause utilities to switch to natural gas because it produced less carbon dioxide. However, he also stated without emphasizing the point that natural gas generation still produced an unacceptable amount of carbon dioxide.

In subsequent conversations with utility executives, I made the point over and over that they should not allow themselves to be misled into thinking they would not eventually be under attack for having natural gas-fired power plants. Many utility executives did not really believe that natural gas would become the subject of environmental attacks, although they certainly know better now. That, of course, is exactly what has happened and continues to happen right up to the present. As I was writing this part of my story, Biden Administration extremists were still trying to do just that with their war on gas-fired electric power plants, as well as gas stoves, heaters, and furnaces. If or when they again get political power to do so, there is no doubt in my mind they will resume this same nonsense. After leaving the Reagan Administration and Washington, DC, I wrote about these disingenuous maneuvers.

In 1993, Regnery Publishing President Al Regnery, who was a friend and on whose governing board I sat, approached me about writing a book, which was a new thought to me. Al found a professional writer, Bob Deitz, with the understanding that while I would be responsible for all of the content, Bob would take my thoughts and put them into readable prose, while doing background research and filling the gaps in what I knew personally about the industry from my years as Secretary of Energy. The book was released in 1994 and titled *Crisis in the Oil Patch.*

I wrote about the damage done to the energy industry in the 1980s during the Reagan Administration. Essentially, the US had persuaded Saudi Arabia to increase its supply of oil in order to drop the world price to around $10 per barrel to deprive the Soviet Union of hard currency, thereby crippling its ability to engage in an arms race with the US. The strategy was successful, but it played havoc with the US oil industry, especially oil producers, causing the loss of jobs for hundreds of thousands of people who worked in the industry and reducing the volume of oil produced in the United States. I presented some ideas about how to defend the US oil industry against future outside attacks in the form of raising and lowering the price of oil.

My foreword to the book also provided a good summary of my eight years working for President Reagan:

> *From January 1981 to January 1989, I spent all my time in the Departments of the Interior and Energy of the United States. It will always be a frustration to me that an administration supported by the American oil and gas industry could not do nearly enough in return. This is true especially because I believe that the energy industry forms the backbone of our economic system and our much-envied way of life.*
>
> *Many people did not know that the Department of the Interior, where I was Under Secretary and, later, Secretary, has more to do with implementing energy policy than*

the Department of Energy. The Department of Energy, where I served as Secretary for nearly two years, simply talked about energy policy; it recommended action, but had no power to dispose of energy issues. Interior, on the other hand, is charged with managing one-third of the United States that is owned by the federal government, plus the Outer Continental Shelf where vast energy resources lie. The Interior Department has jurisdiction of the leasing, exploration, and development of truly huge potential energy supplies—not only oil and natural gas, but coal, geothermal, tar sands, oil shale, and other resources of power available to our energy-dependent modern civilization.

During my tenure in the Reagan Administration, I came to know and respect many of the key players in the oil and gas industry. They were, almost without exception, dedicated patriots more interested in the nation's future than in their bank balances. These independent oil and gas producers were prepared to do whatever was required, within reason, to keep essential energy flowing to Americans.

I often described the difficulties of being Secretary of the Interior with an example of what could happen on any given day. He could be faced with a decision as to what to do with 400,000 acres, or even four million acres, of federal land, usually in the western United States. The National Park Service would want to make it into a national park; the Fish and Wildlife Service wanted a wildlife refuge; the Bureau of Reclamation wanted to dam up any water in sight and sell it to someone. And the Bureau of Land Management wanted to lease the land for cattle grazing, or for mineral development, or logging, or recreation, or all of the above!

Meanwhile, as that battle was raging, in came the Bureau of Indian Affairs and said, "Forget it, folks, it's belonged to the Indians all along." (Note that I used the word *Indians*, not *Native Americans*, or *Indigenous Peoples*, as are common nowadays. The agency was—and is—named the Bureau of *Indian* Affairs so I will use that term—respectfully—in this book.)

The Secretary, therefore, found himself among several rocks and hard places with no way to win. If he agreed with one of the agencies, he offended the other four constituencies. If he insisted on a compromise, he offended all five!

When I became Secretary of the Interior in the second Reagan Administration, I wanted to learn more about the history of the Department—and we had an employee of the Department of the Interior (DOI) who had made it his avocation to examine that history. From time to time, I asked him to make presentations at my weekly staff meetings so that the top staff could learn DOI's history. As a result of one of his lectures I learned an anecdote I could use in my speeches: After talking about some of the difficulties of being Secretary of the Interior I would pause and then say, with apparent relief, "It was the greatest consolation of my life to find out that this job has never been a stepping-stone to anything!" (This was a twist in perspective on what was said to me years earlier by Oregon's national committeewoman when I served as state party chairman.) I would continue, "The second Secretary resigned after only eleven days. He wrote to President Millard Fillmore that his 'peculiar nervous temperament could not stand the stress.'"

Before I became Secretary of either Department, of course, I served as Under Secretary of the Interior to my friend James Watt for twenty-one months. Here is how that came about.

After leaving Bonneville Power on December 31, 1977, I opened an energy consulting firm called Hodel Associates. The company began to grow as I worked with clients and, for three years, I was happy to be living in Oregon and working with Barbara in a *much* smaller enterprise than BPA. Suddenly, that was about to change.

Shortly after the 1980 Presidential elections and Ronald Reagan's landslide victory over incumbent President Jimmy Carter, I received a phone call from Oregon US Senator Mark Hatfield. He was influential both with the Reagan people and, of course, inside Oregon, and he knew of the important job responsibilities held by the Administrator of BPA. Mark asked if he could put my name in the hat for Secretary of the Interior.

I was flattered both by the offer and by the fact that Hatfield thought enough of me to recommend me for a Cabinet post, even though we had not always seen eye to eye (remember my battle with his handpicked Republican state chairman, Pete Gunnar). However, I attempted to decline his request, because I did not want to leave Oregon and, although I did not say it, I knew that Barbara loved living in Oregon and had really disliked living in the heat of the Eastern Shore of Maryland, not far from Washington, DC. Senator Hatfield and I discussed the situation back and forth for a considerable time before he finally persuaded me to let him enter my name. When I hung up the phone, I cried.

Shedding tears was a very untypical response for me. In fact, it startled me. Then I realized that even though the odds were very much against my being chosen (there were so many ambitious people seeking these top jobs who were much better connected politically than I was), by agreeing to let my name be put on the list I had agreed to change my life, and uproot Barbara and me, and move to Washington, DC, if I were selected by President-elect Reagan

A short time later, I learned that Jim Watt was also on the short list of potential nominees for Secretary of the Interior. After he interviewed me for my first post at BPA back in late 1969, and I got the job, we worked together very closely. He was essentially my boss at the Interior Department in his role as Deputy Assistant Secretary for Water and Power. BPA officially reported to Jim's boss, Jim Smith, of course, but as he had let Watt interview me initially, he basically delegated BPA to him, which they both preferred. This was another of those unplanned happenings that served to further my career, as Watt and I got to know each other well and became friends along the way.

Watt had moved on at Interior to head its Bureau of Outdoor Recreation, which dealt with recreational land and water resources, and during the Carter Administration, he became president of the Mountain States Legal Foundation (MSLF) in Denver, a nonprofit legal firm which protected individual property rights from government intrusion. Joe Coors, one of President Reagan's Kitchen

Cabinet (Reagan's closest confidants, including influential donors who had helped finance his Gubernatorial and Presidential campaigns), was the primary donor behind MSLF.

I called Jim and said that I was withdrawing my name, offering any support I could give to him. But Jim, with his typical analytical approach, told me that I should leave my name on the list. He said that would increase the chance that one of us strong conservatives would be chosen, adding, "If one of us gets it, the other can be his Under Secretary." (The Under Secretary was equivalent to the chief operating officer in a business.)

I was well acquainted with that number two role, having been deputy to Russ Richmond at BPA, and I did *not* want to be Jim's Under Secretary. I knew him well and my instinct was that he might be difficult to work with and that even though he was my friend, he was going to be controversial and therefore it would be a difficult job. So, I made no response to his comment. He also knew me well enough to realize that my silence meant I did not want to be his Under Secretary.

When I hung up the phone and told Barbara what I had done on the call with Watt, I expected her to be pleased because it meant that we were not moving to Washington, DC. Instead, she set aside her own strong personal preference for staying in Oregon, looked at me and said, "Do you mean to tell me that after all these years talking about what ought to be done in Washington, you're being offered a high-ranking policy position, and you're *going to turn it down*?"

Her question opened my eyes to my shortsightedness. After further discussion with Barbara confirming that she really was willing to move to Washington if I got the job, I called Watt and reminded him that I did not *want* to go to Washington, but I told him that if he became Secretary and could not find someone else who was satisfactory to him as Under Secretary, I would do it. "But," I pleaded, "please don't do me any favors."

Reagan's victory coattails had been long enough to sweep Republicans into the majority party in the United States Senate, although Democrats retained control of the House of Representatives.

With a new majority Republican Senate taking office on January 3, 1981, the Senate pre-confirmed nominees for key positions even before Reagan would be inaugurated on January 20. New Cabinet Secretaries would officially take office only after President Reagan was sworn in at noon, January 20, at which time, new Department heads and their top staff could occupy their offices and start to work.

President-elect Reagan chose Jim Watt to be his Secretary of the Interior, and Jim's nomination was approved by the Senate on Friday, January 9. The next morning, Saturday, January 10, 1981, as I sat eating breakfast with my family at our home in Lake Oswego, Oregon, the phone rang. I answered to hear Jim say, "This is that phone call you've been dreading." He was, of course, following up our prior conversation about each serving as the other's number two with the request that I come to Washington to become his Under Secretary. He assured me he had found no one better, admitting that he had not even looked.

I was both dismayed and excited. Dismayed to be leaving Oregon as my home for the first time since boarding that train for Harvard when I was 18; but thrilled to have the *unexpected* opportunity to serve at a very high level in our government. Without further discussion I told him I would be there the following Wednesday. By coincidence I had a meeting for my consulting business Tuesday in Boston, Massachusetts. I arranged to fly down to Washington after my meeting in Boston rather than immediately returning to Portland as I had originally planned.

I could not resist calling Don Pearlman to tell him what had happened. He was pleased and immediately told me that I needed to negotiate what my role would be and what the scope of my authority would be. That is typical of Don's very careful approach to such matters, and it would normally be very good advice. However, I knew Jim Watt, and I knew that if I handled the job the way it should be done, the scope of my authority would never be a question.

Don's reaction was similar to that of a good friend and stalwart Reagan campaigner named Frank Whetstone, who later came to see me in my new office and told me that my office was too far from the Secretary's office (at the other end of a long corridor). He believed that it was necessary for me to be right next to the boss's office to avoid being left out of important meetings. Neither Don nor Frank knew, though, how close Jim and I were and how inclusive Jim would be with me.

My previously planned trip to Boston was to meet with a major prospective client of my consulting business. Continental Hydro was proposing to put small electric generating plants on small streams without altering the environment, which seemed to be very appealing at the time. However, I packed my bag for the trip with the expectation that I would take the job in Washington, anticipating that I would have to tell Continental Hydro that I would not be able to work with them. However, to my surprise, while I was in Boston, I became so enthusiastic about the prospect of working with this new client that I decided that I needed to tell Jim Watt that I simply could not accept the job at Interior.

Watt and I had agreed to meet in the lobby of the venerable Mayflower Hotel, on Connecticut Avenue, NW, that Wednesday and talk over lunch. As I exited the taxi and approached the hotel, I saw Jim walking toward me with a big smile on his face. He extended his hand to shake mine and the first words out of his mouth were, "I cleared you with the Kitchen Cabinet this morning, and I'm meeting with the Senate Republicans this afternoon."

My stomach immediately filled with butterflies. I had an instant recognition that there was no way I could take back my commitment to him after he had gone that far, no matter how badly I wanted to build my consulting business by working with the client in Boston.

So, after a lunch where we had our first of many discussions of what needed to be done at Interior and how to do it, Jim left for the Senate Republicans meeting and I quickly called another energy consultant, Bob Mooney, and connected him with the Boston opportunity. Bob was a longtime friend who had been doing similar work back in the Pacific Northwest. As it happened, Bob made quite a success of the opportunity over the next eight to ten years, so my instinct that Boston was a big opportunity was accurate.

Only later did I learn that Watt had to fight for me to be nominated as his Under Secretary. The White House Presidential Personnel Office had suggested several prospective nominees to Watt, and my name was not on their list. He went directly to Helene von Damm, Director of Presidential Personnel, and asked bluntly, "Helene, am I going to be the Secretary, or are you all going to try to run the Department from over here?" My name was then approved for nomination by the President

Earlier in life, whenever successes happened, my mother cautioned me against hubris. "Don't get a big head, Baby," she'd say. Often as a married adult, I still found that when I did something that I was proud of, I characteristically kept myself from enjoying it because I heard her well-intentioned voice in my head. I have learned that some psychologists call this haunting aspect "the committee in your head," voices of anyone in one's past whose unsolicited counsel persists, and help their patients learn to turn off that audio.

Mom simply had a strong personality, and she was exceedingly proper in manner. As most any mother would do, she shared her opinions with her children—and her grandchildren. I learned from my son Dave after the summers he lived with her that she had a similar impact on him, as later, when he did or said something, he would often hear Grandma's voice giving him advice.

When I was in the Cabinet, I began to feel uncharacteristically burdened by the job. Fortunately, I have always been self-analytical, and I realized that if I could not enjoy the most prestigious job I had ever had or ever would have, something was wrong. What I figured out was that I was not able to feel *good* about my successes, hearing "Don't get a big head, Baby," but I was able to feel *bad* about my mistakes or failures. Therefore, the job had no upside and was unrewarding (or worse), and it was no fun at all. Once I realized what my reaction was, I knew that I needed someone with whom I could freely share my successes. I described my problem to Barbara and told her what I needed: someone to whom I could brag without having to appear to be modest by downplaying my pride in my success. She was very understanding and said she was willing to play that role—which she enjoyed far more than laboring to critique my speeches earlier in my career. I could trust Barbara to listen without her suggesting I was getting a big head. This allowed me to enjoy, at least in private, my successes, which offset the discouragement of being all too aware of my failures.

My mother was also a big cheerleader, however. After I had moved to Washington, DC, to work at Interior, she told me, "If I have to put up with you being so far away, at least I could see your name in the paper now and then."

I told her: "Mom, if my name is in the paper, it means I'm in trouble. If my picture is with it, it means I'm in *deep* trouble!"

"Oh!" she said, looking alarmed, "then I don't want to see *that*!"

In fact, in Washington, I avoided media attention for myself, especially after seeing the attacks they made on Jim Watt. I was so good at keeping a low profile that *The Oregonian,* Oregon's leading newspaper, once wrote that I was as quotable as Harpo Marx (the Marx brother who pretended to be mute while performing).

A Cabinet Secretary has essentially unlimited authority to divide up responsibilities of those reporting to him, and his top staff have not historically been those of his own choosing. For instance, the Under Secretary has not always been someone the secretary even knew beforehand. We were told that under Jim Watts immediate predecessor, Cecil Andrus, the sole responsibility he assigned to the Under Secretary was overseeing the protection of a single species of endangered whale, and nothing else.

As far as I could tell Andrus's Under Secretary wasn't even included in many of the Secretary's meetings. Fortunately for Jim Watt and me, we were already friends. He trusted my loyalty and my management skills. He wanted me to work with him and his other top staff in discussing and deciding what to do on all the issues confronting the Department, and then it was my responsibility to see that his decisions were implemented. This was a role that I loved, being second in command, the implementer of decisions made by a good leader—like Frank Breuer at G-P, Russ Richmond at BPA, and now, Jim Watt at Interior. Although Jim always corrected me when I said I was his number two man. He said, "Hodel, I think you are my number one man."

There were occasions on which it seemed to me the discussion was moving in the wrong direction, and Jim was getting close to making a decision that could create problems. My usual approach at such a time was to say nothing, which was different from my normal full participation in the discussions. If I remained silent, as the decision was nearing completion Watt would notice my silence, and he'd look at me and say, "You don't agree with this, do you, Hodel?"

I never acknowledged that I disagreed with his decisions. What I would say was something along the lines of, "It's not that. It's just that I'm trying to figure out how we would answer this question…" Or "…how we would deal with this problem when it comes up…" I would then state my concern.

On every occasion where I did this in our two years together at Interior, Jim would immediately see the implications and say something like, "You're right! We can't do what we were thinking about." Ever after, he was generous in his praise. Whenever he mentioned the decision I had raised concerns about, he would always give me credit for avoiding a problem and say something like, "I was going to do [such and such] until Hodel pointed out that would be a big mistake." Again, I never made any such statement. I simply asked a question that Jim answered quickly and correctly in his own mind. He was a gifted decision maker but, unlike many leaders in positions like his, he did not have to claim credit for every decision.

I would always demur and say, "I never said it was wrong. I just asked a question, and you provided the answer."

Also, Watt never did anything to limit my authority as his Under Secretary. On one occasion, he and I were sitting at a large round conference table while a Deputy Assistant Secretary made a presentation to Watt, seeking his approval for some idea the deputy had. He sat to my left across from Watt who sat to my right. As the deputy neared his conclusion, he attempted to slide a memo across the table to Watt. Without thinking, I instinctively reached out and slapped my hand down on the memo, saying, "I haven't seen that yet." Neither man said anything, and the meeting ended.

As Watt and I were walking away and out of earshot of the other man, he turned to me and said, "Hodel, I'm so proud of you. If you had let him do that, you would have lost control of the Department." I was relieved to know that Jim understood what I was doing and supported it. It was essential that I be seen as totally aligned with the Secretary and that I was someone whom he wanted to look at everything that was being presented to him.

One of the key staff people in Watt's Interior Department was Stan Hulett, our head of Congressional relations, who had known Watt much longer than I, and had been his deputy when Watt ran DOI's Bureau of Outdoor Recreation years earlier under President Nixon. Stan was highly competent and was very close to Watt. It was a significant day when Stan came to me and asked me to persuade Jim to do a particular thing. Prior to that time, Stan would have assumed that his long association with Jim was more influential than mine. It made me realize that Jim showed all his key people that he viewed me as his chief operating officer and that they should, also.

Watt was justified in placing that trust in me. Once he made a final decision, I would never ever have even considered doing something that I knew he didn't want, even if I thought he was making a mistake. I strongly felt that he was the ultimate decision maker and that I owed him either my loyalty or my resignation. Too many appointees in Washington are quite happy to undercut or manipulate their bosses—their loyalty, if any, being only on the surface.

One of my strengths was in reading people. I knew from my years of working with Jim that if I told him I disagreed with him on an issue, his natural tendency would be to dig in and defend his position. That's why I chose to let him ask me why I wasn't speaking up in support of a decision that was being made.

Occasionally, though, I had trouble understanding why Watt made the decisions that he did. He was highly intuitive, by which I mean he did not consciously analyze a situation and then reach a conclusion but saw the key factors and just knew what needed to be done. Since my job was to carry out decisions Jim made, I needed to understand why it was the right decision in order to be able to execute it properly.

In those instances when he made a particular decision and I could not figure out why, I would go home and Barbara and I would get together to discuss it. I would stand at the flip chart and try to analyze with her why he made the decision that he did. Almost always we came up with a solid understanding of Jim's outcome. And, unlike the meetings in my office that she attended, where she could not say anything, she was a full and helpful participant in these sessions.

I would go into his office the next day and tell him what I had figured out. He would smile broadly and say, "What's so great about you, Hodel, is that I make a decision, and the next day you come in and tell my why it was right!"

A practice that I learned from Russ Richmond when I was his deputy at Bonneville Power was something that I continued with Jim Watt. Russ explained that before I got to BPA, whenever he was traveling and called in from the road and asked, "What's going on?" the staff person he left in charge would customarily reply, "Nothing," or "Everything's fine," which, he said, "drove me nuts." He knew BPA well enough to expect that everyday there were issues to be decided or problems to be dealt with. He said that when he himself had been BPA deputy (to Chuck Luce), he would keep a list of almost everything that happened so that when Chuck called in he could give him as much information as Chuck had time for.

So, I followed that practice for Russ as his deputy and I did the same for Watt at DOI. With all the complexities of a federal Cabinet agency, sometimes I had the entire side of a 3x5 index card covered with lists of things I had written in very small handwriting on which to update him or on which to get his input. Sometimes, Jim had time only for one or two of the most important items, and occasionally he had time for all, but he always left the call feeling like he was fully aware of the most important things happening in his absence.

When I became Secretary—in each Department—I asked Earl Gjelde to do the same for me, having learned from those experiences that no boss wants to call the office and be told "nothing's happening" or "no, we don't need you just now." After I left government, I continued that practice and hope that many of my former direct reports are now using the same system in their current roles.

One of the things I was most pleased with as Under Secretary was the follow-up system I developed—of course using my flip chart—in which each decision was broken down into written action items and a timeline for completing them. I called it Management by Objectives (MBO), using the well-proven management term for the system that I had learned years earlier in the American Management Association course I took in 1973 after becoming BPA Administrator. This resulted in a rather informal looking list of assignments and dates for completing them. Each week, I sat down with the head of each of the ten agencies of the Interior Department and their top staff and would go through each of the action items to find out how they were doing in meeting the timeline.

I discovered two important aspects of government agencies right away. First, I learned a lesson about asking the right question. The Bureau of Indian Affairs was scheduled to produce a long-term plan by mid-June 1981, and each week I asked about the various things they were working on. On the long-term plan, I asked, "Will you have something for me to review?" as the deadline came nearer. Each time I was told that they would. And it was true, but what I got was not a long-term plan. It was a request for a multi-month extension of the deadline! I never made that mistake again.

Next, I learned that as rudimentary as my MBO approach might have appeared, it was much more effective than a detailed, computer-based system. One of the DOI Assistant Secretaries, Garrey Carruthers, a former professor and, later, the very successful Governor of New Mexico, proposed that he and his team develop a much more detailed, computerized set of tasks than I had constructed. It was so detailed, however, that no overview at my level was even possible in a timely fashion and, therefore, it was not useful.

From January 1981 until October 1982, when I learned that I was actually going to become Secretary of Energy, I was entirely engrossed in my job. Serving as Watt's Under Secretary gave me great satisfaction in doing a job that was important and totally demanding. Barbara, in her typical 100 percent supportive manner, told me that she would manage all of our personal affairs, and I should devote myself full time to my job. She was magnificent and sheltered me from crises, such as arranging for all the repairs after a tenant had trashed our house in Lake Oswego. I only learned about the damage long after the cleanup was done.

Barbara enabled me to focus entirely on managing the Department and supporting Jim Watt. It meant long hours going through multiple documents, lengthy meetings, and strategizing on how to deal with specific issues that arose along the way and trying to accomplish the policy objective that Jim and I, and his other top staff, had agreed to. Sometimes, we would have one or more long meetings attempting to boil down an issue to its essential elements so that we could present it to the Secretary in thirty minutes or less for his decision. This was the opposite of the "bury the boss under details" used by some to keep the boss out of their affairs. I worked from 8:00 a.m. or earlier each day until 10:30 or 11:00 p.m., six days a week, taking time off for church on Sunday mornings, followed by an afternoon nap, and then digging into my briefcase for a few hours before bedtime.

Barbara was unwavering in her steadfast support and her successful efforts to be with me. Many nights and weekends she came to my large and comfortable office and sat there reading or doing her beautiful crewel work (a type of embroidery) much as if we were sitting in a nice home. I also made it a practice to invite her to come to my office for any meeting she *could* attend—either where all participants were Interior employees or a meeting with an outsider who was a personal friend of ours. There was only one rule we agreed upon: she could not say anything whatsoever in the meetings other than pleasantries such as "Hello," because if the

Secretary's wife contributed an opinion, it would immediately change the dynamics of the meeting and cause staff to wonder what input she was giving to the boss, as well as whether they were allowed to disagree with her. As a result, she became friends with the staff, and they became comfortable with her. Also, it meant that she was fully up to date on many of the things with which I was dealing, so that I did not have to try to repeat what had happened that day. She also was an active participant in meetings of the committee that scheduled my events (speeches, meetings with various groups, and travel) as Cabinet Secretary. She knew me well enough to know how much I could do and when I would need a break in my schedule. She protected me against staff overscheduling me.

Watt had a couple of interesting things to say about my workload. About three months into the job, after all the major decisions on policy matters had been made and it was my job to shepherd them through, he walked into my office and, with a big smile, said, "Ya' know, I've figured it out and I'm jealous. You have the *fun* job around here." He meant, of course, that once the policies and programs had been agreed upon with his participation and final approval, implementing those decisions fell entirely to me and the rest of the staff—the "fun" part of the job.

On another occasion Jim came into my office and told me that he was very much bothered by the fact that while he was going home exhausted at the end of the workday, leaving about 6:00 p.m., he knew that I was staying late into the night. I pointed out that my job was time-consuming but relatively stress free. He had to contend with so many things, such as ceremonial meetings and other events which required his presence as Secretary, Congressional demands, testifying at hearings, giving multiple speeches, dealing with endless news media assaults, and the like, as well as being constantly under hostile attacks. "That's what's really wearing on the boss," I told him. "Sitting here for long hours running the Department does not create at all the same kind of stress." When I became Secretary of Energy and then later returned to

Interior as Secretary, I experienced firsthand what I had seen Jim dealing with.

One other thing Barb and I very much enjoyed in Washington, beginning when I was Under Secretary, was attending fundraising receptions for Republican members of Congress—both Representatives and Senators. We adopted that practice after going to our first reception for the Alaska Congressional Delegation—Senators Ted Stevens and Frank Murkowski, and Congressman Don Young. It was great! Lots of fresh Alaskan salmon and king crab, plus piles of other goodies. The next day Young called to thank me for attending. I replied, "Oh, no. I need to thank you for inviting me." He then explained to me that I was doing him a favor because as soon as my staff told his office that I would be attending, his office would call the lobbyists who dealt with the Department of the Interior to tell them "Under Secretary Hodel will be there." That encouraged those lobbyists to pay the fee to buy a ticket, and such fees went to the campaigns of the candidates. For Cabinet and sub-Cabinet level officials there is no prohibition on attending political functions because they are Presidential appointees and exempt from the restrictions against political campaigning which apply to other government positions.

From that day forward I viewed it as part of my responsibility to assist where I could by attending as many of those functions as possible, and it was great because Barbara and I ate better than we would have at home—and often, at multiple receptions in an evening, although, the food was always more plentiful at the earlier events than at the ones we got to later in the evening. I was always busy mingling, and Barbara would kindly visit the food tables and bring me a plate.

More importantly, I found that I was often able to learn things at those receptions by talking with people who would never have been able to get an appointment to see me in my office. Finally, as I wrote in an earlier chapter, since I did not drink alcohol, my driver could drop us back at the Department and I could still be sharp and get back to work after such affairs. All in all, it was a mutually beneficial and, for Barbara and me, an enjoyable arrangement. There were, however, other things that were not quite so enjoyable.

As I've indicated, Jim Watt was often under attack in the media as Interior Secretary, and there were times when attacks were made against him without any foundation whatsoever. Many of Jim's comments that were reported as "outlandish" happened in hearings where the listeners understood that he was being humorous, but which the media and others seeking to hurt him misquoted or treated as serious statements in order to ridicule him.

One awful example of this was at a hearing before a House committee shortly after he became Secretary. I recall this instance differently from the version that was reported by the *Washington Post*. The common theme is that Jim's Christian faith was ridiculed. As I recall, Congressman Jim Weaver from Oregon asked, "Mr. Secretary, is the reason you don't believe in conservation because you believe in the second coming of Christ?" Jim was shocked and had long vowed that he would not defend his faith if attacked for it. All he said was something like, "Congressman, I'm shocked by what you said."

The next day several environmental groups put out fundraising letters proclaiming, "Secretary Watt opposes conservation because he expects the Second Coming soon!" There was at that point no way of catching up with that story and putting a stop to the total falsehood which exists to this day. (In my personal experience, none of the mainstream media are honest about Republicans in general, but especially not about those they target for ridicule, like Jim Watt.)

A funny side to this, however, occurred as a result of the newspaper articles about this issue. Secretary of Defense Caspar Weinberger's press secretary was asked if Secretary Weinberger believed in the second coming, to which his press secretary replied, "I assume he does. He's a Christian." To which the reporter responded in amazement, "He is? I thought he was an Episcopalian."

Perhaps the most well-known assault on Jim was in 1982 when the National Park Service canceled future July 4th rock and roll concerts on the National Mall. I recall the day the story broke in the *Washington Post*. When I walked into Jim's office that morning, he looked at me and asked, "Who are The Beach Boys?" "I have no idea," I said. We obviously were unaware that they had performed in earlier years' July 4th celebrations. We only knew that the US Park Police had reported assaults, rampant drug use, and other crimes committed during the 1982 July 4th concert by a rock band, The Grass Roots.

As Jim later wrote in his book *The Courage of a Conservative*, in order to attract a different crowd, he instructed the Park Service to announce that future July 4th concerts would feature inspirational and patriotic music to appeal to a family audience. The Beach Boys were not mentioned. He never said The Beach Boys were unpatriotic. He did not even know who they were.

News stories began to accuse Watt of personally cancelling The Beach Boys by name, which was not true, and which ignited a firestorm of protest. Claims were made that The Beach Boys performing on Independence Day was a tradition. They had performed at least twice previously, but that hardly qualified as a tradition, and the facts made no difference when the object of attack was Watt. A story highly critical of Watt included a quote from Nancy Reagan saying that she had "raised her kids on The Beach Boys." This, of course, was told to the press to make plain that the White House was not endorsing Watt's supposed criticism of this popular group.

The furor would not die down. Each day it seemed there were more false stories about the incident. Reagan had an aide, David Gergen, who, in my opinion, never liked Jim Watt. Gergen was among those on the President's staff who wanted to believe that if the President and all his appointees made nice, the mainstream media would come to like the President. Gergen got the bright idea of presenting Jim with a plaster cast of a foot with a bullet hole in it which he called the "Shot yourself in the foot award." It was presented to Watt at a ceremony in the Rose Garden. Afterward, Gergen said to Jim, "Thanks for being a good sport, Mr. Secretary." To which Watt replied, "I'm not. I'm a good *soldier*."

Watt wrote in his book that if having knowledge of pop music was essential to serving as Secretary of the Interior, the Senators should have asked him about that at his confirmation hearing. The National Park Service was right about the rock and roll environment. In 1983, incidents of attendees seeking medical treatment were a tenth of the previous year, and there were no reports of assaults or injuries from drug overdoses or broken bottles.

In the fall of 1983, Watt finally resigned in spite of the President's support for him, after almost two weeks of attacks following his public use of the word *cripple* to describe someone who had a weak or impaired arm or leg. Earlier on the morning of the day he made the statement, there was a small staff meeting during which Jim was discussing the investigative commission he had appointed to evaluate Interior's coal contracts. The contracts, which I had approved and signed, were under attack. The Director of the Bureau of Land Management, Bob Burford, a real western cowboy from Colorado, said something like, "And they always criticize us about lack of diversity. Well, this committee is diverse. We have a woman, a Jew, and a cripple." It was simply gallows-type humor, not meant to insult or harm anyone. The guys around the table laughed at Bob's remark. Had I still been at Interior I would have cautioned Jim not to repeat that joke, but I had already left to become Secretary of Energy.

Jim, later that day, was speaking to a friendly audience that was enjoying his freewheeling presentation. He was a very good speaker, especially when he was on a roll before such a friendly audience. As he entertained his audience with humorous anecdotes, the remark from the morning meeting came to mind and without considering if he should, he repeated it. He told me later that he realized it was a mistake when the audience, rather than laughing as they had been at his other humorous remarks, gasped as if he had said something shocking.

The press hostility to Watt turned that gaffe into a many days' attack. He tried to resign on three different occasions, and each time Reagan turned him down, the third time telling Jim to go west for a while and let things cool down. But things did not cool down.

The press and Jim's ardent critics kept stirring the pot, saying and doing things that kept the story alive. Each day there was another story of somebody's outrage over Jim using the word *cripple*.

Jim and his wife, Leilani, returned to town, and Barb and I went over to visit them as soon as we knew they were home. We often did that on weekends, as we were among the few people with whom they could relax. He and Leilani seldom went out to a restaurant because he was instantly recognizable and people who believed what they read about him were downright hateful, coming up to him and insulting him.

At the National Cherry Blossom Festival Parade with (L-R) Lelani and Jim Watt to my right and Georgie and Barbara to my left (Department of the Interior)

One fun aspect of that was when someone wasn't sure and asked, "You're Secretary Watt, aren't you?"

Jim's reply was to break into a big smile and say, "Wow. I sure must look like him because people tell me that all the time."

When we went to visit, Jim told me that he intended to resign. I believe he resigned because he had simply been worn down by the constant harassment from the media. He had an amazing ability to be steadfast in the face of great opposition, but eventually even he became weary and simply could not stand to continue.

As fate would have it, Jim Watt died at eighty-five, on May 27, 2023, as I was working on the manuscript for this book. He was a wonderful friend, mentor, and brother in Christ. And he was instrumental in so many important things that happened in my life. Every time I spoke with him late in our lives, I would tell him of my gratitude for all that he had done for me, but I still feel like all those words could not adequately express what he meant to me.

CHAPTER 12

MR. SECRETARY

After leaving Washington I found that people were curious about President Ronald Reagan and often asked, "What was President Reagan really like?"

Ronald Wilson Reagan was truly one of the world's most congenial men. He was as nice a person in private as he appeared to be in public. His good guy image was more than just that. He really was a kind and gracious man. But even more so, he believed in principle and in the goodness of the American people. I was startled once in a Cabinet meeting when he uncharacteristically interrupted someone who was speaking. "You're talking politics," he said. "I want to know what you think is *right*." Like many others who worked for President Reagan, I tried to emulate him—first to determine what was the right thing, and then to pursue it with courage and determination.

There were all sorts of theories suggested by the press and others in an effort to explain what made the President the way he was. My belief is that it was three things: his abiding belief and confidence in God, a fundamental commitment to human freedom everywhere, and a love of country. He was a patriot to the hilt.

Reagan believed that the human spirit is capable of greatness, and he inspired Americans to strive to make America a shining city on a hill. Better than any President in my lifetime, he illustrated that ideas matter, values have consequences, and good leadership is important. He lived the principle that the quality of every citizen's life in every nation will be affected for good or bad by ideas, by values, and by leadership.

Ronald Reagan had a strong faith in God, albeit a more private faith than many have come to expect of political leaders. Once in a Cabinet meeting while I was Secretary of Energy, the new Health and Human Services Secretary, Margaret Heckler, suggested that he begin the Cabinet meetings with prayer, a somewhat bold move for a new member of a Cabinet that had been assembled for over two years.

Reagan calmly answered, "I do," and in those two words he both answered her question and closed the issue.

As I wrote in an earlier chapter, I worked quite closely with then-Governor Reagan's appointments secretary, Tom Reed, while running Reagan's unofficial 1968 Presidential campaign in Oregon. We became friends and I remained in touch with him during the Nixon years when he was Secretary of the Air Force, visiting him on some of my visits to Washington, DC. In May 1982, while I was serving as Under Secretary of the Interior, Tom called and invited me to join him after work for cocktails at the Metropolitan Club. I was a teetotaler, but I was more than happy to meet with my friend Tom, who I had heard was back in town, rumored to be working on the MX Missile Program, trying to find suitable sites for the deployment of missiles for national defense. I didn't know why he wanted to meet, but I thought that maybe he wanted to discuss possible missile sites on federal land, much of which was under the jurisdiction of one or another of the agencies in Interior. I prepared myself appropriately and quickly for the meeting.

I arrived at the club with a quite comprehensive list in my head of what I thought might potentially be suitable sites for MX missiles, but it turned out that was not his reason for meeting. After we caught each other up on our families, Tom told me that he had been in the Oval Office in the last day or so with the President when Reagan was informed that his Secretary of Energy, former South Carolina Governor Jim Edwards, wanted to return home immediately after the November 1982 Congressional midterm elections. The President asked, "Well, who are we going to get to be Secretary of Energy?"

Tom said he told the President, "I have just the man."

The President replied, "Well, good, why don't you take care of it."

Then came the shocker. Tom said, "*You* are my candidate to succeed Edwards."

I was completely taken by surprise! This was so far beyond anything I had ever considered possible that I was stunned, especially since Jim Watt had recently come into my office one evening when he was headed home and said, "Y'know? One of the things that bothers me about all these attacks on me is that *you* won't ever get to be a Cabinet officer." I told him without any hesitation that I had not come to DC to become a Cabinet officer. I had come to help him turn around the Department of the Interior and then go home. I added something more which came straight from my heart: "And, if I had had any idea of how successful you would be at getting that done, instead of hanging back, I would have been begging you to bring me with you."

Our meeting in May was the last I heard from Tom on the subject. Of course, there are few secrets in Washington, and word began to spread that Secretary Edwards was planning to resign in November. Several people who wanted to replace him began active campaigns to garner support among members of the Senate. I heard rumors about that but nothing more about me. Finally, in mid-August, thinking that the White House *might* be mulling over my chances of being confirmed by the Senate, I called Helene Von Damm, at the White House, and asked her if she needed to know anything about my relationships on the Hill (thinking that there might be some concerns about whether I would have trouble getting confirmed). She promptly shut down that conversation, saying, "There's no vacancy to be looking at." I went home that night and told Barbara that the Department of Energy thing didn't appear to be happening.

At some point partway through the summer, as rumors continued to swirl about Edwards's replacement, I was called by a reporter who asked if I had heard that my name was being mentioned. I promptly said that I was happy being Under Secretary of the Interior and that as far as I knew Secretary Edwards was doing a good job. My name did not show up in the story, which confirmed my belief that whenever such stories included the names of people being considered for key positions, *they* were the ones actually stoking the fire of their own possibilities.

As the summer waned with nothing happening, I pretty much concluded that nothing *would* happen, as far as I was concerned, and I went on about the business for which I had gone to Washington—helping Jim Watt and President Reagan by managing the Department of the Interior.

One day in early October, however, I unexpectedly got a call from a woman in the White House Personnel Office. With very little if any lead in, she simply said, "The President is planning to appoint you Secretary of Energy right after the election."

Although this was a surprise after the "silent" summer, my immediate reply was, "Well, I need to talk with the President before he does that."

"Why?" she asked.

"Because the first question the press is going to ask is, 'What did the President say to you?'"

"Oh," she said. "We'll set it up."

And that was it. No campaigning, no meetings to seek the position. It apparently was a done deal.

Almost immediately I began receiving information about the job. I also knew that I wanted two people from my past to join me: Earl Gjelde, who had been on the team that educated me about electricity at Bonneville Power when I was first appointed Deputy Administrator there; and Don Pearlman, my college roommate, who was a successful lawyer in Portland and who had done such terrific work filling out the myriad forms that had to be completed before I could be confirmed as Under Secretary of the Interior.

I asked Earl to come to Washington and be the chief operating officer of the Department of Energy. There was no such position in the organization chart for DOE, but I knew that the Secretary could hire assistants and give them whatever assignments he wanted, and I wanted him to use his experience from BPA in the role that I, similarly, had filled for Watt. I don't recall whether Earl said yes immediately or whether he took time to talk it over with his wife, Sandra. It involved sacrifice on their part because there was little that could be done to increase his pay and he would need to find housing in the Beltway Area, and so on. But very shortly he agreed, and I asked him to help me get ready for the transition.

Earl quickly became my alter ego. He saw to it that the decisions we made were carried out as intended and did not let them be passive-aggressively sidetracked by someone on the staff who had other ideas. Potentially, this appointment of Earl would be very upsetting to those six or eight of the top staff of the Department who were Presidential appointees confirmed by the Senate. I was putting this young (he was thirty-eight) career bureaucrat over them in the chain of command. What was truly amazing and is an incredible testimony to how effective and congenial Earl was, only one of those Presidential appointees ever objected. All the others quickly figured out that if they persuaded Earl that they were doing the right thing, I would approve it.

Next, I called Don Pearlman and told him that I needed him to again help me through the documentation required for confirmation. Don had a lucrative law practice in Portland, and this move entailed a significant financial sacrifice, but I knew his intense interest in politics and government would make it nearly impossible for him to decline. He managed to work out a three-month leave of absence from his law firm to help me get started at DOE. Of course, that meant he gave up earning his living for three months and he was simply a volunteer with me and could not be paid.

Shortly after Don arrived, Barbara and I took him and his wife, Shirley, to dinner, where I told them, "My intentions are strictly dishonorable. I hope to persuade you to *stay* in DC." I wanted him to serve as my right-hand man for political and tactical advice, again under the title of executive assistant, which did not require Senate review. Executive assistant now is the title for what once would have been called a secretary, or an administrative assistant, someone who assists an executive. But then, it meant someone who was also an executive, assisting a more senior executive, and that described Pearlman to a *T*.

One week after I had become Energy Secretary and Don was in DC working and living in a hotel, I went home and told Barbara, "Don is going to stay."

"Oh," she said. "Did he say that?"

"Nope," I said. "He doesn't even know it yet." But I did, because I knew him so well and knew that the atmosphere in Washington was terribly appealing to him and I knew that Shirley thought being in DC was vastly more interesting than Portland, Oregon. I could tell from the enthusiasm with which he entered into his role assisting me that he would never be able to give it up willingly.

The Assistant Secretary of Energy for Administration was Bill Heffelfinger who was a "supercrat" (someone who knew all the ins and outs of operating the government bureaucracy). I knew him slightly from when I was at BPA and he did some work for Assistant Secretary of the Interior Jim Smith. As soon as I had gotten the word from the White House that I was going to be appointed Secretary of Energy, I asked Bill to assemble some briefing books on DOE, and soon he delivered two big boxes full of twelve to fifteen thick, black, three-ring binders with an incredible amount of detailed information about energy generally and about the Department in particular.

One of the perks of being Under Secretary of the Interior was that I had access to some of the cabins that were maintained by the National Park Service in various national parks. One of these was just south of Washington, DC, in Prince William Forest Park, and I arranged for Barbara and me to use it for several days while I prepped myself on the history and workings of the Department, using those three-ring binders—and a flip chart.

I would read the binders on a particular subject for a time and then go to the flip chart and list bullet points of the important parts of what I had read. Then I would tape the pages to the wall of the rustic cabin. Barbara was my all-in participant. She was amazing and never showed any boredom or lack of interest, and asked useful questions, both of which helped me enormously in staying at the task. Regularly, we would take a break and take a walk through the surrounding forest or go canoeing on the small lake beside the cabin. I knew from experience that taking frequent, brief breaks helped my ability to retain what I was learning.

Thinking of perks, any Cabinet Secretary has access to certain niceties that are made available. These include a very nice office, a driver and a security detail, as well as things like the opportunity to reserve seats in the President's box at the Kennedy Center for the Performing Arts and access to the White House mess for lunch. I often saw those things, such as the Kennedy Center seats, as an opportunity to include those among my staff (drivers, security, etc.) who otherwise would never have that opportunity.

One day the park superintendent came by as a courtesy to make sure I had everything I needed. I am pretty sure he was totally perplexed to see the walls of the cabin covered with flip chart pages, showing red, blue, and green writing. He must have wondered what in the heck was going on.

Having plowed through the essential binders and having at least a grounding in the organization and responsibilities of the Department of Energy and a renewed grasp of the facts of the world and US energy pictures, I felt I was ready for the next phase of preparation, which was to get together with the people who were going to join me at DOE when I went there.

As soon as Gjelde and Pearlman got to Washington, as well as others who were available to come in that timeframe, we began meeting. Don had arrived partway through October. Earl and Don comprised my inner circle, along with two others.

Danny Boggs was a brilliant man who would be Deputy Secretary, my *official* number two at DOE (a different title than when I was number two at Interior, as DOE was a much newer agency and the government titles changed), had been a key player at the White House Policy office and was a natural student of any subject he studied. He had a great sense of humor and did an excellent job of overseeing and shaping the development of the national energy policy for which the Department of Energy was responsible. Just a few years later, he was appointed by Reagan as a judge on the US Sixth Circuit Court based in his home area of Louisville, Kentucky. It was always my hope that he would be nominated to the Supreme Court because he was a solid, clear-eyed conservative. Over the years we have stayed in touch. He has remained a stalwart conservative throughout his career, not "growing" in office by becoming more liberal.

Finally, there was Martha Hesse, recently Associate Deputy Secretary at the Department of Commerce under Secretary Malcolm Baldrige, whom the White House had tapped to move over to DOE as Assistant Secretary for Management and Administration. Prior to joining the Reagan Administration, Martha had had a very successful career in the private sector as COO of a large information technology company.

We met in my Under Secretary's office at DOI on a regular basis. Of course, many of us still had other jobs we had to do while getting ready for the new ones. We began an organized discussion of how to begin my term at the DOE and get the Department on the course that we thought would be the most important and productive.

There was a leak right away, as one of the newsletters that covered DOE had an article that reported the rumor that I was meeting with people in anticipation of being nominated as Secretary of Energy and that one of the participants was someone named Jodi. This puzzled us until one person in our group figured someone must have overheard talk about our meetings and thought that "Gjelde" was "Jodi." We did nothing to confirm or deny the rumor, as nothing good comes from responding to that kind of story.

Presidential appointments require approval by a majority vote of the Senate; however, Reagan had another option regarding my appointment. The Senate had gone into recess for the November 1982 midterm elections and for some weeks after, and while the Senate was in recess, the President had the authority to make interim appointments, that is, he could appoint someone to a vacancy and then submit the name for confirmation afterward. In the case of an interim appointment, if the Senate failed to confirm the person within a year of his appointment by the President, the appointee was removed from office. So, without Senate confirmation, my interim appointment would run out when the Senate adjourned at the end of 1983.

On Wednesday, November 3, 1982, the day after the November midterm elections, I found myself in the Oval Office, meeting with President Reagan. It became apparent that he wondered why we were having this meeting because, as I found out later, he had made the decision to nominate me in August. In any event, the meeting accomplished its purpose, giving me the ability to answer any questions about what the President had to say to me.

Two days later, on Friday, November 5, 1982, Barbara, Earl and Sandra Gjelde, Don and Shirley Pearlman, and I were in the Roosevelt Room at the White House, where I was sworn in by William French Smith, Attorney General of the United States. The Chief Justice of the Supreme Court customarily swears in the President, Vice President, and other Justices, while any federal official is able to swear in others.

After the formal swearing in, a clerk came to me and said that I should follow him into the next room to sign something. Someone with federal judicial credentials then swore me in, again, saying that he was doing so just in case it turned out that the Attorney General didn't have authority to do it! I thought that was both amusing and amazing.

Because mine was an interim appointment, my Commission (the official document signed by the President and the Secretary of State) shows that on November 5, 1982, I became a member of President Reagan's Cabinet, which I thought at the time would be the crowning achievement of my career, being the United States' fourth Secretary of Energy. My Commission read:

> *Know Ye, that reposing special trust and confidence in the Patriotism, Integrity and Abilities of Donald P. Hodel, of Oregon, I do appoint him Secretary of Energy and do authorize and empower him to execute and fulfill the duties of that Office according to law, and to have and to hold the*

said Office, with all the powers, privileges, and emoluments to the same of right appertaining, unto him the said Donald P. Hodel, during the pleasure of the President of the United States for the time being and until the end of the next session of the Senate of the United States and no longer.

On occasion, in speeches, I would quote those last twenty-two words from my Commission, "… for the time being…," and comment, "That's what's called 'job security' in Washington, DC," which usually received the laughs it deserved.

A month later, on December 8, the United States Senate was back in session and confirmed me as Secretary of Energy. It was not unanimous, with eight Senators voting against my nomination, led by Senator Edward Kennedy of Massachusetts. To this day I can tell that story to conservatives and receive attaboys from them because Senator Kennedy was such a notorious, left-wing, objectionable person. Being opposed by him was a badge of honor.

The confirmation process is that after the President sends the Senate a nomination, the appropriate Senate committee holds a hearing (or hearings) and approves or disapproves the nominee by a majority vote. If it approves the nomination, the name is forwarded to the Senate floor for a vote. Nominees for Secretary of Energy and for Interior are reviewed by the Committee on Energy and Natural Resources. Often, the first witness to speak to the committee is one (or both) Senators from his home state formally introducing him to the committee, which basically means they sit before the committee and say nice things about the nominee. Both of Oregon's US Senators, Mark Hatfield and Bob Packwood, introduced me that day, as they had done for my hearing to be confirmed as Under Secretary of the Interior. The introductions are not designed necessarily to be partisan occasions. If a nominee came from a state with Senators from different parties, and if he had good relationships with both, it would be possible for each to introduce him to the committee.

The nominee is called and sworn in, promising to tell the truth, the whole truth, and nothing but the truth, "so help me God." He may be asked any question, about anything, by the committee and I spent a lot of time being briefed beforehand by staff at the Department of Energy about possible questions. Since in 1980 the Republicans had won a majority of the seats in the Senate, the committee chairman was a Republican, Senator James McClure of Idaho, who was friendly to the President, to Jim Watt, and to me.

I later learned from Watt that McClure told him he was going to tell the White House not to nominate me because he did not want the controversy of trying to get committee approval for a new Under Secretary of the Interior to replace me. He felt that Watt was so controversial that it would be a battle. Watt assured McClure that he would choose a successor to me who would be overwhelmingly approved. McClure asked how he could do that. Watt told him that his nominee for Under Secretary was Jake Simmons, a friend of Watt's who was well-connected, then serving as a commissioner on the Interstate Commerce Commission. He was also Black and a Democrat, which meant he did not face partisan opposition. Jim knew that Republicans in the Senate would support the President's nominee, and that Senate Democrats would not oppose a nominee chosen from their party, and one who was also a minority. Jake was confirmed instantly and unanimously almost as soon as his name was sent to the Senate. Without Watt's wise choice, I'm fairly sure that McClure would have tried to dissuade the White House from nominating me.

In getting ready for my hearing, part of the process of being confirmed is making "courtesy calls," which are visits to all the Senators who are members of the Committee. This is a very important part of the process. It allows Senators who do not know the nominee to become acquainted and for those who do, to renew or deepen their relationship. Much of politics is about relationships and how people view others. In these visits, some Senators made it plain that they were going to support me, and others played the game of considering whether they would do so or not, as they talked about the things they wanted from the Department of Energy. But it seemed apparent that most or perhaps all nineteen members of the Committee, including the Democrats, were going to support me.

The confirmation hearing, held on December 1, 1982, was quite interesting. Thanks to the interim appointment, I was, in fact, already Secretary of Energy and I would be so until the end of that Senate session, in about a year. That meant, of course, that the committee members addressed me not as "Mr. Hodel," as would have been the case with a typical nominee, but as "Mr. Secretary," a major difference in deference and civility. I *was* the Secretary and even if they refused to confirm me, I would be Secretary for the next year, with considerable power over projects and activities within their states. And while I would be distressed over not having been confirmed, I would have gone home after my three years of service in Washington, with Secretary of Energy on my resume forever.

The two Senators from my home state said a lot of very nice things about me in their introduction. Senator Hatfield was Oregon's senior Senator, meaning he had served in the Senate longer than Packwood. He and I were well acquainted and on reasonably friendly terms. If he had ever been upset with me for my role in removing his chosen Oregon GOP state chairman, Pete Gunnar, it seemed to be long forgotten. He, like Packwood, had also appeared before the same committee to introduce me in January 1981, on my nomination to be Under Secretary of the Interior.

Prior to the hearing Hatfield convened a meeting for me with key environmental leaders in a room in the Capitol. He introduced me to the meeting participants, saying that even though he and I came from different wings of the Oregon Republican Party, we had always been able to transcend those differences. Over the years we worked collegially together from a position of trust. He indicated that I was totally trustworthy, which was about as high a compliment as I could have received, especially from someone with whom I did not always agree.

Hatfield repeated his kind comments from the private meeting for the committee members to hear. And, seeking to say something complimentary and different from his prior appearance on my behalf, decided to make the point that Barbara was my constant companion. He said, "Really, we're getting sort of two for the price of one, because Barbara, his wife, has been a very constant companion and associate of his professional life as few wives have been able to do over the years." Barbara and I both nodded in agreement.

Senator Packwood spoke next, explaining our long history of knowing each other, going back to Grant High School in Portland. And he defended my honor but highlighting the attacks I had undergone from the single-interest environmentalists while at BPA, where I was exposed to death threats, at one time had police protection, and that after a dinner at our home he witnessed me checking to see if a pebble I had laid on the hood of my car earlier in the evening was still there hours later, my way of ensuring that my engine had not been tampered with.

Chairman McClure began the hearing by recognizing Senator Scoop Jackson of Washington to speak next. He commended my integrity and said that I would "restore to the Department a sense and dignity of respect for the public servants who compose(d) the agency." Jackson was "Ranking Member" on the Committee, the most senior Democrat present, which meant that if the Democrats had controlled the Senate, he would have been committee chairman, as he had been before Republicans won control of the Senate. He was fond of me, of course, as we had worked together during my years at Bonneville Power, and he made it clear that he would vote in my favor. And after he spoke, Senator Frank Murkowski, Republican from Alaska, made similar comments.

An exception to calling the nominee as the first witness after the Senators from his home state introduce him occurs if any other Senator, not a member of the Committee, wishes to testify. Senator Max Baucus, a young, liberal Democrat from Montana, appeared unexpectedly (to me) to testify against me, no doubt, urged on by the professional environmentalists.

The environmental leaders who fought Ronald Reagan and Jim Watt tried to derail me. They tried to stop my nomination by distributing to all the members of the committee copies of my

Bonneville Power era "Prophets of Shortage" speech, where I was harshly critical of extreme environmentalists. This was done at the last minute before the hearing, perhaps, so that I did not have time to meet again separately with members of the committee to try to smooth things over.

Baucus's attack was based on allegations about my management of BPA and particularly the Washington Public Power Supply System (the aforementioned WPPSS or Whoops) nuclear plants that, by 1982, had encountered very serious problems with construction costs that were out of control. Senator Baucus made some outrageous and erroneous statements that were designed to put me in a deep hole when I began to testify. He, no fewer than six times, encouraged the committee to question me on Whoops, along the line of, "I hope that you will ask him to explain why..." "I hope you will ask him this question..." concluding that they should get on top of "the Whoops mess." I sat there, mind racing, preparing for a lengthy and difficult hearing.

But a most unusual thing happened, another young Democrat, Senator Paul Tsongas of Massachusetts, pointedly asked Baucus how he planned to vote. Baucus answered that even if the hearings cleared me of the "glaring mistakes" in managing Whoops, he would be voting no. Next, another member of the Committee, a Democrat, Dale Bumpers of Arkansas, asked how distant BPA had been from Whoops, and what exactly was my role. Baucus tried to answer, showing he really had no direct knowledge of either matter.

And then, as Baucus finished a sentence and took a breath, Scoop Jackson took over. He explained to the committee and to Senator Baucus that in reality Whoops was a Washington State chartered operation and the federal government through BPA had no authority over its management. In making his points, Jackson added, "And I think Senator Baucus would agree." Scoop was in control of the discussion at that point.

McClure interrupted Jackson, explaining more about BPA and Whoops, adding that even the citizens of the Pacific Northwest did not understand what Whoops was, and Jackson chuckled, adding,

"[I] couldn't agree with you more." McClure then thanked Baucus for appearing and dismissed him from the hearing.

These comments were recognized by knowledgeable observers as a form of public rebuke of Baucus by a very senior and respected Senator of the same party and were, in my experience, unprecedented. Not only did it send Senator Baucus away in disarray, but it sent a very strong signal to the rest of the Democrats on the committee that Senator Jackson was supporting me, and no nonsense from them would be tolerated. Not one question suggested by Baucus was asked of me and neither were any questions asked about my "Prophets of Shortage" speech.

Barbara and I maintain our composure as Senator Max Baucus opposes my nomination to be Energy Secretary (© Michael Lloyd/*The Oregonian*. All rights reserved. Used with permission.)

Chairman McClure then invited me to the witness chair where he swore me in and asked what he said were admittedly four perfunctory questions about how I would manage the Department of Energy. Satisfied with my equally official answers, he invited me to begin my opening statement.

Senator Tsongas requested permission to speak before it was his turn because he had another commitment, and as he stood up to leave, he made an astonishing statement. During my courtesy call to his office, he and I had found much common ground and seemed to have the basis of a potentially warm friendship. He was quite an interesting person and not the typical politician. His question was not a question at all. It was an explanation of what he was going to do. "I am going to have to leave, and I want to say that I think you will do a very good job as Secretary of Energy, but I am going to vote against your nomination because my wife has never forgiven me for voting for Secretary Watt." And with that he left!

I did not know it at the time, but as the various Senators questioned me, Senator Jackson leaned over to Chairman McClure and said, "We (meaning the Democrats on the committee) have no objection to voting on this candidate right away." The committee practice was usually to wait to vote for two weeks to allow written comments about a nominee to be filed with the committee. Here was Jackson saying they would waive that practice and vote right now.

When the hearing was over, Barbara and I went to the offices of Senator McClure's committee staff to be sure there were no further things to be done. While we were there, word reached us that the committee had already voted to send my name to the Senate floor with eighteen votes for me and one against (Tsongas). A committee confirmation vote happening that fast was quite unusual and a testimony to Jackson's influence and support.

In my car a few minutes later, on the way back to my office at DOE, my car phone rang. There were no cell phones in those days, of course, and only high government officials and wealthy citizens had phones in their cars. It was Jim Watt, saying, "Congratulations! I understand the committee has already approved you!"

"Yes," I said. "It was unanimous."

"Oh?" Jim said. "I thought there was one 'no' vote?"

"No, Jim" I said, laughing. "There were eighteen votes for me and one vote against *you*." We both laughed often over that one.

In most cases, appointees enter the building where they will work knowing almost nothing about where their offices are, or the restrooms, or the other officials' offices, and so on. My inner circle, however, went to DOE on Saturday, November 6, the day after I had been sworn in as Secretary of Energy, after the President made my initial appointment, and toured the building, saw where their offices were to be, and where everything else was. Since I had already been sworn in, my team and I had been preparing for this day for over a month before my confirmation hearing. And we had been meeting and planning, even earlier, beginning when I learned that I would be nominated by the President. This included a careful, detailed plan for taking charge at the DOE. We had laid out a detailed schedule for the first couple of days we were going to be there as well as having established the main things we wanted to accomplish.

The remaining top staff from Secretary Edwards's administration came in on Monday morning, November 8, knowing there would be a new Secretary and a few other new people (Boggs, Hesse, and so on), but probably expecting that there would be a few weeks' adjustment as we settled into our jobs. Instead, they found that they were expected to be at a staff meeting at 9:00 a.m. in the Secretary's conference room that very morning.

After everyone was introduced, I explained what we were going to do and how we were going to do it. I told them that Earl Gjelde would occupy the new position of chief operating officer for the Department. Earl was truly gifted in his ability to get people to cooperate and would run day-to-day affairs. Danny Boggs, as Deputy Secretary, would have all responsibilities regarding energy policy. Don Pearlman would be my executive assistant, which meant that he could pretty much look over anything that was going on.

DOE was basically a contract management agency, but neither Earl, as COO, nor any of the Assistant Secretaries had any contracting authority, all of which, because of the way the Department was organized, resided in the regional offices of the DOE. Even if an Assistant Secretary of Energy wanted a contract signed, he had to get it done by one of the five Regional Managers.

The energy installations in Oak Ridge, Tennessee, Savannah, Georgia, Hanford, Washington, and so on had what were called Regional Managers, and those executives had the authority to negotiate and sign the contracts and oversee the contractor activities that made DOE function. We set things up so that the Regional Managers reported directly to Earl, so he had total control of what was done. However, instead of being circumscribed by this the

Assistant Secretaries found that Earl facilitated getting done the things they sought to do.

Earl also had a very deft hand when it came to managing and protecting me as Secretary. And he used it with both grace and deference.

I had once said to Jim Watt while I was his deputy, "I hope that you never look at an office wall as you are leaving the office and say something like, 'I wish there was a door there.' Because before you get back, there will be a carpenter cutting a hole in the wall." I told him that to remind him of how responsive his staff wanted to be to him, and to help him remember that he could not just speak his mind if it was not something that he really cared about. I knew that of course and got a firsthand example from something I did.

One day Earl came into my office, to which he had walk-in access at any time, and, looking questioningly at me, asked, "Did you really say that you wanted all the Department of Energy field offices to have lavalier microphones?"

I was momentarily confused by the question because I could not remember ever saying anything like that. Earl explained, "Well, I've just received a request to acquire several hundred lavalier mics for the field offices."

"What?!" I said, flabbergasted.

Then we figured out what had happened. On a recent trip to the Idaho National Engineering Laboratory (INEL) in Arco, Idaho, I spoke in the auditorium to the employees there. They had a lavalier mic, which I pinned on my lapel. This allowed me to walk about on the stage as I spoke, which was very comfortable for me and seemed a much more personal way than standing behind a lectern and speaking into a fixed microphone.

I always tried to find something complimentary to say to the people who were hosting me at field offices, so afterward I said, "That was really nice to have that lavalier mic. Thank you." Apparently, the head of INEL let the word out that, "You better have a lavalier mic available in case the Secretary shows up." Had Earl not known that I would be very unlikely ever to make such a request, he might have gone ahead and ordered the purchase of thousands of dollars of microphones that I never asked for nor wanted. If he had done so, it would have been the kind of story that when it reached the press would have been joyfully reported as proof of how "foolish" and extravagant I was.

In the same vein, at one visit there were bottles of fruit juice available for me, and I commented how nice that was. Barbara noticed that from then on, at every visit I made to field offices, there was fruit juice, showing good—but far less expensive than microphones—staff initiative.

As Secretary of a Cabinet agency, it became a necessary part of my duties to be available to meet with the press, to greet foreign dignitaries, to give many speeches, and to generally be visible and available. In addition, as a Republican Cabinet Secretary, I was a key fundraiser for Republican candidates running for office. In 1983 (I think it was that year), I received the award from the Republican Eagles (the high donor group of contributors) as the fundraiser of the year. A prior winner had been none other than President Gerald Ford.

As Under Secretary of the Interior, I had not done press conferences, interviews, or issued statements. In my opinion, depending on the subject, the Secretary, an Assistant Secretary, or an agency head were the officials who were appropriate to appear in public representing the Department. On my first day in the office as Secretary of Energy, after meeting with the top staff of the Department, I had my very first press availability.

One of the reporters afterward told me that he was pleasantly surprised at my availability because he had made a prediction that, based on my actions at Interior, I would not meet with the press after coming to Energy. What he did not know was that I believed the Secretary had a responsibility to make himself available to the press. I allowed the Assistant Secretaries to announce good news about things in their divisions. The White House, of course, always had the President announce good news, and the Cabinet officials responsible for any bad news announce it themselves.

While I had not spoken with the press while at Interior, I watched Jim Watt many times and developed my own ideas about how to handle myself. Where Jim loved to parry with reporters, I knew that none of them were my friends. A crafty reporter would write a negative story about his own grandmother if it got his story on the front page. So, everything I said I weighed for its possible misinterpretation. In my view the press went out of its way to distort and criticize Watt. I did not need to follow in those footsteps.

The first press question I received was prompted by an editorial cartoon appearing in the *Washington Post* shortly after I was announced as the next Secretary of Energy. It showed a caricature of Jim Watt in his suit, wearing his glasses, with his arm around someone who looked exactly like him, bald with glasses, and he was saying, "Let me introduce you to your new Secretary of Energy." Jim of course was very bald on top of his head. A reporter asked me, "Are you a Watt clone?" I genuinely smiled at the reporter and said, "I don't know what you mean by 'clone.' Do you mean do I comb my hair with a washcloth?" He and the rest of the reporters laughed, and I went on to the next question.

The reporter asking the question was not serious. He was testing to see how I handled a hot potato, and if I made the mistake of taking it seriously and said anything that separated me from Watt or sounded critical of him, that would be news. On the other hand, if I told them how close I was and how much I admired Watt, they would have dredged up any old story about Watt and tied it to me. By deflecting the question with humor, no damage was done.

The name, Department of Energy, is really a misnomer, implying that the Department has control over energy matters, but that is not the case. The Department actually has several functions, the more significant three of which I will discuss below.

First, it produces the nuclear materials and weapons for the US military. This may at first seem strange since nuclear weapons are strictly military, but early in the Atomic Age, it was decided that it was better in our Constitutional Republic not to let the military produce and control everything related to nuclear weapons. However, in practice the decision on how much weapons grade uranium and plutonium are produced and how many weapons are made is approved annually by the President based upon a recommendation of a committee made up of generals and admirals, in addition to one committee member designated by the Secretary of Energy. In my case, my representative was a major general in the Air Force! So, I guess that shows how much civilian control there actually was.

The next big responsibility for DOE was to oversee and manage the national laboratories, such as Fermilab, Lawrence Livermore, Brookhaven, etc. These were fabulous experimental and scientific laboratories doing amazing studies and tests of all kinds of things especially related to atoms and sources of energy.

Finally, the DOE gathered and published enormous amounts of information about energy production and use in the United States and the world.

Notice what I did not list: DOE has *no* authority to produce or sell or control the production or sale of any energy products, which led to confusion in at least two ways. First, in the US there was a common misconception that, if there was a Department of Energy, it had some authority to take direct action to help solve energy problems. Therefore, when there was a problem, people wanted *us* to fix it.

Second, foreign governments operated very differently. In many cases their departments of energy, by whatever name (often it was Ministry of Energy), had authority either to produce and sell energy or to closely control those companies that did so. I once received a phone call from the Energy Minister of Algeria, with whom I had become acquainted. He asked me to force an American company to honor a contract it had with his country to build a Liquified Natural Gas facility off the coast of Louisiana to receive liquified natural gas from Algeria. The company was running into fierce and ultimately insurmountable opposition from opponents of the project. I explained that I had no authority whatsoever to order a US company to do anything. I could tell from his reaction, however, that he really did not believe me.

The third situation I kept running into was that when I met with the Energy Ministers of OPEC (Organization of the Petroleum Exporting Countries) countries, they wanted to have a "multi-lateral conference," involving all the countries that were major oil producers, to decide how to handle the world's oil problems. They did not really understand that if I went to such a conference and a majority of the countries agreed to do something, I had no authority to carry out an agreement in the US. Knowing this, I took the position that I would meet anyone at any time but only one on one. I refused to meet in groups because any decision the group made, even if I agreed with it, could not be enforced in the United States.

One of the tasks of the Department of Energy required of it by Congress was to produce a national energy policy. The problem with that was just what I have been referring to above. If the person who makes the policy has no ability to enforce it, the policy is only advisory and may be meaningless. In reality, if DOE, or I as Secretary, said, "Our energy policy is such and such, therefore do this or that," absolutely no one had any obligation even to read the statement, much less to follow it.

So, Earl Gjelde, Danny Boggs, and I decided after much discussion that we could not really publish a policy that was binding. Danny was in charge of such statements, and he was well-suited to working out the wording. He and the staff tried several versions and finally came up with an absolutely brilliant solution: *The National Energy Policy Plan*. Danny's team added the word *plan* to make plain that this was not an action plan but a statement of what ought to be the goal of the US Government regarding energy.

Next, after many attempts to draft a detailed plan spelling out the role of oil, gas, coal, wind, hydro, solar, nuclear, geothermal, and all other possible sources of energy, plus conservation, we never forgot that we could not require anyone to do anything. We could just say what we thought ought to be. Danny did a brilliant job of presenting a fairly complete analysis of what could and should be done. Our hope was that by stating good ideas at least some of them would be adopted.

I ended up summarizing that policy with a very brief statement which, to this day, I believe is the best that can be done in stating broadly what the US policy should be. Sadly no one seemed to pay any attention to it. The wording, as I recall, was something like this:

The policy of the United States should be to provide an adequate supply of energy at an affordable price to everyone in the United States and that in doing so there should be a balanced and mixed source of energy including conventional resources, such as coal, oil, natural gas, nuclear, and renewable sources such as solar and wind as well as conservation.

Our statement was resoundingly criticized by everyone who was attempting to develop any kind of energy project because each one of them wanted a policy stating that *their* preferred source of energy was the best. Further, most of them wanted their favorite to be promoted by the United States Government. There was no way to satisfy all the constituencies because each was almost solely focused on its own favorite.

As 1984 came to an end, and after discussions with my top staff, I decided I would devote the coming year, 1985, to traveling across the country, trying to sell the idea that the best thing for government to do was to *state* a policy such as ours, and then *do* all it could to enable the many brilliant and wise scientists, engineers, and businesspeople in America to make it happen for the benefit of all. That process may not have succeeded, but if we had tried and had an impact, it is interesting to think how different things might have been in the way energy developed thereafter in the United States.

Finally, it was my plan at the end of 1985, after spending the year trying to "sell" our energy policy, that Barb and I would return to the West and go back to private life, retiring—again—from government. I felt that I would have made as much of a contribution to my country as I was able.

But others had a different idea, and President Reagan soon requested my service again, which changed everything.

CHAPTER 13

BACK TO INTERIOR

Barb and I went to Oregon for Christmas 1984 and stayed with my mother in her condo in Lake Oswego. We had our usual extended family Christmas dinner, which happened that year on December 30, with my brother, Les, and his wife, Gladys, their three sons, Tom, Bob, and Jim, plus a few others—aunts, uncles, cousins, Mom, Barbara, Dave, and me. Everyone was pitching in to get the table ready when my mother's phone rang. In the day before cell phones and caller identification, she had no idea who it was. To our surprise, a White House operator was calling for me. When I got on the line, she asked, "Will you hold for Secretary Clark, please?"

William (Bill) Clark was Secretary of the Interior, having replaced Jim Watt in October 1983. He was a close personal friend of the President and had served as Executive Secretary when Reagan was Governor of California. Before leaving the Governorship, Reagan appointed him to the California Supreme Court. When Reagan became President and, within days, had trouble keeping a rein on his first Secretary of State, Alexander Haig, Reagan persuaded Clark to come to Washington as Deputy Secretary of State, the number two man to Haig.

The Washington press corps savaged Clark, ridiculing his lack of experience in foreign affairs and belittling him when he was unable to name obscure leaders of countries you and I have never heard of. Judge Clark, as he preferred to be called, however, was a super good guy. He was totally loyal to the President, and as a solid conservative, shared Reagan's philosophy. He is credited by some (and I believe it likely to be true) with urging the President to put pressure on the Soviet Union, which ultimately led to its collapse.

When Bill was at the State Department and I was still Under Secretary of the Interior, we became well acquainted when, about once each month, all the Cabinet "number twos" (as we called ourselves) would meet for dinner, just to get to know each other. This was very useful because in most cases we ran the various Departments for "our" Secretaries, and it enabled us to pick up the phone and talk to the person managing a department and get things done. Clark and I hit it off and became working friends.

By the time I went to Energy, Clark had left State to become the President's National Security Adviser. We no longer had occasion to meet on business matters. Then, Jim Watt resigned in October 1983 and the President nominated Clark to be Secretary of the Interior, and soon he was confirmed by the Senate. That made us fellow Cabinet officers and our relationship grew even closer, as our two agencies had multiple points of contact, and we could cooperate to help accomplish the goals of the President. Bill and I worked together to make sure that the policies we thought were best for America were consistent with the rules and regulations that the Department of Interior under Watt, and then under Clark, promulgated. Working with such a fine and honorable man, who seemed to take almost a fatherly interest in me and my efforts, was a true pleasure. Now, suddenly, without any prior indication that he would be calling me, Bill was on the phone—and at Christmas!

If you wonder how he could call me at my mother's house, you should know that another of the wonderful perks of being a Cabinet officer was that you could dial the White House switchboard at (202) 456-1414, identify yourself, and tell the operator that you needed to speak with whomever you needed in the government—or otherwise—and they would find him or her anywhere in the world. A few minutes later, your phone would ring back, and you would hear, "Mr. Secretary, I have [so and so] on the line." Obviously, Clark had done that, and the White House operator had tracked me down at my mother's house. We greeted each other warmly, and then he said, "Don, I am going to be with the President tomorrow night at a party and I intend to tell him that I am going to leave Interior."

"Oh! No!" I exclaimed. "Bill, it is such a pleasure to work with you at Interior with me at Energy."

"Well, I really don't want to discuss it, because, for personal reasons, I have to get back to my affairs in California," he said.

I made a few more respectful objections, but he brushed those aside. He assured me that he was not in a hurry and that he would probably depart in April. That timing calmed me a bit, but then I found myself wondering, *Why is he calling me?*

Then Clark explained, and it was a blockbuster, "The reason I'm calling you is to tell you that I will be telling the President that you need to succeed me as Secretary of the Interior."

I was stunned. My immediate reaction was that my nomination for that position would be controversial in the extreme because I had been Under Secretary to the dreaded James Watt. The President didn't need that kind of turmoil going on over one of his appointments, and I said as much to Clark. He reiterated that we had time to talk it over, as he did not plan to say anything publicly yet. He just wanted me to be informed in advance.

I still could not believe it. On the one hand it was a signal honor to be identified by someone as close to the President as Bill Clark as the best qualified person to succeed him in a key Cabinet position. On the other hand, Interior was a real can of worms compared to Energy, and leaving would interrupt my plans to market our *National Energy Policy Plan* for a year and then go home.

If I went over to Interior at the beginning of Reagan's second term, I knew it would be highly inappropriate to leave before the full four years were up, because to depart around the 1986 midterm Congressional election would force the President to get a new Interior Secretary confirmed afterward by a lame-duck Senate (one that would soon be gone) or, worse, if we lost the Senate, by Democrats, which is exactly what would have happened because the Republicans lost control of the Senate in November 1986. I believed the obstructionists would have a field day slowing down or blocking my successor. Further, it would be a terrible disservice to that nominee, the short-term appointee who would assume the role in exactly the same timing and fashion as I had at Energy two years earlier. He or she could barely get into the job before it potentially would end, but he would have an even more difficult time since Reagan could not run for reelection again and everyone would believe the new Secretary was a lame duck.

This meant that if I went back to become Secretary of the Interior, I was going to be in the Administration until after the 1988 elections, not leaving Washington before January 1989, whereas I could have left my position at Energy at the end of Reagan's first term in January 1985. *Oh, well,* I thought, *we'll see how this plays out when we get back to Washington.*

New Years came and went and two days later, on January 2, *The Oregonian*, the state's leading newspaper, had a headline to the effect of, "Clark to Leave Interior" with the sub-heading: "Hodel Rumored Successor." So much for Bill Clark's attempts to keep it quiet. I was sure that he had not leaked it. At the time, I believed one of those close to Reagan who did not like Clark's influence on him heard what Bill had told the President at the White House New Year's Eve gathering and leaked the story to encourage Clark's early departure.

All this was brewing as we traveled back to Washington a couple of days later. I learned that several meetings and discussions had been planned regarding my potential appointment, including a sit down with Deputy Assistant for Presidential Personnel John Herrington. John had been a big Reagan supporter in California when he ran for Governor and President.

In the first meeting it became apparent that White House Chief of Staff James Baker had his own candidate for Secretary of Energy. I cannot recall the name of Baker's candidate at this point, but it was someone who knew nothing about energy. This showed that in Baker's opinion anyone could be Energy Secretary—no energy background necessary. I sat in a meeting with him, Clark, Herrington, and a couple of other people where his candidate was discussed. The disregard for DOE was not spoken outright, but the fact that his candidate had no knowledge of the subject spoke volumes.

In the end, it was John Herrington who replaced me as Secretary of Energy. The good thing about Herrington was that he was totally loyal to the President. Unfortunately, he did not have an energy background, but by that time the main thrust of President Reagan's policies on energy had been established in the Department, so he needed to do what I was doing back at Interior: stay the course.

After about ten days of my attempting to decline the appointment to Interior, I got a call from my friend Bill Rusher, our relationship going all the way back to 1954 and the Harvard Young Republican Club. He was the first president of HYRC, while I was the tenth. He had stayed in touch with those who followed in his footsteps after he became a national conservative personality. Bill did not often phone me, and as soon as we had finished our opening pleasantries he said, "I was talking to Mrs. Reagan this morning at a meeting and your name came up."

I was pretty sure what he was going to say because I had refused to get involved in the political infighting at the White House and kept a low profile over there, so I said, "Yeah. Yeah. And she didn't even know who I was, right?" I figured Bill was going to lecture me on the need to get into the political game.

"To the contrary," he said. "She said, 'Oh, yes. We want him to be our next Secretary of the Interior, but he's dragging his feet.'"

Bill said, "I asked her if there was anything I could do to help, and she said, 'Yes. Call him and persuade him to take the job.'"

At that point, I cut in and simply said to him, "Bill, you can tell Mrs. Reagan that you've accomplished your mission." My opinion—then and now—was that if your boss wants to give you an important job you either take it or resign. You simply must not say, "No thanks. I think I'll stay where I am." And this is especially true if your boss is the President of the United States!

As soon as I hung up the phone, I called Barbara to tell her that we were going to go back to Interior, and we would be staying in Washington for four more years.

I then began the process of assembling those people I needed and wanted to take back with me to Interior. Clearly that included Earl Gjelde and Don Pearlman, who would continue in their now well-established roles for me.

At my desk at Interior with (L-R) Don Pearlman and Earl Gjelde (Department of the Interior)

I also selected Mary Ann Wilkinson, my confidential assistant (an actual title then) from DOE. As I wrote earlier, she had been Jim Watt's assistant at Interior who showed me into his office the first time I ever met him for my interview to be Deputy Administrator at Bonneville Power back in 1969. When I became Under Secretary of the Interior and needed to select my own assistant, I was given a list of the senior assistants in the Department from which to choose and Mary Ann's name was on that list. I knew how good she was after dealing with her in order to see—or even talk with—Jim Watt or his boss, Jim Smith, while I was at BPA.

She had the ability to say no in the most pleasant way. I wanted *that* in my own confidential assistant. When I moved to the Energy Department as Secretary, I had to persuade Mary Ann to leave Interior, where she knew everyone and had good connections that would protect her when Reagan left office, to take the risk of joining me. She prospered as the confidential assistant to the Secretary of Energy, after taking a risk that enhanced her career notably. Then, she got another professional advancement by going with me back to Interior as the confidential assistant to the Secretary in the Department where she had worked for years. Taking a risk often opens the door to bigger things. I had a similar experience in moving from the Davies law firm to join the legal department at Georgia-Pacific, which was a huge boost to my future.

One amusing aside is that just after Reagan's reelection in November 1984, I had hired a public relations specialist named David Prosperi for the position of Press Secretary to the Secretary of Energy. Planning to begin work in January 1985, he left his prior position at the end of December and took his wife on a trip to Europe before returning to Washington to take his new job with me. While David was in Europe, he picked up the European edition of an American newspaper and saw an article announcing that I was going to be the new Secretary of the Interior. There he was, having accepted a position that no longer existed. When he returned, he was pretty nervous for several days, until he contacted me and learned that I wanted him to join me in the same role at Interior. Whenever David and I saw each other, even many years later, it was always something over which we had a good laugh.

For me to return to the Department of the Interior as Secretary, it was necessary to once again be nominated by President Reagan and confirmed by the Senate, including, again, a hearing in front of the Senate Energy and Natural Resources Committee, still presided over by Chairman James McClure.

On February 1, 1985, Oregon Senators Mark Hatfield and Bob Packwood again made introductions on my behalf. Hatfield, referring to the novelty of doing so a third time, once for Under Secretary and now for a second Secretariat, humorously said that he and Packwood had appeared a number of times before the committee on my behalf and that we all talked together just before the hearing. "[W]e came to the conclusion that if [Don] could hold a job we wouldn't be required to do this so often," which brought laughter from the entire room.

Senator Hatfield again made a tribute to Barbara and her role in my life when he said she was "an additional dimension to Don Hodel," adding that "to know him and to like him is to love Barbara." The way he said it caused general laughter throughout the audience. His kind comments about Barbara were very pleasing to us both.

The hearing and committee vote went forward rapidly, as did the floor vote (I think, later that same day). There was only one negative vote in the full Senate as opposed to eight votes against my previous appointment. Again, Senator Edward Kennedy of Massachusetts voted against me, and, again, I took it as a badge of honor. We listened to the vote from my office at DOE. I jokingly asked Barbara, "How many husbands can tell their wives that by a vote of the US Senate they are seven-eighths better than they were only two years ago?" I probably thought it was funnier than she did, but she laughed.

I was better prepared for my new job as DOI Secretary than for any job I had ever held. In my service as Under Secretary, I sat beside an excellent Secretary and had personally managed the Department for twenty-one months. Thus, there were no inherent surprises. I already had a thorough knowledge of the Department and of the projects and plans which had begun under Secretary Watt and were carried forward under Secretary Clark because, of course, I had been a part of their formulation. So, I understood the why of each policy and, under Watt, I was the one who implemented them, so I understood the how.

In later years, when author Perry Pendley, a former Deputy Assistant Secretary of Interior under Jim Watt, allowed me to help edit his book *Sagebrush Rebel: Reagan's Battle with Environmental Extremists and Why it Matters Today*, I learned the reason why Judge Clark was so determined that I would follow him as Secretary of the Interior. After the November 1984 elections, Clark wrote a twelve-page, handwritten letter to President Reagan summarizing what he had done as Secretary, emphasizing that he "had faithfully worked to carry on the programs that Secretary Watt had begun."

Perry used the letter to prove that Jim Watt was doing what Reagan wanted and was not just off on his own, as so many wanted to believe. I saw it as a full explanation of why Clark was so determined that I should go back to Interior. He knew I was a rock-solid conservative, that I knew everything about the policies that Jim (with my help) had established, and I would follow through and not cave to those who were trying to push Interior to the left. Sometime after taking office, I sat for an interview with a journalist who, as we ended the interview, said in a kind of surprised fashion, "Wow. It sounds to me as if you are pursuing the same policies as Jim Watt." To which I replied, "Well, I hope so. I work for the same President."

As I wrote earlier, the Department of the Interior was a can of worms because of the conflicting mandates Congress had given over the years to the ten agencies that make up the DOI, including the Bureau of Land Management, the Bureau of Indian Affairs, the National Park Service, the Fish and Wildlife Service, and the Bureau of Reclamation, to name five with significant competing responsibilities. We were committed to trying to balance the various competing responsibilities of the DOI in a way that recognized the value of each of the various activities. Under President Jimmy Carter, Secretary of the Interior Cecil Andrus had said that whenever an issue involved the environment, no matter what the other considerations were, the environment wins. That seemed to me to be both wrong and counterproductive, but it was quite true then—as now—under Democrat Presidents.

President Reagan, of course, believed in conservation, as did I, by which we meant maintaining and protecting the great lands and resources of America. We must take good care of the resources the Creator put on and under the earth for our use. But that does not mean they should be set aside and never used for the benefit of mankind.

Reagan believed that with many, many millions of acres of public land in America, we had ample room for national parks, wildlife refuges, and wilderness areas, literally millions of acres for each purpose, all without in any way reducing the land needed for and set aside for the protection of endangered species. In addition to these purposes, there remained enough acreage for production of oil and natural gas, for mining of other minerals, for recreation, and for grazing of cattle that provided affordable meat for all Americans to eat.

When Jim Watt and I arrived at DOI in 1981, one of the key questions we faced related to the New Melones Dam on the Stanislaus River in California. The dam had been built at the cost of over $100 million, but then-Secretary Cecil Andrus had refused to allow it to be fully filled because of environmental opposition to interfering with recreational rafting that would be flooded out by the dam. When we arrived in Washington, we were told that someone had threatened to chain himself to a big rock in the bottom of the valley so that if we allowed the reservoir to fill, he would drown. Watt and the rest of the top staff agreed when I said, "Then we announce that if he does that, we will have to deal with his estate." We let the reservoir fill, and he did not drown himself. The same man claimed previously to have chained himself to a rock somewhere in what would be the reservoir, and that caused Andrus to stop filling the reservoir well below full. The man must have concluded that if it had worked once, it would work again. Well, not this time!

While I was Secretary, another project involving a dam came to light, and it had an odd dovetail with the other. Ike Livermore, who had been then-Governor Reagan's director of natural resources for the State of California, visited with me during one of my trips to California and suggested that I propose removing the O'Shaughnessy Dam on the Tuolumne River that runs through Hetch Hetchy Valley inside Yosemite National Park. The dam was built as a reaction to the 1906 San Francisco earthquake out of concerns the city would run out of drinking water. Conservationists believed, and when I looked into the matter, I agreed, that approving the dam was a gross overreach that greatly damaged the natural, majestic beauty of Yosemite.

I asked the Bureau of Reclamation to make a rough assessment about whether it would be possible to capture the water downstream, outside the park, if the dam were removed. The Assistant Secretary, Dave Houston, came and told me that the "back of the envelope" look led them to believe that all the water could be captured and used outside the park. He also said there were several things that needed to be done to reduce waste being caused by the way San Francisco was operating the system, thereby actually increasing water availability.

If I wanted to do this, I needed to line up local support. I called the chairman of the Sierra Club, Mike McCloskey. He had been one year ahead of me at Harvard and a year behind me at Oregon Law School, having spent two years in military service in between. I told him of my genuine intentions with regard to the proposal. It was important that he know I was not just floating a big public relations proposal to pretend to be an ardent environmentalist. (Although, a sarcastic cartoon in an environmental magazine later portrayed me as just that.) Fortunately, although we were hardly close, he knew me to be a man of integrity and was very supportive of my plan. What I hoped for was that the environmental community would support the study and therefore allow even Democrats to support it.

I then called the Democrat Mayor of San Francisco (and later US Senator) Diane Feinstein and told her that I was going to propose that we *study* how to do this and actually increase the water supply, while restoring Yosemite National Park. She went ballistic. She was immediately hostile to even studying the idea.

I persisted in hopes of getting her acquiescence, and later we met at O'Shaughnessy Dam, where she, in a television interview, continued to be totally opposed to even studying my proposal. She then went to Democrat Congressman Sid Yates of Illinois, Chairman of the Subcommittee on Appropriations, and convinced him to add language to our Interior appropriations bill stating, "no money in this act may be spent to study whether or not O'Shaughnessy Dam may be removed from Yosemite National Park." That made it unlawful for me or anyone on my staff to spend time on the matter. And most assuredly, anyone who did so would have been prosecuted by the Democrats—unlike the things they themselves did and continue to do, and whose handpicked prosecuting attorneys simply do not see anything to prosecute.

And the struggle over Hetch Hetchy continues. As late as 2014 at the request of proponents of removing the dam, I appeared in a promotional video about the valley that was narrated by actor Harrison Ford. It was shot in one day as we alternated turns in front of the camera.

At the O'Shaughnessy Dam joking with Harrison Ford, along with (L-R) the Environment Defense Fund's Tom Graff and California State Senator Lois Wolk (Courtesy Restore Hetch Hetchy Foundation)

As an example of the strange coincidences that can occur, one of the key conservationists I met while trying to get approval to study the removal of the dam in Hetch Hetchy became a friend, and after I had left Washington, one day over lunch he told Barbara and me about a friend of his who, a few years earlier, had threatened to chain himself to a rock to prevent the filling of the New Melones reservoir. Barb and I looked at each other without flinching and respectfully kept quiet about my role in the decision to fill the reservoir, as well as my comment about his threat.

Barbara and I had an interesting realization when I went back to the Interior Department. We had always known that what Jim Watt said was true: "The people who were your friends before you got one of these exalted positions are the ones who will still be your friends after you leave office," i.e., beware of those who only want to be friends while you are in office. When I was Under Secretary, various industry lobbyists made a point of getting to know me well. They were wonderfully friendly to Barbara and me, and they were congenial and helpful when it came to representing matters affecting their clients. I always kept in mind when considering what they said that they represented particular interests, even though most of them were very trustworthy with regard to the facts. Nonetheless, I followed President Reagan's well-known and oft-spoken adage, "Trust but verify." When I left DOI and went over to DOE, those old friends were gone, and I suddenly had a whole new set of lobbyist friends. They also were very good, informative, and attentive. Twenty-seven months later, when I returned to DOI, my "new" friends were gone and my "old" friends were back!

Each lobbyist's job was to be a "friend" of whomever was in the key jobs at those Departments. Some government officials did not understand that, and when they left their positions, they were devastated to find out that these supposed friends were gone. It was particularly difficult for wives who were socially oriented to find out that it was not their own wonderful personalities that led to all the invitations to teas and garden parties and so on. Fortunately, Barbara was never bothered by that. First, she understood the reason why she was getting those nice invitations to wives' events, and second, she did those things because she thought it was part of her job as the Secretary's wife. She never thought it was more than a part of her job.

Back at Interior, as was the case when I was Energy Secretary, I could not just stay in my office and run the Department—the fun job, as Jim Watt had termed it, that I had done in my previous role there. I had to appear in public, give speeches (sometimes three or four in a week, and, occasionally, more than one in a single day), testify before Congressional committees, meet with dignitaries, and pose with them for pictures, which my staff would later bring to me to sign and inscribe with a note before they mailed them out.

But if I had been able to just stay in my office as Secretary, I would have enjoyed it because it was a really nice office. Harold Ickes was FDR's Secretary of the Interior throughout his Presidency. At the same time, Ickes was also head of the General Services Administration, which was the agency responsible for approving the design and overseeing the construction of federal government buildings. The legend was that he designed the Interior building as Secretary and approved the design as head of GSA. So, basically, he approved his own building design.

The Secretary's office was impressive: elegant wood paneling, a very high ceiling, and a lovely balcony. There was also a beautiful marble fireplace, which the National Park Service made sure was well-stocked with firewood. And there was the Secretary's private dining room, which Jim Watt reopened after Secretary Cecil Andrus had closed it, admitting to Jim when they met during transition that he regretted the decision ("worst decision I ever made" or something akin to that), but at the time he wanted to make a show of being frugal or humble. I made great use of that dining room as Secretary as a way to honor visiting dignitaries or to bring my staff together over lunch.

I also had a weekly, voluntary staff Bible study, usually around the fireplace, which was led by Mark Petersburg from a ministry called Christian Embassy and sometimes included people from outside the Department who heard about it from another attendee and asked if they could come. Barb often joined and we found it spiritually refreshing.

At both Energy and Interior, when I was in town, I almost always had what I called open time, when top staff could wander over to my office and participate in conversations about what was going on. It was informal and almost always attended by Earl Gjelde and Don Pearlman. At Interior it was held on the sofa and wing chairs in front of the fireplace. Usually, this included Barbara and either of the other two spouses who happened to be there. We reviewed the day and asked ourselves whether there were things we needed to do that were not yet done, and then we could plan the next day. It was a wonderful way to end the day and to set priorities for tomorrow. We would ask ourselves if something we had heard made sense or not. If not, Earl or Don would pursue it to find out and verify whether I, as Secretary, was receiving the correct information from a bureaucracy or whether it maybe was trying to push us off course.

This kind of trust and support is why, whenever we placed a new leader in one of the bureaus that reported under DOI, we insisted that they hire one or, preferably, two close—and competent—friend(s) with whom they could sit down at the end of the day and do as Earl, Don, and I did. There is nothing like having someone you can totally trust and who you know will always be honest with you.

On one occasion, we installed a new head in a bureau that badly needed redirection. Because he already was totally distrustful of the bureaucracy, it seemed unlikely that he could be hoodwinked or "captured" by the system so, because we were in a hurry to get him in the job and begin making the needed changes, we decided that if ever there were someone who could handle it without the two trusted aides, it was he. The joke was on us, however, because in only a few days he was back in my office telling us how great those bureaucrats were. "Why these people are really good! They are not like bureaucrats elsewhere," he exclaimed. "We don't need to change direction." He had been completely captured by them in less than a week! And he never could be persuaded otherwise. In this case as in others, in managing a bureaucracy it is essential to understand how it functions.

I was always fascinated by computers and technology. To improve its operation of the Columbia River power system, in 1969, the Bonneville Power Administration had installed a supercomputer. When I ran the Department of Energy, I used technology to communicate with my direct reports, and for international meetings a team was sent ahead to be sure the secure connections were established and working.

In January 1981 when Jim Watt and I arrived at the Department, the administrative staff in the Secretary's office were still using typewriters with carbon paper. As I walked into my Under

Secretary's office, I noticed a Lanier word processor, apparently unused (and possibly *never* used), sitting on top of a filing cabinet. One of my administrative assistants, Becky Mullin, learned how to operate it, giving us the only such capability in the entire Secretary/Under Secretary wing of the building.

When I went back to Interior as Secretary, I used a local area network (LAN) form of email to communicate with my direct report team. A couple of Assistant Secretaries could not even use the system until I started emailing them, and, when they did not reply, as soon as I saw them I would ask if they had received my messages. I knew that they hurried back to their offices and got help from their staff in finding and replying to my emails. Over time they became comfortable with this technology which enabled much quicker and more frequent communications between and among us.

I had access to the LAN on my computer at home so that in the evening I could check my emails. This allowed me to catch up, so that the next day those who had emailed me could have my answer in their inbox at the start of the day. On one occasion, Steve Griles, an Assistant Secretary, sent me a message late at night. It just so happened that night that I was restless and got out of bed shortly after midnight and decided just to check my emails—mostly out of habit. I came across Steve's email and responded to it. The next day in a staff meeting, Steve came in with mock upset and said, "Doggone it, Mr. Secretary! I decided to send you an email so late at night that for once you would not be able to answer until today, but I got to the office this morning and you had answered it in the middle of the night!"

Unlike Jim Watt, I went out of my way not to be combative with the media in my role as Secretary. I never contradicted a questioner in a hearing, but instead would rephrase the question, or otherwise answer in such a way that no dispute occurred. Whereas Watt's speeches and Congressional appearances would draw two large tables full of reporters and a row of cameras all the way across the back of the room, my hearings quickly became almost ignored by the press, who knew there would be no fireworks.

On one occasion, a Senator whom I knew to be quite vain asked me a particularly hard question which a staff member had written for him. I knew and liked the staff member and believed that he liked me, but the question was a zinger. Instead of responding to the substance of the question, I said something along these lines: "Senator, I appreciate that question. It is what I expect from you because I know how interested you are in such matters, and it is why we are trying our best to be responsive to your interests. It is important for us to work with you and your staff on such matters and I assure you we will continue to do so under your excellent leadership." As I was speaking, the Senator was smiling broadly at my almost obsequious tone and wording, while the staffer, sitting behind him, was gnashing his teeth. When I finished my comments, which in no way answered the question he asked, I paused and waited for the next question. Now, if that had been the Senator's own question he would simply have said, "Well, thank you for that nice compliment, Mr. Secretary. Now, what is the answer to my question?" But since the issue was something his staff was pushing, not the Senator himself, he didn't. He just went on to the next question on his staff's list.

As a result of my purposely straightforward and somewhat bland hearing "performances," very soon I was only invited to Capitol Hill to testify on matters that required the Secretary's personal attendance, such as to introduce our budget to the Appropriations Committee or regarding substantive legislation before the Committees on Energy and Natural Resources. This approach saved me a lot of time—and a lot of pressure. Committee members were not really interested in holding hearings that did not get *them* a lot of press coverage.

One of the biggest controversies during my Secretariat involved the Statue of Liberty restoration in preparation for its one hundredth anniversary in 1986. The saga began in 1982 when Jim Watt was Secretary and a man named Richard Rovsek, an unusually creative man who ran the White House Christmas ceremony for President Reagan—and who later became a good friend of Barbara's and mine—contacted Jim's office to set up a meeting for him and Lee Iacocca, chairman of the Chrysler Corporation. Iacocca was viewed as almost single-handedly saving Chrysler by getting a government loan and restoring the company to profitability. Iacocca was very dynamic and someone who attracted a lot of press because he was always "good copy."

When the four of us met, Iacocca made his pitch to Watt that the Statue of Liberty should be refurbished for its centennial, and the money for it should be raised from private donations. The statue had been allowed to fall into disrepair by the National Park Service under prior Administrations and Iacocca knew that there would be insufficient funds in the future (DOI budgets were public information) to correct the situation. The arm holding the torch was so unstable that no one was allowed to climb its inside stairs to reach the torch. The statue's elevator that went up to the crown did not work, which, like the stairs, was secondary to the fact that it was no longer deemed safe for the public to even be inside the statue. They were restricted to the visitors' center in the base and even that area badly needed to be upgraded.

Iacocca made a brief statement about how Lady Liberty needed to be repaired and proposed that a commission be appointed by Watt to advise on what to do and that a private foundation be created by Iacocca to raise funds from the public to pay for it. Watt did not hesitate for a moment. He said, "You're on. Let's do it."

Although the meeting was only a few minutes old, Iacocca stood up and prepared to leave, saying, "Great. I learned a long time ago that when I've made the sale, get up and leave." Watt, of course, asked him to stay and a good discussion followed regarding how to proceed. The upshot of that meeting was the creation of an advisory commission for the Department, the Statue of Liberty-Ellis Island Centennial Commission, chaired by Iacocca, and the selection of Iacocca to create and lead a companion foundation to raise money to pay for the restoration. Initially, there were twenty-one high-profile Americans on the advisory commission, including Bob and Dolores Hope, former US Commerce Secretary Peter G. Peterson, then chairman of Lehman Brothers, Armen Avedisian, chairman and CEO of Avedisian Company, recent UN

Ambassador Jeane Kirkpatrick, sports and business executive Peter Ueberroth, and others, officially appointed by President Reagan, many of those at the recommendation of Rovsek or Iacocca.

Two years later, when I returned to Interior as Secretary, the Statue of Liberty and Ellis Island restoration was going strong with less than two years to go before the summer of 1986, the one-hundredth anniversary celebration of completion of the statue (Ellis Island began receiving immigrants in 1882), when Iacocca and the commission were planning a huge, star-studded ceremony in New York City.

Ann McLaughlin, wife of well-known PBS talk-show host John McLaughlin, had become Under Secretary to Bill Clark and remained in that position when I became Secretary. She later left Interior and became President Reagan's Secretary of Labor. One day, Ann came to me and raised concerns about Iacocca dominating the advisory commission and not asking them for advice or recommendations on the restoration. Being both chief fundraiser and head of the advisory commission, Lee was basically dictating what would be done, as well as how it would be done. Ann thought he should be removed from chairing the commission, and I agreed. Ann's concerns were later confirmed in an unpublished GAO (Government Accountability Office) report in June 1986.

One problem for the Department was that a major reason for an advisory commission is to provide broad advice on matters that stir controversy. When dealing with a statue or a monument, everyone has a different idea and often feels very strongly about the outcome. So, the best way to avoid having irreconcilable battles is to get recommendations from a credible commission. Critics would still complain bitterly about the commission's advice, but the Department could legitimately follow their advice without having to become engaged in a battle with the various factions who were demanding that their proposal be adopted. However, once it became clear that the commission was not being given a chance to offer advice, we realized that we had a larger responsibility to restore the balance between the commission and the foundation.

I already had other concerns. The National Park Service staff in charge of the physical aspect of the restoration was determined to make an authentically restored Statue of Liberty. They even planned to create identical mastic to that which was used originally to glue the tiles to the ceiling of the main hall at Ellis Island. That seemed incredibly costly and foolish. There were many much better mastics available than there were one hundred years earlier, and they were much cheaper, too. That was further indication that the project needed an advisory commission that was independent of the chairman of the fundraising effort. We had to find a new chairman of the advisory commission and not interfere with Iacocca's role as head of the fundraising effort, where he was doing an excellent job. (Eventually the foundation raised in excess of $350 million.)

About the time that we had made the decision to remove Iacocca as chairman of the advisory commission, he was in town for a press conference at the White House, talking about various things, including the Statue of Liberty. Immediately following that press conference, he came to my office to see me. He was all excited and exclaimed about how terrific it was! He excitedly said that the lectern was so jammed with microphones that "I had no place to put my notes," and he was obviously thrilled by all the attention. As he told me this, the thought crossed my mind, *This man is not going to go quietly*. He loved the limelight.

After much discussion of how to approach the subject, my team and I decided that the best thing to do was for me to write to Iacocca, thanking him for the great job he was doing with fundraising, and requesting his resignation as chairman of the advisory commission. I explained my reasoning in the letter. I wanted the advisory commission to give separate advice from him as funding chairman. The next day I got his response. He refused to resign. After I repeated the request and he again refused, we decided I had no choice but to outright remove him as chairman of the advisory commission.

It happened that years earlier Iacocca had been fired as the head of Ford Motor Company by Henry Ford Jr., and he was a prominent enough figure that it was all over the news at the time, and many people remembered that event. Within a day or two after my letter to him, he held a televised press conference to announce the most recent financial results for the Chrysler corporation and then he turned his presentation into an attack on me for this latest firing.

He began by saying that he had gotten a letter from me firing him as head of the Statue of Liberty-Ellis Island Centennial Commission. He said he'd had to call his mother and tell her that he had been fired… again. He claimed she was very worried about him. This was strictly theater, very good theater, and made for news stories sympathetic to him. He did not mention that he remained as head of the *more important* fundraising effort. Listening to his presentation, one could easily have thought that he was being summarily fired by me without any reason after he had done a terrific job.

Then Lee asked me a series of rhetorical questions, each one prefaced in imperative tones with, "Mr. Secretary, tell me why…" There were about six such questions, and each of them highlighted an aspect of the great job he had been doing to restore the Statue and Ellis Island.

In the meantime, Lee had turned lobbyists loose on the White House, trying to persuade the President to reverse my decision, including one who had a reputation as being highly influential, and who was said to have direct access to the President. So, it is entirely possible that the President was being urged to intervene. The White House Cabinet Secretary (the liaison between the President and the Cabinet agencies), Alfred Kingon, called to tell me about pressure on the White House to force me to keep Iacocca.

Kingon seemed alarmed and even said that some were saying that I had just created a situation which would allow Iacocca to run for President as a Democrat! At the time, articles had been showing up in magazines and newspapers about how he might make a good President of the United States. And there are always people inside any White House who are upset by any bad publicity and want all possible criticism to go away, so they were no doubt cringing, as well.

At that point I said to Kingon, "We should be so lucky... He would make a terrible candidate." I had made several joint appearances with Lee at fundraising events, and I had seen how abrasive he was with staff and how they were intimidated by him. He also did not listen to his advisers. That is the kind of thing that makes it very hard to run an effective campaign for President, and finally, I had seen that he was extremely thin-skinned. He would be easy to upset and push off course.

At that point Al asked, "Well, can you withdraw your letter?"

"Al," I said, "of course, if that's what the President wants, I will do it, but remember Lee Iacocca will never say, 'I rolled Don Hodel.' He will say, 'I rolled Ronald Reagan.'"

When I said that it seemed Al almost audibly gulped before saying, "Well, do what you think you have to."

I went home that night and told Barbara that I might have to resign to protect the President. Actually, I was amazed to realize that I was very relaxed about it. If it meant I had to go home, fine. I had done what I thought was right and needed to be done and was not sorry about it.

Years later, my statement about how Iacocca would view my reversing myself was confirmed to me when I read part of his (updated 1984) biography where he talked about being fired from the advisory commission chairmanship by Ronald Reagan. If he mentioned me, I don't remember it. It did not suit his ego to think that someone less than the President could fire him.

My firing of Iacocca made big news in Washington. The front page of one of the newspapers had caricatures of him and me in a boxing match. My staff was very concerned, and Ann McLaughlin came into my office when she arrived on the morning the story broke and was highly agitated. I felt that she was terribly concerned about her position and may have felt some guilt for having urged me to remove Lee.

However, I told her and the others that I was not worried, and that if I needed to protect the President by resigning, I was ready to do so. This of course would create a problem for all of them, since they might lose their jobs under a new Secretary.

David Prosperi, my press secretary, came into my office and told me that the *MacNeil-Lehrer News Hour* on PBS, a very popular and influential broadcast, wanted me on the program that night to talk about Iacocca. I told him to accept.

There was little preparation that was needed for this program. I knew what I had done and why I had done it. I arrived at PBS with David and my security detail, and was ushered into the studio with Jim Lehrer, while Robert MacNeil co-hosted from New York. Lehrer and I were acquainted from my previous appearances (on less controversial matters). After a few pleasantries, Lehrer said that they had some questions for me, and the monitor on the set showed Lee Iacocca asking the first of his six questions: "Mr. Secretary," he demanded, "tell me why..."

The tape was stopped after the first question and Lehrer asked in his typical calm fashion, "What do you have to say about that, Mr. Secretary?" I was truly relaxed and simply gave a straightforward answer. Then the second question was played and again I responded. Along the way I was able to explain my dilemma of having Iacocca doing a great job of raising funds to restore the statue, but in not giving independent advice, the advisory commission was ineffective. Iacocca was too important to the fundraising effort to let him leave that position, so I removed him from the advisory chairmanship.

The interview ended and I left feeling that the problem would not go away, and I might still have to resign, but I was calm and satisfied that I had done my best to explain my reasoning, and I could leave without embarrassment or shame. However, the next day the issue was gone! There were no additional stories! And there were no more statements from Iacocca! It was over. I could hardly believe it. This huge controversy disappeared in one night. Life went on as if the Iacocca firing and his reaction had never occurred. Those were exciting—and tense—days, especially for someone like me who did not like to see my name in the paper.

Shortly after that, I saw a friend who mentioned to me that he had seen me on *MacNeil-Lehrer*. I asked him what he thought of what I said. He replied with a laugh, "Oh, I didn't listen that closely, but you looked so calm that I figured you had to be right."

His reply captured the essence of what I had often said about Washington, DC, that 80 percent of your grade as a politician was based on style and only 20 percent was substance. So, if you did the right thing in an awkward fashion and got only a few style points, you might have 100 percent of the substance right, but you still wouldn't get a passing grade. On the other hand, if your style was good (e.g., President Bill Clinton) it did not matter if your grade for substance was zero. You still got a high rating for your performance.

It reminded me of a joke often told in politics: *In Washington sincerity is everything, and once you learn to fake that, you've got it made.* I was genuinely sincere in my responses to Jim Lehrer, and that must have come through for the broadcast to have had such an immediate and satisfactory result.

Even after I fired Lee Iacocca from the advisory commission our problems did not go away; however, as he continued to exert his preferences regarding how to spend the money that was raised by the foundation, he continued to chair. The agreement had been that money raised would go toward the restoration, while Lee wanted to use it also for a concluding celebration. That was not what we had agreed to and I, again, had to step in, even offering to help him raise money for the celebration. That action also brought a public reaction from Iacocca. The July 4, 1986 weekend celebration was lavish. It was a star-studded bash on national television. In the spotlight were President and Mrs. Reagan, French President François Mitterrand, and, of course, Lee Iacocca. There were thousands of spectators on the grounds, a fantastic fireworks display, and tall ships in the harbor. But in my opinion, it was not something the donors had intended to fund when they contributed to the restoration project.

CHAPTER 14
FINISHING WELL

In August 1985, six months after I became Secretary of the Interior, Congress took its customary month-long summer recess. Knowing that would happen, I decided this was an opportunity to travel out west and visit other Department of the Interior facilities, especially the nation's national parks. Since we in Ronald Reagan's Administration were always under attack for not supporting the environment, this would give me a chance to show that I was an outdoors person who loved the parks, those Crown Jewels of America, as Jim Watt called them.

The trip would also be extremely useful when speaking with members of Congress and others about the West and the condition of all the public lands for which the Interior was responsible, including the parks and their needs. It gave credibility to my statements that I knew what was needed and what was appropriate.

My political purpose had the luxury of also being true, as my parents had taken me to many national parks and national forests in my youth. And when Barbara and I were tent campers before going to Washington, we visited many federal campgrounds and parks. We truly loved those experiences. I was not faking interest.

I worked with my top staff to make plans for spending a month in the West. My first thought was that we would set up a field office in Denver as a hub, and take trips from there, but as the plans developed it became apparent that I didn't need a field office for the trip. I would have various staff traveling with me all the way, although the individuals would change from time to time so that many of the top staff would get some of the same experiences I had. A few went along on all of it, including Joe Kyrillos, my personal "advance man." If something needed to be arranged or a problem with tickets arose or anything about the trip needed to be discussed with headquarters, it was Joe's job to fix it. Also, we had two security people—members of the US Park Police—who went on the whole trip. One handled the security advance, going to the next stop ahead of us and making sure that there was adequate protection and always some way to communicate with Washington, while the other traveled with our party.

We visited numerous national parks: Redwoods in northern California; Bryce Canyon and Zion, both in Utah; Glacier in Montana; Grand Canyon in northern Arizona; Grand Teton in Wyoming; and a couple of others, though this many years later I don't recall them all.

At the Grand Canyon, our group of twenty-three included security, various staff, such as Under Secretary Ann McLaughlin, COO Earl Gjelde, a couple of Assistant Secretaries, the park superintendent and one or two other park personnel, as well as David Prosperi, plus a female *Los Angeles Times* reporter. Due to her presence, I had told Barbara that it was "alright if I die on this trip, but I dare not falter." I knew that the hostility of the *Times* toward President Reagan would mean that anything bad they could write about one of his key appointees would be the subject of a negative article.

We rode mules down Bright Angel Trail, from the rim of the canyon to the bottom, which was, without a doubt, the most terrifying thing I had (or have) ever done. One reason for riding mules rather than walking down was so we could have the same experience as many canyon tourists. For me, there was an added reason. I was suffering from arthritic knees. The pounding I normally experienced when walking downhill became very painful after a fairly short time and doing it for three miles and 5,000 vertical feet was pretty much out of the question.

What I did not know was that starting on the south rim of the canyon meant that at the very beginning of the descent, perhaps less than one hundred yards after mounting the mules and starting down the narrow trail, we would encounter a series of sharp switchbacks cut across the face of a sheer 1,000-foot rock cliff, which would prove to be a panic-inducing experience.

As soon as we were in the saddles, we were given switches made of braided wire with a leather thong on the end. The "mule skinner," i.e., the guide or driver of a mule, a slim and tough young woman, told us that the switches were for the purpose of slapping the rump of our mule so that it kept its nose right at the rear end of the mule that was directly in front. This functioned as a blinder of sorts, so that nothing startled the mule, such as a bird or a hiker coming up the trail. The danger was that a startled mule might bolt, and the mule and its rider fall off the trail into the canyon—a long way down.

Her statement really got our attention! She assured us that they had never lost a mule and its rider. Although someone in our party passed along a story he had heard about mules, while packing loads, not riders, sliding off the trail during a winter trek out of the canyon. Fortunately, we were there in August.

What the mule skinner didn't tell us was that each switchback was fifty to seventy-five yards in length, with a rock wall rising up one side and a sheer drop of hundreds of feet on the other, and as the mule worked its way around a turn its head extended out over the canyon. As we came to the first such turn, the panic in my chest was almost overwhelming. I thought for a moment that I might pass out. Had it not been for the reporter who came along, I think I might have backed out at that point even if it made my staff think I was a coward. But I knew I could not do that and risk public ridicule in the *Los Angeles Times*, so I had no choice but to continue.

Not quitting took greater courage than I thought I could muster. At the next turn, I had the same rising panic. I don't know how many switchbacks there were, maybe a dozen or even more, but each one was gut-wrenching. Slowly, as each successive turn was completed without a stumble, I became less panicky and, finally, I began to sense that I really could trust my mule. At that point, feeling increasingly relieved, I began to make lighthearted remarks to the other members of the group.

When we got to the bottom of the canyon and were dismounting, I said to the staff around me, "That was the scariest thing I have ever done in my entire life!" At that point the floodgates opened, and it became apparent that everyone felt that way, and most were very angry with me for subjecting them to such a harrowing experience. A couple of them told me in no uncertain terms that they were absolutely frightened out of their wits, and it was no help at all for me to be making jokes! The reporter, who had been white as a sheet, said almost nothing.

I need to add that Barbara was amazing. I knew from her face that she was as fearful as I was, but she was a total trouper. She never said one word of complaint or criticism toward me for getting her into such a scary situation. Her courage and her loyalty and support were wonderful.

Riding my mule down into the Grand Canyon (Department of the Interior)

The National Park Service had sent four inflatable rubber rafts down river from the launch point that was miles upstream. They were not motorized, but were propelled by oars, and the lack of motors would have increased the full trip from one week to two. I did not have time to spend two weeks on only one activity so, because I was Secretary, we were privileged to take a very short version so that we could experience at least some of what other visitors to the parks enjoyed.

After a brief rest, approximately six people in our party boarded each raft, and we began our trip down the river. As Secretary, I led the way, so Barbara and I were in the first raft, sitting across the front bench seat with the park superintendent. It was an exciting ride with many rapids and water splashing all over us in the larger rapids. Of course, each wave that broke over the bow of the raft shocked us with the frigid water, about fifty-two degrees, even on a ninety-degree day.

Drifting with the rapid current and with our guide rowing in the quieter stretches, we were awed by the cliffs of the Grand Canyon rising a mile or more above us, shining yellow, orange, and red in the sun as the day progressed toward sunset. As evening came, we pulled over to a gravel bar where we camped for the night. This was rough camping, more rustic than what Barbara and I were used to when we camped on our own; but back then we drove and could fill our car with supplies. Here we were in rafts, with lots of people along, and limited carrying capacity. It was, however, a great experience, the memory of which is lingering vividly these forty years later.

We slept in sleeping bags on the ground in small tents. We had plenty of food and cookstoves expertly managed by the park rangers who were with us.

We continued downstream in the rafts the next day and, a little before midday, approached Crystal Rapid, a relatively new rapid that had been formed in 1966 when a huge rainstorm (over fourteen inches in a few hours) washed a massive number of huge boulders down from the south-side cliffs and partially blocked the river. As the smaller rocks were washed away downstream several large boulders remained in the river, which caused the water to pile up into a large and dangerous standing wave.

Upstream, the guides rowed our rafts to the north bank of the river alongside a large boulder. Everyone got out and walked downstream about a quarter of a mile to look at the rapid and scope out how to get through it safely. The river was quite wide at this point—maybe 250 feet—and the water was funneled toward the middle where it formed a V-shape, leaving a standing wave that was twelve to fifteen feet high in the center of the river. The water was moving fast, and anything approaching was forced toward the middle and that large, standing wave. The challenge for the guide was to be able to stroke hard enough to fight the current and take the raft over the smaller, side wave and not get caught and swept by the force of the water into the standing wave, which could capsize the raft.

We were told that only one person other than the guide would be allowed on board each raft and that person's job was to bail out the water surging into the raft over the sides while shooting the rapid. I said that I would be bailer on the raft in which I had been riding. Each of the other rafts was claimed by staff in order of their position in the Department. Thus, Ann McLaughlin, Earl Gjelde, and one other person were the bailers in their respective rafts. Other than the guide and the bailer, all others, including Barbara, had to walk downstream on a narrow foot path.

I heard several of the younger staff quietly scoffing at all this drama. It didn't look that serious to them, which made me think they had no experience with white water rafting. I later learned that Crystal Rapid is responsible for more injuries and deaths than any other of the many large rapids in the Grand Canyon.

My guide and I went first. He was strong and an expert oarsman but, though he rowed strongly, we drifted closer and closer to the standing wave. Finally, just before we were swept into it, we popped over the side wave and safely passed the danger. We took on a lot of water, however. I was bailing furiously, and I kept turning my head to look upstream behind us, watching Earl's raft which was next in line. I was horrified to see it slide closer and closer to the standing wave. I alerted my guide, who turned just in time to see that raft get caught in the main current. I can still picture the bottom of Earl's raft as it went vertical, appeared to hesitate for a moment, and then flipped upside down, landing downstream from the standing wave.

We knew we could not go back to help, so we had to position ourselves to catch that raft, the guide, and Earl. My guide took us downstream about 300 yards to a boulder jutting out into the river to which we could moor, and we waited to assist Earl and his guide. Meanwhile the other two rafts launched and headed toward the rapid so they could also be available to help retrieve the flipped raft and its passengers. Those rafts made it without mishap.

The upside-down raft, with Earl and the guide hanging on and kicking it toward our side of the river, moved rapidly to where we were, but it was very difficult for them to get it to our side. Finally, over the last few dozen feet they were able to get close enough so that we could reach them. A few park rangers who had walked down the side helped us get Earl and the guide out of the water. Both were already suffering from hypothermia, losing muscle functions from being in the terribly cold water. Once they were out of the water, each seemed to be OK, although they were very cold. But it turned out that the guide had been hit on her head by a large equipment box in the raft as it flipped over. Fortunately, even though the park ranger determined that she had gotten a mild concussion, she did not have to be evacuated out by helicopter and was able to complete the trip.

We were able to continue downstream after one of the other park staff took over as guide and did the rowing in Earl's raft. Midway through the day, we reached the landing point on the south side of the river for the trail we would follow to hike out of the canyon. Again, because of the reporter, I felt I had to show that I was not faking it in the outdoors. I set a rapid pace and soon was asked by several in the party to stop so that they could rest.

I had not known if I would be able physically to do everything that I thought was needed under the watchful eye of the reporter, so Barbara and I had prearranged that if I needed to take a break, I would ask *her* if *she* needed a rest. Of course, her answer was to be yes. Fortunately, we never needed to employ that plan.

In the end, no article ever appeared in the *Los Angeles Times* about that trip. This was a small victory because a story would only have been printed if it had been negative or demeaning. I was pleased that the fact there was no story meant I had not given the reporter anything negative to report.

After hiking about halfway out of the canyon, I was met by a helicopter which flew me around to view various ancient Indian cliff dwellings carved into the side of the canyon walls. That people successfully thrived in such a place was a fascinating thing to see.

All in all, the summer trip to the national parks was a great experience. I drew on these experiences on many occasions afterward while speaking or simply meeting with key people. There is no substitute for an opinion which includes, "When I was there and saw it…"

While things like that trip to the Grand Canyon were fun, most of my four years as Secretary of the Interior were spent in the office, testifying to Congress, going to meetings, including Cabinet meetings at the White House, and making speeches. And there were always contentious and controversial management issues.

Budgeting for the Bureau of Reclamation

One of the major responsibilities for a Cabinet officer is to oversee and approve the Department's annual budget proposal that goes to the Office of Management and Budget. OMB tries to keep spending in line with the President's desires and to keep it from creating too much of a deficit. The process of putting the budget together is time-consuming, much more so than I had dealt with at Bonneville Power because whereas BPA was one agency, DOI encompassed ten agencies, most of them bigger than BPA. The budget is discussed and shaped through multiple meetings over the course of the entire year. And during one such meeting with the Bureau of Reclamation (BuRec) I was given an insight into one of our major problems.

BuRec was responsible for building and operating many dams and large irrigation systems throughout the West and for producing electricity from some of those dams and building the power lines that moved the power to the ultimate consumer. The power from the dams that is sold over those power lines is managed by one of six power marketing agencies around the country. These were sister agencies to BPA, but none was as large or complex.

BuRec had thirty or forty major projects at some degree of planning or construction in its budget each year. Usually, each of these projects would cost multiple hundreds of millions of dollars to build. They were mostly very large concrete and steel projects and most of them had many millions of dollars to go before they would be finished.

As I was being briefed for the first BuRec budget after I returned to Interior, we discussed the amount of money requested to keep building the huge Central Utah Project that was authorized in 1956 to transport large volumes of water from Colorado to Utah. I recall being told that over the years it was continually revised downward in scope from a high of one-million acre-feet of water down to something in the range of 100,000 acre-feet, at a cost of roughly $1 billion.

I listened to the presentation as to why the proposed amount of money was needed in the next budget year and continually became more frustrated with what I was hearing. Finally, I asked, "When will this project be completed?"

There was an uncomfortable silence as the staff looked at each other before responding. I was shocked by their answer: "Never."

"What?!" I demanded.

It was explained to me that the amount of money Interior was spending on the Central Utah Project was *not enough to make any* progress toward completing it. All we were doing was paying enough money to keep the equipment at the site and pay the employees, but we were not spending enough money to get any work done toward completion of the project. I was literally stunned.

"You mean that we're just throwing money at it to keep it going, but never to make any real progress toward finishing it?"

I was dismayed that we had not discovered this when Jim Watt was Secretary and done something about it then. Since I was the one overseeing the operations as Under Secretary, I was the one who should have caught this. Of course, the main bureaucratic consideration in doing such a thing was the desire of BuRec to satisfy the Senators and Congressmen from each state and district where the projects were being built. They wanted the money to be spent and the jobs maintained in order to keep their constituents happy.

That started me on a whole new line of questioning about all the projects. I learned that BuRec, in order to placate supporters of each project and their members of Congress, was doing the same thing with numerous projects that were never going to be finished with the amounts of money appropriated for them each year.

So, I instructed BuRec to go back to the drawing board and give me a new budget that listed the projects in order of how close each one was to being finished. Then, I wanted to know how much it would take to finish the one closest to being finished, then the next, and so on down to the last one that was furthest from completion.

I directed that moneys be reallocated to the projects that were nearest to completion so that one, two, or three of them could be finished in a year or two if we put enough money into them. Others would be slowed down for a time, but each year we would whittle down the list and keep having more money for the projects which were next in line.

Of course, when our budget proposal became public, I had to cope with multiple calls from Senators and Congressmen who wanted more money for their hometown or state projects, and I had to reallocate some of the money to placate them. However, we did make progress by proceeding in this fashion. This was an effective change that I was pleased to have identified and instituted, although I understand that sometime after I left Interior in 1989 the bureaucratic system resumed doing things the old way.

I have wondered why they would abandon such a practical way of finishing the projects instead of keeping all of them barely alive and with completion dates far into the future. My guess is that it was partially due to the political pressure to spend more money on projects in states represented by the more powerful members of Congress. I had fought the hard part of that battle, however, in getting the turnaround started and generally navigating around the objections of those who were potential roadblocks in Congress. All my successors needed to do was to hold the line and make small adjustments that were politically necessary to keep things going. I'm guessing that sooner or later one of my successors had no inclination to do that, which meant that future Secretaries likely never even heard about my approach, with no one at BuRec willing to risk their self-preservation instincts to tell them. It could have simply been the bureaucracy protecting its future. As long as none of these projects was finished, all of the engineers, planners, administrators, and whoever else was involved, would have ongoing job security. If the number of projects were whittled down, eventually (and maybe sooner rather than later), there would be less need for all of these bureaucrats. Somehow, I'm reminded of Will Rogers's comment, "Just be glad we don't get all the government we pay for."

Leasing for Oil and Gas Exploration

Among the many tasks given the Department of the Interior is to try to lease areas off the US coast for oil and gas drilling. The US is surrounded by a continental shelf, which extends in some places 230 miles offshore and is claimed by our government as part of its sovereign territory. Attempting to lease such areas is almost always a highly controversial process because every state, except oil producing Louisiana and Texas, opposes such exploration, with many voices strongly protesting against the risk of oil spills from wells gone wrong. However, it is also true that a fundamental hostility to any kind of fossil fuels is at the core of much of the opposition.

Faith in renewable sources of energy—such as solar and wind—allows opponents to claim that America's entire energy needs can be supplied without reliance on coal, oil, natural gas, or nuclear energy. The truth is much more complex than that. The energy system is intricately interwoven and interdependent. Even after all the government stimulus for clean energy, it is doubtful that the US can sustain its economic well-being without many more years of dependence on the old-fashioned or traditional sources.

The callousness of the advocates of clean energy toward the negative economic impact on poor people of increasing energy costs as a result of substituting these higher cost resources for the older "dirty" ones is shameful. Our entire economic system is totally dependent upon a reliable supply of electricity. Computers, communications, lighting, etc., cannot operate without uninterrupted power supply. You can't pump gas, recharge your phone, iPad, or electric vehicle, get your airline boarding pass, or check out at the grocery store, and so on if the electricity supply is interrupted.

Also, regarding offshore drilling versus importing oil, the fact is that there is greater environmental risk when importing. Multiple tankers bringing refined oil from foreign countries are a greater risk of oil spills than domestic drilling because refined oil is toxic to wildlife, while crude oil is found in nature and dissipates through microbial action.

When Wally Hickel was Richard Nixon's first Secretary of the Interior, a well was being drilled in the Santa Barbara Channel off the coast of California. It "blew out" (which means that the pressure of the oil in the ground was so great that it forced the drill pipe out of the hole and spurted tar-like oil into the ocean). A lot of that oil ended up on the beaches of California. Ignored by most reports that triggered public expressions of outrage, however, was that that channel had been a known source of leaks from natural seepage to such an extent that there was a section along the shore named "Coal Tar Point." None of that mattered in the political battle that developed, and there was a great deal of opposition to offshore leasing for oil production.

The Montreal Protocol

In 1987, a major issue for the Reagan Administration was the Montreal Protocol, which would prohibit the use of hydrofluorocarbons (HFCs) because of their presumed damage to the ozone layer in the atmosphere. The theory was that damage to the ozone layer would result in an increase in destructive ultraviolet rays hitting the earth and causing increased skin damage among humans and animals. One estimate that was used to support the ban said that in fifty years there would be 750 more deaths from skin cancer because of the hole in the ozone layer.

My science advisers thought that very little was known about both the facts of the ozone hole and the causes. The use of HFCs was essential to the washing of computer chips and there was no known substitute for them. So, the proposal to ban HFCs, based on scientific guesses at a known cost to society was the issue. I argued that we ought to have valid, reliable science to rely on before making a multi-billion-dollar decision.

The EPA and the State Department were desperate to sign the Montreal Protocol because they wanted President Reagan to look like an environmentalist. A "green victory" was the goal—even if the science was not settled.

One of the underlings from State, who was about as far Left as you could get, told the *Washington Post* that I was opposing the signing and said, "Hodel's position is that the solution to the ozone layer is sunglasses and hats." Those words never passed my lips! David Prosperi got wind of the *Post's* plan to publish a story about my supposed views the day before it was to run. He called the reporter, Cass Peterson, and said, "Would you like to hear Secretary Hodel's side of the story?" "No," she said, "I have my story."

The next day on the front page of the *Post* was the story "quoting" me as saying that sunglasses and hats were the solution to the ozone layer problem. This was, of course, false—because I never uttered those words or anything like them—but that story made it impossible for me to continue the fight because few in the White House wanted to be associated with someone who was accused of having made such a ridiculous statement. Even though I did not say it, they were afraid to support me and be painted with the same brush.

At some point, though, the White House Cabinet Secretary, Nancy Risque, who had succeeded Al Kingon, wrote a letter to the editor defending me, stating that I said no such thing, but that was neither newsworthy nor was it deemed significant enough for the *Post* to print.

Years later, someone sent me a copy of an editorial from a newspaper in Florida where there was a statement like, "Why, one

Cabinet officer in the Reagan Administration even went so far as to suggest that the solution to the hole in the ozone layer was to wear sunglasses and hats." Right then I knew it would be my epitaph. But at least here in this book I can detail the true story, so that my grandchildren and their kids know the truth, even if no one will ever believe them.

Yellowstone Fires

In the summer of 1988 one of the most publicized events of my tenure as Secretary of the Interior occurred when Yellowstone National Park suffered massive forest fires. What began with multiple fires caused by lightning strikes both inside and outside the park, along with at least one fire caused by sparks from a logging operation near the west entrance to the park, became a national news story covered nightly for weeks as many of those multiple fires merged into one huge conflagration. The forest suffered from pine beetle infestation, causing large areas of dead trees, which was a tinder box for the fires. Added to that was unusually low humidity and high winds, which caused the fires to quickly get out of control.

Nightly, dramatic news footage and photos showed trees exploding in flames and many thousands of Americans living in Idaho, Montana, and Wyoming suffering enormously from terrible smoke. Yellowstone, with its forests, animal life, and tourist attractions such as Old Faithful, was—and is—a national treasure and the entire country was aghast.

Of course, the media sought a scapegoat, and it was natural for them to blame the Secretary of the Interior, the National Park Service, and the Reagan Administration in general, for not putting out the fires. When placing blame, it is always better to accuse a person than an organization since it is harder to visualize an organization, but a person at fault is something everyone understands.

I flew out to Wyoming to see the fires myself. Once there, I took a helicopter to fly over the park and get a feel for the severity of the fires. What I saw was both tragic and amazing. Immediately apparent were the different kinds of forests inside the park, including areas composed of very old trees that were kind of grayish green in color—I recall that the park ranger with me said the oldest were perhaps 400 years old—and other areas of much younger trees that appeared to be bright green—estimated by the guides to be 200 years old or less, the younger in most cases growing in areas that had burned sometime during the prior two centuries. The older trees were highly flammable, like a Christmas tree that had been left up for three weeks after Christmas, and they exploded when exposed to a spark. It was apparent when looking at the park from the air that it was the older forests that provided the fuel that fed the rapidly spreading flames.

At that time the long-standing Park Service policy had been to not fight forest fires that had natural causes, only to protect infrastructure, while fires with man-made origins would be combated. These Yellowstone fires were both natural and man-caused, and they merged with no way to separate them. So much of the park became jeopardized that the Park Service decided—and I agreed—that they must try to stop it, no matter the cause. In other words, this was a lot worse than the usual situation and a more aggressive approach was deemed necessary; it could be argued that once several of the fires of mixed origin merged fighting the fires was appropriate.

With all the attention on the fires in Yellowstone there was widespread desire to help. Over 400 fire trucks and personnel had come to help from all around the western United States. And I was told that the Department of Defense sent over 9,000 troops to assist the Park Service fight the fire. It truly attracted national attention! As an example of how people responded, a few years later I met a local fire chief who proudly told me about how he had brought a truck from Silverthorne, Colorado, to help fight the Yellowstone fires.

DOD Deputy Secretary William Howard Taft IV, the great grandson of the former President (and, later, Chief Justice), and I met with President Reagan in the Oval Office to update him on the situation and to describe our joint efforts to put out the fire and save the park. As we briefed the President while the television cameras were running, we explained what was going on using a map of Yellowstone. The President was gravely concerned, and he knew how important it was to show everyone what he was feeling over what was happening.

I found it interesting to learn from Taft that fighting the fires was a significant team-building experience for the servicemen and women who participated. However, in spite of everyone's best efforts, nothing was successful in stopping the fire.

As the timber continued to burn, those on the ground worked to protect infrastructure (buildings and bridges), as troops removed fallen trees and other debris from getting close to those structures. We were largely successful in that effort, particularly with regard to the more historic structures that were symbols of Yellowstone National Park to the millions who had visited the park over the years.

The Park Service told me that wooden buildings that got hot enough would explode into flames if a spark landed anywhere on them. In order to reduce this risk, when water was available it was sprayed on roofs and siding on any structure in the path of an advancing fire. I observed that buildings surrounded by green grass for a distance of at least twenty-five feet between them and the forest seemed to be pretty much safe.

Due to the high winds, there was the added difficulty of not being able to have firefighters in the path of a fire because the fires were spreading rapidly and could easily engulf anyone if sparks landed around them, and almost all of those sparks would start a new fire which also would trap the firefighters.

I recall that in late July, the director of the National Park Service came to me with good news: The fire was almost under control. We were greatly relieved. However, the very next day the winds picked up to speeds that I was told reached fifty miles per hour and the largest of the multiple fires advanced many miles in one day. So, the battle continued.

I again flew out to survey the scene, this time accompanied by Mike Sullivan, the Democrat Governor of Wyoming. Mike was a really good guy and a longtime friend of Jim Watt's and therefore was instantly friendly toward me. While we were flying over the fire, I told Mike that liberal voices, especially from the environmental community, were demanding that I fire the head of the National Park Service (as if that would have done any good). I said that my response to them was that if anyone should be fired, it should be the Secretary of the Interior—me! We both laughed, and then with a big smile he said, "That's what I've been saying, too!" I've always thought he was kidding. But who knows? In truth, much of the animosity and criticism we encountered came from those hoping to hurt the then-active candidacy of Reagan's Vice President, George Bush (since known as George H. W. Bush after his son George W. served two terms as President), in the 1988 Presidential election.

In truth, there was little that could have been done from Washington, DC, to fight a forest fire in the West, other than to do everything reasonably possible to supply the necessary resources on the ground. At one point I was faced with a major decision when asked by the Park Service whether to approve the use of bulldozers to create a broad "fire line" in front of the advancing fire. I was told that that fire line would need to be at least the width of five highways, and even that did not guarantee the sparks would not go past that and start more fires. Once I understood the implications, I said no. Fires had been part of the history of Yellowstone long before it had been made a national park, even before the country came into being, and such a man-made swath would leave a scar for the next two centuries. Even if it was guaranteed to stop the fire, the difference between that sharp cut through the forest by bulldozers would be more visually disturbing than the aftermath of a fire. So, we did what we could to protect the park facilities and let nature do what it had done for centuries, that is, burn the old, dead trees, fallen limbs, and underbrush in order to allow a burst of new growth.

Finally, cooler weather arrived in early September, and soon rain and snow began to fall, and the fire finally died out. The Park Service at that time estimated that about half of Yellowstone's two million acres of forest was burned, although I have subsequently read that the total acres burned within the park were just under 800,000 or about 36 percent of the park.

The decision was made to review the National Park Service's own policies regarding firefighting in America's national parks. As soon as that policy review was announced—after the election—the professional environmentalists who had been so critical of us for not fighting the fires adequately (i.e., to their satisfaction) went ballistic because they actually favored the policy that was already in place. These same people had said nothing about how fire was natural and a long-term benefit to the park, as I described above, but instead had attacked the Reagan Administration for not stopping the fires.

Briefing Reagan in the Oval Office on the Yellowstone fires, including among others Gen. Colin Powell, Nancy Risque, and Marlin Fitzwater to my left and Dick Lyng, Judy Black Ogelsby, and Ken Duberstein to the President's right (Reagan Library/National Park Service)

In November, with Bush's victory secured, the environmental extremists no longer were trying to influence the election, so they spoke the truth about what they believed. In the end, the policy that was in place was maintained, because it was the correct policy, and not a peep was heard from the former complainers.

The politicization of the fire was reprehensible. They should have honestly acknowledged the long-term benefits of such fires and credited the Park Service and all those who were fighting these, which, I believe, would have reduced the personal abuse that was heaped upon the Park Service during the fires.

I was very appreciative when Bob Barbee, then-Yellowstone superintendent, and several of his career employees came to my office in Washington and presented me with a plaque for the support I had given them during the fire. They knew that I had taken a lot of personal abuse because I was willing to shield them by not trying to pass the blame. Nonetheless, the legacy lived on, and to some I would always be known as the Secretary who let Yellowstone burn. The joys of public service!

Winding Down an Administration

The last thing to discuss in this chapter is what happens at the end of a Presidency. For a two-term President, as was Ronald Reagan, the moment he is reelected his future is settled. The Constitution requires that he must leave the White House in four years. His ability to sway the Congress, therefore, diminishes rapidly. My personal view is that he has only two to three months, maybe one hundred days, to initiate anything new or significant in his second term. After that the system bogs down in the anticipation of a change of leadership, even if the same political party is expected to win the White House again.

In terms of the line of succession to the Presidency, the Presidential Succession Act of 1947 stipulates that the agency (Cabinet) Secretaries follow after Vice President, Speaker of the House, and President Pro Tempore of the Senate, in the order their agencies were founded. Interior, therefore, comes eighth in line, while Energy falls in at number fifteen. At Cabinet meetings as DOI Secretary, I sat on the same side of the Cabinet table as the President, separated from him by only one person, the Secretary of State. On the President's left was the Secretary of Defense. Directly across the table was the Vice President, and next to him were the Secretary of the Treasury and the Attorney General.

With Senate Democrats back in power after the 1986 Congressional elections, as well as their continued dominance of the House, we lost the ability to generate any significant legislative initiatives, and the Democrats had renewed ability to pass bad bills and send them to the President. I remember the Cabinet meeting immediately following the 1986 midterm election. President Reagan told us, "I have my veto pen ready!"

Reagan instinctively recognized that we had to present a clear philosophy in our upcoming battles with the Democrat-controlled Congress, and the only way for us to show the differences between Democrats and Republicans would be to present clear, strong proposals for what Reagan thought was best and then let the Democrat Congress tear them apart and do nothing or, instead, pass something else which the President could then veto. Such actions would have presented the American people with a clear picture of the difference between what the Democrats wanted and what we conservatives wanted.

However, the White House people around the President did not seem to understand what had happened. They were said to be so smart and wise, but they failed to recognize that Reagan had won and was a popular President because he had successfully presented a vision for America that was different—and better—than what the Democrats were proposing.

People like Don Regan, who had switched from being Secretary of the Treasury to being Chief of Staff, and James Baker, who had traded jobs with Regan, kept right on doing what had been done since 1981, namely, they went to Capitol Hill and met with the committee chairmen and tried to negotiate legislation that would pass the Democrat Congress. This meant that they were forced to compromise on all key issues, so that when the legislation got to the floor of the Senate or the House, it was not a clearcut proposal which could be shown by the White House to be flawed. Yet Reagan still vetoed legislation he did not like, over twenty times in the second term, in addition to several "pocket vetoes" where a President simply allows the time to run out without addressing a bill sent to him by Congress.

It might have been that President Reagan was so affected by the Iran-Contra controversy in his second term—even in the eyes of those around him—that they were unwilling to have him take strong stances on philosophical grounds. If that was indeed their thinking, I believe they were wrong. The American people will respond to clear leadership which soundly expresses what it stands for and believes.

Another aspect of a second term is at first manifested by the behavior of the bureaucracy, where it begins to make the system slow down. This happens because very few bureaucrats are willing to take any risk that the incoming party might dislike something they did and thereby take their job away.

Until the midterm Congressional elections, some work gets done. Almost immediately after those elections, however, the White House begins to signal that we should think about not rocking the boat before the Presidential election two years hence.

Then, in the spring of the following year—roughly eighteen months before the next Presidential election—the message is stronger: "Don't do something too controversial before the next election." Then, finally in the fall of the year before the election the word is, "Don't do anything that *might* be controversial." In other words, do nothing.

Knowing this in 1987, I instructed my Assistant Secretaries to take all the steps necessary to complete the process for making whatever decisions they thought needed to be made, but to not submit them to me for final action. Instead, I requested that they put the almost completed decisions "in the bottom drawer of their desks," and we would deal with them the day after the election.

In November 1988, Vice President George Bush won the Presidency. The next day at Interior, we began what turned out to be three days of meetings considering and deciding seventy-two administrative decisions, which were required to be published in the Federal Register for a period of time before they became effective. By Friday of that same week, all the decisions had been made.

A surprising sidenote was that when then-Vice President Bush arrived at the Republican Convention in New Orleans in August 1988, he had not yet chosen his running mate, and someone floated my name to the media. I gave it no serious concern and declined to comment when asked. And seeing the vicious attacks against the eventual nominee, Senator Dan Quayle of Indiana, during the general election campaign, it did not take me long to be very thankful that I had not been Bush's choice. Further, I doubt he would have wanted me, coming from the more conservative wing of the party. In an offhanded comment picked up by the media he seemed to lack confidence in "the vision thing."

It was apparent that as a Cabinet Secretary with no more decisions to be made, I was superfluous. No speeches or Congressional hearings were left either, as no one wanted to hear from a lame-duck Secretary. There was literally nothing for me to do. So, I decided that I would move my official office to the Denver area Federal Center in an office made available to me by the Bureau of Reclamation. Barbara and I found a condo to rent (at personal expense) in Frisco, Colorado, in Summit County about an hour's drive up in the Rocky Mountains. This was because we were planning to move to Summit County and enjoy its wonderful skiing opportunities for one year while we opened a consulting business.

In those days remote work was not as easy because the internet was only getting started, which meant that I could not be present in the office from a remote location. So, each morning we left Summit County in a vehicle driven by one of our security detail members on the way to my office in Lakewood, near Denver, while I used the car phone for business along the way. I don't recall what I did to keep busy once in the office, but I did.

After a couple of weeks of doing this, someone must have told the *Washington Post,* because one of its Beltway gossip columns included a short piece to the effect that Interior Secretary Hodel "apparently has lost interest in his job and was officing in Denver."

As I recall, that was only a day or two before all seventy-two of the decisions we had made immediately following the election were published in the Federal Register. The deluge of decisions was noted in the press but having already said that I was gone from Washington, they had no one to attack for making these decisions, so mostly they went into effect without the Democrats and their spokesmen in the media naming me as responsible. They had already told the world that I was not involved.

Barbara and I returned to Washington in January 1989 to begin packing our things for our move to Colorado. Knowing that I did not particularly like to attend the big events in Washington, I got a call from Cabinet Secretary Nancy Risque asking if I could be the "designated survivor" for the Inauguration. I happily said that I could, provided that they would permit me to stay at my home in Arlington, Virginia, that day—January 20, 1989—packing a moving van, rather than being sequestered away from Washington, DC, as I had done when previously serving in that role.

I did not seek the limelight while I was in Washington. At the President's annual State of the Union Address to Congress each winter, one Cabinet member is chosen to stay away from the Capitol to step in as President in the highly unlikely—but devastating—event that the Capitol suffers an attack of terrorism or war wiping out the President and all of those who are statutorily designated as successors to the President. With other Secretaries, Supreme Court Justices, the Chairman of the Joint Chiefs of Staff, and other generals sitting front and center while the President spoke, during my six years in the Cabinet I served as the designated survivor three times. On those nights Barbara and I waited and watched the President's address on television, which was much more enjoyable than sitting in the front row at the speech with cameras ready to put you on national television if you yawned or in any way reacted in a way that allowed them to make you look bad.

The Secret Service showed up outside my home that 1989 Inauguration morning in six official looking black vehicles. The colonel in charge of the detail had the nuclear "football" (the briefcase containing nuclear codes and the ability to launch), so that if the unthinkable occurred, I would, as the "successor President" be able to direct the use of nuclear weapons to retaliate against an attacker. About midday, I was busily involved packing the moving van when he appeared at my door and announced, "Sir, the President (i.e., Bush) has cleared the area (i.e., the Inauguration site) and we are leaving." I have often teased, holding my thumb and index finger about half an inch apart, "I was this close to being President of the United States."

Three days after President Bush's inauguration, on January 23, 1989, Barbara and I left Washington forever. We visited occasionally for work-related reasons, but we never lived there again. We both were fifty-three years old and ready to be away from the Beltway. We flew back to Denver and then drove up the mountain to Summit County and never looked back.

An interesting aside is that in February 2001, former Reagan Domestic Policy Adviser Kenneth Cribb told me that when then-Attorney General Ed Meese announced that he was leaving the Justice Department near the end of Reagan's second term, there was a ground swell of support inside the Administration for me to succeed him. Of course, the President's final decision was to select the moderate former Pennsylvania Governor Richard Thornburgh—aides already planning for him to do nothing risky with another staunch conservative—but it was interesting to consider that I had also been that close to becoming a Cabinet officer for the (very rare) third time. It would have been a signal honor to succeed my friend and mentor, Ed Meese, and I would have been proud to continue General Meese's policies on behalf of the President.

CHAPTER 15

LIFE AFTER WASHINGTON

Many people who go to Washington for federal positions fall in love with the excitement and try to find ways to remain in the city after their government service is over, often as lobbyists. Those who are attorneys might enter private law practice, while others may establish or get hired by think tanks, or cling to hopes of subsequent government posts. The more important their government position, the easier it is for them to find a high-paying job with a law firm or lobbying firm. As a former Cabinet Secretary and a lawyer, I would have had a good chance to find such a position.

Right from the start, however, Barbara and I knew that we did not want to remain in the Capital once my stint as Under Secretary to Jim Watt was over. My moving from that to becoming Secretary of two agencies prolonged our stay but did not change our plans for the future. A standard part of her speech when we gave our Christian testimony was to say, "we never caught Potomac Fever but always had our bags metaphorically packed while we were there." Our thinking on that never changed even though our stay was much longer than we first thought it would be after President Reagan asked me to serve as Secretary of Energy and then of Interior.

As the Reagan Administration was drawing to a close in the summer of 1988, after George Bush became the Republican nominee, I phoned his Chief of Staff, Craig Fuller, to let him know that I did not want to be considered for any posts in the anticipated Bush Administration. Interestingly, he asked me if I would tell that to my fellow Cabinet officers since many of them were already lobbying to be retained.

As I wrote in the last chapter, Barb and I planned that when I left Washington we were going to be ski bums in the Colorado sunshine before moving back to Oregon (where the sun didn't shine much)—at least for a year. We decided to live in the community of Silverthorne in Summit County, but we could not seem to find a nice place to rent that we could afford, and we didn't want to live beyond our means. So, instead, we reached agreement with friends of ours, Dave and Mary Kay Morgan, to purchase one-half of their duplex in Wildernest, a cutesy named community at 9,300-feet elevation overlooking Silverthorne. We continued to rent the condo in Frisco, about three miles away, until the sale was complete; and we moved in in February.

Barbara and I are enjoying a ride on Air Force Two with then Vice President George Bush (The White House)

I had no job and no visible means of support after leaving Washington—with very little savings left—so I calculated the minimum we needed each year to live in the half duplex and concluded that we would have to earn at least $36,000 per year. I was comfortable that Barbara and I could earn that much if we both found entry-level jobs, for example, working as lift attendants at the local Keystone ski resort. Having skied at Keystone over the former six years, we had gotten to know several of its key executives, and I was optimistic that we could get some kind of jobs there. That was a backup strategy, however, because I had another path in mind, but there was no guarantee it would succeed.

Earl Gjelde and I had agreed that after we both had left the Interior Department, he and Sandra would move to Summit County and he and I would form an energy consulting firm. This was the same plan we had years earlier after I left the Bonneville Power Administration but had to abandon when I joined the Reagan Administration.

Instead, Earl was asked by the new Bush Administration to stay on as Under Secretary of the Interior because the new Secretary, Manuel Lujan, although a very good guy, knew nothing about running a Cabinet Department, and by that time everyone knew that Earl was an expert at doing so. In fact, Earl was, as far as I can recall, the only *true* Reagan appointee who was retained in the new Bush Administration. He stayed at Interior until June or so, when he had had enough of trying to advise Lujan, and then he left.

Earl was very, very good: savvy, exceedingly nice, and creative. He was immediately snapped up by Waste Management (WM) to create and lead their (new) federal division. The goal was to obtain major contracts with the federal government cleaning up sites that had been used by the government, particularly in the production and testing of nuclear weapons. For the next couple of years, he was a full-time vice president with WM, heading the division which eventually had over 800 employees and many contract proposals outstanding. Thus, during this time he was unavailable to participate actively with me in a consulting operation, although he had fully disclosed his relationship and had permission from WM to work with me as long as it did not conflict or interfere with anything he was doing there.

So, once again, Earl and I put our consulting partnership plans on hold. I went about the business of forming Summit Power Group (SPG), a name I chose after learning that my early choice,

Summit Energy Group, was already in use, and to avoid a conflict with the many Summit company names already in use in Colorado. I registered its name and completed the necessary steps to have a legally recognized corporation. And I reached out to various people to let them know that I was available for consulting. Before I could really get started on that, however, another opportunity came along.

I had become acquainted with a Houston oil man named Terry Looper when Barbara and I had given our testimony at his church shortly after the November 1988 election. We were sponsored at the time by the Christian Embassy and had agreed to do a fund-raising luncheon with about twenty of their potential major donors after speaking at the three morning church services. Terry was the host of the luncheon.

Sometime in early January 1989, while I was still technically in the Cabinet but no longer doing anything (because there was nothing for me to do), Terry approached me about a business opportunity. I told him that I would not talk about a future business while I was still Secretary because I did not want to do anything that would give the extremely hostile press anything at all to report as a conflict of interest.

After Barb and I had moved back to Colorado and were living in Frisco awaiting the duplex to become available, Terry contacted me, again. His proposal was that I become part of a new oil-aggregating company he wanted to form. He concluded that having a former Secretary of Energy as a partner would give a new company greater credibility. He was definitely correct in that thought.

At the time, I did not even know what an oil aggregator was. It was a simple concept: Oil refineries paid more money per barrel of oil in larger quantities than for small ones. This made good sense for them because it took just as much time and effort to make large purchases as it did smaller ones. Many oil wells were producing a few to a few dozen barrels a day and could not command the higher prices paid for larger quantities. An oil aggregator would buy oil from many small producers and combine those barrels for a larger sale. The aggregator would pay the producers slightly more per barrel than they otherwise could get for their small quantities of oil and, also, arrange to pick up and ship their oil. The aggregator would then turn around and sell that larger quantity of oil to refineries at enough of a higher price per barrel to pay the extra to the producers and to pay the cost of transportation and still make a small profit per barrel.

Before meeting with Terry, I had calculated that an arrangement paying me at least $3,000 per month would be entirely acceptable because it would meet Barb's and my minimum living expenses for one year. He flew out to Colorado in early February to make his offer. After skiing together in the morning and meeting in the building lobby of our rental condo, Terry offered me a retainer of $2,000 per month (*Oops, not quite enough*, I thought) until the company became consistently profitable, at which time he would increase the amount to $4,000 per month (*Oh, my goodness*, I thought. *He bracketed my minimum goal exactly!*) Terry also offered me a 5 percent interest in the company. Without any negotiation or quibbling, I accepted on the spot and what became a very successful company, Texon, was born.

As Terry and I discussed the business plan further we used my trusty flip chart analysis. He explained that a typical oil aggregator operation had from twenty to fifty buyers (employees of the company) who were paid roughly $60,000 per year and earned a 2 percent commission on the profit each buyer earned for the aggregator.

I suggested that he seek buyers who were proven stars and to pay them much larger commissions, such as 20 percent. I pointed out that if a buyer was really good, a star, and he earned $1 million for Texon, and was paid 20 percent ($200,000) in commission, Texon would retain $800,000, while virtually guaranteeing that the buyer would remain highly motivated. If the buyer made $5 million for Texon, he would get a $1 million commission, a huge payment compared to what was the standard, and Texon would retain $4 million.

Terry found the suggestion difficult because it was such a departure from the general practice in the industry. But finally, he agreed to try that approach. Eventually, he modified it in some ways; however, it was successful, and it allowed Texon to hire a few very talented buyers and never have the large number of average buyers that was the practice in the industry. Over time, thanks to Terry's outstanding executive capabilities, Texon became perhaps the most successful oil aggregator in the business and, one year, had the largest gross income—over $6 billion—of any company headquartered in Houston—which was amazing considering that Houston hosted some very large industrial enterprises and oil companies.

Former Cabinet Secretaries are often much sought-after for posts on corporate boards of directors, and I was no exception, receiving invitations from both the for-profit and nonprofit sectors. One of the offers that was quite appealing to me was from Taylor Energy, a New Orleans independent oil company that operated oil wells in the Gulf of Mexico off the coast of Louisiana. Pat Taylor and his wife, Phyllis, were a remarkable couple, yet he was an extreme example of the hard driving businessman, and quite irascible. My income for serving on Pat's board was $1,000 per meeting, held in New Orleans three to four times each year (which amounted to at least one month of our budgeted living expenses). One of my favorite things about attending the meetings was that I could arrive the night before and treat myself to a big dinner of boiled crawfish on Bourbon Street.

By late spring 1989 Texon had begun to generate a small amount of revenue. Terry had signed up a few small producers as customers but nowhere near enough to become profitable. In June, I mentioned my partnership with Terry to Pat Taylor. Much to my surprise, he began telling me in no uncertain terms how much he distrusted oil aggregators, saying I would damage my reputation by associating with one. Playing my protector, he went as far as to presume to forbid me from working with Terry. (I told you he was hard driving!) I did a great deal of explaining about what a wonderful man Terry seemed to be and how much the potential income meant to me when, finally, Pat grudgingly agreed to meet with Terry, who was elated and set the meeting. Afterward Terry was exhausted, telling me that it was one of the most stressful sessions he had ever experienced. He had really been run through a ringer.

It turned out to be an almost all-day meeting where Pat cross-examined Terry vigorously for several hours. Terry politely and carefully explained again and again how he operated. After meeting in the morning, Pat told him to come back a couple of hours later. Terry did so, and they met for several more hours of Pat's questioning and Terry's careful and competent explanations of how he operated. Terry was finally able to satisfy Pat that he was supplying a legitimate service to smaller oil producers. Amazingly, Pat then agreed to allow Texon to purchase barrels of oil from Taylor Energy—for a higher price than Pat had otherwise been able to obtain, after which Texon aggregated and sold the barrels to customers.

Soon after Texon began buying Taylor Energy oil, my monthly envelope arrived from Texon. It contained a check for $4,000!

I immediately called Terry. He said that July had been a profitable month. I reminded him that his promise to raise my fee when the company became consistently profitable did not mean profitable for only one month. Terry replied that he was so grateful for the Taylor Energy introduction that he wanted me to begin the higher retainer immediately—from that month forward.

This was a huge moment for Barbara and me! It meant that we were now solvent—and things only got better from there. Over the next decade and a half, Taylor Energy was Texon's best customer and because of the very large total number of barrels exchanged, the earnings were substantial for both companies. As it happened, after that first month of profitability, Texon was consistently profitable.

One of the remarkable things about Terry Looper was that he never forgot that his contract with Taylor Energy, which was only possible because of my relationship with Pat Taylor, was what made Texon an almost instant success and established the platform from which a much larger and successful company was built. Typically, after a few years (or even less), the person in Terry's position of receiving such assistance seems to forget how much help someone was at a key moment in his life—but not Terry.

Finally, after over thirty years of my being associated with Terry Looper and Texon, in 2020 Terry bought out my interest in the company and our business association ended. Texon had been hugely beneficial to Barbara and me, a significant source of my income over those thirty years. From a personal standpoint, Terry's openness about his commitment to try to follow Christ's leading in his life had been a wonderful example to me as well.

Other board opportunities that I accepted included the advisory committee for the Electric Power Research Institute (EPRI), headquartered in Palo Alto, California. I served on the board at EPRI while I was Bonneville Power Administrator in the 1970s, where I learned of the coming attacks on natural gas, and those five years on the EPRI board led to the invitation to serve on the advisory committee years later after I left the Cabinet.

I also joined the board of Integrated Electrical Services, American Electric Power, Columbia Gas, MAPCO (which owned and operated the mid-American pipeline system), Eagle Publishing, and Salem Communications, a Christian radio network.

In 1991 after I had been on the board of American Electric Power for a year, Pete White, chairman of the board and CEO, made a special trip to Summit County to ask me if I would be willing to come to work for AEP full time with the expectation that I might succeed him. I felt honored that a man of such stature in the electric utility industry would consider me a potential successor, but I didn't even have to pretend to consider it. With great deference to Pete, I thanked him for such a wonderful offer, but I told him honestly that I was unwilling to give up the life I was now leading and return to the electric utility wars. I did not say it to him in those terms, but I had no desire to carry on the same battles with the mindless people who fought every single thing that increased US energy supply.

I very much enjoyed being on the board of Eagle Publishing, which owned several monthly business newsletters, and also owned Regnery Publishing, which produced high-quality, conservative-themed books, including, in 1951, the landmark *God and Man at Yale*, by a young William F. Buckley Jr. The Eagle board included noted conservative journalist and pundit Robert Novak who had interviewed me in 1968 in my office at Georgia-Pacific when I ran the 1968 Reagan campaign in Oregon. Regnery, of course, published my book *Crisis in the Oil Patch.* Regnery was so successful that many of its titles appeared on the *New York Times*'s bestseller list year after year—although the *NYT*'s bias meant that they never reviewed any of those bestselling books.

Regnery also owned *Human Events,* a solidly conservative newspaper. Tom Winter, the paper's editor, had been a freshman member of the Harvard Young Republican Club when I was its president. At a meeting where Maryland Governor Theodore Roosevelt McKeldin spoke, Tom, after listening to McKeldin, raised his hand and asked, "Governor, after what you have just said, how can you call yourself a Republican?" To which McKeldin replied, "My granddaddy was a Republican. My daddy was a Republican. And that's good enough for me." Now, some forty years later, Tom and I had once again crossed paths.

Sometime in 1991 or 1992 I had a realization, about which I talked with Barbara. A bit lightheartedly I described it to her as understanding what I wanted to do when I "grew up." I realized that I did not want to simply earn a good living in order to support us. I still wanted to do good, just as I had as a five-year-old boy. I had some experience in Summit County working with a church consultant, and I learned from him that the churches needing the most help could not afford to pay and those that could afford to pay didn't need help. Knowing that, I said to Barb, "What I'd like, if the Lord blessed us with the money to do so, is to consult with Christian organizations without charging any fee or accepting expense reimbursements."

I really didn't think a lot about it after that, but a couple of years later I realized that God *had* so blessed us. The consulting business was going well, as was Texon, and we had the income to do exactly what I had said, work for charities for free and pay our own expenses. However, I didn't know how to go about finding clients. I knew I couldn't just pick up the phone, call a nonprofit organization or church, and say, "Hi. I'm a consultant to charitable organizations, and while I have no experience in doing it, the good news is I don't charge a fee, and I cover my own expenses." I could imagine how long it would take for someone to say, "Um… yeah," and hang up.

Things began to change in early 1994 when I became a member of the board of directors at Focus on the Family, located in Colorado Springs. We had heard of its founder, Dr. James Dobson, a child psychologist, way back in 1974 in Lake Oswego not long after we lost our son Philip. Then around 1985, while I was Secretary of the Interior, Barb and I attended a dinner meeting in one of the major Washington, DC, hotels. As we were leaving with my security detail, we saw another large gathering in one of the hotel's ballrooms. The speaker's voice caught our ears, and Barb thought she recognized it as Dr. Dobson's. So, we stepped inside the room and stood at the back, listening to his speech.

Dobson spoke about child-rearing and the troubles encountered by parents of young and teenage children. Frankly, he was fun to listen to with his compelling voice and meaningful, commonsense approach based on solid Christian values; and he was humorous. At one point that night, he told a story about how he loved to play basketball even as an older man and during a break in one game a young college kid came over to him and said, "You sure must have been something in your prime!" That, of course, brought the house down and it tickled me because I, too, loved to play basketball and almost the exact same thing had happened to me. The speech ended and we left, sharing with each other how much we had enjoyed it. I remarked to Barbara that if we had known about Dobson when our son Philip was young, we might have been able to save his life. The next day, I wrote to Dr. Dobson, telling him that I had had a similar experience to his in-your-prime story, and I invited him to come and play in the gymnasium at the Department of the Interior the next time he was in DC.

Shortly after the Interior building was completed, WWII began and a swimming pool that had been constructed in the basement (approved and overseen by Secretary Harold Ickes) was decked over and converted into a secret intelligence office for the duration of the war. After the war it was discovered that the pool had a large crack and would be too costly to repair, so a basketball floor was constructed over the space.

Dobson enthusiastically accepted my invitation, asking a top aide, a man named Peb Jackson, to be the contact point for the arrangements. I invited enough additional players to round out two teams of five, including a couple from the White House staff, and on Dobson's next trip to Washington, we had a highly enjoyable full court basketball game. A photo of the group of ten in our sweaty gym attire graced the wall of the entrance to the Focus on the Family's headquarters for years afterward, and a similar one of just Dobson and me was displayed upstairs in the boardroom.

In coming years, Dr. Dobson hosted Barb and me as guests on his very popular daily radio program, also called *Focus on the Family*, in 1992 and again in 1994, talking first about our son Philip's suicide and later about our marriage.

In early 1994, a couple who lived in Holland, Michigan, Edgar and Elsa Prince, invited Barb and me to come over to Vail for a couple days and ski with them and a few of their friends, including Jim Dobson and his wife, Shirley. Ed had become a billionaire as owner of a company that sold parts to the automobile industry, having developed a method of molding an entire plastic dashboard in one piece. He and Elsa gave millions of dollars to Focus, including paying for the building to house its welcome center, children's play area, and bookstore.

Of course, we were quite flattered to be included in that ski trip. We had met the Princes in Washington while I was still in the Cabinet and had immediately liked them. We had a great time with the Princes, the Dobsons, and several of the officers from Ed's company, at which time we got to know Jim and Shirley better and we enjoyed firsthand Dobson's personal warmth and humor. Also, I felt honored to be in the presence of such a high-profile public figure, and I was impressed by what he stood for and the way in which he was an advocate for so many things I believed to be important. All in all, Barbara and I felt privileged to be included with the Princes and the Dobsons.

There are many people who cross one's path during life who make an indelible impression. I had more than a few in my life, as is clear in this book. Ed Prince was certainly one of those. In addition, Elsa later served with me on the Focus on the Family board. Ed and Elsa vacationed in Vail for a month or so in the early spring of each year, where they rented an entire floor of the Hotel Gasthof Gramshammer, one of the oldest Vail hotels, and located right in the heart of Vail Village, a short walk to the ski lifts. Barbara and I were invited to join the group for two or three days each year for several years. I quickly learned that when Ed was the host he paid for everything. He was generous to others, to a fault, paying for his guests' stay at lodging, meals, and lift tickets. Also, he arranged that we would ski with an instructor every day so that we never had to wait in long lines. If the group was larger than six people, he would arrange for however many instructors were needed to ski in two or three groups of similar ability levels. We were always invited at the same time as Jim and Shirley Dobson, and once when I told Jim that I wanted to pay my share and not always have Ed pay for Barb and me, he said there was no point even in trying. When Ed was there, Ed would pay. As we became able to do so, Barbara and I tried to emulate Ed's example.

By August or September of 1995, in addition to working as an energy consultant, and traveling around the country to meet with clients, sometimes twice a week, I was also doing volunteer work for our church and for people who needed help in our community. I began to feel burdened and thought I was working too hard. My immediate thought was that I needed to reduce my involvement in Summit Power Group. However, I decided that before I told that to my business associates (particularly Earl Gjelde, our long-planned partnership finally in place), I ought to keep a careful time sheet for a month so that I could clearly show him the problem. For several weeks, I kept track of my time in five-minute segments for business, charitable, and personal, and for miscellaneous, which included anything that did not fit into the first three categories.

When I totaled up my time, I was astonished to see that I was spending only about ten or twelve hours per week on business. The rest of my sixty- to seventy-hour week was spent largely on charitable activities. I had been taking every little issue that came along from someone with a problem. I was really amazed as, until I kept those time sheets, I had not realized how my time was actually being spent on nonbusiness activities. I said nothing to my partners at that point, but I did tell Barb, "If I'm going to spend that much time on charity work, I should spend it on things that are really significant." This was a watershed moment for me, and when I later looked back on the decision, I realized that was another turning point in my life.

At about the same time, after getting to know Jim Dobson from a few of those ski trips, I was approached about becoming a member of the Focus on the Family board. I was interviewed and accepted the offer when it came, which was instrumental in my plans to give my "work" to charity. Although I really did not know the details at the time, Dobson was nearing sixty and his body was suffering from his incredible work ethic. In 1990 he had suffered a heart attack. I learned later that his father had died from a heart attack when he was in his early sixties, and that loomed large in Dr. Dobson's mind.

In 1994, Dobson had agreed, at his board's urging, to take on a senior executive to run the day-to-day activities, allowing himself to focus more on his radio program and on the fast-growing public policy shop that had a staff of about fifty out of the over 1,000 total employees. However, as studies have found, founders of highly successful enterprises, whether businesses or charities, are rarely willing to turn over management of their baby to anyone, and the landscape of America is littered with rubble from founders who could not let go. But at least he was willing to try, and that was a very good sign.

However, just over a year later, at the October 1995 board meeting, Dobson made a presentation to an executive session about how that senior executive, Dick Mason, was not working out. He also felt that Mason was unresponsive to his concerns, having ignored numerous memos from him, which convinced Dobson that the organization was being mismanaged.

I listened with great interest and felt a strong desire to help. After all, I admired and liked Dobson, and I really liked helping organizations function properly. It was both my gift and a great source of satisfaction. From my time sheet exercise, I knew that I had charitable time available for a really important cause. After the board meeting, as we were walking out, I caught up with fellow member Bobb Biehl, who was a management consultant, and told him that I had a couple of days a week for a few months that I could spend with Focus as a free consultant. But I also told Bobb that I was reluctant to push myself on anyone, so I asked him to think about what he thought of the idea before mentioning it to Dobson.

Not five minutes later, as Barbara and I were about to leave, we heard, "Yes! Yes! Yes!" echoing from Dobson as he quickly came out of his office looking for me. When he caught up with us, he looked pleased and excited, saying, "Bobb just told me what you said. Would you *do* that?"

We worked out the details and beginning in late October, and for the following ten weeks or so, Barb and I spent two to four days a week in Colorado Springs working at Focus. Earl agreed to assume more of the Summit Power Group responsibilities while I did this. When I tried to express how wonderful I thought he was for that, he said modestly that it was a way *he* could make an important charitable contribution, too. Just one more example of what a tremendous friend and supporter he was throughout our years together.

Barb and I drove about two hours down from our home in the mountains on Mondays and returned on Thursdays, spending nights at the local Drury Inn, less than a mile from the campus. Shirley Dobson often commiserated with us, calling it the dreary inn. It was hardly lavish but met our needs quite well, and best of all, was close to the office.

In keeping with our desire to be together as much as possible after losing our son, Barb joined me in the office at Focus, as she had done during our years in Washington. She helped the woman who served as my assistant with correspondence and getting to know how I liked things to be done, and she traveled with me at our personal expense. Jim Dobson welcomed Barbara into all meetings (including executive sessions of the board). He became so used to our arrangement that when I entered his office without Barb along, he would ask, "Where's Barb?" Even if I just needed a quick answer and stuck my head in to ask a question, he would insist on Barbara being located and brought into the meeting, overriding my protests about not wanting to take up his time.

My first task was to learn what was going on in the ministry—at a much more detailed level than a board member would ever see. I met with Dick Mason for a detailed discussion. Dick was a straightforward person who struck me as a good and experienced manager. I promised him that if I ended up believing that the situation between him and Dr. Dobson could not be fixed, I would be honest with him. Barb and I also met with many among the staff, and I asked a lot of questions, learning all I could about Focus, its business processes, and its culture.

What quickly emerged was the classic case of a founder-entrepreneur who was carrying much too heavy a workload. Consequently, he had been pushed by his friends, board members, and advisers into turning over the operating responsibility for "his" organization to an outsider, but doing so was clearly very uncomfortable for him. As soon as he heard things that were disturbing to him, he either internalized them (thus allowing them to grow and fester) or, occasionally, he wrote Mason notes (about even small issues). Dick simply did not answer many of them because, to him, they appeared to be about insignificant matters. But Dobson cared very much about details both big and small, and any time Dick failed to respond to a note, it simply confirmed Dobson's conviction that things were out of control. Unfortunately, once he began to have doubts about Dick's management, it would have been almost impossible to change his opinion.

I tried gently to begin the rehabilitation process with Dobson by suggesting that Mason was focusing on serious problems of organizational procedure and performance and felt he had no time for answering minor questions raised by Dobson. Of course, it became very clear that with a founder, there are *no* minor issues. Dobson's view of Mason had hardened into one of doubting his ability to manage.

I believed that Dick was a solid manager with much better organizational skills than I had. He was well-schooled in MBA level principles, and he was trying to institute them at Focus. But the organization—and its founder—were resisting. One of the ways the staff pushed back against Mason was by complaining to Dobson behind his back. On the other hand, some of the staff might have feared reprisal from Dobson for following orders and making changes requested by Mason, especially when they knew Dobson would not like such changes.

Dobson very much valued how people were treated by others. After some staff told him that Mason was insensitive, Dobson told me in a frustrated voice (on more than one occasion), "Dick just doesn't get it!" I never knew to what extent, if at all, some of the staff comments were made by people who were resistant to what Mason was trying to do. They knew Dobson well and also how he would react to comments about Mason being insensitive.

Mason was further damaged by a gross misunderstanding—on both his and Dobson's part—about what his job actually was. He had been told that he was to be the top administrative executive, with the final operational decision authority on nearly everything. So, he jumped in with both feet, began taking control, dealing with specific areas of concern (staffing, order fulfillment, backlog, etc.), and establishing a much more structured and standard budget process. But apparently no one had discussed in advance with him and Dobson what their roles were to be, and they most assuredly did not even try to work it out between themselves, probably because their styles were so different that neither realized there would be a very serious problem in a fairly short time.

Within my first month volunteering at Focus, it was clear to me that Dobson would never restore to Mason the authority he needed in order to do his job, and that the maximum Dobson would tolerate would be for Mason to serve as a high-priced assistant to him. And I felt that even if Mason had wanted to do that, Dobson probably would not have accepted him for long. By mid-November, having made little if any headway in reconciling Dobson and Mason, I realized that the best solution for the good of everyone was for Dick Mason to leave Focus.

I asked board member Tony Wauterlek, a former Marine fighter pilot and successful financial entrepreneur from Chicago, who had recruited Mason, to fly into town and join me in a breakfast meeting with Dick. I filled Tony in on my conclusions and, knowing Dobson better than I did, he agreed with my conclusion that Dobson would never accept Mason.

I also told Dr. Dobson what I was doing. He disliked that kind of calculated confrontation and obviously felt bad about the situation. I assured him there was no alternative unless he would be willing to give Mason the authority that he needed. He hesitated only briefly before agreeing that he would not. "Well," I said, "then we have no alternative but to be honest with Dick. I believe he will not want to stay under those conditions." Dobson was relieved that I would take on the task of speaking with Mason.

Our breakfast meeting, held at the nearby Embassy Suites, was lengthy. I spent considerable time telling Dick truthfully how I admired him and his management abilities and how much he had done for Focus, as well as how much there was left to do. I also told him, honestly, that Dr. Dobson was not able to allow him to exercise the authority he needed and that I was pretty sure that that would not change. Tony Wauterlek, knowing Dobson better than I, confirmed my message. By the end of this very cordial but serious breakfast, Mason concluded that he did not want to remain at Focus. With Tony's advice, we agreed to create a suitable and amicable transition plan. Dick loved the ministry, Dobson, and the Lord, and he was an honorable man, which made our negotiations easy.

I then met alone with Dr. Dobson to bring him up to date. And he surprised me by asking *me* to assume Dick Mason's duties. No doubt I was flattered that he thought enough of me to enthusiastically urge me to stay longer at Focus. I felt a desire to help him and Focus, and I was excited about the chance to try to improve the organization. It didn't hurt that Barbara really admired him, too, and was willing to be with me full time, if I decided to stay. I wanted to enable him to be there for other parents in similar circumstances, as we had experienced with Philip, so I accepted his offer—for an indeterminant length of time. After talking things over with Earl Gjelde and tidying up several issues both at Summit Group and at home, on Tuesday, January 2, 1996, Barb and I arrived at the Focus on the Family headquarters to try to help manage Focus and lift some of the load off Dr. Dobson.

Mason and I had agreed on a six-month severance package, and I continued to consult with him on-site early in that period. He was knowledgeable and very helpful, and he spent a lot of time getting me caught up about many issues he saw at Focus, knowing so much more about the inside details than I. We had previously discussed that the organization desperately needed to undergo a reorganization. And as soon as I walked in the door, I was fully engaged in trying to begin that process. The first step had to be to understand the existing organizational structure.

By Wednesday of my first week, I thought that by the weekend I would be ready to talk to Dobson in a general way about a possible reorganization, of course, subject to his approval. He was not available that weekend, however, and so Dobson asked to meet on *Thursday* evening—*the next day!* Dick and I had only a day and a half to organize some general thoughts on a plan! We worked furiously to create our presentation, in my characteristic fashion, flip-charting our way through the process. Dick played the major role.

On Thursday night, Barb and I dined with Jim and Shirley Dobson, where I laid out on a yellow pad a proposal for reorganization. As I did so, Jim kept saying things like, "Oh, yes!" or "That's great." At one point, he said, "It's as if this is what I've been wanting to do, and you have spelled it out." I was thrilled at his strong, positive reaction to the proposal. Both Barbara and I knew how much of this proposal was the direct result of Dick Mason's excellent knowledge of Focus and his advice. Although I wanted to give him the credit, I knew that if I mentioned his essential role in this proposal, it might have prejudiced Dr. Dobson against it. So, I felt I had to remain silent about the crucial role Dick had played.

The main structural change was to divide all of Focus into three divisions, each presided over by an executive vice president. Diane Passno, a vice president who had been with Focus over ten years, was made EVP over Correspondence, Fulfillment, and Human Resources. The other two divisions fell to me on an interim basis until we could find two new executives to come in.

Dobson and I had an interesting debate over my title. I knew that he would set strict limits on anybody in my role, so I said my title should be staff assistant. He would have none of that, insisting that I should be an EVP. I balked, because I did not intend to stay for very long after putting the reorganization in place and, therefore, my departure when I did so would appear to be another executive leaving on the heels of Mason. Finally, we agreed that I would be called "acting EVP."

Next, Dobson wanted to work out my pay arrangements. I declined to be paid, explaining my pledge to the Lord that if He provided the means, I would charge neither a fee nor expenses for my work. If I were paid, it would be like reneging on my promise to the Lord. Barbara and I had somewhat recently also decided to give more of our finances to others—beyond the customary 10 percent (tithe) described in the Bible. And there was one other motivation for me: not to stay longer.

On the morning of Barb's and my drive down from our home to Colorado Springs to begin my temporary job at Focus, I phoned Tony Wauterlek, who offered much encouragement to me but said, "You need to realize that your relationship to Dr. Dobson may not survive this job." He thought of those who had gone before me with whom Dobson had become disenchanted. I understood the risk.

It turned out that I did not wear out my welcome with Dr. Dobson. It may be that it was because I was there for only seven months and got out while he was still happy with what I was doing for him. Dobson and I became even closer, and he developed and frequently expressed both his appreciation and support for me. As with Russ Richmond and Jim Watt before, I was always respectful of him and deferred to him in all things. It was easy for me to do because he was truly a gifted and wonderful Christian man. It was another case of enjoying the role in which I felt most comfortable, supporting an able leader in an important organization to help him achieve his goals.

With my friend Dr. James Dobson at a Focus on the Family staff party (Courtesy Vurl Watkins)

At the end of each day, I would do a report to Dobson about what was going on with five or six lines on each issue that needed to be dealt with. Sometimes this list would be several pages long. I would state the issue as I saw it and often say what I thought ought to be done, or I would ask what he wanted to do about it. The next morning, I would get that paper back from him with his notes in the margin—mostly he wrote "I agree" or "Agreed." Sometimes he would say to check with someone who had more information.

Basically, I served Jim as I had intended, as his staff assistant, not as an EVP who had decision-making authority. Years later, we laughingly disagreed on whether I had made all those decisions or whether I had only sought his approval or advice.

Whenever I disagreed with something Dobson said in a group meeting, I used the same approach as I had with Watt. Rather than contend with him in front of others, thereby forcing him to dig in his heels due to his strong personality, I waited and told him in private that I would follow his leading but wondered if he had thought about such and such. Though not as flexible as Jim Watt, Dobson responded fairly well to that approach. Overall, it was a great working relationship. But I knew his personality, and, like Watt, he could nitpick any decision that was made if he had not made it himself—even if he would have agreed to it if asked about it before it was made.

Dr. Dobson was astonishingly capable of monitoring virtually every detail and nothing was too small for his attention. In that way, he could have been called a micromanager, but he actually had the mental capacity to pull it off. Most people cannot do that successfully in a large organization, and they complicate everyone's lives simply by trying.

To assure himself that things throughout the ministry were handled to his satisfaction Dr. Dobson had developed what he called the "hot pending" system. I believe he conceived of this system himself, and it allowed him to pursue the most minute question until he got a satisfactory answer. He would write a memo to someone, which was attached to a form showing the deadline by which they were to respond (usually a week or, at most, two). His office staff kept a careful record of all hot pendings sent out and when the replies were due. As soon as a response was late, they would notify the staff person that his hot pending was overdue. Doctor (as the staff affectionately and respectfully called him) would not let go and no issue was too small if he had asked about it. The staff felt the pressure of him looking over their shoulders regarding the smallest details of their jobs, which they sometimes resented. His theory was that if he smelled smoke, then fire had to exist somewhere and a late response to a hot pending was big smoke.

It was the best management follow-up system I had ever seen or heard of, but, of course, it was loathed by the staff, mostly, I think, because there was no filter to remove his examining little things. It made them feel that he did not trust them to do their jobs. Everything was inspected by him, from the big issues affecting the entire ministry to things as small as why some employee Dobson knew (and did not think was very effective) was getting a very minor raise.

Often the response, even if timely, would generate additional questions or directives from Dobson. The next answer would bring another question, and so on until sometimes the back and forth went on for several pages, not unlike some of today's lengthy email chains. It was (many of) these hot pendings sent to him that Dick Mason had chosen to ignore. His personal assistant at the time knew how crucial they were to Dobson, and tried to get Mason to respond, but she was unsuccessful. Fortunately for me, I understood that "JCD" (another way in which the staff referred to him, usually in writing) put a high priority on replies to his hot pendings.

In the first two months I was at Focus, I received sixty hot pendings from Dobson, an unprecedented number, double what most staff members would get in a year. But it was the result of how concerned he had become. I decided, therefore, to make responding to them my top responsibility. If I did not, he would lose trust in me as he had in Mason, and then he—and the concerns over his and the ministry's health—would be back to square one. I felt that my sixty hot pendings, plus the dozens of others that he scattered around the ministry, were way too big a burden for him and also led to a lot of wasted time and effort by the staff. I pulled together some of the key people and said, "We're going to figure out what is causing so many hot pending memos, and we're going to fix it!"

I found that staff had become so resistant to his memos that they were sabotaging the system either by responding with partial answers or overwhelming him with so many documents that he would be forced to wade through them to find the answer to his question. I viewed those behaviors by staff as verging on insubordination, and I insisted they begin sending Dobson complete, yet succinct, responses to his questions, which, over time, changed the entire dynamic around his hot pendings. By the time I left Focus in mid-August 1996, I was receiving only two or three hot pendings a month—a dramatic reversal of form.

In May 1996, the board of directors met at Triple Creek Ranch, several miles north of where Barb and I lived in Summit County. At that meeting, Dobson unexpectedly looked across the room at me and told the board, "If something happened to me, that man right there could step in and run the place." I was enormously flattered and emotionally touched by his expressing such a high level of confidence. Since my goal was to lighten his workload while providing proper management to the ministry, I felt that his reaction made all of Barbara's and my sacrifice worthwhile.

At some point that summer, a man named Bob Hamby came along. Bob was ten years younger than I and had recently served as chief financial officer of a very large company, Multimedia, which among other things, owned the very popular (Phil) *Donahue* television show. He had successfully negotiated the sale of Multimedia. His financial reward for doing that had enabled him to retire early. Bob had joined the Focus board, having met Dobson at a donor event. He soon began to work with me, also as a volunteer. We hit it off right away. Bob had enormous regard for Dobson, and he and I saw every management issue the same way, which was very pleasing to me as Bob was better organized and better versed in management than I was.

In early August, Barb and I went to her family's cottage on Haskell Island off the coast of Maine for a long-scheduled, two-week vacation. On our first morning back at Focus, during a staff meeting I confirmed that the delegating had worked very well. Everything I had been doing was successfully delegated to someone else while I was gone. As soon as the meeting was over, I said to Barb: "We're out of here. If I stay, all that will come back to me, and I'll be stuck. We need to leave today." She was surprised, but typically supportive.

I went into Dobson's office and told him, "Things are running well. Processes are in place to support your management. I am no longer necessary. We are leaving."

Probably thinking that I meant in a month or two, he said, "When?"

"Today!" I answered.

Dobson was shocked but finally agreed when he saw that I was determined, and by 8:00 that night Barbara and I had left Focus to return to life in the mountains. Bob Hamby was able and willing to take my place, which he did for the next six months, moving temporarily with his wife, Rebecca, to Colorado Springs from their home in South Carolina. In early 1997, Dobson hired Tom Mason (no relation to Dick), a recently retired international vice president with General Motors, to be the third full-time EVP, and when he had gotten his feet on the ground, Bob was able to leave.

The results of my time there were substantial, however. First, Dobson and I established a great working relationship based on mutual trust and admiration. Second, he said the management structure of Focus that was put in place was its best ever, which knowledgeable board members such as Tony Wauterlek confirmed. Third, the Dobsons, the board, and much of the staff, saw me as someone who had stepped in, set things right, and left without hanging around trying to run the show.

When Bob Hamby left, however, the EVPs were on their own with Dobson and, after a time, things began to be troubled again. That was when Shirley and others started saying, "What you need is someone like Don Hodel to *permanently* run Focus for you." Dobson mentioned that to me a couple of times as a possibility. But I had done it already, I knew how hard it was, and it was apparent that he really did not *want* to relinquish control. The EVPs were allegedly running things, but by diving in occasionally in true founder fashion, he undercut their authority and made them less effective. More and more things had to be decided by Dobson. I had no intention or desire to step back into my former role under those circumstances. I knew enough about management and human nature to know that it would be nearly impossible to achieve such success again. And worse, Tony Wauterlek might then be proven right about the outcome of my friendship with Dr. Dobson.

So, I remained in private life, back trying to contribute to the success of Summit Power Group, which Earl was guiding. I did not suspect that another opportunity was coming soon.

CHAPTER 16

RETURN TO POLITICS

In mid-spring of 1997, I was perfectly content at Summit Power, living a great life in Ski Country USA, and serving on the board at Focus on the Family, when, one day, I received a call from a woman named Barbara Johnson, religious broadcaster, Pat Robertson's longtime executive assistant.

Robertson, founder of the Christian Broadcasting Network (CBN) and host of its daily television program, *The 700 Club*, and I were acquaintances. I knew little about him and his organization, but I was impressed by his successes, including the creation of Regent University, located on his headquarters' sprawling campus in Virginia Beach. I also had not forgotten that he had paid me a high, though discomforting, compliment during his unsuccessful campaign for President.

In 1988, he sought the Republican nomination, coming in a distant third behind then-Vice President George Bush and Senator Bob Dole, of Kansas. Barbara and I attended an event where Pat was the speaker and, without talking to me first, he told the gathering that should he become President, I would be his choice for White House Chief of Staff. While this was a great compliment, it also embarrassed me terribly, since I was serving at that time in the Reagan Cabinet and working alongside Vice President Bush, who was clearly going to be the Republican nominee.

Though I knew Pat could not win the nomination, I actually thought I would enjoy being White House Chief of Staff. While being in the Cabinet is prestigious, the fact is that the person who sits near the President's office and sees him many times each day has a great deal more influence on the course of government than any one Cabinet officer. Cabinet officers need to pay attention to their relationships with the Chief of Staff because he has the President's ear many times every day.

In March 1988, Barbara and I were interviewed about our Christian testimony on *The 700 Club* from the deck of the Mercy Ship *M.V. Anastasis*, which was berthed at a Norfolk, Virginia, pier at the time. Pat Robertson did not do the interview, as he was on leave while running for President.

After the campaign ended, Pat invited me to attend an August 1988 founding meeting of his political action committee, Americans for the Republic. And later, he also sounded me out about various roles, including the Presidency of Regent University.

In late 1989, Robertson founded Christian Coalition, a 501(c)(4) grassroots organization (such a group's income is exempt from taxes, but donors' contributions are not tax deductible), which would keep his campaign followers involved in politics. He planned for Christian Coalition to recruit ten pro-life activists in each of America's 175,000 precincts. The group would be run on grassroots power to distribute voter guides in churches on the Sunday before each election. To run the organization, he hired Ralph Reed, a twenty-seven-year-old PhD student at the University of Georgia who had led a group called Students for America and had been mentored by the venerable conservative strategist Paul Weyrich, who had earlier coined the term, "Moral Majority."

Using a $20,000 seed gift from Robertson, the Coalition repeatedly attempted to use the 1988 campaign's mailing list to solicit ground-level donors for the new effort. Reed told me later that that mailing list produced very few donors, so he turned to other direct mail fundraising. These fundraising efforts also provided funds to Robertson to settle the leftover 1988 campaign debt. Pat, obviously unaware of Ralph's actual experience with the list, once told me how very *valuable* his list from the campaign was. In addition, hardly any—not more than three—of the campaign's state directors had signed on in a similar role for the Coalition. What

Ralph was telling me was that he had built the new organization with the use of Pat Robertson's name, using new tactics.

Reed led the organization to significant public prominence in only eight years of activity, peaking with the 1994 Republican takeover of Congress, claiming over thirty million voter guides distributed in churches. After the 1996 elections where President Bill Clinton was reelected, Ralph perhaps felt there was nothing left for him to do at the Coalition. So, in a surprise announcement (to them) on an April 1997 conference call with the Coalition's state directors, he said he would be resigning and forming a new political consulting firm, while remaining on the Coalition's board of directors.

After Barbara Johnson's call, Pat next invited me to meet at his new vacation home near the famous Homestead resort in Hot Springs, Virginia, where he, Reed, and I would discuss the possibility of my taking over leadership of the Coalition. Hot Springs is a remote location, accessible only by driving or by small aircraft which land at a strip on top of the mountain near Robertson's home.

Pat had arrived early from his home in Virginia Beach, while I flew commercial to Virginia—in a rare trip without Barbara—and then drove on I-81, turning west on I-64, and then following a circuitous route up the mountain to the house. I was unaware of how Ralph planned to get to Hot Springs, but it turned out that he was late, and so Pat and I drove down the mountain to talk over dinner at The Homestead.

When we arrived back at Pat's mountain home, Ralph was there, waiting for us. Years later I learned that he had been in Nashville that afternoon for a Christian Coalition event and flew via chartered plane into the tiny Hot Springs airport. However, the pilots mistakenly took him to Hot Springs, Arkansas, delaying his arrival in Virginia by about three hours. I recall the three of us standing and talking in the vestibule of Pat's house. Intrigued by the opportunity to be involved with a grassroots political effort and impressed with the results that Ralph had achieved, I was leaning toward taking the job.

I had learned to trust such inner leanings, and after talking with Barbara, I felt strongly, as I thought about Christian Coalition, that I should accept the role. So, I did. Throughout my career I had felt pulled or led to take on new challenges. These included leaving the Davies law firm for Georgia-Pacific in my twenties, leaving that role for Bonneville Power in my thirties, and abandoning Hodel Associates (and leaving Oregon) to work for Jim Watt at the Department of the Interior in my forties. With Christian Coalition, on the one hand, I was pleased for the opportunity to be able to do grassroots politics because I have always believed that successful door-to-door or person-to-person campaigning is the most effective way to win elections. On the other hand, I was not eager to move to Virginia so far away from my responsibilities at Summit Power and the ski slopes of Colorado. Once again, Earl Gjelde could not have been more encouraging and supportive, although that meant he had just that much more of the Summit Power workload on his shoulders.

Pat introducing me to the media as the new president of Christian Coalition (Richard Ellis / Alamy)

On June 11, 1997, I stood alongside Pat at a news conference on Capitol Hill in Washington, DC, as he introduced me as the new president of Christian Coalition, a title he previously held. Pat would now be known as Founder & Chairman. With us were Ralph Reed and Randy Tate, a very young, former Congressman from the State of Washington, who had first gotten involved in politics during Pat's 1988 Presidential campaign. Washington was one of three states that Pat had won in the Republican caucuses and primaries, along with Alaska and Hawaii. Randy carried Reed's old title of executive director. Pat never wanted to run the daily activities of Christian Coalition, as CBN remained his main interest; thus, our working relationship would be quite different from what I had experienced under Dr. Dobson at Focus on the Family. One similarity was that I would again keep my commitment to the Lord and work without a salary and pay my own travel expenses.

The *Washington Post*'s report of the announcement included that Pat had talked with two other national figures as well, US Senators Dan Coats of Indiana and William Armstrong of Colorado, both friends of mine. It may be that someone inside the Coalition wanted it to be clear that I had not been the top choice and had leaked that information. That mattered little to me, as I had a career-long practice (although not an exclusive practice as evidenced by my moves to Georgia-Pacific and to Bonneville) of accepting positions only when those who might have been better qualified would not take the job.

A couple of days after Pat's announcement of me as the group's new president, I flew from Washington to Norfolk International Airport on United's shuttle. Joel Vaughan, a longtime staffer at the Coalition, met me at the gate (in pre-911 America) and drove with me to the headquarters at 1801-L Sara Drive, in nearby Chesapeake, Virginia, about ten miles away, so that I could take a look around. I was eager to get started. He respectfully referred to me as Mr. Secretary, but I wanted none of that, telling him and everyone else in the office to call me Don.

I admired Joel's demeanor, his knowledge of the staff and mission of the Coalition, and his writing skills, which he quickly demonstrated, and I soon promoted him to the role of assistant to the president. He had written for both Robertson and Reed, and he quickly learned my style as well. I would take him with me to future posts, beginning with a similar role at Summit Power Group after we both had left the Coalition. I officed in my home, where he had access to my finances, my personal files, my computer, etc. He was invaluable, as when he traveled with Barb and me on a speaking trip for Campus Crusade for Christ to Austria and the Eastern European nations of Ukraine, Croatia, Moldova, and Slovakia in April 2000. The level of trust it takes to have someone working in your home is enormous, and the fact that I was comfortable with him having total access to everything, even while I was absent, is the highest compliment I could pay to his integrity.

I am a firm believer in grassroots political action and, as I mentioned earlier, that is a big reason Christian Coalition held significant appeal to me, considering Pat Robertson's goal to identify over a million precinct activists nationwide. Getting to each voter and turning them out on Election Day, those were the things that could win elections. Perhaps this attitude was an outgrowth of my early political job of filling precincts in Clackamas County, Oregon. I also appreciated Christian Coalition's prestige on the national stage and the effect it apparently had in 1994.

I did not know, however, that the preceding eight years' media success had replaced the goal of organizing precincts in favor of large, spectacular, and very expensive events, with top Republican speakers on the agenda. The group's finances had been rerouted away from the main priorities. In truth there was a lot of hype, which increased the visibility and *apparent* impact of Christian Coalition, but the actual grassroots organizing had been neglected. Ralph did an outstanding job of making the Coalition seem much more influential than it probably was, and he impressed many people, including Pat Robertson and me.

My first objectives at the Christian Coalition were to get to know the headquarters staff and to reach out to the grassroots supporters, including what I was told were 2,000 county chapters across the country. They surely were uncertain of the national organization's future in a post-Reed era. I traveled and met with several leaders in their home states.

I also had to get a handle on the finances, both revenue and spending. Fundraising, which had already been lagging—and might have contributed to Ralph's decision to leave—had taken a deep dive after Ralph's announced resignation in April. Meanwhile spending was barreling along, having been set to match 1996's election-year high of about $26 million. The Coalition had started a slick magazine and launched two sister organizations in the past year or so, an outreach to conservative Catholics and one to African Americans, both run out of the group's rapidly growing offices on Capitol Hill in Washington, DC.

The organization was in horrible financial shape and there was no one with enough financial experience to know it. A year earlier the CFO had been fired for releasing confidential documents to the government as part of a personal backlash against Ralph Reed. The fallout cost the services of a very successful direct mail vendor, which helped crash the fundraising. The same week that Reed announced his departure, an accountant at headquarters discovered that the controller was embezzling money. Losing the top two financial executives was akin to a death blow. By the time I took over, the mounting bills were far outpacing receipts.

Before I accepted the Christian Coalition presidency, I had been told that there was approximately $500,000 in the bank, which was true. However, once I was there, I learned from COO Ken Hill, a former staffer in President George Bush's National Security Council, that Ralph had required him to keep that as a minimum balance for the two months or so before the reins were passed to me. In order to do that, the Coalition had simply stopped paying its bills.

I was completely blindsided. I had not done adequate due diligence before accepting the job. Then, it took me too long after coming on board to get a handle on spending. By the time I learned how bad the financial problem was, I decided it was too late to resign my position in protest, and there was nothing to be gained from my reporting this to Pat and the board, so I did not do so. I'm quite sure that Pat had no idea how bad things were.

In retrospect, I should have done my due diligence, discovered the problem sooner, and resigned, while being factual with Pat about why. However, I cannot complain about the course that my life took thereafter. It is just that as I look back, I take little pride in what was done. As I think about it, however, I don't know that there was anything I could have done differently that would have saved or restored the group to its previous position. It may be that the Coalition's time had passed and trying to revive it was no longer possible although that is purely speculation. It is even possible that Ralph's change of direction for the organization from grassroots organizing to high-visibility events came as a result of his recognition of the futility of actually trying to achieve the massive precinct-by-precinct goals originally set out for Christian Coalition.

While there I also realized, based on feedback I received, that reported numbers for the Coalition's massive voter guide distribution had been overstated. While multiple millions of guides were sent out to the grassroots network, it was in many cases far more than they could possibly distribute, and many ended up rotting in garages and trunks of cars around the country, never making their way into church pews on the Sunday before Election Day or delivered door-to-door.

In October 1997, Ken Hill brought a new CFO on board, a fine auditor named Steve Wolkomir, replacing both individuals who had been fired. It took him several weeks to dig in and get command of the books, which were not in good order when he arrived.

A month or so later, Steve presented me with a frank appraisal of the situation. We were approximately $3 million in debt and that was increasing daily. I instructed him to take immediate corrective measures, including that he personally approve all purchasing, but it was not enough as income continued to fall. In the end, revenues in 1997 came in at around $17 million, 35 percent less than the previous year. And matters would have been worse without both Pat and me making significant stopgap contributions. He wrote a check for $500,000, and Barb and I made two gifts amounting to a total of $200,000, perhaps not my best decision from a personal standpoint, but I wanted to help as much as possible. Income began to rebound by mid-1998, fortunately, after we got the direct mail operation back on track with a new vendor and list management company.

After Steve presented me with the group's stark financial situation, I contacted Pat Robertson to let him know how bad the situation was, which was news to him, and which motivated his large donation. He had Barbara Johnson contact the Coalition's four board members and set a meeting for December 16, which would be held on the CBN campus.

Members of my immediate staff, having more history in the various Robertson organizations, and to whom I was already growing close, warned me that layoffs would be coming. And they were right. In all, approximately 20 percent of the total workforce was let go almost immediately. The board, as part of the reductions, decided to slash its sister organizations focused on Catholics, the Catholic Alliance, and on African Americans, the Samaritan Project, along with related staff. The Samaritan Project's executive director, Reverend Earl Jackson, wanted to spin off rather than close that organization, and I agreed that he could do so, along with its small bank account, most of which, $25,000, had been a donation from Barbara and me.

The Coalition's full-color monthly magazine, the *Christian American*, was reduced in size and scope, with most of the staff being laid off. This was a fine magazine, well done and professional. However, it was bleeding money, and the benefit was very hard to calculate since we could not reliably tell how many dollars of contributions resulted from having such a magazine. Its new editor was a young woman named Stacy Mattingly, who had been a recent hire from author John Grisham's staff. When she was let go along with others, I got a call from Grisham, who was really upset that we had treated her so badly. I regretted what we had done to the magazine and the team there, along with the others, but I told him that I felt there was no option. The call ended without my being able to convince him that I had treated her properly.

Among the reductions in spending I planned, I told the board that I would forgo future chartering of private aircraft, thereby slashing that line item by at least $200,000 annually, the amount spent during the previous year. Since these expenditures occurred during Ralph's tenure, and he was on the board and in the meeting, it was awkward to bring this up there. That was when I realized it would be helpful if he were no longer a member of the board. After that revelatory board meeting, I spoke with Pat Robertson and then had similar conversations with the other three members. All agreed that it would be better for the organization if Ralph left the board.

An even more significant reason Ralph should no longer have a formal relationship with the organization was his role as a consultant to Republican candidates for public office. I was concerned that with the hostile eyes of both the Internal Revenue Service (IRS) and the Federal Election Commission (FEC) ever upon us—and an ongoing lawsuit from the FEC accusing the Coalition under Ralph's leadership of illegal electioneering activities already in progress—his partisan work while serving on our board could endanger our non-partisan status with both federal agencies. When the FEC and the IRS get you in their crosshairs, even if you are vindicated in the end—which ultimately the Coalition was—the trouble and cost that come with that can devastate an organization.

I'll never forget my meeting with IRS, when I pointed out that the exact things for which they were proposing to remove our tax-exempt status were used by left-wing organizations. The IRS was nonplussed, asked for a recess in the meeting, and fifteen minutes later reconvened, after which they gave me this answer: "What is done with other organizations is not relevant. The only issue before us is your actions." It's the same answer a traffic cop gives the driver who is in a long line of speeding cars and is pulled out of that line and given a speeding ticket. There is no question in my mind that Christian Coalition was targeted by the IRS because of its Christian and conservative activities.

Again, problems like the FEC lawsuit and the IRS's hostility are things I would have learned if I had taken time to ask important questions before agreeing to accept the job. But, unfortunately, I had not.

Although income was declining, Christian Coalition's political clout was still very high, and both Randy Tate and I received numerous media requests. We were offered and undertook a weekly television program on the revamped National Empowerment

Television's cable channel, which had been founded by Paul Weyrich. Our hope was that such visibility would assist the Coalition in reaching more grassroots supporters, although it never appeared to have any visible effect.

In August 1997, *FORTUNE* magazine published its annual "Power Rankings" of the top twenty-five groups in America that affected public policy, and Christian Coalition was placed at number seven—the highest of all pro-family organizations—right behind the behemoth National Rifle Association. We maintained the seventh spot in 1998, as well. This ranking was testimony to Ralph Reed's skill in achieving public recognition for the presumed successes of the Coalition.

We released a legislative agenda for 1998, called *New Freedom for America's Families: A Blueprint for the 21st Century.* The plan focused on six key areas, including: national security, restrictions on abortion, and correcting something called the marriage tax penalty that gave a tax break to couples living together but not to those who were married. Our proposed legislation on the marriage tax was passed by Congress into law. In addition, I was back testifying before Congress on behalf of Virginia US Rep. Frank Wolf's international religious freedom act that was also passed by Congress and signed into law.

However, none of this successful political and public policy activity mattered in comparison to the fallout from the impeachment trial of President Bill Clinton.

Clinton had been charged with articles of impeachment by the House of Representatives in December 1998, and his Senate trial was set for the following February. Christian Coalition called on all its supporters to press their US Senators to vote for conviction.

Before the trial, however, came Clinton's annual State of the Union address to Congress, held Tuesday evening, January 19, and he delivered what the media proclaimed a masterpiece. Although I did not like him or fall for his phony smile, the press and many Americans seemed to feel that he was unmatched as an orator. (I used to say that if you turned off the sound on your television when Clinton was talking on camera, you could not tell from his facial expression if he was saying something happy like, "My family and I just returned from a delightful vacation," or some awful thing, such as, "The Marine barracks in Lebanon has just been bombed." He had a seemingly genuine, soft smile across his face no matter what he said.) Clinton left a hugely impacted television audience across America, by promising new spending and putting his own positive spin on every issue.

He also made a huge impression on Pat Robertson. On the next morning's *The 700 Club*, Pat basically called for retreat regarding the impeachment effort, telling his audience that it was over. "Clinton's won… We might as well get on with something else," he said, dejectedly.

Both Randy Tate and I immediately began receiving troubled and angry calls and faxes—no email in those days—from the state leaders and county chairmen asking why Pat had done that. They had spent weeks going out on a limb, at our urging, and, presumably with Pat's approval, calling for Clinton's impeachment and conviction by the Senate and they felt, rightly, that Pat had pulled the rug out from under them.

I called Pat to discuss the situation and suggested that he go on television the next day and try to put the toothpaste back inside the tube. But he was unwilling. He surmised that the Senate would never convict Clinton after that speech so why bother fighting any further? He eventually agreed to go on ABC's *This Week* program the next Sunday morning, but he basically repeated the same defeatist analysis.

Pat was proven correct in his assessment of the situation—the Senate acquitted Clinton two weeks later—but the Coalition's supporters did not care. They were fighting for principle. And that is what I told Pat on the speakerphone from my Coalition office when Randy and I called to discuss it with him.

My heart was with the grassroots activists. In my first speech to the Coalition's nationwide network I was upfront with my motivation for taking the job: "We are called to be faithful to God… And in that cause, we are united strongly."

Pat's response to my asserting the need to hold up a standard startled me and caused me to do something, after which I knew there was no recovery. In reply to my argument that we had to fight for the principle that a corrupt and immoral person should not be allowed to remain as President, Pat said, "Principle doesn't matter," which infuriated me. I slammed my hand down on the desk beside the speakerphone. I could not believe my ears! Now, of course, Pat was not referring to principle in general. He was assessing the efficacy of continuing to fight for what would be a certain political loss. But I knew that his giving up publicly was the equivalent of a football coach telling his team at halftime that they didn't have a chance to win the game. Every player would stop giving his best efforts. Sometimes it is critical to fight hardest in a losing battle in order to make your opponent realize that you are not going to fold and run away if the going gets tough.

However, by that action of slapping the desk, something I had done only twice before in my career, I felt I had disrespected the chairman of the organization—with a subordinate (Tate) listening—and that it was inevitable that I needed to leave the Coalition. I had lost my temper, which also left me feeling defeated and embarrassed, and I had also lost too much of my respect for Pat.

I wrote and delivered a letter of resignation to Pat, which he did not immediately accept. He saw that my leaving would look bad, and he genuinely seemed to want to find a way to solve the problem.

After I cooled off somewhat, I tried to think of ways in which the situation could be turned around. I did not want to run away from the Coalition, because I still believed in what it was set up to accomplish—getting good, solid citizens involved in the day-to-day political process—and I hated the thought of leaving simply because we had run into a problem. The following few days involved back and forth memos between Pat and me, where we discussed a way of making things work, including my suggesting he become chairman emeritus, thus distancing himself somewhat more visibly from the day-to-day management of the organization so that he could continue in his role as an analyst, which was how he explained to me why he had given up on trying to oust Clinton. However, in his final memo, he accepted my original resignation and resumed the group's presidency himself.

I regretted the state of the Coalition when I left, as well as my breached relationship with Pat, but knew I had fought hard for the approximately eighteen months at the Coalition's helm and had put a lot of my own money into trying to shore up the finances. My leaving did not alter my conviction that grassroots activity is the way to win elections.

Barbara and I continued to spend time that year at our home in Chesapeake, Virginia, and also back in Colorado: four to five months in Colorado during ski season, from early November through early April, then April to mid-June in Chesapeake, followed by June to late August in Silverthorne enjoying the glorious Rocky Mountain summers and then back to Chesapeake until early November. That way we minimized our time in Chesapeake when it was too hot for Barbara as well as our time in Summit County when skiing was not available, but the weather was still mostly winterish.

I tried to help several of the laid-off staff who had hardships and others to begin new careers, most notably buying a struggling Virginia tabloid newspaper, the *Charlottesville Observer*, and hiring former *Christian American* editor Jeff Peyton to run it for a couple of years before we eventually shut it down. Jeff was a committed Christian and a conservative in a liberal college town. The last nail in the lid of the coffin for the newspaper was when he wrote an excellent editorial opposing unlimited abortions—his stance was absolutely correct, and I supported him—but that editorial in a liberal town proved to be a disaster. Advertising dried up, revenues slumped, and I could not continue to invest good money after bad with no prospect of recovering.

I also found ways to stay involved in political matters. I invested heavily in a dot-com startup that was run by my son's college roommate, Gabe Joseph, who had lived with Barbara and me for our last five years in Washington, becoming like another son to us. His initial idea was to use outbound automated phone dialers to market products, but he soon found a way to use it to identify and turn out voters.

The company was instrumental in the 2001 state legislative elections in Virginia, beginning with a State Senate special election that August for future Virginia Attorney General—and later unsuccessful (by a whisker) Republican candidate for Governor—Ken Cuccinelli, who became a national figure as Deputy Secretary of Homeland Security for President Donald Trump. Gabe's system was also quite effective in several 2002 elections for Congress.

In 2002, I accepted the Presidency of the Council for National Policy (CNP), a group founded early in the Reagan Administration by a combination of some wealthy conservative donors and key leaders of conservative and Christian organizations in an effort to bring together doers and donors for three meetings a year at which ideas could be discussed and relationships built. I had been a member for several years. The list of past CNP presidents included the names of several Reaganites. CNP had an excellent staff and wonderful members, and it was a delight to preside over for those two years.

Shortly after leaving Christian Coalition, I ran into conservative columnist Cal Thomas while on a layover in the Chicago airport. Thomas had been a vice president for Reverend Jerry Falwell's Moral Majority, which had closed shop about the time Christian Coalition started. Most recently, he had coauthored a book, *Blinded by Might*, which was a critique of the Christian Right, highlighting some failures and manufacturing others. "Hi, Don," he said, "Are you still shilling for Pat Robertson?"

I later learned that Thomas had been critical of Pat in the past, and although I was not exactly on the best of terms with the broadcaster at the time, his scornful words touched a nerve. Upon my return to Chesapeake, I dispatched Joel Vaughan to buy the book and to analyze it in depth. He presented me with a report on the book's inaccuracies, but by that time I had cooled off and decided to let the matter lie.

In that book, Thomas also named and criticized Jim Dobson. At that time, I was already active with Focus, again. Thomas's reported thesis seemed to be that since the "Christian Right and moral conservatives" had been fighting for decades and the country was still headed in the wrong direction it was time to give up. It looked to me like an effort on his part to curry favor with his left-leaning media outlets that might publish his column. I basically told him what I thought in Chicago that day. When I became president of the Council for National Policy, I instructed the staff to not invite Thomas to attend or speak at any of its meetings for as long as I was in that role.

One low point during my and Barbara's years living in Virginia had nothing to do with Christian Coalition. It was June 18, 1998, when Dr. James Dobson's assistant, Karen Bethany, phoned to tell me that he had suffered a stroke during the night. Knowing he had endured a heart attack eight years earlier, I was overcome with sadness for my friend and concerned for his life. However, he miraculously did recover—truly miraculously—in less than a week and surprised the entire Focus on the Family staff by walking out from behind a curtain at their June 23 monthly staff chapel service. "Lazarus has returned!" he beamed to a cheering crowd.

Jim Dobson's stroke would eventually lead to my own return to Focus on the Family—this time, to be his successor as president.

CHAPTER 17
BACK IN FOCUS

In 1997 when I became president of Christian Coalition, I resigned from the Focus on the Family board of directors in order to avoid any implication that the Coalition and Focus were collaborating, and to avoid any claims of a conflict of interest. The media at the time bantered back and forth about who was the more influential voice of the Christian Right: Pat Robertson or James Dobson—often including the Reverend Jerry Falwell—and I felt that I could not effectively serve Pat and Jim at the same time. Dr. Dobson continued to invite me to board meetings, and I may have attended one or two. Sometime after I left Christian Coalition in 1999, I rejoined the Focus board.

I also resumed helping Earl Gjelde at Summit Power Group, really throwing myself back into things, in part trying to make up for the almost four years I had been away volunteering at Focus and then at Christian Coalition. Barb and I moved back to Colorado to live full time in the late spring of 2000.

When I reached age sixty-six in May of 2001, however, I began turning down new work because I thought I was too old and needed to retire. But before long, I saw an ad in a ski magazine which posed the question, "How old would you be if you didn't know how old you were?" My immediate thought was, *I'd be fifty-two!* And with that, I became energized again.

In October 2001 at the fall Focus on the Family board meeting, Dr. Dobson informed the board that he felt he was carrying too heavy a workload, which he had never phrased as directly or as strongly before. With my renewed energy I felt this might be an opportunity for me to again be of charitable help, so I quickly asked Barbara if she was OK with my offering. She answered as I expected: "Yes." And when I spoke with Jim, he was delighted at my offer.

We soon made a few trips back to Colorado Springs where Barbara and I met with the three executive vice presidents. Diane Passno and Tom Mason were holdovers from the 1990s, along with a new EVP, Del Tackett, an Air Force veteran who had worked in the first Bush White House. I was not acting in any official capacity, neither staff assistant nor acting EVP, but everyone knew of my relationship with Jim and that I was only there trying to help.

Because the EVPs trusted me and truly wanted to improve things at Focus, they were entirely candid with me, sharing things that if told outright to Dobson would have ended their relationship with him immediately. I found that they were enormously distressed and surprisingly candid about their shared frustration with the situation. At least one of the three was always in the doghouse with Dobson over something. It was apparent he had lost confidence in them and was therefore suspicious of everything they did, and sometimes he found a problem where none existed. If they tried to explain that he was mistaken, he viewed their defensiveness as further proof that he was right not only about the incident in question, but about their general inadequacy as well.

Del Tackett once described to me how Dobson, and perhaps founders in general, see their closest staff members. Del's assessment was that when a new executive began at Focus that person was like a shiny new coin in Dr. Dobson's eyes. He or she came in with a stellar performance record and brought great promise to the ministry. But eventually that person did something that caused Dobson to have just a bit of doubt, the result being that a small piece was lost off the edge of their coin; and once removed, that portion could never return to make the coin whole again. Del said that the nibbling at the coin just kept happening until, finally, it was so reduced in size and value that the person—one way or another—had to leave the ministry.

I then began to look at Dr. Dobson's personal workload. I reviewed the dozens and dozens of documents Dr. Dobson took home every night and the large file box full of paperwork he took home on the weekends. It became obvious he was working incredibly hard, with many long hours. Often, I would see notes he had written well after midnight on Sunday, which meant that he could not have gotten a proper night's sleep, coming in to begin a new workweek on Monday morning already tired.

Next, I wrote Dobson a detailed seven-page memo suggesting that at least 20 percent of his workload could be removed if only he would delegate some of his responsibilities to the EVPs. I knew I could not urge him to do anything without risking a defensive response. Therefore, my ideas were couched as things I thought might possibly be helpful in reducing his crushing workload.

I laid out how he could make more and better use of his three EVPs and included a paragraph in which I wondered if, by his not giving them the chance to utilize their very excellent abilities more fully, they were occupying themselves with other activities. I was not simply speculating about that because I knew about what was happening. Diane Passno was writing a book for Focus; Tom Mason was going to seminary on his own time; and Del Tackett, in his off hours, was teaching in at least two other organizations, while also trying to work on his doctorate.

Sharing that information with Dr. Dobson, however, sank my memo. None of my efforts to put my thoughts in the least possibly offensive manner was successful. After he had read it, Dobson told me, "I only agree with *one* part of your memo," and he became very defensive about even *that* paragraph.

Jim knew me well enough to know that I was frustrated by his response to my memo. It almost seemed to me that he did not *want* to do anything about his workload. From observing what was going on, I knew that if he truly wanted relief, he had to be willing to delegate responsibilities—something very difficult for any founder to do. Until he was willing to do that, my pushing him to delegate would simply be an irritant to him, simply nagging him without result, and likely be troubling to our relationship.

As a last resort, I told him that the board needed to intervene and reduce the amount of work that he was personally carrying. But he would not follow their direction either, so I, very frankly, told him that I was unwilling to stay around and watch him die an early death. He had already been diagnosed with prostate cancer, in addition to the 1990 heart attack and the 1998 stroke. It was quite possible that he was going to kill himself (literally) and leave Focus without his crucial leadership.

At about that time the board decided to rearrange its membership terms. I saw my opening, and I took it, rotating off at the end of my current one-year term. The October 2001 meeting was to be my last.

The ministry's twenty-fifth anniversary celebration occurred the following summer, in 2002, and it was an elaborate affair that got out of control in terms of scope and cost. Recriminations followed, mostly through memos and email exchanges between Dr. Dobson and the EVPs.

In the aftermath of "the twenty-fifth," as it was thereafter referred to internally, came a crucial board meeting, held in October 2002. Dobson sent a special invitation to Barbara and me to attend, even though I was no longer a board member. We decided to accept without knowing that the main subject would be the twenty-fifth, because we were interested in what was going on generally at Focus. As a former board member at the time, I had not known about things as they occurred.

As the meeting convened, the board members were unusually subdued. There was the usual, pleasant exchange of greetings and casual catching up on each other's lives, but the meeting was otherwise full of negative energy, focused almost entirely on the twenty-fifth celebration. The subjects discussed were awkward because the EVPs were, as usual, in the room. My sense was that the board members were upset about the extravagance of the celebration.

As the discussion before the board continued, I began to understand what must have happened. Dr. Dobson would request and receive an update about plans for the celebration. He would then ask if it would be possible to do something more. And similar to a change order in a building project, such additions usually add to the cost.

Dr. Dobson was quite subdued, almost abashed, during the board discussion about the twenty-fifth, as were several others at the table. My sense was that in retrospect everyone involved felt that they should have taken some appropriate measures early on to ensure that the scope of the celebration would not exceed the budget. The expectation was that thousands would attend and be awed by a fantastic event, and this would encourage their ongoing and increased support of Focus. In fact, however, turnout was less than anticipated and the response of participants fell short of expectations.

I also knew from my experience at Focus in the past that, most likely, those staff involved felt that if they had objected to the scope creep, they would have been further diminished in Dr. Dobson's eyes. I thought of (as I described in an earlier chapter) the way Earl Gjelde had come to me when I was in Washington and asked if I had actually said I wanted all the Department of Energy field offices to have lavalier microphones on hand in case I visited them. If I had been a different style of leader there might have been no one who would have dared to raise a question—as I'm pretty sure was the case at Focus.

At one point during the meeting, I left to visit the restroom, and when I returned, I was informed that I had been reelected to the board! I felt that Dobson was personally offended by my having left the board a year earlier and, in part, he wanted me back as vindication.

I immediately objected, saying I did not have the time. In truth, I did not *want* to rejoin the Focus board because I felt the twenty-fifth debacle was a direct result of his own management style. I did not say that then and there because I felt it would have been disrespectful. But after more halfhearted protests on my part, which were discounted by the board members and Dobson, I finally, against my better judgment, accepted the reappointment.

Things were quiet thereafter until late February 2003, when Dr. Dobson's self-imposed workload continued to weigh on the minds of the board, and we became even more concerned over his health. At the February board meeting it was clear that my fellow board members were ready to act. And, more importantly, we saw that Dobson was finally and truly ready, as well, and not only to delegate to the EVPs, but to hire a new president of Focus on the Family.

Shirley's words to her husband from years earlier, "You need someone like Don," began to ring true. I also felt he wanted to get away from the unpleasantness of the flagrant use of resources on the twenty-fifth. The evening at the end the first day of the meeting, all the board members, other than the Dobsons, got together for an unofficial dinner. And there was only one topic of discussion: how to find a new president of Focus.

After at least two hours of disappointingly fruitless discussion, any way the group could think of to find a president was both discussed and discarded. Anyone who had the experience for the job would not be willing to come in and spend their first eighteen months being tutored in Focus style and management principles by Dr. Dobson, which is what *he* actually had said would be necessary. Not even a search firm could solve that problem for us. There also was no one *inside* Focus whom Dobson would accept, because by that time he had downgraded the "coins" of his top staff.

At one point, we all needed a break. Barbara and I drifted off to a corner to talk privately. Eventually, Tony Wauterlek came over smiling and said, "You know there is *only one* person Jim would accept as president without having to mentor him, don't you?"

My heart sank. I knew that Tony was referring to me. The seven months I spent there in 1996 had created the image in Dr. Dobson's mind that I *could* do the job to his satisfaction and without the eighteen months of training by him. Remember, he had said years earlier, "If something happened to me, that man right there could step in and run the place," although I could not help but think of my lengthy memo that he had dismissed a year earlier.

I was very reluctant to accept the suggestion. First, it meant an extended time in Colorado Springs and a lot of ongoing financial expense. Further, I would again be less productive for my partners at Summit Power Group, which was my *paying* job. Finally, Barbara and my lives would be greatly disrupted here in our late sixties.

Tony walked away, while Barbara and I remained huddled waiting for the other members to come back together. She agreed with Tony that I was quite possibly the only person who could step in, and further, if Dr. Dobson was to continue his remarkable ministry through Focus on the Family, he must have relief from his workload. We agreed that I would do it, but only long enough to find a successor who, perhaps, could step in without requiring the mentoring that Dobson visualized. (It is remarkable as I look back on that time, that this late in life I was once again getting a job that I did not seek because there was no other qualified candidate willing to take it, and I was taking it only until a suitable successor could be found.)

As we returned to the meeting, I whispered to Tony that Barb and I were willing if that was what the board wanted—and if Dr. Dobson would agree. The remainder of dinner was spent working out the details of who would approach Dobson the next day with the information that I was available to replace him as president and CEO—if that was what he wanted. To his credit, considering how difficult it is for a founder to give up any control over his creation, Jim could not have been more positive or supportive. The roles of president and chief executive officer are not always held by the same person, with the former title sometimes, even often, resting on the person running day-to-day affairs while the CEO remains the boss. So, Jim's willingness to relinquish both titles was a very positive sign.

He had written a ten-year plan for succession that was signed by every board member and mailed out in the form of a trifold brochure to the ministry's supporters sometime in 1999. So, his stepping down as administrative leader was the first domino to fall as part of that progression. He told a story about an older pastor he knew many years earlier who left a church pulpit but then stayed in the church and caused turmoil for his successor. He emphasized that he did not want to make that same mistake himself: stay around and cause trouble for his successor.

Once Dr. Dobson, the board, and I were in agreement, I wrote him a lengthy memo laying out how I visualized the arrangement would work. With the title of president and CEO, I could not operate as I had as acting EVP in 1995–1996. While I would continue to consult him on major decisions, I had to be free to handle day-to-day without consulting him or he would not get the workload relief we were attempting provide. This placed a real obligation on my part, though, to ensure that anything of major importance be cleared with him. Also, I added a stipulation that there be no more hot pendings (his system of follow-up I described two chapters earlier) sent by him to me or to anyone on the staff.

My memo confirmed the board's discussion and centered around these key points: primarily, that Dr. Dobson would retain control over the content of radio, public policy, and his monthly fundraising appeal letter, as he called it, while I would handle day-to-day operations, finance and budgeting, and personnel. I would relieve him of the daily management duties while he would retain the board chairmanship, the broadcast host's chair, and, importantly, for him and appearances, his large, corner office in the building. I would occupy what was at the time Tom Mason's office, the nearest to Dobson's, which Tom graciously and willingly relinquished, moving to an office three doors away in the executive wing,

I planned to keep Dr. Dobson up to date as I had when I was acting EVP, which meant that we would meet at least once a week. While doing all this, I had to avoid the landmines stepped on by Dick Mason in the previous decade when he ignored Dobson's inquiries or interests.

In keeping with my ongoing promise to the Lord, I again insisted on working without a salary, I reimbursed the ministry for my travel expenses, and I paid for all expenses involved with having Barbara with me full time. I remained unwilling even to consider an arrangement that separated us. Jim kindly protested my no-salary-and-no-expense-reimbursement arrangement, but he also knew of my resolve.

BACK IN FOCUS

Barbara and I arrived at Focus, officially this time, on May 19, 2003, and were joined by Joel Vaughan as assistant to the president, a familiar title from my years in the Executive Branch, a frequent senior staff level designation in both the Department of the Interior and the Department of Energy. I knew that having someone with Joel's skills and loyalty as my right hand would be immensely helpful.

Joel was ideal in the role. First, he was a dedicated Christian. Second, I had worked with him three times already: at Christian Coalition as my right-hand man, at Summit Power Group, and at the political advertising firm I funded. I trusted him completely and had great confidence in his capabilities. Third, I knew his personality would fit well with the people at Focus. For my management style I wanted someone who I could trust to sit in all my meetings and keep track of all the commitments that were made by me and others and be able to remind me later of the things I needed to do and the things I expected of others. This was in a way similar to—but not exactly like—the role I played with Dr. Dobson in the 1990s, as well as that of Peb Jackson with Dobson a decade before that.

I had offered Joel a job in Colorado with Summit Power three years earlier, when in mid-2000 Barbara and I moved back from Virginia, but he was single at the time and did not want to leave his native Virginia for a small community like Silverthorne. But when I invited him to join me at Focus, he accepted.

In early April I had called Joel, where he was then working as vice president of the political firm's Beltway Area office. I made him the offer to leave that and join me at Focus, adding that if he accepted, he had to walk in the door with me on my first day as president. He could not arrive even one day later or he would diminish the influence he would otherwise have as the president's right-hand man.

Joel and I had a couple of lengthy telephone conversations during which he asked me questions about Focus and how I envisioned his role, when, finally, on a Thursday in late April, I felt that I needed to have his answer by the following Monday—just over three days away! I knew his nature was to be very careful about such decisions and take as much time as was available in making them. But I felt that there was nothing more for him to learn. All that was left to do was for him to decide.

For me, if Joel chose not to accept the job, I needed all the additional time to figure out how to find a substitute, which was likely impossible because of Joel's unique gifts, and we had already worked closely together for several years by that time, which made him unusually qualified for the position I envisioned. Barbara and I were greatly relieved—and pleased—when Joel told me on Monday that he accepted my offer. He was absolutely essential to me if I were going to do that job. And he became an even closer friend, like a son to both Barbara and me. His loyalty and support were unquestionable and unmatchable.

I knew that few people at Focus at the time had ever seen that kind of arrangement at the top of the organization. So, I told the management team right away that if Joel asked them to do something, they should assume that it was coming directly from me. I believed in—and tried to exhibit—a chain of command where people are given authority commensurate with the degree of trust I had in them, which was expressed implicitly in that directive. Joel and I worked so well together that, not long after we began at Focus, Shirley Dobson told me, "*Jim* needs a Joel." Jim Dobson had plenty of assistants, but he did not utilize even his closest man in the same way. That was the difference between a founder and a manager.

Right away, I dove in as I had a half-decade earlier and reacquainted myself with the inner workings of Focus. I had been gone from management involvement at Focus since August 1996, in part running the Christian Coalition and in part participating actively in Summit Power Group.

I saw my top duties as president as three-fold. First, freeing up Dr. Dobson from the administrative load that I feared was killing him must happen. Second, working to convert the ministry from a founder-driven organization to one that was more in line with a traditional, management by objectives model which would allow Focus to continue to thrive when Dobson was no longer a part of it. And third, assisting Dobson and the board in identifying his future replacement as the voice of Focus.

I was briefed by the top staff and learned that they had been working on two reorganization plans: one they thought they might have a chance to get Dr. Dobson to agree to, and a second one that they thought would be a much better plan but which they did not think he would ever accept. After listening to the details and looking at the two plans, I made the decision to adopt their preferred plan. I agreed with their assessment, but I approved that plan primarily out of a belief that they knew better than I, a substantial outsider, what would make the most sense as an organizational structure.

It was no surprise that, even in matters of daily management, it was easier said than done to be in charge, as Tony Wauterlek had warned me years earlier. My close friends and advisers Jim Watt and Terry Looper warned me not to make any small decisions that might loom large in Dr. Dobson's eyes. They were committed Christians who served on what I referred to as my "Informal Advisory Group" along with Terry's friend Jim Wise and my son David, plus Barbara, of course. We emailed back and forth as a group, and they all flew into Denver airport for a Saturday morning meeting about a month after I started back at Focus.

I almost made that *large* mistake on one occasion regarding a *minor* change to Dobson's strict dress code for the staff. He required women to wear closed-toe dress shoes, stocking hose, and, unless the high temperature forecast for the day was forty degrees or below, they had to wear skirts or dresses. Men had to wear dress shirts and neckties. He simply felt that was appropriate dress for the office. Frankly, I agreed with the need to dress nicely because we had many visitors coming through the offices on tours every day. Many if not most of them were financial supporters of Focus. People who give to charities sometimes wonder how their money is being spent and if they visit the offices and see the employees all dressed casually, it is easy to think of them as relaxed and not working hard. So, I felt that proper attire sent the right message.

Barbara and I were living Monday through Friday in a new Homewood Suites hotel across the street from Focus and parking outside in the elements both at the hotel and at Focus. The Dobsons, however, got into their cars (she had an office as chairman of the National Day of Prayer, which was headquartered at Focus) in a garage at home and then parked inside a private garage at Focus. Having had a chauffeured car while in Washington, I remembered how easy it was to forget what it was like for even my closest associates to find parking and get to work on bad weather days. After clearing snow off my car one frigid morning before driving the two blocks to Focus, I decided that it mattered little what the high temp for the day would be. What mattered was the temperature in the early morning when women wearing skirts were getting into their cold, snowy cars and driving to work. I called Jim at home to say that I was changing the policy to whether the temperature was thirty-two degrees or below at 7:30 a.m. rather than forty degrees as the projected high for the day. He sounded very reluctant but said, "Well, Don, you are the president, and that is your decision."

Later that morning I had a meeting with the top staff of Focus. I had barely sat down when Patty Watkins, my executive assistant, knocked at the door to tell me that Shirley Dobson was on the phone for me. After I left the meeting to take the call, Shirley told me that changing her husband's long-established dress policy, even that small amount, would be an embarrassment to him in front of the staff. I thanked her but was noncommittal. As I shared that with the group, Del Tackett said, "Don, you know, of course, that even if you make this change, some staff will still complain about the dress code."

Immediately I realized that Del was right. I decided that there was little to be gained from doing something that upset the Dobsons if it did not alleviate the staff complaints. Thus, the dress code stayed the same.

Other things went very well during my first months back at Focus, although I was not having as much fun as I had during my last tour, somehow always (consciously or subconsciously) waiting for Jim Dobson to become upset with something I was doing.

I worked closely with the executive staff to further the reorganization and align the various ministry departments under three group vice presidents (GVPs), while targeting the EVPs to tasks that I felt were instrumental to the future of Focus.

Tom Mason did an excellent job as COO overseeing business matters, while Diane Passno did an amazing job running what we called the "office of orthodoxy," i.e., being sure that everything published or aired by Focus continued to echo the teachings of Dr. Dobson. I was not willing to have the change in leadership result in even a minor variation from the biblical, tried and true, message that Dr. Dobson had established for the ministry. Del Tackett undertook the development and presentation of *The Truth Project*, Focus's most auspicious and successful content-related project since Dr. Dobson's legendary film series in the late 1970s that had helped launch the ministry.

But soon, turbulence began, although I did not see it coming. Board member Bobb Biehl called me one day and suggested that I meet a friend of his who was a fundraiser. Bobb said that this man had done a tremendous job in greatly increasing the funding for the child-advocacy ministry World Vision, and that if I retained his firm, he could do likewise for Focus.

After more calls and meetings, I took Bobb's suggestion and engaged the consultant and things went extremely well. The response to the new fundraising strategy was very effective, raising the contributions to about $140 million for fiscal year 2004. The previous year's total had been about $130 million. It turned out that this disturbed Dr. Dobson. He told me he felt that we were being too aggressive, saying that he knew that money was out there but that he had not wanted to be as pushy with the donors as the outside firm was recommending. He liked the idea of leaving some on the table.

What Dr. Dobson did not seem to realize was that in the past when money was tight, he used his radio program to ask for money in dramatic terms, saying that without greater support it would be the end of Focus on the Family. He would say words such as, "This has always been the Lord's ministry, and if He does not want it to continue, so be it," a tactic more aggressive than anything the fundraising firm had been doing. This lack of awareness, in the midst of complaints about how I had changed the fundraising approach (which was far less aggressive than most any other ministry, by the way), was very distressing to me. Worse, it was beginning to affect our friendship, which was really the main reason I had gone to Focus the second time. My primary motivation was trying to help prolong my dear friend's life.

My financial goal for Focus had been to reach the point where Dr. Dobson did not have to be the primary fundraiser, so that Focus could survive his eventual departure. I knew that someday he would no longer be alive, and if raising funds was heavily dependent upon his personal appeals, as in "Give to *me*," then Focus would be doomed.

Further, more funds meant greater ministry outreach. That, too, seemed like a good thing. After thinking about it, I concluded that (perhaps subconsciously) Jim really did not want the organization to prosper without his direct intervention. He was the founder, and Focus was entirely the product of his vision and leadership. Add to that his aversion to what he saw as the typical fundraising activities of ministries and, incorrectly in my opinion, he was sure I had taken Focus into that mode.

At the June 2004 meeting of the board of directors, things were amazingly upbeat. The vice presidents presented a glowing report on ministry to the board. Fundraising numbers were strong, and we had just had a very favorably received mailing on the subject of judicial tyranny. After the members left town, Barb, Joel, and I sat in my office comparing notes on the most positive Focus board meeting we had ever attended.

Suddenly, Jim Dobson knocked on my open door and walked in holding an envelope and seeming quite distressed. "Don, did you approve this?!" he asked. It was the cover envelope for a second round of the judicial tyranny mailing, which had a photo of him on the outside that he did not like. His cousin (Focus's vice president for church relations) Reverend H. B. London had sent it to him with a teasing note along the lines of, "Were you really this angry?" Jim was upset that I had allowed the photo to be used without his approval. He had a rule that he had to approve each use of a photo of himself, even if the same image were being used a second or third time. Although I was pretty sure I had gotten his approval, I was unable to find the documentation; therefore, there was no way to refute his criticism.

It is fair to say that I never spent another wholly happy day at Focus on the Family. In minutes I went from the incredible high point of the best Focus board meeting I had attended to the terrible low feeling that I had let down Dr. Dobson, at least in his eyes—although unintentionally—the very friend I had come to serve. Making matters worse, this mistake having reduced his confidence in me, I was fairly certain that our working relationship had turned a corner and would never be fully restored, making it much harder for me to do my job—and accomplish the goal of helping him release the reins. I recognized at once that my *primary* responsibility had suddenly shifted from finding a long-term replacement *for him* to finding a replacement *for me*—and to do so *as soon as possible*!

After much reflection, I became convinced that after the June board meeting Dobson saw how pleased everyone was at the string of successes for Focus. It seemed that we were making real progress at creating a ministry where donors gave because they saw what their dollars did in the way of helping families. I said to Barbara that it might have been that the founder was not comfortable seeing his baby beginning to be weaned from his ever-present guiding hand. The photo on the envelope was simply a way for him to have something to call me on and release his overall frustrations, and if it hadn't been that it would have been something else.

The remainder of that summer consisted of further implementation of the reorganization, more contention over fundraising (now that Dobson no longer trusted me and, therefore, got much more closely involved himself), and some August vacation time for Barb and me on Haskell Island in Maine.

August 2004, our last family photo, vacationing on Haskell Island with (L-R) Dave, his wife, Tanya, and our grandsons, Aaron, Brennan, and Christopher (front). A very happy day (Family photos)

When we returned from vacation, I asked the vice president over direct mail fundraising, Katy Vorce, to give me a review of all of the funding appeals Dr. Dobson had made over the years, which I referred to as the "hard ask" report. My suspicions were confirmed. It turned out that he had on several occasions been far more pleading with his supporters than any funding appeals I had approved. On multiple occasions when funds were running low, he went on the radio with a desperate appeal as I described above. On every occasion the funds flowed in due to the donors' deep love and respect for Dr. Dobson. I was tempted to show him the hard ask report, but I finally decided that it was pointless. And he had a point. As the beloved founder, he enjoyed the leeway to do things that would have been unacceptable to his supporters coming from anyone else.

The search for a new broadcast host had not gone any better, with two early candidates who came in on a trial basis quickly ruled out by Dobson. The board's plan called for someone from the "help sciences," either another psychologist like Dobson (although there was no psychologist *like* Dobson), a physician, or a minister. The board and its chairman discussed name after name after name, but none were right. It was not a crisis, though, because Dobson was only in his late sixties at the time and not ready to turn over the microphone by a long shot, plus the ministry needed him and his gravitas for fundraising purposes.

Things crept along until I decided that something had to change with my own situation. In addition, my personal businesses were suffering, in need of my attention, and my partners were unnecessarily carrying too much of the burden. I went to Dr. Dobson and told him that it was time for me to leave—finally admitting to myself and informing him of what I knew earlier in the summer. I said that the board should immediately form a search committee for a new president and CEO, strongly concerned that he would simply resume both roles and my months there—as well as the strain on our friendship—would have been for nothing.

I suggested a few names as potential successors for me, stressing that one person internally would do a fine job in leading the ministry, then-GVP Jim Daly And I was delighted with Dobson's response when he said, "Don, if we think Jim Daly can lead this ministry why do we need a search committee?" And that was it. We both agreed that Jim Daly could step in and do a very good job as president and CEO. From that moment on, with Dobson's blessing, I began to pull Daly into the role.

Dobson's only concern was that Daly had no hands-on political or public policy experience. I assured him that I would work to give him some mentoring on that subject, which I did not expect to be difficult at all. His values were the same, and he was adept at dealing with all types of people—and I was correct. In the ensuing years Jim Daly has continued to carry the Focus message into the halls of power, although with a different approach than Dr. Dobson had done before him.

I let the board know the direction things were going and there were some who at first were concerned with Daly's youth—forty-four at the time. I remember telling Barbara that I had headed Bonneville Power when I was thirty-seven and was a Cabinet Secretary at forty-seven. I did not think someone with business experience like Daly, having come to Focus from International Paper and earning an MBA degree at night while working for the ministry, plus his almost twenty years with Focus in various leadership roles, which gave him knowledge of many aspects of the ministry, was too young.

I promoted Daly to the position of COO for a while, reporting to me and supervising the other GVPs and the CFO, as well as the EVPs to whom he had reported previously, as I began planning my eventual exit, at the time targeted for the May 2005 board meeting.

By December, I felt the board was becoming more comfortable with Daly. Barb and I went to Hawaii for Christmas, and I had time to ponder things at Focus. I realized that I needed to get away because I felt there were growing problems between Jim Dobson and me.

After talking further with many on the board and finding them to be increasingly supportive of Jim Daly, I phoned him from Hawaii and asked if he was still interested. When he said yes, I sprung February on him—a time which was then only two months away! I told him that I thought that might be the time for him to succeed me.

At the February 2005 board meeting, the final approval of Jim Daly as my successor was on the agenda. Dr. Dobson's first thought was that the transition to Jim Daly should occur in September after he and Shirley returned from an extended summer trip they had planned. He loved the big surprise and dramatic announcements (e.g., "Lazarus has risen"). He suggested to the board that once we decided that Daly should take over in September, he immediately would announce that my successor had been chosen but would not be named until the May meeting. He really liked the idea of the excitement that would build from such an announcement: Daly chosen secretly in February, an unnamed new president announced in May, and finally, the name of Jim Daly revealed in September.

The board strongly disagreed, especially those who had executive experience in running businesses of their own knowing that there is no way to keep such things secret for a long time. And they reached total agreement on that point as soon as Dobson stepped away from the meeting. I certainly agreed with the board because I had learned over and over that in organizations there are no secrets, especially in matters of such significance. Sooner rather than later, and probably very soon, perhaps even within minutes of the meeting adjourning, word would leak that Jim Daly had been chosen to become the next and long-term president of Focus. And once the staff learned of his impending succession, they would realize that the prudent thing for them to do would be to take anything important to Jim and make sure he was OK with it since he would soon be the president. I would, therefore, become superfluous—a lame-duck president.

The board's transition committee and a few other members talked things over and decided that Daly's announcement and installation should be done as soon as possible. Bobb Biehl pointed out that there was already an all-staff monthly chapel service planned for the very next morning and, of course, the entire board was already in town. The next time we were all scheduled to be together was not until the June meeting. So, it was decided that "as soon as possible" meant at the next day's all-staff chapel service with the board in attendance.

When the board gave Dr. Dobson its decision, it startled him, even though, of course, he strongly agreed with the choice of Jim Daly as my immediate—and his long-term—successor, but the sudden announcement, removing the summer of anticipation, was disappointing to him. However, since the board was convinced that its reasons were sound, and he saw that its decision was unanimous, he accepted the board's decision.

Jim Daly was advised and also accepted the idea. The investiture service was held the next morning in an all-employee meeting—over 1,000 staff members—and when the announcement was made, it received a highly favorable reaction from them. Jim Daly's wife, Jean, was present and sat on the stage with him, alongside the Dobsons, and Barb and me. The board members gathered around the Dalys, and they and the staff prayed over their new president.

I cleared out my office and Jim Daly's then-assistant began moving in his belongings. I was pleased that he soon decided to retain both Patty Watkins and Joel Vaughan in the roles they had with me. This is not a typical move for an incoming president, and it showed that he felt comfortable in his new position and showed the trust he had in them. Some years later Patty retired but Jim and Joel are working together as of this writing after Jim promoted Joel to a senior executive role as Focus's chief of staff.

I returned to my work with Summit Power Group, happily no longer commuting to Colorado Springs on a weekly basis. Being in our home full time again was wonderful.

As would be expected of any new leader, Jim Daly, after a few years as president, began new ways of doing things. One such change was relaxing the dress code. His rationale, which was correct, was that it would make it easier to hire younger staff, especially in the tech area. But I am sure this did not sit well with the Dobsons, just as it hadn't a few years earlier when I started to make dress code changes of my own. I am not aware of whether or not he said anything to Jim Daly at the time.

A second change came when the board voted (with the Dobsons in agreement) to accept management's recommendation to modernize the ministry's historic logo. Again, I suspect that change was not desirable to Dr. Dobson simply because as the founder he was comfortable with those things that he had personally chosen and become accustomed to over many years.

The third event was far more major, and that was when Daly found it necessary, during the decline in revenue projected with the national economic recession in 2008 as the US Presidency was about to change hands from George W. Bush to Barack Obama, to prune Focus programs that were deemed nonessential to the overall mission of the ministry, which also meant reducing the number of employees. Yet almost any program that had existed under the leadership of Dobson would have been sacrosanct in his eyes because all programs at Focus had begun with his personal approval, so they were his. Thus, it inevitably created a further rift between the two. Consequently, Daly's "coin" had begun to diminish in Dobson's eyes.

I knew from personal experience that such changes were fundamentally unacceptable to the founder and that, while one or two might have been survivable, the cumulative impact would eventually lead to a rupture, which ultimately happened when, upon

Daly's recommendation, the board voted in late 2008 to reduce the ministry's budget and an authorized number of employees for 2009 due to the worsening recession. Dobson wanted the decision to be postponed until after the end of year financial giving season, which usually produced a very large share of Focus's annual revenue. A majority of the board, however, agreed with Daly that waiting longer would make the impact of the reductions even worse. I concurred with that opinion, as I was hearing directly from some on the board about what was going on. I did my best to ease the situation while supporting all involved: the board, Jim Daly, and my friend Jim Dobson.

Over the next year I received occasional updates on the situation directly from some board members. It all came to a head in 2009 at that fall's board meeting, where it was agreed that the time had come for Dr. Dobson to enact the final step of his ten-year plan and depart Focus at the upcoming February 2010 board meeting. He had considered three dates in 2010 by which he wanted—and expected—to depart, with February being the earliest. The Board chose February.

The decision caused Dr. Dobson a great deal of personal regret and hurt, which he expressed to the nationwide radio audience in his first broadcast that aired after the agreement had been reached. Founders in church and ministry, and in business, routinely have second thoughts when faced with handing over the reins of the organization they founded, and Dr. Dobson was no exception.

I continued to receive input from board members, and from Dobson himself, which convinced me that he really did not want to leave Focus. While continually reassuring him about my ongoing respect and admiration for him, I did all that I could to encourage him to complete the plan for Jim Daly to do the job that Dr. Dobson ultimately had chosen him to do. I really believed that it was in Dobson's and Focus's best interest for the change to be completed. I would say that subsequent events have proven that judgment to be correct. Focus has flourished under Jim Daly's leadership.

For his part, Jim Daly remained respectful of Dobson, often complimenting him afterward, saying, "He got it done" (i.e., the ten-year plan Dobson enacted a decade earlier). Dr. Dobson soon began a new radio ministry with his son. With these events, Dr. James Dobson completed his years of service at Focus on the Family.

Focus expressed its admiration for Dr. Dobson by making a very substantial gift to his new ministry, as well as mailing introductory information on his new venture to the Focus list of supporters. Focus also ceded to the new ministry ownership of recordings of over thirty years of daily radio broadcasts that had been aired with Dr. Dobson as host—an invaluable asset. It had been my belief that those broadcasts were almost crucial for Focus in that they could be aired for many years by Focus to remind listeners of the great things Dr. Dobson had said, and to continue to link with him as the founder of the ministry. I had hoped thereby to cement the donors' ongoing loyalty to Focus. With Dr. Dobson gone, Jim Daly succeeded to the host's chair and microphone of the *Focus on the Family* daily radio program in addition to serving as president and CEO.

My main goal as president of Focus was to assure a smooth transition to the leader who would follow Dr. Dobson. While the transition did not occur as I had pictured it, the results are better than I could have hoped, because Jim Daly has filled the role with exceptional skill and success. I know him well enough to know that he would be the first to give the glory to God for granting the wisdom and guidance to achieve the following list of highlights, which I am sure are only a portion of the full story.

As I do the math into his twentieth year at the helm, I estimate that Jim must have hosted something over 3,000 daily broadcasts. He has personally engaged with the ministry's donor base and radio listenership, while thriving in the role of an interviewer. He has authored several books on family issues, appeared on major television news programs, and launched an orphan care ministry touching almost 5,000 families. In addition, he guided the ministry through a founder transition, a pandemic, and a national economic downturn.

Finally, a few years ago when I was visiting Colorado Springs, I noticed new construction on the campus as I drove by. I later was told that he has engaged private commercial development of vacant property owned by Focus into a source of income for the organization so that those revenues cover almost all of the overhead expenses, allowing virtually every donor dollar to go directly into ministry. Those, to me, are outstanding achievements. I am very pleased, for him and for Focus.

As I write this, under Jim Daly's presidency the ministry not only has survived but has grown in outreach and prospered. It was not always easy, I am sure, particularly the reductions in programs and staff. He also reemphasized family issues over public policy, and to some extent removed Focus from the political arena—a major departure from Dobson's high-profile participation. This was something that Dobson feared would happen. However, it would be hard to say that it was not the right decision. Dobson's increasing politicization was affecting some of Focus's key constituents who were reluctant to see Focus be involved in politics. Overall, it seems clear to me that the decisions made by the board were the right ones.

As I reflect on my own two years at the helm of Focus, in terms of ministry to families alone, those years were well worth the time that Barb and I spent there, for several reasons. Among the things of which I am most proud were that we championed the development and launch of *The Truth Project* by Dr. Del Tackett, which took a Christian worldview curriculum into small groups gathered in homes and churches across America.

We also converted Focus from a founder-driven management system to a more conventional strategic approach, and in doing that we freed Jim Dobson to do those things which only he could do—for as long as he was there—and prepared Focus for when he was not. We launched a 501(c)(4) lobbying arm (later spun-off) to allow Dr. Dobson, also its then-board chairman, to speak out on political matters without endangering Focus's 501(c)(3) tax status as a ministry.

We allocated significant wage increases for the staff, many of whom were struggling. And we set in place new salary structures for the future. Upon the institution of 2 percent across the board raises in 2003, I received a letter of thanks from a staff person who said that until that time he and his wife did not think they could afford to buy a new rake.

And I may have been a very useful and, possibly, an essential help to the future of the ministry in helping transition the leadership to Jim Daly. It is hard to see how he would have been selected in anything like the same time frame without my involvement. After all my one major goal was to create a transition plan that would allow the ministry to continue after Dobson was gone.

Finally, nothing pleased Barb and me more than championing a staff-initiated program now called Option Ultrasound. When I arrived at the ministry, there was a tendency to look at a proposal for a new project and ask, "Will it pay for itself?" But I told the staff that the first question we should be asking was, "Is this a desirable project for the Kingdom?" And second, "Is it appropriate for Focus?" If the answer to both questions was yes, then we should seek ways to fund it.

When Focus's vice president of women's ministries, Yvette Maher, came to me with studies suggesting that if a mother with an unplanned pregnancy saw her baby on either a conventional black and white ultrasound or, much better, a four-dimensional ultrasound screen, one where the image of the baby appeared more like a photograph, she was likely (up to 70 percent of the time) to carry the baby to term rather than to abort it. Yvette's proposal was that Focus should offer to provide free ultrasound machines to crisis pregnancy clinics across the country, at a cost of about $30,000 each. CFO Mark Buzzetta, who was always appropriately cost conscious, came with Yvette that day, which spoke volumes about his view of the financial viability of the idea. By the end of the meeting, we all were in tears at the opportunity.

My immediate reaction was positive. Of course, we had nothing in the budget for such a project, and with thousands of pregnancy resource clinics around the country the cost would be very large. The initial numbers indicated we would need several million dollars annually for this project. However, I was absolutely confident that many major donors would leap at a chance to help fund such a wonderful, life-saving project and that proved to be the case.

Under Option Ultrasound, Focus helped pay for ultrasound machines and related medical services for pregnancy resource clinics across America. It was a much more difficult and complex effort than first thought, but it had a profound impact. Clearly it was the right thing to do, and it was also totally within the scope of Focus's mission.

As I am writing, Focus has raised and spent multiple millions of dollars on Operation Ultrasound, contributed by faithful donors with a heart for life. The program is estimated to have saved over 500,000 innocent babies from being terminated by abortion. Sometime after the program had been in operation for a few years, Jim Daly sent me an update on the project with the estimated total of babies saved at the time. I replied that launching Option Ultrasound might be "the most important thing I have ever done." Even if there were no other reasons for thinking that I did the right thing by committing so much to serving the Lord by working at Focus, this program alone would be enough.

Commentary

This and the preceding chapter have been difficult for me to write. My earlier experience at Christian Coalition, followed by a somewhat similar result at Focus—although Focus continued to flourish after I left, whereas the Coalition soon fell into obscurity—were hard for me to include in this autobiography. As I have thought about my service with the Coalition and with Focus, I have felt that I, likely, should have said no to each opportunity, thereby not accepting the two assignments that ended unhappily for me. On the other hand, I thought then and still believe that in both cases I was seeking to be responsive to what I believed was the Lord's calling on my life.

My eventual confrontation with the founder in each case suggests to me that the flexible and supportive person I had been through most of my life had changed. I was no longer willing to stand aside and let others substitute their managerial judgment and their reality for mine. I am not concluding that I was better or worse than before—just different. I had much more experience in managing large organizations, and greater confidence in my own judgment about how to make them effective and successful. I have no doubt that had I behaved in that way earlier in my life, before I had such experience, many of the great things that happened in the way of an incredible career would not have happened.

Regarding my personal feelings about Focus on the Family in particular, had I known in advance the way things would eventually turn out there, considering my long and close friendship with Dr. James Dobson, I surely would have passed up the opportunity, letting my 1990s era service as acting executive vice president be my final working memory of that phenomenal leader and the organization he founded. While the ministry has continued quite well without him, it was not in the fashion I had imagined, and I had lost a friendship with a man I greatly admired. My friendship with Jim Dobson became threatened while I was Focus's president, and I left sooner than planned in order to preserve our relationship. However, my strong support of the board during the events that occurred after I left brought the bond I had treasured to an undesirable end.

I truly believe that Dr. Dobson was a great man and a great Christian leader, who revered God and loved people and only wanted to help them. I will forever regret losing our warm friendship and close working relationship.

Now, all these years later, I am reminded of something I have often said to others: As Christians, we are not called by God to be successful *in human terms*. Rather, we are called to be *faithful to Him and to His calling*.

I am not the one to judge whether I succeeded in doing that, but I did what I did because I believed I was called by God to do those jobs. In that judgment, Barbara was wholeheartedly supportive. Had she indicated even the slightest doubts, I would have been much less inclined to take on these roles because I had such great trust in her judgment and relied so heavily on her unlimited support. In the end, neither she nor I regretted the enormous time, energy, and money that we invested in these efforts.

In early March 2005, shortly after I departed as president and long before Dr. Dobson's disagreements with Jim Daly and the Focus board—and before the worst of our disagreements with each other began to rear their heads—he invited Barbara and me back on the program for a retrospective on our time there. In answering one of his questions, I commented that laying down our private life and businesses had turned our lives upside down. I continued:

> *It was hard work... it consumed us, really. But what a tremendous privilege it was for us to be here. That [Barbara and I] were in this together... (Often) [a]s the evening was getting late, I could tell that she thought it was bedtime. But she never once said to me, 'Don't you think you could button that up now? We could go back and go to bed; or I could go back, and you walk (next door) to the Homewood Suites...' Not once. Not once. Wholly supportive. And I can't talk about her without breaking up.*

Barb quickly spoke when I finished that statement, saying she never minded the late hours and never thought it was about her druthers, saying, "Wherever Don is, is home."

CHAPTER 18

ANOTHER TRAGIC AUGUST

As Barbara and I reached our seventies, we often expressed to ourselves and others how thankful we were that our health was strong. While most of our friends in our age range had either suffered major illnesses or had major surgeries—or both—we remained healthy. We lived in a home that we loved in Summit County Colorado. We continued to ski among the wonderful Colorado resorts, occasionally played golf (badly) in warm weather, and jogged, bicycled, and walked in the mountainous terrain.

We exercised every day, jogging outdoors when the weather permitted or on a treadmill or riding a stationary bicycle in our basement furnace room. On December 10, 2006, we celebrated our fiftieth wedding anniversary—and fifty-two years together—over brunch at Denver's Brown Palace hotel with two other couples. And we traveled often.

I turned seventy-two in May 2007, and Barb would do so in September. She often complained (humorously) that as soon as I reached my birthday each year, she immediately thought of herself as my age without waiting the extra four months. Then, when her September birthday arrived she felt like she was yet *another* year older. With a big smile she declared that was, "Unfair!"

Moving to Summit County after my time in Washington had been glorious. We loved the mountains, the sunshine almost every day, the beautiful summers, the clear blue skies, and on and on. I recognized however that it was coming to an end because, as we aged, living at an elevation of 9,000 feet was beginning to take its toll on us physically, especially on Barbara. As a result, I scheduled several upcoming vacations to areas in southern California because I liked the weather there, but Barbara had the mental picture of that area as too hot. I wanted those vacations to begin to show her that there were lovely areas around San Diego where the summers were cool, and the winters were comfortable.

With Barbara on our 50th Anniversary (Courtesy Kellie Vaughan)

In June 2007, we spent a wonderful ten days in the vacation home of our friends from Summit County Ed and Carol McVaney. The home was located on the famous Balboa Island off the coast of San Diego. Ed was a very successful software mogul, having sold the company he founded, J. D. Edwards. That made him almost a billionaire, and he had more than one residence. We ate out at night and strolled around the island. It was idyllic. Joel and Kellie Vaughan also flew out to join us for a few days, staying in a casita on the property. The four of us had a wonderful time, including my driving us around the island at Ed's insistence in an old, yellow, classic Rolls-Royce convertible that he kept there.

But those ideas of living close to sea level were shattered—forever—on Tuesday, August 14, 2007, at 7:15 a.m.

That morning, I was planning to leave home on an overnight business trip at about 9:30. It was to be such a short trip, Barb was not traveling with me. At the time, my company, Summit Power Group, was doing well. I sometimes flew to attend meetings where a deal was anticipated and having Secretary Hodel present went a long way to prove ours was a substantial company. In 2010, I was awarded the National Energy Award by the United States Energy Association as chairman of Summit Power Group and in recognition of the work SPG was doing.

Before driving down the mountain to Denver International Airport for my flight that day, I went downstairs to exercise. Our basement was sixteen carpeted stairs below the main floor of our home and the stairs descended by the wall that was adjacent to the furnace room. That morning while working out, I suddenly heard something go "thump, thump, thump" down the stairs. Immediately I knew that it had to be Barbara.

I cried, "Barb!" and ran to the door where I saw her lying at the bottom of the stairs with her hands at her throat. She was grimacing, trying to breathe, but she could not. So, I tried to do mouth-to-mouth resuscitation, but it was not working. I had not been trained in CPR and did not know that I needed to hold her nose closed. She was losing consciousness. Fortunately, my cell phone was nearby. I called 911 and the operator talked me through the process of forcing air into her lungs, while he sent the emergency medical team. His instructions allowed me to keep her alive while waiting for the EMTs to arrive.

There was an empty suitcase and three paperback books at the foot of the stairs beside her. Barb evidently had been carrying the suitcase in one hand and the books in the other as she started down to the basement. My guess was that she caught her foot on the carpet at the top of the stairs and with both hands full was unable to reach for the handrail. Her injury was such that we concluded that her head buckled under, and she crimped her spinal cord between vertebrae C3 and C4 although, amazingly, without fracturing her neck.

Barb had been having problems with her knee and had caught her foot and fallen—or almost fallen—several times in recent weeks, including during our early August vacation at the cottage in Maine. In fact, it was those falls that might have led her to say on the morning of our departure from there, only two days before she fell down our stairs at home, “I think this is the last time we need to visit 97” (the name given by the family to the cottage).

The ambulance seemed to be taking forever but finally it arrived. Rob Mitchell, our next-door neighbor, saw it and came over to see if he could help. He tried to calm me as I became increasingly upset that the medics were painfully slow in getting oxygen to Barbara, spending time verifying that her bronchial tube was open, something that I felt was obvious from the fact that I had been able to keep her alive via mouth-to-mouth resuscitation. They took her to the only hospital in Summit County south of Breckenridge, about twenty minutes south of our home. There she was X-rayed, and the doctors concluded that her injury was very severe and that she needed a full-service hospital, which meant she had to be moved to Denver.

They decided to transport Barb by helicopter to St. Anthony Hospital in Denver, and offered for me to fly with her, but rather than do that, since I was pretty sure that I was going to be in Denver with her for the foreseeable future, I went back home to cancel my business trip, to notify my business associates of what had happened so they knew I was unavailable until further notice, and to pack a bag for an extended stay in Denver.

As I did that, it occurred to me how blessed we were, even in the midst of this tragedy. Thank God I was exercising when Barbara fell and that I had my phone with me. If I had already left for the airport, I would have returned home the next day and found her dead at the bottom of the stairs. Or even if I had finished working out and gone up to shower before she started down the stairs she would have died before I discovered her.

After canceling my trip, and the three flights and hotels for upcoming vacations we had planned, I drove to Denver, fighting panic and praying all the way. While driving, I called our son Dave, who, with his wife, Tanya, immediately made plans to fly in from Seattle.

I arrived at the hospital at the same time as Joel and Kellie Vaughan, who had driven from Colorado Springs after learning the horrible news from Gabe Joseph, and they took care of parking my car so that I could get to Barb as soon as possible. When I saw her, it was alarming. She lay on a bed in the emergency room, her neck in a brace, and totally unresponsive. I knew then that our lives would never be the same, even if Barb survived, which was very much in question at that moment.

Eventually the hospital moved her to the intensive care unit which had a somewhat comfortable waiting room for families. I staked out a corner, as my friends and I waited for news. Dave and Tanya's friend Dale Watne, who was their close friend from a few years earlier when they lived in Lakewood, Colorado, had received word from Tanya, and also came to the hospital and sat with us. Dave and Tanya arrived the next day.

That night, Barbara had regained some degree of consciousness, and Tanya came out of intensive care to get me, having read Barbara's lips and urging me to go in. I went in and could see that Tanya was right. Barb looked up at me beseechingly and mouthed, "I want to go home." I wept. I tried to explain to her that she could not go home yet, because she needed all the help from the people and the machines she was getting in the hospital. When I explained the need for the respirator, she looked reproachfully at it as if to say, "I'm not sure I like that thing!" But with the incredible serenity with which she had been blessed throughout her life, and which she would exhibit for the next five years, she seemed to accept it.

Around noon the day after her fall, the neurosurgeon, Dr. Brown, came to me and said, "Her neurological functions are rapidly declining. I think we need to operate on her neck." He wanted to perform a laminectomy, which would remove some of the bone in the vertebrae and allow her spinal cord to expand, thus releasing the pressure.

I knew nothing about such things, so I was very reluctant to allow such a surgery. It sounded very risky. Fortunately, Kellie was there, and she amazed me by saying that she had had the same surgery decades earlier. I could see her, talk with her, and observe that she was totally fine. *Thank You, God*, I thought. It calmed me so that I hesitated no longer in telling the doctor to proceed with the surgery.

Unfortunately, it took almost two more hours for them to schedule the operation. When it was over the doctor came to me and said, "I'm really glad we did the surgery. As soon I removed the bone, the spinal cord swelled into the space." That meant, of course, that her spinal cord had been under severe pressure. As it turned out, the effect was essentially the same as if the cord had been severed. She was paralyzed from vertebrae C3 all the way down through the rest of her spine. This meant that she had some—although weak—control of her diaphragm, which meant she could somewhat breathe, but she could not move any part of her body below the neck.

In subsequent years I became convinced that the proper procedure for spinal cord injuries was immediately to ice the point of injury and operate as soon as possible, not a day or two later. That would, I thought, relieve the pressure on the spinal cord and prevent strangling the nerves that operate all bodily functions below the point of injury.

Fortunately, Barb regained consciousness after the surgery and was able to mouth words to me. She even retained her sense of humor. On one occasion she mouthed, "Thirsty," and I wet a small, blue sponge cube that was affixed to a small stick, like a lollipop, and started to put it to her mouth so that she could suck out the water. "Don't bite it," I warned. She immediately bit down on the sponge and looked up at me with an impish grin.

She could not talk, however, because she had tubes going down her throat. Kellie suggested that we create a sheet of paper with the alphabet on it so that I could point to letters and spell out words in the instances when my lipreading ability failed. We used that system until a few days later when the tubes were removed, and Barb's voice somewhat returned.

After the laminectomy, Barb heard the doctor talking with me and asked via the alphabet tablet, "Why am I here?" Later, she asked, "Where was the surgery?" Becoming weary of the alphabet board, she asked, "Why don't we try words?" which led me to ask the hospital if they had any better ways for us to communicate.

At least, all these questions from her were good early indications that Barb's brain was functioning pretty well, for which I was immensely thankful.

Dr. Brown basically said that following the laminectomy we could only wait, provided that no other complications arose, and that it might be a few days before we had any indication of how things were progressing, or it could be much longer. The doctors clearly tried to dampen our expectations, but we hoped the swelling in Barb's spinal cord would reduce, which might allow her to regain movement.

Next, the doctors inserted a feeding tube directly through the belly into Barb's stomach. That greatly reduced her discomfort and lessened the risk of infections by allowing them to stop feeding her through a tube in her nostril. And about the same time, they saw the necessity of performing a tracheostomy to allow a breathing tube to be inserted in her windpipe, below her voice box, and allow her to be on a ventilator. Breathing unaided was very hard for her, however, and at one point she begged me not to let them unhook the breathing machine.

Three days after performing the tracheostomy, the medical staff adjusted her tubes in order to allow air to pass through her vocal cards, which enabled Barb to make sounds for the first time. What a joy it was to hear even the faintest whisp of a voice come again from my beloved wife. A pacemaker had to be installed after Barb suffered a sixteen-second heart stoppage one night during sleep, and it proved its worth several more times over the course of the next few weeks.

At times like this, friends wish to show support, and I was grateful for the many well wishes and prayers that came in. We quickly ran out of space, however, for flowers and other gifts, and I soon sent out a message asking for any gifts to be made in honor of Barb to Patrick Henry College (PHC), a relatively new undergraduate college in Virginia, where she was a member of the board of trustees.

Barbara had been quite surprised when she was asked to join the board by the college's founder, Constitutional attorney and co-founder of the Homeschool Legal Defense Association, Michael Farris. Her reaction was, "Don is the one who serves on boards, not me." I urged her to accept the invitation. She had a great deal of executive experience from the years of sitting through so many of my various meetings where significant issues were debated and resolved. She brought the wisdom and know-how from all of that together with her intelligence and calm demeanor to her role on the board.

About a week after the accident, Barb and I sat alone. I tried to give her something positive or upbeat to think about, trying to avoid the dreadful truth about our future. I reminded her that we had agreed that we had done all the travel we really wanted and that she herself had said that our recent trip to the island in Maine (97) was probably our last. What we enjoyed most in life was just *being together*—reading, watching television, or just doing nothing, "dumbing around," as we called it: walking down a city street with no particular destination in mind. We agreed that it looked like we would get the chance to do a lot of just being together in the future and we would love that.

Also at that time, Kellie sat with Barb while Joel and I made a quick trip to Silverthorne to get more clothing and pick up a few necessities for Barb and me. But when I walked inside our home, there at the bottom of the stairs, I saw the blood-stained carpet where Barb had landed and lay while I gave her CPR. I quicky got out cleaning supplies and tried to make it look better, but it had been there too long, a grim reminder that things would never be the same again.

After a few days, Barb was released from intensive care and transported just a mile or so away to Colorado Acute Hospital, more of an intermediate facility for accident victims. The time there included her first solid food since the accident. She mouthed to me the words "ice cream." Although she was silently mouthing, it was nonetheless music to my ears. But the nurses were wary of introducing something so cold into her diet at that point.

The first solid-like food she ate since falling actually was chocolate pudding, but that was close enough to ice cream for her. Days of eating pureed meals followed, and she had to be taught to drink through a straw. I could not help but reflect on decades earlier when our son Philip was twelve and broke his jaw in the bike accident and had to eat his meals through a straw.

I started an online journal in order to allow our family and friends to stay abreast of Barbara's condition and to allow myself to be able to tell it only once. The night I reported that she had eaten chocolate pudding, I wrote:

> *Free advice. (My friends know how I love to give free advice.) Tell your loved ones how you feel about them while you can. While planning for tomorrow, live for today. Nothing is certain; just because something is entered in your calendar does not mean it will happen. (Right now, after canceling flights and hotel reservations, meetings, etc., for the foreseeable future, I am glad I only wrote things in pencil—which is a good reminder that every plan has an invisible "tentative" in front of it.) Don't encounter a "tragedy" and wish you had done things differently or shared your feelings with your husband, wife, son, daughter, mother, father, etc. For some things, there is no second chance.*

As I canceled more flights and hotel reservations, I had serious twinges of regret at how different things were from what we thought they would be when I entered those arrangements in our calendar. I recalled how Barbara would lightheartedly quote the old saying, "Life is uncertain; eat dessert first!" But regardless of our situation, we constantly felt upheld and blessed by all the messages and prayers which were being said for her recovery, and by the extraordinary generosity and support of my business partners at Summit Power.

Barb was at Colorado Acute for several weeks, where she continued to improve slightly, at one point even moving a toe, which was a great encouragement but eventually proved to be a false hope of greater recovery. I learned to read lips better each day, although occasionally we got our wires crossed. Barbara's mental acuity continued to improve, and I could tell that she was following my conversations with others, even more closely than when she had asked about the surgery.

One day, as she and I reminded ourselves of how blessed we were to have each other, and how she was still the Barbara I had known and loved, adding that if we had to we could live like this for the rest of our lives, she suddenly mouthed, "Superman," reminding me of actor Christopher Reeve who played Superman in the movies and who had become a quadriplegic after being thrown from a horse. Barb and I had met Reeve once, when he and I were in the same New York hospital in 1986, each having had our appendix removed. Barbara later heard me telling someone in her hospital room that story and when I gave the year as 1996, she corrected me quickly, saying, "1986."

In early October we went outside, which was her first experience in the open air and sunshine in over seven weeks! I pushed her in a wheelchair around the hospital property, and we had a wonderful time, given the circumstances. At that time, I was still optimistic that she would substantially recover movement in her arms and legs.

At the time it seemed like there were never more than five minutes in a twelve-to-fourteen-hour day when I could just sit and catch my breath. That was how it had to be, and I would not have had it any other way, but at my age I was aware of how demanding it was. I thought back to my mother's constant attention to my father over the seven years of his decline and death from Alzheimer's and realized that at that time I only *thought* I knew what she was going through, and, even then, only superficially. Then I thought of all my friends who were undergoing struggles of painful, agonizing times with loved ones, and while I had been sympathetic, it was not with the understanding that I now had.

At about this time, friends affirmed what I already knew: the necessity of a caregiver to take care of himself. If I kept up such an intense pace without a break, I would soon be no good to Barbara. So, I took time to exercise at the hotel and even got away several times for nine holes of golf with Joel, while Kellie sat with Barb. Eighteen holes was too long to be away, but the time it took to play nine was OK.

One very special day occurred at Colorado Acute Hospital. It was when Barbara was finally able to be weaned off the respirator and breathe only through a small cannula attached to an oxygen tank, which left her nose visible for the first time since the accident. At one point, doctors had told me that they did not believe that a woman her age would ever be able to breathe on her own again after what had happened to her. Getting off the respirator was only about a week or so after she was able to wiggle her toe slightly and both instances brought great interest and glee from hospital staff. That day, Barb looked at me and mouthed, "They used to come to see my toes, and now they come to see my nose."

I moved into an extended-stay motel, like the one Barb and I had occupied while working at Focus on the Family a few years before, only it was much different this time, with no Barb by my side. Later, Ed and Carol McVaney offered their spacious home in Denver's Cherry Hills neighborhood while they were away. Through Barb's accident and recovery Ed and I became even better friends. Later, once Barb was out of the hospital and we had caregivers in our home, Ed made it his mission to get me out two or three times a year to play golf. He was a dear, dear friend. Ed passed away a year or so before I resumed work on this book, and I always think of him with sadness because he is greatly missed in my life.

The prime facility in the western United States for spinal cord and brain injury victims is Craig Hospital in Englewood, Colorado, a suburb on the south side of Denver. As soon as I learned of it, I began making plans to try to get Barb accepted as a patient there, because I wanted her to have the very best care possible. I was still hoping that she could improve significantly.

On her last day at Colorado Acute, as we went for a walk around the grounds, we reflected on how our lives had changed. We also realized that we needed to move from Silverthorne down to a lower altitude and to the proximity of Barb's doctors. From my online journal:

> *During our stroll today, we stopped many times to bask in the sun and talk. We reflected on how we had had eighteen wonderful years in Summit County, Colorado, but we knew it could not last, or, more accurately, we could not last—at 9,000 feet altitude. We loved it; we'll miss it; we'll really miss the people; but it is time to go, a decision we might not have made so soon if it had not been forced upon us. We have no real regrets. We are looking forward to a new adventure as Barbara learns how far she can go in getting back to normal. We are thankful to God for all the wonderful friends and prayer partners who have supported her this far. We are blessed. In the last few days, I have had conversations with two other people whose family members have not had so happy an outcome. One woman has brain damage from which she is not recovering, and the prognosis is not good. Another, a man who hit a tree while mountain biking, has reached the limits of his recovery and there is nothing more to be done for him as he lies in a coma. He will probably never have that conversation with his wife that she wished for in our talk a number of days ago. On earth there are not answers to the question, "Why me?" whether good or bad things happen. We must trust in the Lord whose mysteries we will not know, this side of heaven. We are, therefore, even more thankful for His unmerited blessings in Barbara's situation.*

At one point, I noticed that my daily online journal had changed from being a quick update on Barb's condition for our friends, into more of a personal journal, where I processed my thoughts, shared my grief, and asked for the prayers that sustained both of us. Some entries were very short, especially if I was very sleepy after leaving Barb's room late at night, and others were quite long, several paragraphs, some even cowritten by Barb herself, after she regained her voice loudly enough for me to hear, giving me insights as I wrote.

The day we moved Barb into Craig was bittersweet. I was thankful to have her at the best facility possible, but seeing the other patients around who were not able to walk was daunting. One good aspect was that I was able to move from the McVaneys' into a little apartment Craig had on campus for families, which meant that I could walk three minutes to Barb's room rather than drive several miles from Ed's home. I could do laundry there, and it had a refrigerator. While my gratitude to the McVaneys for their generosity was in no way diminished, the proximity to Barbara's room at Craig was a significant improvement.

We spent both Thanksgiving and Christmas 2007—as well as our fifty-first wedding anniversary—in the hospital at Craig, but at least we were together. We truly loved each other, which we knew was a tremendous blessing, especially in these trying circumstances.

Craig threw a big Thanksgiving celebration for its patients and their families, with several varieties of turkey and all the fixings. Barb's sister, Debbie, and her husband, Norman, came from Ann Arbor, Michigan, for the second time since Barb's accident, and we invited Rob and Jude Mitchell from Silverthorne, along with their two adult children, and Joel and Kellie Vaughan, making our party ten in all. Norman even made his famous (and very tasty) applesauce. It was a time of giving thanks for everything with which we had been blessed, in spite of Barbara's tragic injury.

That year began a new tradition, as subsequent Thanksgivings were held at our home with the same group—and occasionally others—for the next seven or eight Thanksgivings. In addition to the original group, Dave and Tanya came and usually brought their sons, Aaron, Brennan, and Christopher. Our high-attendance year came to over twenty family, friends, and neighbors. Usually, we had a gathering on Tuesday evening for local friends and Barb's nurses I had hired to assist me in caring for her and to provide round-the-clock coverage. That was followed by a full Thanksgiving Day dinner on Thursday. The ladies brought their favorite preparations, and from Whole Foods Market I bought the precooked turkey and other "fixin's" such as mashed potatoes and gravy.

After ten weeks, Barb had her first meal outside of her hospital room, when Dave and I took her to the hospital cafeteria. Also, at about that time was the first day in the hospital when she remained off the respirator all day. But we also were slowly coming to realize that those would be the only physical improvements, as caretakers and I watched over Barb twenty-four seven, day after day.

At whatever of the three hospitals Barbara was in before she was released to go home, I remained very alert as to how she was being cared for, and at times I was critical of the various doctors and nurses who cared for her. On one occasion, a doctor came into the room and was extremely nasal with a reddish nose (although no longer coughing or sneezing into the crook of her arm as she had been the night before). When she reached for her stethoscope, I asked why she was not wearing a mask. She said that she was "better." I became very upset and challenged her because "better" does not mean "well."

"Are you *well*?" I asked. I soon found myself basically telling her to leave Barbara alone unless she was well. I was embarrassed afterward because I had allowed myself to show how upset I was. But it seemed outrageous to me to take any chances on exposing Barbara to a bad cold.

I also insisted on speaking with each new nurse after a shift change so that she heard directly from me of Barb's experiences during the previous shift. I left nothing to chance concerning communication.

I have many times since reflected on how differently I managed Barbara's care compared to how I managed the Bonneville

Power Administration, or the two huge federal organizations—the Department of Energy and the Department of the Interior—and, much later, the major nonprofit organizations Christian Coalition and Focus on the Family. In each of those roles I was a delegator. That is, I worked with staff to agree on what needed to be done and then gave the person with the assignment great leeway in how to get it done.

In contrast to that, in managing the care for Barbara, I watched over and checked every detail and tried to be present whenever anything significant was being done. This was especially true once she was in our home, and I was overseeing her twenty-four-hour care by the nurses I hired. Multiple times every day I checked the medication chart to see that the many medications she was taking were given at the right time and in the right dose.

If I found that a nurse was not doing Barb's care the way I had been taught to do it at Craig Hospital, I insisted she do it the "Craig way." If she failed to do that, I terminated her involvement. Some of the nurses I hired myself, but when nurse Robyn Kindahl came on board, she fairly quickly became Barb's lead nurse, as my trust in her grew.

Increasingly, I relied on Robyn's evaluation of people applying for a job as one of Barb's nurses. Interestingly, Robyn found it very difficult to let someone go, even if it was necessary, so we shared the responsibility of relieving someone who was not satisfactory. She would tell me someone was not up to the job, and I would handle the dismissal—as nicely as I could, but I had no compunctions about removing someone who was not doing the best possible job for Barbara.

Not long after Barb's accident I received a call from Mike Farris at Patrick Henry College, asking if I had any objection to the board's naming the college's new student life center, which was then under construction, in Barbara's honor. I assured him that I would be delighted, and that Barbara would be greatly honored.

On October 31, Mike flew to Denver and drove to Craig, where he made the formal announcement that the board of trustees had voted to name their new building "The Barbara Hodel Center," bringing along a framed artist's rendering of the building—a magnificent federal period brick building with tall white columns and The Barbara Hodel Center carved above the columns. It was truly thrilling to see what was planned and to realize what an honor was being bestowed on Barbara. Dave and Tanya flew in from Seattle for the occasion, and I invited three other couples, Jim and Shirley Dobson, Diane and Paul Passno, and Joel and Kellie Vaughan, to join us for the occasion. When I rolled Barbara into the hospital's conference room and she saw Mike Farris along with Dave and Tanya, and our friends, she knew something special was happening, of course, though she could not imagine what it was.

Mike took the floor and explained that Barbara had made major contributions to the conduct of the affairs of the college by her service as a trustee, and that she had lived an exemplary life in which she manifested her Christian values, and many more comments in that same vein. By then I was all choked up because someone was singing Barbara's praises. Here was Barbara, truly reluctant to be in the spotlight, being given tremendous recognition. No one who knew her could not be excited for her.

Barbara was overwhelmed, of course, being the only person in the room for whom this news was a surprise. She made brief remarks via mouthing the words, and in it she said that she had never thought that something like this would happen, and if she had, she would have thought it would be for me because of my governmental activities. Never in her wildest dreams had she thought she might be the one to be so honored. I marveled at how wonderful it was that a person who was so modest and willing to work behind the scenes would be honored in this fashion.

Barbara had spent her life being the complete team player, quietly supporting me in everything that I did—and then doing the same for Patrick Henry College—with everything she had in the way of experience, without any thought of recognition or reward. Her life was a true example of selfless devotion.

Mike said the center's completion would be in about nineteen months, sometime in October 2009, when it would be dedicated, which gave us something to plan for and look forward to. Our hopes and prayers were to get Barbara well enough so that she could fly to Virginia for the dedication.

I was concerned as to how to get Barbara there. It was obvious to me that we could not travel by commercial aircraft. Ed McVaney eased my angst early on by saying that he would make available, at no cost to us, a private jet for which he had a time-share type arrangement. When the time came, however, a wonderful and generous friend of both Barbara's and mine, Phyllis Taylor, offered us the use of her Gulfstream IV. Phyllis had taken over Taylor Energy after her husband, Pat's, death, and I, of course, had sat on their board of directors for several years.

Ed assured me that I should accept Phyllis's offer. It was good that we did, because we were barely able to get Barbara into the larger aircraft, and it would have been very difficult if not impossible in a smaller jet.

Before all that happened, however, there was much to do. Barb was finally discharged from Craig on February 8, 2008, almost exactly six months after her fall. I had rushed to purchase a house in the local area and found one in the city of Lakewood that had been designed to be wheelchair accessible by a man who suffered from a condition which meant that he would soon be in a wheelchair.

At first, we slept in the same room with my (twin) bed beside Barb's hospital-style bed. The amount of medical equipment we had to find and acquire was staggering. I barely slept because I was constantly listening to (and monitoring) the ventilator. The sounds of the ventilator indicated whether she was breathing satisfactorily. Meantime the nurses sat in the living room and attempted to keep track of Barb's status in the bedroom via a baby monitor. Finally, we recognized that I could not continue to try to sleep beside Barbara. I needed to move my bed into our bedroom's large walk-in closet and allow the nurses to sit in the room with Barbara for the night. I could be available in a moment, if called, but until called, I could get some sleep.

We had to take things one day at a time, even each hour or minute, such as having to perform a weight shift every twenty minutes when Barb was either in bed or in her wheelchair in order to prevent pressure sores from forming on her skin. The weight shift when she was in her wheelchair meant that we would recline her wheelchair for sixty seconds while she lay almost flat on her back. In her bed it meant turning her from her back to her side, alternating from left to right.

This weight-shift routine was distressing to Barbara. Apparently, it was uncomfortable for her. Finally, a nurse at a clinic we went to periodically told me about a bed made by a company named Hill Rom. That bed was amazing. It consisted of an inflated edge like a kiddie swimming pool surrounding an area that was about four feet long and two and a half feet wide, with a bottom that was pierced by tiny holes. Thousands of very small glass beads filled the "tub." Though small, they were too large to go through the even smaller holes in the bottom of the bed. That allowed warm air to be blown through so that the patient was "floating" on the sheet over the tiny glass beads and there was no pressure concentrated on any single spot on the skin. This was a great blessing and saved Barbara so much of the hassle involved in turning her every twenty minutes while in bed.

I purchased a new Toyota Sienna van, and had it outfitted with a ramp for an electric wheelchair, which enabled us to travel easily whenever we wished. I could load Barbara into the van by myself. We went out to eat, alone and with friends; we drove to nearby Westminster to one of Barb's favorite venues, the Butterfly Museum; and we sometimes simply parked beside Clear Creek in the town of Golden, Colorado, and watched the water, the birds and the kayakers and tubers passing through the rapids on a lovely summer day.

Costco was one of our favorite places to visit, and some weeks we went there as many as three times. Their food samples were part of the attraction, tasty treats always available and fun for us to try. The "sample ladies" got to know Barbara, and if I happened to go to Costco without her, as happened once in a while, I would be asked by them, "Where's your wife?"

There were many ups and downs over the years after Barbara's accident. We learned to consider some days as ordinary, even in the extremely extraordinary times in which we found ourselves. We were elated when she could move her fingers and toes, and then slightly raise her arms, or pedal a stationary set of bike pedals, called a Motomed. The device lets the patient pedal if able, and, if not, it picks up the pace to a preset speed. At one point I saw that the physical therapist had set the Motomed for seven RPMs, but the screen showed that Barb was clearly pedaling it herself at a pace of thirty-six! That was a very good day. It did not continue, however. These movements declined, and then finally ceased, and slowly it became apparent that she would never recover any significant ability to move her arms or legs.

At one point, funding for The Barbara Hodel Center at Patrick Henry College lagged and it looked like construction might slow down considerably, thus postponing the dedication which we so eagerly anticipated. But our dear friend Elsa Prince Broekhuizen (who had remarried after her husband, Ed, died) heard of the dilemma and made a sizable gift, and Dr. James Dobson followed up with one of his own. His love and respect for Barb were evident, notwithstanding any of our personal disagreements, which, at the time, were still minimal and our friendship still intact. Elsa's extreme generosity so impressed Barbara's fellow PHC board member Dr. James Leininger that he stepped forward and made a matching gift that was large enough to complete the building, basically telling Mike Farris that he would ensure that the building was completed. I still am amazed at the kindness of our friends—financially and prayerfully. It is also testimony to the loving high regard these fine people had for Barbara.

On Friday, October 9, 2009, and accompanied by two health care workers, nurse Robyn Kindahl and physical therapist Patti Sellers, and four Colorado friends, the Gjeldes and Vaughans, Barb and I flew on Phyllis Taylor's Gulfstream jet to Leesburg, Virginia, the closest private airport to PHC, in preparation for the next day's ceremonies. Dr. James Dobson, who had great fondness and respect for Barbara, gladly agreed to be the guest speaker at an event which featured scores of our family, friends, and associates. The remainder of the auditorium was filled with students and faculty. Barb was regal that day and I could not have been prouder of her or of the occasion.

The next two years were more routine, as Barb's condition leveled out and, over time, I had to accept that her ability to move was not going to get any better. I worked hard to try to give Barbara as good a life as was possible, considering her enormous handicap. Whatever success we achieved in that regard would not have been possible without the help of a cadre of caretakers. To this day I give thanks and am grateful for the financial ability to hire those wonderful nurses and to do whatever might possibly make Barbara's life better.

One of Barbara's early nurses, Courtney, was the daughter of a racehorse veterinarian. Her mother encouraged me to bring Barbara to the Colorado racecourse located east of Denver and watch the races during the sixty-day race season each summer. This seemed to me to be a very good idea because Barbara had taken riding lessons as a teenager and was very fond of those magnificent animals. Once we discovered how much Barbara enjoyed it, we often attended the races on Sunday afternoons and would invite friends to join us for lunch at the track. It was a great way to get out of the house and have an adventure.

Friends and family were supportive during those years, of course. Dave and Tanya visited when they could from Seattle, as did their sons. The eldest, Aaron, actually lived with us for about a year and a half, and he could not have been more helpful.

We had good days and bad days, each with constant reminders of Barb's condition. There was the ever-present wheelchair, and the mechanical hoist which we used to lift her between the bed and the wheelchair. She suffered from neck pain, bladder infections, muscle spasms that were agonizing to her, and what felt to her like a tight band around her chest, which hardly ever went away. One very good day was when she was able to support her own weight while being steadied by two helpers who had gotten her standing beside her bed on a rotating disc on the floor. She then could be rotated while standing and then be seated in her wheelchair. That was wonderful because it increased her ability to be out of that bed.

Once again, I found myself hoping that she might regain the ability to move her arms and legs, although I think in my heart I knew that she would never recover.

At times, I joined conference calls for my company, made one speech in Denver to a coal transportation conference, where I talked about our proposed Integrated Coal-Gasification Combined Cycle electric power plant and how important it would be for the country's clean energy supply.

Several times during these years Robyn would tell me that I had to get away for a few days. This meant that I was showing signs of unusual impatience with the nurses resulting, no doubt, from fatigue. On the first occasion I went into the mountains to Beaver Creek, Colorado, and spent two nights at a time-share up there. Other than getting out of bed to eat and take a few walks, I spent almost the entire time sleeping. I returned refreshed to the task of caring for Barb. I took time off like that several times, when I was told by Robyn that it was needed.

Then, on a Wednesday in early October 2012, Robyn thought that Barbara was showing symptoms of a possible infection. We took Barbara for tests at Swedish Hospital, which was adjacent to Craig and connected via underground tunnels. We had gone to Swedish for similar tests several times over the preceding five years.

The tests showed that she had a bladder infection, and blood was drawn to see if she had an infection in her blood. Urinalysis provides results within minutes, but blood tests require a day or two for the culture to develop before an infection can be identified. We were allowed to return home with Barbara.

The next morning, however, at about 9:00 a.m., I received a call from the hospital telling me that Barb indeed had a blood infection, and I needed to return her to the hospital for treatment as soon as possible.

Robyn and I got her there promptly, and the hospital immediately gave Barbara an injection of multiple antibiotics. Later I learned this was the technique used to try to combat any one of a number of antibiotic-resistant infections. The problem is that each strain may respond to treatment from a different antibiotic, but if the doctors wait until they are sure which infection is involved before giving the antibiotic, it is too late, and the patient may not survive.

Barb remained in the hospital overnight. On Friday morning our nurse and I began Barbara's normal morning routine. Barbara was in a mellow mood and made a special effort to tell the nurse how much she appreciated how she took care of her. As the nurse worked on her I stood near the head of the bed watching Barbara. She closed her eyes. I tried to wake her but got no response. Immediately, I realized that Barb had stopped breathing. Alarmed, I told the nurse immediately to call for help. The nurse rang the emergency button on the wall. Within fifteen seconds a hospital nurse arrived and quickly the room filled with medics. For the next twenty agonizing minutes I watched the horrifying process of staff attempting to restore her breathing using CPR. Finally, her heart resumed beating, but she remained in a coma from which she never woke up.

Dave and Tanya came from Seattle and spent the next two days with Barb. Debbie came from Ann Arbor as soon as she could. By the time she arrived on Thursday, it was obvious to me and all the others who came to visit that Barb was unresponsive, being kept alive solely by the machines to which she was attached.

After Debbie saw this, I suggested to her that it was time to let Barbara go. She agreed that it was hopeless. I told the nurse in the intensive care unit to disconnect the machines. In the past Barbara had tolerated being independent of machines quite well, often going for hours before she became tired and needed to be back on the ventilator. This time, however, within fifteen minutes, all of her systems shut down and she was gone. I cannot find the words adequately to express the total sense of loss felt by everyone who knew Barbara.

Barbara and I had purchased side-by-side burial plots at Riverview Cemetery in Portland, Oregon, where her parents and mine, together with several other relatives, and the ashes of our son Philip are interred. We had a burial service there within a week. Then, considering our almost quarter-century of living in Colorado, we held a memorial service at the church we had been attending in Lakewood, where Mike Farris delivered a warm and fitting eulogy.

As I hugged David during the service, tears flowed. He had his own family of course, Tanya and their three sons. But I am sure that neither of us had ever felt quite so sad, losing my wife and his mother. But even then, I knew that God was with me and that I had more to be thankful for in life than I had ever deserved.

Barb and I learned several lessons through the ordeal of her accident and its aftermath, including that one has to deal with the urgent matters that are in front of them and not worry or even think about what might happen tomorrow or what might yet go wrong. As Jesus assured us long ago, each day of ours truly had enough trouble of its own.

We were always very thankful for what we had. Barb retained her faculties and her personality even though paralyzed. She remained substantially herself, even though she was a quadriplegic version of herself. We remained able to communicate throughout the entire time. Our physical relationship changed, of course, as it was even difficult to hug her in the wheelchair, but emotionally, we were closer than ever. I think that what had always been a close and strong relationship became even stronger. I was intimately involved in every detail of her care for those five years, and she was totally dependent upon me for everything.

I would tell her that I loved her multiple times every day because it seemed to me that had I been in her situation I would have wondered if my circumstances would have been such a burden that my caregiver would be tired of it. I wanted her never to doubt that this was a labor of love. Barb relied on and trusted my being there. Several times during the day our caregivers would hear her ask, "Where's Don?" if I were not visibly nearby.

On the two-year anniversary of Barbara's fall, August 14, 2009, she at one point said, "I don't want to think about it." That was one of only two times she ever came close to saying something that showed how sad she was about what had happened. The other occasion was when I was thinking how amazing it was that she seemed so serene about her situation. I said, "You are amazing. I can't believe that you are not bitter." She looked at me gravely and said, "Oh, *I'm bitter*." That was the only other thing she ever said or did to indicate what a burden she was living through. She was truly amazing.

Barbara was such a gentle and good person, with such a quiet and unassuming nature, that it was particularly painful for me to see her as she was. Yet I reminded myself that it could have been much worse. She could have suffered severe brain damage or died when she fell. We knew many couples who never had as many years of marriage as we did, or such a warm and loving relationship. Her lack of mobility did not fundamentally alter the blessed, loving relationship we enjoyed for over fifty years.

One day at church, a year or so into the saga, we were approached in the coffee area by a man who obviously had mental deficiencies. He asked me what was wrong with Barbara, and then, why I took care of her. Without even having to think about it I responded, "Because I love her." Hearing that, Barb cried the first tears I had seen since her fall. In my online journal I titled that evening's entry, "Happy tears."

She explained to me later that I could have given other reasons: that she was my wife, that we had been together over fifty years, etc., but saying it was because I loved her was the best thing she could have heard.

As an aside, we learned of other couples who did not have such a positive story. One man we heard about took his paralyzed wife home from Craig Hospital and then walked out and left her to die, never to return. Only the miracle of her sister stopping by saved that woman's life.

I loved Barb unconditionally. She had wonderful qualities, but those were not why I loved her. I simply loved her. And she loved me and would have done for me what I was doing for her had our situations been reversed. When we were together, we were complete.

Finally, we tried to remember to be thankful. For years I had been trying to condition Barbara to the probability that I would die before her. I would say that when one of us died the other needed to be thankful for the wonderful blessing we had of a lifelong happy marriage.

Some people never experience a day of what we took for granted year in and year out. Therefore, we must not let ourselves become bitter or sad about the things which would not continue, which would never be the same again, but be thankful for the many blessed years we had had. As it turned out it was not Barbara who needed that advice—I did. Even in her tragedy, Barb said she was among the blessed because God had lined everything up that morning that was necessary in order for her to live. She knew that God had a purpose remaining for her, and that He was her strength and fortress afterward.

Skeptics or honest inquirers might ask that if God did all that, why did He allow her to fall in the first place? We could not answer that question. Nowhere does God promise that if we believe in Him we will not have problems. The world is a fallen and corrupt place, and bad things happen. Further, God's ways are higher than our ways and we do not always know how He plans to receive glory out of our suffering in order to provide a witness of His love to others, likely to those who are unsaved, perhaps even someone who is reading this book right now and desperately needs to know the love of the Savior.

In my online journal entry on Thursday, December 10, 2009, our fifty-third wedding anniversary, I wrote the following:

> *I wished Barbara a Happy Anniversary and assured her that even if we had been able to foresee this day and all of her current problems, I would not have hesitated to marry her. We had 51 years of married bliss and great excitement and challenges before her fall, and we still have each other and the love we share. What has been driven home to us is it's not the things we do in a relationship that matter nearly as much as how we relate to one another and how we feel about each other. Because we love each other, those aspects of our relationship are entirely intact. The doing has been severely curtailed, but so, too, has the doing for a lot of people our age.*

Looking back to that 1954 December afternoon in Boston, when I was at Harvard and met Barb in what seemed like such a serendipitous encounter, I have no doubt that God was smiling on me—on us. Through Barb and her love, He gave me a life of which I never could have dreamed, or planned, and certainly more than I ever believed I deserved.

EPILOGUE
AFTER BARBARA

I continued to help Earl Gjelde and our partners in Summit Power Group as much as possible, including one very memorable occasion in October 2012, just before Barb passed away.

We had been awarded a $450 million grant by the federal government for a coal gasification project in Texas. Such grants to corporations are not taxable, however SPG was an LLC (Limited Liability Company), a different type of business designation, thus we faced about $137 million in taxes. The IRS claimed that they sympathized, yet without legislation by Congress they would demand SPG pay the taxes. Texas US Senator John Cornyn was also sympathetic but unwilling to approach Senate Majority Leader Harry Reid because he knew that Reid would want something in return.

I learned, however, that US Senator Orrin Hatch of Utah was to be in Denver on October 4, speaking at the Western Conservative Political Action Conference (CPAC). He and I had been cordial friends during my years in Washington. I decided to try to talk with him. Hatch was ranking member on the Senate Finance Committee and, therefore, essential to any effort to get legislation on this matter.

My friend and business associate Gabe Joseph called Hatch's office and requested a meeting for me with the Senator after Hatch addressed the Western CPAC. Hatch's staff quickly agreed.

As I drove from Craig Hospital to the hotel near Denver International Airport where the event was being held, I encountered the motorcade of GOP Presidential nominee Mitt Romney, who was also speaking that day after completing the first debate with President Barack Obama the evening before in Denver. By my count, I was the twentieth car in line before Romney's motorcade forced the closing of the highway. I figured that I had lost the meeting, but I called Gabe, who in turn called Hatch's chief of staff and explained the situation. "The Senator will be happy to wait for Secretary Hodel" was the response.

I arrived and had a very warm meeting with Orrin, who quickly understood the dilemma and said, "We can help with that." And he did. The correction was eventually approved in both houses of Congress, as Senators and Representatives agreed that it made no sense to make a government grant to an organization and then turn around and insist on collecting taxes on that money.

Even though I was chairman of Summit Power, for the last five-plus years I had worked far less than the other executives due to having an invalid wife. In addition, I was seventy-seven years old. I had an idea that some in the company resented my sizable salary, even though it was less than some of the others. Yet those who questioned my pay quickly understood the value of having a former Cabinet Secretary on the letterhead. As an outgrowth of that one brief meeting with Senator Hatch, SPG saved $137 million.

I was tremendously gratified by that outcome, as I had felt badly about not shouldering my share of the work for SPG. This occurrence illustrated to my associates—at least somewhat—that it was not how *many* hours I worked that was important, and that my distraction because of caring for Barbara did not mean I was not valuable to the company. After I finally decided to retire, my partners named me to the post of chairman emeritus.

After Barb died, I planned our usual Thanksgiving celebration with friends and family, and after dinner I told them that I had decided to endow the new chapel which was planned at Craig Hospital, and it would be named The Barbara Hodel Chapel. I could not think of a better way to memorialize Barbara and the life she had lived. Of course, she was already mightily honored by the naming of The Barbara Hodel Center at Patrick Henry College in

Virginia. For over a year I discussed plans with the hospital staff and donated a large, abstract painting that I loved and had purchased during a trip to Hawaii. My one stipulation was that a Christian cross be placed somewhere in the multifaith chapel, even if it was removable at times of services for those of other religions.

As I have gotten older, I have noticed how easy it is to think that other people are living happy, uncomplicated lives, especially when we ourselves are suffering in the aftermath of a loss of something precious. When we get to know those people no matter how well off or happy they seem to be, however, we learn that everyone has burdens. That is simply a fact of life. To live is to have cares and concerns, problems and crises, loves and losses. We either learn to go on with life or we collapse. As I said to my son Dave within an hour after we learned of Philip's death, "Life is for the living," meaning those who survive have to go on living and striving. They cannot dwell on their losses or quit because of their grief, no matter how profound it may be.

The morning after Barbara died, I awoke to a twin realization. First, I no longer had anything that required me to go on living. For over five years I had prayed daily that I would live longer than Barbara because she *needed* me to be alive to help her survive. When she was gone, I no longer had that reason. I was free and ready for the Lord to take me. I was ready to go—and I still am. Second, I realized that I did not want to be alone for the rest of my life—however long that might be.

As soon as I had completed the arrangements for Barbara's interment service in Portland and a public memorial service in Denver, I knew that I needed some time to begin my recovery from over five years of twenty-four seven intensity as a caregiver. I scheduled a trip to the Mauna Kea Resort on the Big Island of Hawaii for the first week of November. Barbara and I had been there several times and had decided that it was our favorite resort.

Ric Redman, who had become president of Summit Power Group, had a house on the South Fairways at Mauna Kea and emailed me about a woman acquaintance of his, Kitty Egan, who lived in Chicago but also had a house near his in Hawaii. He told me how wonderful she was, and I later learned he had said the same kinds of things to her about me. A few days after Ric's introducing us via email, Kitty and I began to correspond by email and, fairly soon, by telephone. After seven weeks of lengthy, daily telephone calls, I decided it was time to meet her. While I knew I did not want to be alone the rest of my life, I certainly did not expect to connect with anyone that soon, and without a more suitable length of time after Barbara's death. I felt uncomfortable with how fast it seemed to happen, but often in life we are surprised by how things transpire.

On December 7, I was in Washington to attend the annual Cabinet Secretaries' Luncheon. This event had been a bipartisan annual tradition, beginning while President Reagan was in office. It was attended by former Cabinet officers from subsequent Administrations and was an interesting event. On my way back to Denver, I stopped in Chicago to meet Kitty in person and take her to dinner. Our conversations had allowed us to become quite good friends, and once we met in person it was apparent that we had much in common and that we could have a solid and enjoyable relationship. Kitty is the second woman I have loved in my life, and we both feel that we are blessed by the fact that we found each other.

Someone in my circumstances might wonder what it is like to find love again after a long, loving marriage such as Barb and I enjoyed. Historian David McCullough discovered a letter written by Colonel Washington Roebling, builder of the Brooklyn Bridge, who found love again late in life after his first wife died, where he explained that a second love "cannot be judged by the standard of the first, because its motives are usually quite different."

I think that is a wise statement. When someone is young, they are likely looking forward to the long term: having and raising a family and building a life together. Late in life, there is a desire to find a loving companion with whom to share one's declining years.

Kitty insisted that I date a few other women as well while we were getting to know each other, being aware of how happily married men who become widowers can easily rebound and fall for the first woman they meet after their wife's death. That was a wise thing for her to do, and it served us both very well as we became closer.

I am amazed and grateful that I have been twice blessed to find a loving and wonderful woman who is motivated to make this latter stage of our lives pleasant and enjoyable. Now, some twelve years later, both Kitty and I often express to each other our utter amazement that we found each other and have been able to have so many wonderful years together, considering that I was seventy-seven and a half and she was two days short of her seventieth birthday on the day we first met face-to-face.

With Kitty (Family photos)

In 2019, my family experienced yet a third August tragedy when my youngest grandson, Christopher, died unexpectedly at twenty-six. He was a wonderful young man, and I thought he was showing great promise. I will forever miss his loving smile and genuine heart. I certainly know from our experience with the loss of Philip what his parents, Dave and Tanya, have gone through losing a beloved son.

Aaron, my oldest grandson, and his wife, Amanda, have made me a great-grandfather, with their two sons, Oliver (born in August 2016) and Jackson (born in February 2023). I can only hope for them to live blessed lives extending far beyond my years. Maybe someday one or both of them will read these words. I hope so.

In reflecting on my decades of service to our great country, I fully believe that the United States became the nation it did in large part because of the spiritual commitment of its Founders. Our foundational documents, the Declaration of Independence and the Constitution (including the Bill of Rights) were written by men who were steeped in the Judeo-Christian value system.

They knew that all men are sinners, but they believed that they were writing those documents for a body politic that would be similarly steeped in that value system and that, therefore, we would seek to do what was right because it was right and avoid doing what was wrong because it *was* wrong, not just because we were afraid of getting caught.

I shudder to think that many in America have jettisoned those high ideals in favor of tearing down America rather than building it up. There was a time when those on both sides of the aisle, Democrats and Republicans, cared about what was best for the American people, and defended them to the hilt. They fought tooth and nail over politics, but in the end, they wanted what was best for the nation, even though they often disagreed about how to bring it about.

President Ronald Reagan had more in common with a liberal icon like FDR than the President who guided us through both a depression and a World War would have with his own Democrat Party today. Liberals in Washington today are more about political expediency, social experiments, and Leftist agendas than about what is best for America and Americans.

John Adams, our second President, wrote, "Our Constitution was made only for a moral and religious people. It is wholly inadequate to the government of any other." He and his fellow patriots believed that the American people, because of their value system, would have an internal gyroscope that would aim them in the right direction. As I approach age ninety and reflect on the America of the last several years, I can only pray that we will return to our proper path as a nation.

I never reached my childhood goal of being President, and the reader can decide whether I became a statesman. I tried to do what was right as God gave me the vision to discern it. It seems to me that I accomplished more than perhaps could have been expected of the son of an immigrant.

I married a wonderful woman whom I loved and who loved me, and who gave me two sons, my family whom I have loved more than life itself. Amazingly, at an advanced age I was further blessed by finding the second love of my life with Kitty. With God's help, I reached tremendous heights in our country's government, serving a President who became a legend. I loved my friends and family, and I tried to leave them and my country better for my having been here.

May God bless America.

ABOUT THE AUTHOR

Donald Paul Hodel served in President Ronald Reagan's Cabinet for six years, as the fourth US Secretary of Energy (1982 - 1985) and forty-fifth US Secretary of the Interior (1985 - 1989). Hodel began his two decades of federal government service as Deputy Administrator and then Administrator of the Bonneville Power Administration. A native of Portland, Oregon, whose parents emigrated from Canada, Hodel is a graduate of Harvard College and of the University of Oregon Law School. He is a recipient of the Presidential Citizens Medal and the National Energy Award. He became a widower in 2012 after an almost 56 year loving marriage to Barbara Beecher Stockman. Retiring in Colorado after a career in law, business, government, and non-profit service, Hodel is the father of two sons, with three grandsons, and two great grandsons.

INDEX